DEFINING TRAVEL

DEFINING TRAVEL
DIVERSE VISIONS

Edited by Susan L. Roberson

University Press of Mississippi   *Jackson*

www.upress.state.ms.us

Print-on-Demand Edition

Library of Congress Cataloging-in-Publication Data

Defining travel : diverse visions / edited by Susan L. Roberson.
   p. cm.
  Includes bibliographical references (p.   ) and index.
  ISBN 1-57806-411-2 (cloth : alk. paper)
   1. Travel. 2. Travelers. I. Roberson, Susan L., 1950–

  G163 .D44 2001
  910'.4—dc21

                                                        2001026905

British Library Cataloging-in-Publication Data available

THIS ONE IS FOR WALLY

CONTENTS

DEFINING TRAVEL: AN INTRODUCTION

Travel, movement, mobility—these are some of the essential activities of human life. Whether we travel to foreign lands or just across the room, we all journey and from our journeying define ourselves. As philosopher Merleau-Ponty puts it, "It is the body in its orientation toward and action upon and within its surroundings that constitutes the initial meaning-giving act" (qtd in Young 147). Meaning, definition, identity, and structure, Merleau-Ponty argues are all derived from motility, movement through space. Because as Rockwell Gray says, ". . . the essence of human life has been wayfaring" (Gray 49), travel is an important metaphor by which we discuss other fundamental activities of life: we speak of our lives as a journey from birth to death and education as the road to knowledge. The journey is the metaphor by which we describe the mind's workings, our flights of fancy and imaginative adventures, our "Traveling in the unconscious" (Cixous 70). Even the word "metaphor" has meanings of transport, of carrying over, that suggests the restlessness of human nature. As your eyes travel through this introduction, as you read my words going across the page, keep track of how often you get up from this reading to move about the room and refresh yourself from your otherwise stationary task. Then you will have a sense of how basic movement, journeying, travel are to human life and why travel books continue to be among the most popular types of literature.

As will be evident from the many examples the authors of this collection use to illustrate their arguments, travel is a defining element of history and of literature, from the ancients to the moderns. Eric Leed argues that ". . . the history of travel is in crucial ways a history of the West" (and, we would add, not just of the West) (14), for it defines territories and boundaries, forms communities, and civilizes. He says, "Recorded history—the history of civilization—is a story of mobilities, migrations, settlements, of the adaptation of human groups to place and their integration into topography, the creation of 'homes'" (4). Indeed, in his essay on American history, George Pierson describes the "M-factor" of "movement, migration, mobility" as elemental in the formation of the American character (121), for movement, he argues, connotes change and transformation. And today we are finding that experiences of globalization and transnationalism describe not only economic movements across nations, but new definitions of culture and nationness. Thus, travel and mobility continue as defining elements of history, place, and people.

The ancient stories of Gilgamesh and Odysseus are plotted around the journey, the heroic venture that takes the protagonist (usually a male) out into the world—or sometimes beyond the "known" world to fantastical places—to test his mental and physical prowess, to gain knowledge of the world beyond the home borders, to achieve selfhood. These stories, like Telemachus's journey to seek news of his father or Gilgamesh's search for eternal life, suggest, even as they illustrate its hardships and dangers, that travel is a freeing and transformative experience from which the untested youth emerges a man, with knowledge, confidence and power. They suggest that travel is emancipatory and subversive, again as Telemachus frees himself from his mother's hold and returns to Ithaca set to subvert the will of the suitors. As Leed and others who study myth and the quest motif demonstrate, these are stories of "male potencies" (Leed 8) marked by "the rites of passage: *separation—initiation—return*" (Campbell 30). These ancient myths assume the sessility, or immobility, of women, the association of the female with place rather than travel. But women's travel is also subversive, even transgressive, for "The limitation of women's mobility, in terms both of identity and space, has been in some cultural contexts a crucial means of subordination" (Massey 179). Regardless, travel is traditionally seen as transformative and freeing, of promoting change for the individual and for institutions because the traveler gains knowledge not only about the wider world but about the self, making the journey a double voyage of discovery.

While modern travelers may not be able to visit the fantastical places Odysseus visited on his long return home—which for him was also fraught with hardship, loss, and grief—or to linger, entrapped, with the goddess Calypso on her island, we continue to use the word "odyssey" to describe travel and extended wanderings to unknown and far away places, like the outer reaches of space. At the same time, modern travel is also being defined to account for rapid globalization and the mass migrations and relocations, often forced, not only of individuals but of whole communities, illustrating again that the road can also be a "trail of tears." Much critical attention is being focused on the dynamics of postcolonialism, transnationalism, and globalization to examine the effects of imperialism and colonization on both the journeying colonizer and the colonized, the negotiation of cultural identity in the liminal spaces created by movement, and the often nomadic, displaced, diasporic quality of modern (or postmodern) life. Homi Bhabha in *The Location of Culture* calls this kind of disjunctive global crossing "the new internationalism" and says of this phenomenon, ". . . the demography of the new internationalism is the history of postcolonial migration, the narratives of cultural and political diaspora, the major social displacements of peasant and aboriginal communities, the poetics of exile, the grim prose of political and economic refugees" (5). Regardless of the kind of travel one undertakes, some commonalities remain in the defining discussions of travel. As the comment from Bhabha suggests, theorists continue to see the connections between the history of travel and the history of the world, and, as we shall see, discussion of travel continues to circulate around the same key issues: what constitutes travel and the homesite, the role of travel in the formation of identity, and the relations between travel, knowledge, and power.

TRAVEL

Sitting here at my desk composing this introduction, the word "travel" brings up images of vacation, of getting away from my work and visiting places different from the one in which I live but to which I will return refreshed and ready to get back to the mundane chores of every day. My mind wistfully conjures up imaginary voyages to Paris, Santiago, Santa Fe, perhaps even Uganda. As well, when Paul Fussell speaks of travel, he means travel "abroad" to foreign lands, the adventures that men (not women) of privilege, freedom, and education engage in and report about in their travel books, which hence take the reader "abroad, into the author's brain, and into his own" (204). Dean MacCannell likewise sees travel as a touristic event, but he finds that one does not have to go to the other side of the globe but can rather tour "society" or the social world and its material manifestations. In his account, a visit to Paris will take the tourist not only to historic and cultural sites (the "must-sees" on anyone's itinerary), but to neighborhoods, restaurants, and public works establishments like the Paris sewers. And Jean Baudrillard engages in travel, not so much to visit new places or to find himself, as to erase place and self in an elitist, postmodern blur that questions origins and authenticity. To that extent, Fussell, MacCannell, and Baudrillard define travel in ways familiar to many and in ways that tend to universalize travel around models of pleasure and escape. But the word "travel" has a multitude of meanings and connotations, not all of romantic tropic islands or exciting foreign cities.

Travel means different things to different people, depending on their reasons for journeying and their positions of gender, race, class, and ethnicity. Writing about tourists, Erik Cohen further argues that a person's relation of closeness to or alienation from society's "world-view" (180) affects not only the kind of travel but the value the tourist derives from the travel experience. While much of the traditional discussion of travel presupposes a male voyager and constructs paradigms of travel based on the free, adventure-seeking male, we must remember that this model does not apply to all journeyers. Relations to place, power, and identity, often based on racial, class, and ethnic backgrounds, make up part of the baggage that the traveler carries. Likewise, women tend to experience travel and mobility differently than do men, in large part because of women's traditional ties to home, family, and domesticity, and because of their sexual vulnerability and objectification at the hands of men. We must also remember that not all travel is voluntary, leisure or adventure travel, that many people migrate or cross boundaries to find jobs or a better life, which may or may not be realized. Indeed, Arjun Appadurai points to the deterritorialization of large sectors of migrant lower-class workers and populations of guestworkers who create a labor diaspora (11). And Norma Alarcón reminds us, ". . . the 'invitation' to cross over, when it is extended, does not ameliorate the lot of women of color . . ." (129), who often still remain in the margins of society.

Michel Butor also extends the activities of travel beyond tourism to include reading and writing as well as nomadism, settlement and exodus, emigration, round-trips, business trips, pilgrimages, and exploration, while Michel de Certeau reminds us that travel is an "everyday practice" (115). Students of the period of exploration and imperialism see travel as a colonizing, exploitive venture fraught with violence and power. For Bhabha, as we have seen, travel is a transnational experience of cultural displacement which is aggravated by the violence of compulsory relocation, refugeeism, and estrangement from home by external forces like natural catastrophes or war. And when anthropologist James Clifford speaks of travel, he connects home and travel together as "dwelling-in-travel" and "traveling-in-dwelling" (108). While most of the discussion about travel marks three stages of the journey—departure, passage, and arrival (Leed 21–22)—Clifford explodes the standard dichotomy between travel and home when he speaks of cultures or homes as "sites of dwelling *and* travel" (108).

HOME

The dialectic between home or place and travel runs through much of the traditional discussions of mobility. French philosopher Gaston Bachelard speaks of the home, the house, as the first location, "our corner of the world" in which we can "dream in peace" (5, 6). For Bachelard, this first home is a maternal site where the individual is nurtured and from which one emerges to experience the wider world. The connection between home and the maternal, shelter, and immobility has a biological foundation, for the female body is in fact the child's first place. As Julia Kristeva remarks, "the biological fate that causes us to be the *site* of the species chains us to *space*: home, native, soil, motherland" (*Nations* 33–34). This then is the home from which one must depart to be a sojourner of life's roads, the point of departure on the way to finding oneself—or of being dislocated from one's true self. Referring to her home as "the source, the mother, . . . my family, *mi tierra, mi gente*," Gloria Anzaldúa says, "I had to leave home so I could find myself" (16). Edward Said, on the other hand, speaking as an exile who longs for the home, connects the "native place" to the self's "true home" (137). Although Said's nostalgic longing for home is much different from Anzaldúa's sense of home as confining, both identify it with the native, the original site that stands in opposition to travel or the road.

This easy and seemingly natural dichotomy between home and the road is unsettled, however, by modern experiences of globalization and homelessness. As I have already pointed out, James Clifford finds he cannot separate dwelling from traveling, for even the most remote peoples have been touched by global commercialism. We have probably all been struck by pictures of the "native" talking on a cell phone, wearing a Mickey Mouse t- shirt, or eating a Big Mac hamburger. Doreen Massey demonstrates (in the essay collected here) how the "local" has become globalized by imaginatively walking her readers through her London neighborhood, which is the home not only of native Brits, but of Irish, Indian, Arab immigrants. Elsewhere, she argues that "we should question any characterization of place which is singular, essentialist, . . ." ("Double Articulation" 114), a point that Clifford Geertz also makes. He shows how even the legal system of Bali is not indigenous, but a mix of influences from the Islamic, Indic, and Malayo legal codes (183). Further, Arjun Appadurai sees the global flows of people, goods, and ideas as disjunctures between what he labels ethnoscapes, technoscapes, finanscapes, mediascapes, and ideoscapes. In other words, more than people move about the world; technology, money, ideas, and images also migrate and contribute to the globalization of culture. Globalization, however, Appadurai argues, is not the same as homogenization, for local cultures adapt and use the instruments of global flow (the five-scapes) for their own purposes, transforming to some extent their original meaning or intent.

The dichotomy between home and travel is also disrupted by people who find a "home" in traveling. Nomadic peoples obviously have made a home, defined as that region of comfort and protection that is a "symbol of self" (Feldman 184), in mobility. And the modern "nomad" who goes from country to country, city to city, traversing cultures and languages, refers not so much to an "original" home as to the latest habitation as "home." Rosi Braidotti, herself a nomadic intellectual, says that "As an intellectual style, nomadism consists not so much in being homeless, as in being capable of recreating your home everywhere." Braidotti sees the condition of the nomad and polyglot as the ideal condition for questioning assumptions of stability: ". . . being in between languages constitutes a vantage point in deconstructing identity" (16, 12). Likewise, Bhabha finds that in transnational displacement "the borders between home and world become confused," again upsetting the binaries of home and travel, of identity, and nationness, leaving a population that while it may be homeless is not necessarily "unhomed" (9). For Braidotti and Bhabha nomadism and transnationalism are not only historical events, but ideal intellectual postures from which to theorize and define the contemporary or postmodern condition.

One pitfall we must avoid when speaking of home—whether as a maternal place of origins or as a mobile home built in the interstices between cultures—is that of romanticizing it. We must remember that not all homes are nurturing, that as Caren Kaplan reminds us, ". . . homes are often sites of racism, sexism, and other damaging social practices" (194). One can be an exile, as was Anzaldúa, a lesbian Chicana feminist, from oneself at home. Likewise, as feminist thinkers have reminded us, our most intimate home, the body, is vulnerable to invasion and appropriation. As Shari Benstock puts it, "[A woman's] very body is the 'native land' on which patriarchy stakes its claims. Thus *matria* need not leave home to be exiled and expatriated . . . " (26). We must also remember that home or the local is not static, but is multidimensional, dynamic, a site of ongoing power relations, as Massey, Clifford, Bhabha, and Braidotti have argued. Put succinctly, "Seeing space as a moment in the intersection of configured social relations . . . means that it cannot be seen as static" (Massey 265). Geographer Gillian Rose describes what she calls a "paradoxical geography" as multiple, contradictory, and different, a "plurilocality" through which the individual must negotiate (151). Women, Rose contends, and we could say the same for everyone, move through layers of geographies or places during the course of a day, going from home, to the market, to the daycare center, the office, each of which has its own dynamics and to each of which she poses a conditional or paradoxical subjectivity.

IDENTITY

As we are beginning to see, there is a correlation between place and sub-jectivity, between the kind of place or position one occupies and one's sense of self. Psychologist H. M. Proshansky asserts that "place identity is an inte-gral part of the self" (in Sarbin 337), that the "who I am" is related to "where I am" (338). When one moves through space, travels, relocates, then the "who I am" undergoes some kind of transformation: the "ecology of the self" is restructured with a change in the environment (Hormuth 3). So strong are some people's ties to their home or homeland that forced reloca-tion can have deleterious effects on self-identity. The grief that many expe-rience when they are uprooted, Edward Krupat explains, is evidence that "forced relocation [is] an attack on 'self'" rather than on property (343). Thayer Scudder, the "dean" of community resettlement studies, points to the trauma of compulsory relocation and the multidimensional stress it pro-duces—physiological, psychological, and sociocultural. Psychological stress, he contends, has two aspects, "grieving for the lost home" syndrome and strong anxiety about the future, both of which adversely affect self-identity.

For those who choose travel or do not experience the trauma of being vio-lently uprooted, travel can facilitate more positive self-transformations. Indeed, it is an axiom of travel theory that with journeying one's sense of self changes, transforms, and that the wayfarer finds inner resources, matures: "Travel is the paradigmatic 'experience,' the model of a direct and genuine experience, which transforms the person having it" (Leed 71–72). In fact, "The connection between travel and the construction of identity has a long history" (Stowe xi). And as Carl Pedersen demonstrates, even the terror of the Middle Passage was transformative, for from it emerged new discourses and hybrid identities. The notion that the voyager reconstructs identity sug-gests the fluidity of identity and the need to "re-find" ourselves by recon-structing the cognitive maps by which we find our way in the world.

Discussion of travel brings into focus the invented, fluid, multiple, rela-tional, and as R. Radhakrishnan contends, intentional qualities of identity (210). For those living on the margins or borders or traveling between cul-tures—the displaced, nomad, immigrant—the question of identity presents itself on both personal and theoretical grounds. Finding herself in "a border culture" in the Río Grande valley of Texas between the United States and Mexico, Gloria Anzaludúa describes a *mestizo* or hybrid identity that is an uneasy negotiation marked by transgression, transition, and terror (3). "Living on borders and in margins, keeping intact one's shifting and multi-ple identity and integrity," she claims, "is like trying to swim in a new element, an 'alien' element" (1). Homi Bhabha, perhaps more optimistically than Anzaldúa, claims that the "'in-between' spaces [of gender, race, locale] provide the terrain for elaborating strategies of selfhood—singular or communal—that initiate new signs of identity . . ." (1–2). The immigrant likewise reconstructs identity, often "on the hyphen" between cultures (Pérez-Firmat), retaining memory of and affiliation to the original culture while adopting usages of and allegiance to the new. Whether through process of acculturation, transculturation, or as Pérez-Firmat prefers, biculturation, the immigrant or exile experiences a kind of double consciousness as both, for example, Cuban and American. Paul Gilroy uses the idea of double consciousness, famously articulated by W. E. B. Du Bois, to describe the "dialectics of diasporic identification" for Blacks living outside of Africa who are doubly identified by geographic dislocation from Africa and racial identification with Africa (9).

Travel abroad or to places different than our own, affects identity, for we often define ourselves in reaction to others. Certainly with new experiences and meeting new people, our world vision changes, but we also tend to define ourselves against the other. Eric Leed explains that "Social being and its chief categories—race, gender, and class—proceed from observations and identifications by others" (264). For example, writing about nineteenth-century Americans, Terry Caesar argues that travel abroad affected "America's imagination of itself as a nation" (8). It can also be said that America's idea of itself is affected by internal migrations—the M-Factor Pierson describes—as well as by the many immigrants who have changed the aspect of America. As well, the traveler's sense of self changes depending on how he/she is perceived. Indeed, one does not become a "stranger" until one leaves home and is viewed by someone else. The position of spectator is double sided, for both the visitor and the visited view each other and contribute to the construction of new identities. Thus, the traveler, a spectator of the native inhabitants, affects their identity, often rendered and codified as "other" than the traveler and a homogenous, stereotyped "they" that does not recognize individual differences (Pratt, "Scratches" 139). Likewise, as Mary Louise Pratt points out, in "contact zones" where colonizer and colonized meet, identity and influence are reciprocal, if uneven (*Imperial Eyes* 4). This reciprocity of influence also plays in the immigrant's effect on the adopted country. Radhakrishnan asks, "If the Asian is to be Americanized, will the American submit to Asianization?" (211). Indeed, Radhakrishnan and Appadurai both argue that national as well as individual identity is liable to be destabilized by the flows of peoples and the ideologies they carry with them from place to place.

KNOWLEDGE/POWER

At least since Telemachus left home to get word of Odysseus, travel and the acquisition of knowledge have been associated. What Telemachus learned, that his father's return was close at hand, empowered him when he returned to assert his will over his mother and to contest the presence of the suitors in his home. The relations between knowledge and power, theorized by Michel Foucault, notably in *The Archaeology of Knowledge* and *Power/Knowledge: Selected Interviews*, and their association with travel has informed the work of several prominent scholars and their investigation of colonialist, imperialist (or Orientalist, to use Edward Said's term), and postcolonialist discourses. What, for example, Said, Mary Louise Pratt, Sara Mills, and J. B. Harley, all influenced by Foucault, stress is the role of the production of knowledge in maintaining imperial rule over colonized peoples. In *Orientalism*, considered to be the foundational text of postcolonial studies, Said focuses on the ways by which the West processed knowledge about the East, the Orient, in ways that asserted and maintained the power of the West over an East continually presented as inferior, a representation which perniciously also plays into the East's conception of itself. Mary Louise Pratt, in *Imperial Eyes: Travel Writing and Transculturation* delineates types of travel writing during the age of European imperialism—manners-and-customs narratives, scientific writing, and sentimental travel writing—all of which codify and normalize the "native" other and territory according to European standards of knowledge and sensibility in order to validate European expansionist and capitalist projects. Sara Mills extends the work of Said and Pratt to interrogate the role gender plays in travel and travel writing and to contend that women's travel writing, particularly of the nineteenth century, also "produc[ed] knowledge that impacts upon the colonial presence," even if it was of a different order than men's (35). And J. B. Harley argues that cartography, mapmaking, is, to quote Foucault, "'a form of knowledge and a form of power'" (qtd in 279), for the mapmaker replicates not only the terrain but also "the territorial imperatives of a particular political system" (279). Anne McClintock problematizes to some extent Harley's understanding of the dynamics of imperialism and mapmaking. While she argues that "The map is a technology of knowledge" that supposedly captures the "truth" about a region, she also points to the "reminders of the failure of knowledge," rendered by the blank spaces on maps or areas labeled "cannibal," evidence to her of the anxiety of male impotence in the face of a feminized landscape (27–28). Regardless of any anxiety about the imperialist project, the person or political system that makes the maps or writes the documents controls to some extent the accepted definitions of place and peoples, and often uses those documents to wield power over the inscribed region.

What is at issue, then, is not so much that the traveler gains knowledge about other places and peoples as well as about the self, but what use the traveler and travel text make of that knowledge. What writers like Said, Pratt, Mills, Harley, and McClintock stress is that travel and travel writing or maps can become instruments of political, military, scientific, and economic power as well as of racism and sexism, themselves tools of power exercised over others. What they also suggest is that the "knowledge" the traveler gains is often "misknowledge" or incorrect interpretations and stereotypes of indigenous culture. But even this misinformation is powerful, for in the hands of the imperial author, it shapes the accepted history of the colony, the accepted identity of the colonized peoples. Chinua Achebe makes this concept come to life at the end of his novel, *Things Fall Apart*, when the District Commissioner, an agent of the British crown, reduces Okonkwo's life, which has taken the entire novel to unfold, to "a reasonable paragraph" in his projected book, *The Pacification of the Primitive Tribes of the Lower Niger*, a book which has nothing to do with the real history or culture of the Igbo people.

At issue in Achebe's novel and in much of the work of anthropologists, who are also travelers and travel writers, is the source of knowledge. Who can best supply information about a culture—local informants or outsiders? Achebe clearly believes that the native African knows Africa better than a European, even an astute one like Joseph Conrad, whose novel *The Heart of Darkness*, he argues in "An Image of Africa: Racism in Conrad's *Heart of Darkness*," gives a fractured and racist view of Africa. But anthropologists like James Clifford and Clifford Geertz contest that position. Geertz argues that the natives may be too close to the culture to interpret it, too "imprisoned within their mental horizons" to produce an ethnography built around a thesis (57–58). Clifford maintains that the "native informant" is a problematic figure because many "emerge as travelers" who are both inside and outside their own cultures. Like the Native American Squanto who greeted the pilgrims in 1620, the informant is often already well-traveled and equipped with an ethnographic agenda that makes his "information" suspect (97). And like Squanto, the native engages in uneasy relations of power with the traveler and the production of knowledge.

POSTMODERNISM

Travel itself has become a metaphor for the postmodern condition where conceptual boundaries are blurred and the unfixed identity of the tourist, the stranger, or the nomad describes the postmodern individual who resists the illusion of unity or is alienated from society. Zygmunt Bauman puts it this way: *"The hub of postmodern life strategy is not making identity stand—but the avoidance of being fixed."* For him "The figure of the tourist is the epitome of such avoidance" since tourists do not belong to the place they visit and are continually on the move (89–90). For Rosi Braidotti the metaphor of nomadism best describes the postmodern condition because it refers to "the kind of critical consciousness that resists settling into socially coded modes of thought and behavior" (5). Other terms related to travel—alienation, homelessness, and exile—also define the condition of the postmodern man or woman of ideas who questions paradigms of knowledge, power, and identity, though actual exiles like Said object to the metaphorization of their particular experience.

Even the kinds of places the postmodern tourist visits, the hyperreal and the simulated, question the possibility of the settled and the authentic. Terry Caesar, borrowing from Jean Baudrillard and Umberto Eco, defines the hyperreal as "having to do with copying, falsity, imitation, illusion, and reproduction" (64). When we visit not Bavarian castles but Disney's version of them (or Euro-Disney's version of Disneyland), we are traveling in the unauthentic (the simulated) which is nonetheless real (or hyperreal) and provides for us a real experience. Our souvenirs, often miniature versions of the original, stand in as signs of an original experience and take on a meaning or value of their own. In fact, the gift shop has become almost as popular an attraction as the sight itself, the t-shirt as valued as the experience. As postmoderns and travelers of the hyperreal, we thus can occupy multiple spaces, experience multiple times and identities, leaving us freer from confining definitions and hierarchies but also a little dizzier and lost.

The alienation of the traveler in "unmapped" territory, speed's obliteration of meaning with the obliteration of place, the transitory, transitional meeting grounds of the hotel, motel, airport, and train station are markers of postmodern aesthetics and identity. "In search of *astral* America," Jean Baudrillard finds it in "the America of desert speed" that erases details in an "aesthetics of disappearance" and yet expands "the mental desert" of the traveler's mind (5). He finds an America of motels and surfaces and a journey that takes on the hyperreality of cinema. Frederic Jameson describes the postmodern aesthetic in terms of "saturated space," like the hotel, where one is "exposed to a perceptual barrage of immediacy" (351) as travelers, luggage, attendants come and go in a perpetual flow and a perpetual din of noise. And Braidotti speaks of "places of transit that go with traveling: stations and airport lounges, trams, shuttle buses, and check-in areas" as "privileged sites of creation for contemporary artists" because they suggest the transitoriness of identities and boundaries (18–19) that mark the postmodern condition.

Moreover, the politics of location and of mobility have informed feminist and gender discussions. Much of the work of feminists has gone towards destabilizing readings of female identity, of arguing for fluidity of identity and the performative quality of gender. Angelika Bammer says, ". . . our sense of identity is ineluctably, it seems, marked by the peculiarly postmodern geography of identity: both here *and* there and neither here *nor* there at one and the same time"; in other words, "displaced" (xii). Ever since poet Adrienne Rich coined the phrase "politics of location" in her "Notes toward a Politics of Location," feminists also have been investigating how specific locations impinge on female identity. Rich maps her own politics of location when she says, ". . . I need to understand how a place on the map is also a place in history within which as a woman, a Jew, a lesbian, a feminist I am created and trying to create" (212). Feminist scholars have extended Rich's understanding to see how "in creating our own centers and our own locals, we tend to forget that our centers displace others into the peripheries of our making" (Probyn 176). Thinking about identity as location (as well as relocation) has thus become a postmodern project that interrogates "the contradictory and complex subject formation in postmodernity" (Kaplan, *Questions* 183–84) and a transnational project that avoids essentializing "woman" across cultural, ethnic, class, and racial boundaries. Because they question the binaries of center and margin, inclusion and exclusion, and pose multiple versions of identity, the politics of location and mobility provide metaphors for the intellectual and cultural displacement caused by rapid, ongoing social change and globalization.

Travel, as we have seen, is a complex matter, encompassing a variety of travel experiences—family vacation, political exile, exploration of distant lands, immigration, mundane shopping trips—and theoretical approaches to defining travel. The field of travel itself "travels" across academic and theoretical boundaries, bringing together sociology, anthropology, geography, history, psychology, and literary criticism. Recognizing the multidimensionality of travel, this book endeavors to provide an accessible entry into some of the defining and definitive discussions going on among some of the best thinkers in this diverse field of study. The authors collected here are those to whom other scholars on travel refer and who refer to each other, making this collection much like an actual conversation among thinkers. In selecting the essays, I have attempted to be as inclusive as possible, to represent a variety of travel experiences, from tourism to immigration and exile to the "new internationalism," and to represent a variety of theoretical and political positions about travel in an effort not so much to consolidate opinion but to open discussion. Thus while there are many excellent essays on any one particular aspect of travel, like the semiotics of tourism, I have selected a representative essay or two in order to leave space in the anthology for other discussions.

The essays are organized into four sections in order both to represent the central concerns of definitions of travel, some of which I have outlined in this introduction, and to question some of our assumptions about travel. As a whole the book moves from the general to the particular, from broad views of travel to close examinations of specific travel experiences or narratives. Beginning with essays that provide readers with categories and definitions by which to understand travel experiences, the collection moves to essays that take up specific issues, such as imperialism, exile, and American migration. The first section, "Travel and Tourism," maps out the general perimeters of travel and provides some definitions. The second section, "Reading and Writing Travel," examines the links between travel experiences and the word, the connections between the activities of travel, reading, and writing. "The New Internationalism," the third section, considers modern experiences in a globalized world—postcolonial migration, cultural and political diaspora, forced dislocation, and exile. The final section, "The Politics of Relocation," examines experiences of forced relocation, immigration, and migration within an American context. The logic of the collection, then, is to engage both readers and authors of the collection in a lively discussion that is sure to enrich the separate essays as well as the reader's understanding of definitions of travel.

Traveling across disciplines and individual experiences, we find that travel is itself an unsettled term, one whose definition depends on the particular "politics of location" of the writer. If, as William Least Heat Moon, author of *Blue Highways*, contends, mobility "has been one of the elemental qualities of the American experience," what constitutes mobility (and, we might add, America) is not so easily defined (20). Mobility, too, is mobile.

WORKS CITED

Achebe, Chinua. "An Image of Africa: Racism in Conrad's *Heart of Darkness*." *Hopes and Impediments: Selected Essays*. New York: Doubleday, 1988, 1–20.

——. *Things Fall Apart*. New York: Fawcett Crest, 1959.

Alarcón, Norma. "Traddutora, Traditora: A Paradigmatic Figure of Chicana Feminism." *Scattered Hegemonies: Postmodernity and Transnational Feminist Practices*. Ed. Inderpal Grewal and Caren Kaplan. Minneapolis: U of Minnesota P, 1994. 110–33.

Anzaldúa, Gloria. *Borderlands/La Frontera: The New Mestiza*. San Francisco: Spinsters/Aunt Lute, 1987.

Appadurai, Arjun. "Disjuncture and Difference in the Global Cultural Economy." *Public Culture* 2.2 (Spring 1990): 1–24.

Bachelard, Gaston. *The Poetics of Space*. Trans. Maria Jolas. Boston: Beacon, 1969.

Bammer, Angelika. Introduction. *Displacements: Cultural Identities in Question*. Ed. Angelika Bammer. Bloomington: Indiana UP, 1994, xi–xx.

Baudrillard, Jean. *America*. Trans. Chris Turner. London: Verso, 1988.

Bauman, Zygmunt. *Postmodernity and Its Discontents*. Cambridge: Polity, 1997.

Benstock, Shari. "Expatriate Modernism: Writing on the Cultural Rim." *Women's Writing in Exile*. Ed. Mary Jane Broe and Angela Ingram. Chapel Hill: U of North Carolina P, 1989. 19–40.

Bhabha, Homi. *The Location of Culture*. London: Routledge, 1994.

Braidotti, Rosi. *Nomadic Subjects: Embodiment and Sexual Difference in Contemporary Feminist Theory*. New York: Columbia UP, 1994.

Butor, Michel. "Travel and Writing." *Mosaic* 8.1 (1974): 1–16.

Caesar, Terry. "Brutal Naïveté and Special Lighting: Hyperspatiality and Landscape in the American Travel Text." *College Literature* 21.1 (February 1994): 63–79.

——. *Forgiving the Boundaries: Home as Abroad in American Travel Writing*. Athens, Ga.: U of Georgia P, 1995.

Campbell, Joseph. *The Hero with a Thousand Faces*. Princeton: Princeton UP, 1949.

Cixous, Hélène. *Three Steps on the Ladder of Writing*. Trans. Sarah Cornell and Susan Sellers. New York: Columbia UP, 1993.

Clifford, James. "Traveling Cultures." *Cultural Studies*. Ed. Lawrence Grossberg, Cary Nelson, and Paula Treicher. New York: Routledge, 1992. 96–112.

Feldman, Roberta M. "Settlement-Identity: Psychological Bonds with Home Places in a Mobile Society." *Environment and Behavior* 22 (March 1990): 183–229.

Foucault, Michel. *The Archaeology of Knowledge*. Trans. A. M. Sheridan Smith. New York: Harper & Row, 1976.

——. *Power/Knowledge: Selected Interviews and Other Writings, 1972–1977*. Ed. Colin Gordon, trans. Colin Gordon. New York: Pantheon Books, 1980.

Fussell, Paul. *Abroad: British Literary Traveling Between the Wars*. New York: Oxford UP, 1980.

Geertz, Clifford. *Local Knowledge: Further Essays in Interpretive Anthropology*. New York: Basic Books, 1983.

Gilroy, Paul. "It Ain't Where You're From, It's Where You're At: The Dialectics of Diasporic Identification." *Third Text* 13 (1990–91): 3–16.

Gray, Rockwell. "Travel." *Temperamental Journeys: Essays on the Modern Literature of Travel.* Ed. Michael Kowalewski. Athens, Ga.: U of Georgia P, 1992. 33–50.

Harley, J. B. "Maps, Knowledge, and Power." *Iconography of Landscape: Essays on the Symbolic Representation, Design and Use of Past Environment.* Ed. Denis Cosgrove and Stephen Daniels. Cambridge: Cambridge UP, 1988. 277–312.

Hormuth, Stefan E. *The Ecology of the Self: Relocation and Self-Concept Change.* Cambridge: Cambridge UP, 1990.

Jameson, Frederic. "Cognitive Mapping." *Marxism and the Interpretation of Culture.* Ed. Cary Nelson and Lawrence Grossberg. Urbana: U of Illinois P, 1988. 347–57.

Kaplan, Caren. "Deterritorializations: The Rewriting of Home and Exile in Western Feminist Discourse." *Cultural Critique* 6 (Spring 1987): 187–98.

———. *Questions of Travel: Postmodern Discourse of Displacement.* Durham: Duke UP, 1996.

Kristeva, Julia. *Nations without Nationalism.* Trans. Leon S. Roudiez. New York: Columbia UP, 1993.

Krupat, Edward. "A Place for Place Identity." *Journal of Environmental Psychology* 3 (1983): 343–44.

Leed, Eric J. *The Mind of the Traveler: From Gilgamesh to Global Tourism.* New York: Basic Books, 1991.

MacCannell, Dean. *The Tourist: A New Theory of the Leisure Class.* New York: Schocken Books, 1976; Berkeley: U of California P, 1999. New York: Routledge, 1995.

McClintock, Anne. *Imperial Leather: Race, Gender and Sexuality in the Colonial Contest.* New York: Routledge, 1995.

Massey, Doreen. "Double Articulation: A Place in the World." *Displacements: Cultural Identities in Question.* Ed. Angelika Bammer. Bloomington: Indiana UP, 1994.

———. *Space, Place, and Gender.* Minneapolis: U of Minnesota P, 1994.

Moon, William Least Heat. "Journeys into Kansas." *Temperamental Journeys: Essays on the Modern Literature of Travel.* Ed. Michael Kowalewski. Athens, Ga.: U of Georgia P, 1992. 19–24.

Mills, Sara. "Knowledge, Gender, and Empire." *Writing Women and Space: Colonial and Postcolonial Geographies.* Ed. Alison Blunt and Gillian Rose. New York: Guilford P, 1994. 29–50.

Pérez–Firmat, Gustavo. *Life on the Hyphen: The Cuban-American Way.* Austin: U of Texas P, 1994.

Pierson, George W. "The M-Factor in American History." *The Character of Americans.* Ed. Michael McGiffert, rev. ed. Homewood, Ill.: Dorsey P, 1970. 118–30.

Pratt, Mary Louise. *Imperial Eyes: Travel Writing and Transculturation.* New York: Routledge, 1992.

———. "Scratches on the Face of the Country; or, What Mr. Barrow Saw in the Land of the Bushmen." *Critical Inquiry* 12.1 (Autumn 1985): 119–43.

Probyn, Elspeth. "Travels in the Postmodern: Making Sense of the Local." *Feminism/Postmodernism.* Ed. Linda Nicholson. New York: Routledge, 1990. 176–89.

Radhakrishnan, R. *Diasporic Mediations: Between Home and Location.* Minneapolis: U of Minnesota P, 1996.

Rich, Adrienne. *Blood, Bread, and Poetry: Selected Prose 1979–1985.* New York: W. W. Norton, 1986.

Rose, Gillian. *Feminism and Geography: The Limits of Geographical Knowledge.* Minneapolis: U of Minnesota P, 1993.

Said, Edward J. *Orientalism.* New York: Vintage Books, 1979.

———. "Reflections on Exile." *Granta* 13 (Autumn 1984): 159–72.

Sarbin, Theodore. "Place Identity as a Component of Self: An Addendum." *Journal of Environmental Psychology* 3 (1983): 337–42.

Scudder, Thayer. *No Place to Go: Effects of Compulsory Relocation on Navajos.* Philadelphia: Institute for the Study of Human Issues, 1982.

Stowe, William W. *Going Abroad: European Travel in Nineteenth- Century American Culture.* Princeton: Princeton UP, 1994.

Young, Iris Marion. *Throwing Like a Girl and Other Essays in Feminist Philosophy and Social Theory.* Bloomington: Indiana UP, 1990.

TRAVEL AND TOURISM

"Travel and Tourism" introduces readers to the place of travel in history and in thinking about human culture. It also brings together essays that explore and define the tourist and categories of tourism. What does it mean to travel? What is the effect of journeying on the traveler and the way humans perceive their place in the world? What does it matter where and how one travels? These questions are essential in understanding not only the condition of the road but the human condition in relation to place, others, and the past. They help us understand the role of mobility as an inherent activity of human nature and in the construction or de-construction of individual and collective identities.

The essays in this section argue for the importance of travel and tourism in making meaning of our lives and society, even if they disagree on the mechanics of meaning-making, the categories of travel, or the dichotomy between place and mobility. Eric Leed's sketch, "The Ancients and the Moderns: From Suffering to Freedom," taken from his extensive history of travel, *The Mind of the Traveler: From Gilgamesh to Global Tourism*, argues that the meaning of travel has changed through time. For the ancients, travel is "an explication of human fate and necessity," often decreed by the gods, in which the traveler is marked, tested, and transformed by the experience. The paradigm of the classic heroic journey continues in modern travel narratives, even if the modern traveler is tested only by inconveniences. For the modern, travel is an "expression of freedom and an escape from necessity and purpose." In this brief selection Leed points to the changes in the self of the traveler, often within a pattern of penance and purification, and to the connections between travel and ideologies of freedom and individualism. Leed's essay is an excellent introduction to travel, travelers, and the issues that concern other writers—the nature of the experience, and the tension between place and mobility—even if not all agree with him.

Moving from heroic journeys to more mundane ones, the essay by Dean

MacCannell, taken from his *The Tourist: A New Theory of the Leisure Class*, outlines the travel experiences of the ordinary tourist who, he argues, is a kind of sociologist of modern society. MacCannell approaches tourism through a structuralist semiotics that defines a "tourist attraction as an empirical relationship between a *tourist*, a *sight* and a *marker* (a piece of information about a sight)." The relationships between sight, tourist, and marker lead to an institutionalized consensus about what constitutes a touristic attraction. MacCannell then outlines the stages of sight sacralization, the means by which a sight is converted into a tourist attraction: naming, framing and elevating, enshrinement, mechanical reproduction, and social reproduction (when groups, cities, regions name themselves after famous attractions). Seeing the system of tourist attractions as revelatory of social systems, MacCannell claims that "taken together, tourist attractions and the behavior surrounding them are . . . one of the most complex and orderly of the several universal codes that constitute modern society." At the same time, then, that tourism is a model of social structure, it converts modern society into a touristic attraction, something subject to the gaze of the outsider, and the tourist into a sociologist.

Arguing against an oversimplification of "*the* tourist," Erik Cohen maps out "A Phenomenology of Tourist Experiences." Reframing the debate over the superficiality or authenticity of tourism, Cohen suggests that there are actually five types of tourists or touristic experiences, each with its own demands for authenticity. Cohen borrows from socio-religious discussion of society as having a moral or spiritual center to argue that one's relation to that center, or the degree of alienation from it, engenders the kind of touristic experience the traveler has. The first type of touristic mode Cohen discusses is the "recreational mode" in which travel is a form of entertainment and endows the tourist with a general sense of well-being which restores the individual to society. For this traveler the authenticity of the experience is irrelevant. The second type is the "diversionary mode," a mere escape from the boredom and meaningless of routine life. Next is the "experiential mode" by which the tourist looks for meaning outside of the home society by experiencing authenticity in the lives of others. The "experimental" tourist seeks authenticity, but rather than being merely content to observe that life (like the experiential traveler), this tourist participates in the different alternative societies encountered in the search for personal meaning. Finally, the "existential" traveler undergoes a kind of conversion experience as a result of travel and switches worlds, temporarily, sporadically, or permanently. This traveler elects a new center for life, much like the religious pilgrim. With this taxonomy of touristic experiences, Cohen counters simplistic views of tourism at the same time that he adheres to a spiritually based reading of society and the journey.

This first section is rounded out by Jean Baudrillard's account from his book *America* of his automobile journey through the American Southwest. In lyrical and elliptical fashion, Baudrillard writes of the "aesthetics of disappearance" that the sameness and horizontality, the surface, of the American desert represents. He speaks of speed as a pure form that produces transparency, dissolves the particulars of the landscape into a kind of nothingness, that produces abstractions against the picturesque qualities of nature. This abstraction allows him to see the desert as empty and primitive (which, of course, it is not) and to imagine a future likewise empty and primitive, even in its hybrid, complex forms. Pure travel, he asserts, is not about seeing the sights but of space and speed where everything is discovered and everything is obliterated, where the specifics become a blur in the windshield of the speeding automobile and speed itself loses meaning. In this way, Baudrillard uses travel to speak of the postmodern condition and to hypothesize about the future, a scene without stable meaning but constituted by "empty, absolute freedom."

As travel for Baudrillard, looking through the "view finder" of his car windshield, seems like a cinematic production, so for MacCannell and Cohen, and even Leed, travel entertains or improves the individual traveler, who they imagine has a certain degree of time and money to expend on adventure travel or tourism. At issue as well in much discussion of touristic travel is the authenticity of the travel experience. While some might insist that the traveler visit "authentic" locations, uncorrupted by contact with a materialistic world, Cohen questions the need for authenticity for all tourists, claiming that for some the simulated constitutes a viable experience. The authors in this section also make assumptions about freedom—the freedom to travel and freedom derived from going out on the road—which are not born out in all types of travel. Indeed, the journeys described in "Travel and Tourism" are by and large entered into freely by the traveler for adventure or recreation. And the traveler is generally assumed to be a male with the freedom and means to visit distant sites in order to experience something out of the ordinary, an assumption that is rather problematic given the many types of travel people engage in, as essays in the following sections will demonstrate.

And while these essays are important statements about travel and tourism, they are not necessarily the last word on the subject. Since travel and travel literature are so popular, much has been written about particular moments in the history of travel and about issues related to travel or tourism. For example, the distinction between "authentic" travel, as Leed assumes, and the "hyperreal" is questioned by Terry Caesar, and the dichotomy between place and mobility, home and away, is rejected by James Clifford, who posits a "dwelling-in-travel." Likewise the reasons for leisure travel and what it means to the tourist are looked at differently by Nelson Graburn, who sees tourism as a part of the cycle of life that alternates between the mundane and the sacred or unordinary, and by Jonathan Culler, who sees it as a search for the authentic. The mechanics of technology in travel, which for Baudrillard in his speeding automobile marks his view of the desert Southwest, is explored by Wolfgang Schivelbusch in his landmark study of the effect of the railroad on travel and the panoramic view of the landscape it afforded. Kris Lackey's *Road Frames* further makes the connection between the means of travel, the automobile, and vision—for American roadsters it is a vision of liberty and individualism.

FOR FURTHER READING

Caesar, Terry. "Brutal Naïveté and Special Lighting: Hyperspatiality and Landscape in the American Travel Text." *College English* 21.1 (February 1994): 63–79.

Clifford, James. "Traveling Cultures." *Cultural Studies*. Ed. Lawrence Grossberg, Cary Nelson, and Paula Treicher. New York: Routledge, 1992. 96–112.

Culler, Jonathan. "The Semiotics of Tourism." *Framing the Sign: Criticism and Its Institutions*. Norman: U of Oklahoma P, 1989, 153–67.

Graburn, Nelson. "Tourism: The Sacred Journey." *Hosts and Guests: The Anthropology of Tourism*. Ed. Valene Smith. Philadelphia: U of Pennsylvania P, 1977. 17–31.

Lackey, Kris. *Road Frames: The American Highway Narrative*. Lincoln: U of Nebraska P, 1997.

Schivelbusch, Wolfgang. *The Railway Journey: Trains and Travel in the 19th Century*. Trans. Anselm Hollo. New York: Urizen Books, 1979.

THE ANCIENTS AND THE MODERNS

From Suffering to Freedom

Eric Leed

> "Here we go, we're all together. . . . What did we do in New York? Let's forgive." We had all had our spats back there. "That's behind us, merely by miles and inclinations. . . . " We all jumped to the music and agreed. The purity of the road.
>
> *Jack Kerouac, 1957*

Ancient and modern conceptions of the "meaning" of travel are very different, as are their emphases on the transformations effected by a journey. The ancients valued travel as an explication of human fate and necessity; for moderns, it is an expression of freedom and an escape from necessity and purpose. Ancients saw travel as a suffering, even a penance; for moderns, it is a pleasure and a means to pleasure. Ancient epics of travel describe those motions through which individuals, in groups and often armed, confirmed an order of the world and demonstrated their status; travel today is marketed as a means of discovery, of acquiring access to something new, original, and even unexpected.

In general, the ancients most valued the journey as an explication of fate or necessity, as a revelation of those forces that sustain and shape, alter and govern human destinies. The travels narrated in the *Odyssey* and *The Epic of Gilgamesh* are god-decreed and thus not wholly voluntary nor pleasurable. Odysseus wanders on a long, frustrating journey toward home, personified by Penelope, the territorialized and virtuous woman whose exclusion of suitors preserves that home. When Odysseus finally arrives in Ithaca, disguised as a beggar, he thanks the swineherd Eumaeus for his hospitality in terms that adequately express the ancient conception of travel as a driven state of exis-

5

tence, a necessitated, even prophesied suffering: "You have given me rest from the pains and miseries of wandering. To be driven hither and then thither—nothing mortals endure can be worse than that, yet men will bear with such utter wretchedness, will accept such wandering and grief and sorrow for the sake of their accursed bellies."[1]

The sufferings of travel clearly frame and intensify the significance of the heroic traveler's actions. When Odysseus accepts the challenge of the nobles of Sphacteria to compete in their games, he cites the wastings and reductions of travel as factors that will make his victory even more significant: "As you see me now, I am ground down by distress and misery; I have had many trials to endure, fighting my way through hostile warriors and battering waves. Yet nevertheless, despite all sufferings, I will try my fortune in your contests. Your insult rankles and you have roused me."[2] The ability to rise to the new occasion despite the losses and frictions of the journey demonstrates, at the very least, that Odysseus, even though reduced, is still superior to the best efforts of the locals. The rhythm of this epic, the recurrent pattern of phallic self-assertion and exhaustion, of freedom and captivity, suggests that it is a narrative of male potencies deployed in the classical journey.

This emphasis upon travel as a test, as a loss that brings a gain of stature and certainty of self, suggests that the changes of character effected by travel are not so much the introduction of something new into the personality of the traveler as a revelation of something ineradicably present—perhaps courage, perdurance, the ability to endure pain, the persistence of skills and abilities even in a context of fatigue and danger. The transformations of passage are a species of "identification" through action, which adds to the being in motion only a consciousness of the irreducible form and individuality of that being. In the difficult and dangerous journey, the self of the traveler is impoverished and reduced to its essentials, allowing one to see what those essentials are.

In this sense, the heroic journey resembles what the critic and philosopher Kenneth Burke has spoken of as a "fictional death" (Personal communication, 1978)—fictional rather than real because death is used as a context for the assertion of an essential and irreducible self; implicitly denied is the reality of death as a dissolution of form and a solvent of identity. The *topos* of the fictional death is prominent in funeral orations, in narrations of epic and heroic journeys as well as in war literature, in which it is frequently assumed that a "true" and genuine self is tried, proven, reduced to its essence by a journey through the valley of death. This *topos*, characteristic of ancient journeys, occurs in modern adventure travels and travels of discovery. Captain James Cook, upon reading the journals of his gentlemen companions, became indignant, believing that they had exaggerated the perils encountered on the around-the-world voyage of the *Endeavour* (1768–71): but he resigned himself to their hyperbole as inevitable:

> [S]uch are the dispositions of men in general in these voyages that they are seldom content with the hardships and dangers which will naturally occur, but they must add others which hardly ever had existence but in their imaginations, by magnifying the most trifling accidents and circumstances to the greatest hardships, and insurmountable dangers ... as if the whole merit of the voyage consisted in the dangers and hardships they underwent, or that real ones did not happen often enough to give the mind sufficient anxiety; thus posterity are taught to look upon these voyages as hazardous to the highest degree.[3]

The dangers and fatigues of travel remain today, in some sense, a test of the heroism of the traveler. The great structural anthropologist Claude Lévi-Strauss, who ostensibly despises the mere tourist and the self-promoting adventurer ("adventure has no place in the anthropologist's profession"), nevertheless makes use of the traditional *topos* in gauging the value of what an ethnographer acquires on a voyage to the peripheries. The anthropologist "may endure months of travelling, hardships, and sickening boredom for the purpose of recording (in a few days, or even few hours) a hitherto unknown myth, a new marriage rule or a complete list of clan names."[4] In some sense, hardship, boredom, and physical effort contribute to the value of the rite or myth recorded, and to the stature of the anthropologist among equals.

Indeed, the fatigues and characteristic dangers of the journey may be precisely calibrated and itemized in one's hotel bill. A hotel in the Ecuadorean Amazon advertises, "The hosts try very hard to meet individual interests and provide levels of adventure according to what you feel you are up to—from easy guided walks on marked trails to strenuous Outward Bound-style overnight hikes through the forest, which make you feel like the real Indiana Jones."[5]

The fatigues of travel, the sufferings of the journey, remain a cause and a measure of the extent to which a traveler is marked and tested by experience, becoming *bewandert*— "skilled" and "wise." It is this factor that distinguishes the mere tourist from the real and genuine traveler, for whom travel is a test rather than a pleasure. This traditional theme persists beneath the modern emphasis upon pleasures of travel, which in any case do not exist, Albert Camus insists, for those traveling on cheap tickets or with no tickets at all.[6] For the poor contemporary traveler, travel retains its ancient significance and is given value by the fear that makes the individual "porous" and sensitive. However ancient the theme, Camus's emphasis is modern: the fear of the wayfarer, the loss of security implicit in unaccommodated travel is a gain of accessibility and sensitivity to the world. Travel, from the moment of departure, removes those furnishings and mediations that come with a familiar residence. It thus substantiates individuality in its sense of "autonomy," for the self is now separated from a confirming and confining matrix.

Today the very vicissitudes, strippings, and wastings that constituted the ancient sufferings of the traveler are prized as an ascetic, disciplined freedom, as the confirmation of an individuality that encounters directly a world held at bay by the walls and boundaries of one's home. "'Being naked' always has associations of physical liberty, of harmony between the earth and men who have become freed of human things."[7] The sufferings of travel constitute a simplification of life that enhances the objectivity of a world within which the traveler becomes aware of an irreducible subjectivity, a self. This contemporary conception of the strippings and wastings of travel as a freedom from mediations is only a present appearance of the ancient conception of travel as a penance and a purification which have a morally improving effect upon the traveler. The conception of travel as a penance is as old as the journey of the primal pair, evicted from the Garden for their sins and enjoined to travel and labor as an expiation for those sins. Departure breaks the bonds between the sinner and the site and occasions of the sin. It is a way of leaving trouble behind. This is perhaps the reason travel, as exile, was conceived to be at once punishment and cure, retribution and purification. The stripping away by the frictions of passage of all that is not of the essence of the passenger, the removal of defining associations, of bonds to the world of place—all effect changes in the character of the traveler that are strictly analogous to a cleansing, the reduction of the purified entity to its smallest, truest dimensions.

The penance of travel was also prescribed to the second biblical generation, as Cain was set upon his course of wanderings for his act of fratricide, the act that alienated him from the soil that had defined him and that he had watered with his brother's blood. Denying him any further attachment to the soil, God made wandering Cain's permanent condition: "When you till the ground, it will no longer yield you its wealth. You shall be a vagrant and a wanderer upon the earth." At the same moment, God decreed the sanctity of the wanderer whose travels and exile are his penance and make him sacrosanct, with the "mark of Cain": "So the Lord put a mark on Cain, in order that anyone meeting him should not kill him."[8]

Pilgrimage is the institutionalization of this transformation of travel, a formalization of the notion that travel purifies, cleanses, removes the wanderer from the site of transgressions. This notion is explicit in the charter of Buddhist pilgrimage, the *Aitareya Brahmana*: "There is no happiness for him who does not travel; living in the society of men, the best man often becomes a sinner; for Indra [Vedic deity of rain and thunder] is the friend of the traveler. Therefore wander."[9] Here the loss of travel may be a moral and psychological gain—as was understood by that modern Odysseus, Neil Cassady, fictionalized as Moriarity, in Jack Kerouac's epic *On the Road*, who left behind any number of sins in a life spent in passage.[10] ****

Implicit in the conception of travel as a penance and a purge is the assumption that "self" and "place" are integrated realities, and that the self may be changed with change of place. The reductive effects of travel begin with the first term of a journey—departure, a separation requiring one to leave behind much that has previously defined the civil self. This event transforms the passenger into a species not unlike Rousseau's savage man, who has his own forces constantly at his disposal and carries himself "whole and entire" about with him. But such stripping away of defining relations and furnishings of the civil self is often painful, evoking protest, grief, and mourning. Departure is an occasion of human suffering. Though celebrated in modern travel, departure was traditionally undertaken only for the most urgent of motives. These may be explicit or implicit, and they change over time. **** [A] particular age places certain motives ahead of others, decreeing the propriety of traveling as a penance, a purification, a test, a liberation, a pleasure, a satisfaction of curiosity. **** [Just as evident is the] transition from the ancient emphasis upon travel as a necessary suffering to the modern emphasis upon travel as an experience of freedom and the gaining of autonomy.

The ancients had no conception of travel as a voluntary and altruistic act. Even ancient tourism, which flourished under the *Pax Romana*, appears to Seneca as a driven state of existence, a distracted wandering:

> This is the reason why men undertake aimless wanderings, travel along distant shores and at one time by sea, at another by land, try to soothe the fickleness of disposition which is always dissatisfied with the present. "Now, let us make for Campania: now I am sick of rich cultivation: let us see something of wild regions, let us thread the passes of Brulli and Lucania: yet amid this wilderness one wants something of beauty to relieve our pampered eyes after so long dwelling on savage wastes. Let us seek Tarentum with its famous harbor, its mild winter climate. . . . Let us now return to town; our ears have long missed its shouts and noise: it would be pleasant also to enjoy the sight of human bloodshed." Thus one journey succeeds another, and one sight is changed for another.[11]

The travels of Odysseus, Heracles, and many other ancient heroes were imposed upon them by an external "command"—from a god, a goddess, fate. The identity-defining travels of the medieval knight were, on the other hand, ostensibly voluntary and undertaken to no utilitarian purpose. The chivalric journey, which is the pattern and model for significant modern travel, is essentially self-referential, undertaken to reveal the essential character of the knight as "free," once the essence of nobility but since the seventeenth century considered an attribute of human nature. The voluntariness of departure and the solitude of the knight identified the new concept of adventure; travel became a demonstration of freedom from necessity, the mark of a status above the "commons." This transmutation of the heroic journey into a freely chosen opportunity to demonstrate an identity—as freedom, self-display, and self-discovery—enters into the very definition of a new species of travel characteristic of the postmedieval world: the voyage of discovery and, later, the "scientific" expedition and the travels of curious and recording tourists. The celebration of travel as a demonstration of freedom and means to autonomy becomes the modern *topos*; clearly evident in William Wordsworth's evocation of the condition of the wanderer:

> Whither shall I turn,
> By road or pathway, or through trackless field,
> Up hill or down, or shall some floating thing,
> Upon the river point me out my course?[12]

The very indeterminacy of wandering, which Odysseus found hard to bear, is the source of the freedom the Romantics prized in travel. This association of travel and freedom may be traced to medieval roots, where it was written into law. According to the laws of Henry II, a lord who wished to free his serf had first to declare that intention in a church, a market, or a county court, to bestow a lance and a sword upon his former bondsman, and then take him to a crossroads to show him that "all ways lie open to his feet."[13] These two features—arms and the right of free departure—long remained the distinguishing marks of the status of "free" man. Their opposites—the forbidding of arms or of travel—were the marks of unfreedom. The right to travel had entered into the Western definition of the free autonomous individual whose associations to others are a result of conscious acts of connection, of allegiance and contract.

In Wordsworth and the Romantics, and in modern travels generally, we find divorced those things with which travel had been inextricably wedded in ancient conceptions. Travel became distinguishable from pain and began to be regarded as an intellectual pleasure. Thus, Wordsworth's "Old Man Travelling" is a portrait of "A man who does not move with pain, but moves/ with thought."[14]

These factors—the voluntariness of departure, the freedom implicit in the indeterminacies of mobility, the pleasure of travel free from necessity, the notion that travel signifies autonomy and is a means for demonstrating what one "really" is independent of one context or set of defining associations—remain the characteristics of the modern conception of travel. Michael Crichton's explanation of why he travels draws upon these themes:

> And I felt a need for rejuvenation, for experiences that would take me away from things I usually did, the life I usually led. In my everyday life, I often felt a stifling awareness of the purpose behind everything I did. Every book I read, every movie I saw, every lunch and dinner I attended seemed to have a reason behind it. From time to time, I felt the urge to do something for no reason at all.

Done "for no reason at all" except to escape a world where all things are a means to an end, travel, in modern circumstances, is prized less as a means of revealing ungovernable forces beyond human control than for providing direct access to a new material and objective world. In the apprehension of that world, the passenger acquires a new awareness of self in the context of a direct experience that "inevitably makes you aware of who it is that is having the experience."[15]

If travel is, as the great African-American writer and folklorist Zora Neale Hurston observed, "the soul of civilization,"[16] then in the history of European travels we may find the soul of the West, its continuities, evolution, permutations. For the history of travel is in crucial ways a history of the West. It recounts the evolution from necessity to freedom, an evolution that gave rise to a new consciousness, the peculiar mentality of the modern traveler.

NOTES

1. Homer, the *Odyssey*, trans. Walter Schewring (Oxford: Oxford University Press, 1980), p. 183.

2. Ibid., p. 89.

3. Captain James Cook, *Journals*, vol. 1, ed. J. C. Beaglehole (London: Hakluyt Society, 1955), p. 461.

4. Claude Lévi-Strauss, *Tristes Tropiques* (New York: Atheneum Press, 1975), p. 17.

5. *Chicago Tribune*, 18 June 1989, sec. 12, P. 6, col. 1.

6. Albert Camus, *Notebooks*, 1935–1942 (New York: Alfred A. Knopf, 1963); pp. 13–14 for epigraph quote on p. 1.

7. Ibid., p. 57.

8. Gen. 4.12, 4.15.

9. Quoted from "Pilgrimage," in *Encyclopedia of Religion and Ethics*, vol. 10, ed. James Hastings (New York: Charles Scribners Sons, 1951), p. 23.

10. Jack Kerouac, *On the Road* (New York: New American Library, 1957); see p. 111 for epigraph quote.

11. Seneca, *De Tranquilitas*, chap. 2, trans. Aubrey Stewart, quoted in Carone Skeel, *Travel in the First Century after Christ* (Cambridge: Cambridge University Press, 1901), pp. 12–13.

12. William Wordsworth, "The Preludes," in *Poetical Works*, vol. 3 (Oxford: Clarendon Press, 1968), pp. 27–30.

13. Quoted in F. W. Maitland and Sir Frederick Pollock, *The History of the English Laws, Before the Time of Edward I*, vol. 1 (Cambridge: Cambridge University Press, 1968), p. 428.

14. Quoted in George Roppen and Richard Sommer, *Strangers and Pilgrims. An Essay on the Metaphor of the Journey* (Oslo: Norwegian Universities Press, Norwegian Studies in English, no. 11, 1964), p. 116. See also Charles Norton Coe, *Wordsworth and the Literature Of Travel* (New York: Bookman Associates, 1953).

15. Michael Crichton, *Travels* (New York: Alfred A. Knopf, 1988), pp. ix, x.

16. Zora Neale Hurston, *Dust Tracks on a Road* (New York: Arno Press and the New York Times, 1969), p. 189.

SIGHTSEEING AND SOCIAL STRUCTURE

Dean MacCannell

THE MORAL INTEGRATION OF MODERNITY
The Place of the Attraction in Modern Society

Modern society constitutes itself as a labyrinthine structure of norms governing access to its workshops, offices, neighborhoods and semipublic places. As population density increases, this maze of norms manifests itself in physical divisions, walls, ceilings, fences, floors, hedges, barricades and signs marking the limits of a community, an establishment, or a person's space.[1] This social system contains interstitial corridors—halls, streets, elevators, bridges, waterways, airways and subways. These corridors are filled with things anyone can see, whether he wants to or not. Erving Goffman has studied behavior in public places and relations in public for what they can reveal about our collective pride, shame and guilt.[2] I want to follow his lead and suggest that behavior is only one of the visible, public representations of social structure found in public places. We also find decay, refuse, human and industrial derelicts, monuments, museums, parks, decorated plazas and architectural shows of industrial virtue. Public behavior and these other visible public parts of society are tourist attractions.

Sightseeing and the Moral Order

The organization of behavior and objects in public places is functionally equivalent to the sacred text that still serves as the moral base of traditional society. That is, public places contain the representations of good and evil that apply universally to modern man in general.

A touristic attitude of respectful admiration is called forth by the finer at-

13

tractions, the monuments, and a no less important attitude of disgust attaches itself to the uncontrolled garbage heaps, muggings, abandoned and tumbledown buildings, polluted rivers and the like. Disgust over these items is the negative pole of respect for the monuments. Together, the two provide a moral stability to the modern touristic consciousness that extends beyond immediate social relationships to the structure and organization of the total society.

The tours of Appalachian communities and northern inner-city cores taken by politicians provide examples of negative sightseeing. This kind of tour is usually conducted by a local character who has connections outside of his community. The local points out and explains and complains about the rusting auto hulks, the corn that did not come up, winos and junkies on the nod, flood damage and other features of the area to the politician who expresses his concern. While politicians and other public figures like Eleanor Roosevelt and the Kennedys are certainly the leaders here, this type of sightseeing is increasingly available to members of the middle class at large. The *New York Times* reports that seventy people answered an advertisement inviting tourists to spend "21 days 'in the land of the Hatfields and McCoys' for $378.00, living in with some of the poorest people in the U.S. in Mingo County, West Virginia."[3] Similarly, in 1967, the Penny Sightseeing Company inaugurated extensive guided tours of Harlem.[4] Recent ecological awareness has given rise to some imaginative variations: bus tours of "The Ten Top Polluters in Action" were available in Philadelphia during "Earth Week" in April, 1970.

This touristic form of moral involvement with diverse public representations of race, poverty, urban structures, social ills, and, of course, the public "good," the monuments, is a modern alternative to systems of in-group morality built out of binary oppositions: insider vs. outsider, us vs. them. In traditional society, man could not survive unless he oriented his behavior in a "we are good—they are bad" framework. Although some of its remains are still to be found in modern politics, such traditional morality is not efficacious in the modern world. Social structural differentiation has broken up traditional loyalties. Now it is impossible to determine with any accuracy who "we" are and who "they" are. Man cannot therefore survive in the modern world if he tries to continue to orient his behavior in a traditional "we are good—they are bad" framework. As man enters the modern world, the entire field of social facts—poverty, race, class, work—is open to ongoing moral evaluation and interpretation. This craziness of mere distinctions forces the modern consciousness to explore beyond the frontiers of traditional prejudice and bigotry in its search for a moral identity. Only "middle Americans" (if such people actually exist) and primitives—peoples whose lives are "everyday" in the pejorative, grinding sense of the term—may feel fully a part of their own world. Modern man has been condemned to look elsewhere, everywhere, for his authenticity, to see if he can catch a glimpse of it reflected in the simplicity, poverty, chastity or purity of others.

The Structure of the Attraction

I have defined a tourist attraction as an empirical relationship between a *tourist*, a *sight* and a *marker* (a piece of information about a sight). A simple model of the attraction can be presented in the following form:

[tourist / sight / marker]
attraction

Note that markers may take many different forms: guidebooks, informational tablets, slide shows, travelogues, souvenir matchbooks, etc. Note also that no *naturalistic* definition of the sight is possible. Well-marked sights that attract tourists include such items as mountain ranges, Napoleon's hat, moon rocks, Grant's tomb, even entire nation-states. The attractions are often indistinguishable from their less famous relatives. If they were not marked, it would be impossible for a layman to distinguish, on the basis of appearance alone, between moon rocks brought back by astronauts and pebbles picked up at Craters of the Moon National Monument in Idaho. But one is a sight and the other a souvenir, a kind of marker. Similarly, hippies are tourists and, at home in the Haight Ashbury, they are also sights that tourists come to see, or at least they used to be.

The distinguishing characteristic of those things that are collectively thought to be "true sights" is suggested by a second look at the moon rock example. *Souvenirs* are collected by *individuals*, by tourists, while *sights* are "collected" by entire societies. The entire U.S.A. is behind the gathering of moon rocks, or at least it is supposed to be, and hippies are a reflection of our collective affluence and decadence.

The origin of the attraction in the collective consciousness is not always so obvious as it is when a society dramatizes its values and capabilities by sending its representatives out into the solar system. Nevertheless, the collective determination of "true sights" is clear cut. The tourist has no difficulty deciding the sights he ought to see. His only problem is getting around to all of them. Even under conditions where there is no end of things to see, some mysterious institutional force operates on the totality in advance of the arrival of tourists, separating out the specific sights which are the attractions. In the Louvre, for example, the attraction is the Mona Lisa. The rest is undifferentiated art in the abstract. Moderns somehow know what the important attractions are, even in remote places. This miracle of consensus that transcends national boundaries rests on an elaborate set of institutional mechanisms, a twofold process of *sight sacralization* that is met with a corresponding *ritual attitude* on the part of tourists.

Sightseeing as Modern Ritual

Erving Goffman has defined ritual as a "perfunctory, conventionalized act through which an individual portrays his respect and regard for some object of ultimate value to its stand-in."[5] This is translated into the individual consciousness as a sense of duty, albeit a duty that is often lovingly performed. Under conditions of high social integration, the ritual attitude may lose all appearance of coercive externality. It may, that is, permeate an individual's inmost being so he performs his ritual obligations zealously and without thought for himself or for social consequences.

Modern international sightseeing possesses its own moral structure, a collective sense that certain sights must be seen. Some tourists will resist, no doubt, the suggestion that they are motivated by an elementary impulse analogous to the one that animates the Australian's awe for his Churinga boards. The Australian would certainly resist such a suggestion. Nevertheless, modern guided tours, in Goffman's terms, are "extensive ceremonial agendas involving long strings of obligatory rites." If one goes to Europe, one "must see" Paris; if one goes to Paris, one "must see" Notre Dame, the Eiffel Tower, the Louvre; if one goes to the Louvre, one "must see" the Venus de Milo and, of course, the Mona Lisa. There are quite literally millions of tourists who have spent their savings to make the pilgrimage to see these sights. Some who have not been "there" have reported to me that they want to see these sights "with all their hearts."

It is noteworthy that no one escapes the system of attractions except by retreat into a stay-at-home, traditionalist stance: that is, no one is exempt from the obligation to go sightseeing except the local person. The Manhattanite who has never been to the Statue of Liberty is a mythic image in our society, as is the reverse image of the big-city people who come out into the country expressing fascination with things the local folk care little about. The ritual attitude of the tourist originates in the act of travel itself and culminates when he arrives in the presence of the sight.

Some tourists feel so strongly about the sight they are visiting that they want to be alone in its presence, and they become annoyed at other tourists for profaning the place by crowding around "like sheep." Some sights become so important that tourists avoid use of their proper names: in the Pacific Northwest, Mount Rainier is called "The Mountain," and all up and down the West Coast of the United States, San Francisco is called "The City."

Traditional religious institutions are everywhere accommodating the movements of tourists. In "The Holy Land," the tour has followed in the path of the religious pilgrimage and is replacing it. Throughout the world, churches, cathedrals, mosques, and temples are being converted from religious to touristic functions.

The Stages of Sight Sacralization

In structural studies, it is not sufficient to build a model of an aspect of society entirely out of attitudes and behavior of individuals. It is also necessary to specify in detail the linkages between the attitudes and behavior and concrete institutional settings.

Perhaps there are, or have been, some sights which are so spectacular in themselves that no institutional support is required to mark them off as attractions. The original set of attractions is called, after the fashion of primitives, by the name of the sentiment they were supposed to have generated: "The Seven Wonders of the World." Modern sights, with but few exceptions, are not so evidently reflective of important social values as the Seven Wonders must have been. Attractions such as Cypress Gardens, the statue of the Little Mermaid in the harbor at Copenhagen, the Cape Hatteras Light and the like, risk losing their broader sociosymbolic meanings, becoming once more mere aspects of a limited social setting. Massive institutional support is often required for sight sacralization in the modern world.

The first stage of sight sacralization takes place when the sight is marked off from similar objects as worthy of preservation. This stage may be arrived at deductively from the model of the attraction

[tourist / sight / *marker*]
attraction

or it may be arrived at inductively by empirical observation. Sights have markers. Sometimes an act of Congress is necessary, as in the official designation of a national park or historical shrine. This first stage can be called the *naming phase* of sight sacralization. Often, before the naming phase, a great deal of work goes into the authentication of the candidate for sacralization. Objects are x-rayed, baked, photographed with special equipment and exam-

ined by experts. Reports are filed testifying to the object's aesthetic, historical, monetary, recreational and social values.

Second is the *framing and elevation* phase. Elevation is the putting on display of an object—placement in a case, on a pedestal or opened up for visitation. Framing is the placement of an official boundary around the object. On
a practical level, two types of framing occur: protecting and enhancing.
Protection seems to have been the motive behind the decision recently taken
at the Louvre to place the Mona Lisa (but none of the other paintings) behind
glass. When spotlights are placed on a building or a painting, it is enhanced.
Most efforts to protect a sacred object, such as hanging a silk cord in front of
it, or putting extra guards on duty around it, can also be read as a kind of enhancement, so the distinction between protection and enhancement eventually breaks down. Tourists before the Mona Lisa often remark: "Oh, it's the
only one with glass," or "It must be the most valuable, it has glass in front."
Advanced framing occurs when the rest of the world is forced back from the
object and the space in between is landscaped. Versailles and the Washington
Monument are "framed" in this way.

When the framing material that is used has itself entered the first stage of
sacralization (marking), a third stage has been entered. This stage can be
called *enshrinement*. The model here is Sainte Chapelle, the church built by
Saint Louis as a container for the "true Crown of Thorns" which he had pur-
chased from Baldwin of Constantinople. Sainte Chapelle is, of course, a
tourist attraction in its own right. Similarly, in the Gutenberg Museum, in
Gutenberg, Germany, the original Gutenberg Bible is displayed under special
lights on a pedestal in a darkened enclosure in a larger room. The walls of the
larger room are hung with precious documents, including a manuscript by
Beethoven.

The next stage of sacralization is *mechanical reproduction* of the sacred
object: the creation of prints, photographs, models or effigies of the object
which are themselves valued and displayed. It is the mechanical reproduction phase of sacralization that is most responsible for setting the tourist in
motion on his journey to find the true object. And he is not disappointed.
Alongside of the copies of it, it has to be The Real Thing.

The final stage of sight sacralization is *social reproduction*, as occurs
when groups, cities, and regions begin to name themselves after famous attractions.

Tourist attractions are not merely a collection of random material representations. When they appear in itineraries, they have a moral claim on the

tourist and, at the same time, they tend toward universality, incorporating natural, social, historical and cultural domains in a single representation made possible by the tour. This morally enforced universality is the basis of a general system of classification of societal elements produced without conscious effort. No person or agency is officially responsible for the worldwide proliferation of tourist attractions. They have appeared naturally, each seeming to respond to localized causes.

Nevertheless, when they are considered as a totality, tourist attractions reveal themselves to be a taxonomy of structural elements. Interestingly, this natural taxonomic system contains the analytical classification of social structure currently in use by social scientists. A North American itinerary, for example, contains domestic, commercial and industrial establishments, occupations, public-service and transportation facilities, urban neighborhoods, communities and members of solidary (or, at least, identifiable) subgroups of American society. The specific attractions representing these structural categories would include the Empire State Building, an Edwardian house in Boston's Back Bay, a Royal Canadian mounted policeman, a Mississippi River bridge, Grand Coulee Dam, an Indian totem pole, San Francisco's Chinatown, a cable car, Tijuana, Indians, cowboys, an antebellum mansion, an Amish farm, Arlington National Cemetery, the Smithsonian Institution and Washington Cathedral.

Taken together, tourist attractions and the behavior surrounding them are, I think, one of the most complex and orderly of the several universal codes that constitute modern society, although not so complex and orderly as, for example, a language.

Claude Lévi-Strauss claims that there is no such system in modern society. I think it is worth exploring the possible base of this claim, which is by no means confined to Lévi-Strauss's offhand remarks. Erving Goffman has similarly suggested that:

> in contemporary society rituals performed to stand-ins for supernatural entities are everywhere in decay, as are extensive ceremonial agendas involving long strings of obligatory rites. What remains are brief rituals one individual performs for another, attesting to civility and good will on the performer's part and to the recipient's possession of a small patrimony of sacredness.[6]

I think that the failure of Goffman and Lévi-Strauss to note the existence of social integration on a macrostructural level in modern society can be traced to a methodological deficiency: neither of them has developed the use of systemic variables for his analysis of social structure. In my own studies, I was able to bypass Lévi-Strauss's critique by working up the very dimension of modernity that he named as its most salient feature: its chaotic fragmentation, its *differentiation*.

Interestingly, the approach I used was anticipated by Émile Durkheim, who invented the use of systemic variables for sociological analysis and who named tourist attractions ("works of art" and "historical monuments") in his basic listing of social facts. Durkheim wrote:

> Social facts, on the contrary [he has just been writing of psychological facts], qualify far more naturally and immediately as things. Law is embodied in codes . . . fashions are preserved in costumes; taste in works of art . . . [and] the currents of daily life are recorded in statistical figures and historical monuments. By their very nature they tend toward an independent existence outside the individual consciousness, which they dominate. [7]

Until now, no sociologist took up Durkheim's suggestion that "costumes," "art" and "monuments" are keys to modern social structure. The structure of the attraction was deciphered by accident by the culture critic Walter Benjamin while working on a different problem. But Benjamin, perhaps because of his commitment to an orthodox version of Marxist theory, inverted all the basic relations. He wrote:

> The uniqueness of a work of art is inseparable from its being imbedded in the fabric of tradition. This tradition itself is thoroughly alive and extremely changeable. An ancient statue of Venus, for example, stood in a different traditional context with the Greeks, who made it an object of veneration, than with the clerics of the Middle Ages, who viewed it as an ominous idol. Both of them, however, were equally confronted with its uniqueness, that is, its aura. Originally the contextual integration of art in tradition found its expression in the cult. We know that the earliest art works originated in the service of ritual—first the magical, then the religious kind. It is significant that the existence of the work of art with reference to its aura is never entirely separated from its ritual function. In other words, the unique value of the "authentic" work of art has its basis in ritual, the location of its original use value.[8]

Setting aside for the moment Marxist concerns for "use value," I want to suggest that society does not produce art: artists do. Society, for its part, can only produce the importance, "reality" or "originality" of a work of art by piling up representations of it alongside. Benjamin believed that the reproductions of the work of art are produced because the work has a socially based "aura" about it, the "aura" being a residue of its origins in a primordial ritual. He should have reversed his terms. The work becomes "authentic" only after the first copy of it is produced. The reproductions *are* the aura, and the ritual, far from being a point of origin, *derives* from the relationship between the original object and its socially constructed importance. I would argue that this is the structure of the attraction in modern society, including the artistic attractions, and the reason the Grand Canyon has a touristic "aura" about it even though it did not originate in ritual.

ATTRACTIONS AND STRUCTURAL DIFFERENTIATION

In the tourists' consciousness, the attractions are not analyzed out as I present them type by type in the next sections and chapters. They appear sequentially, unfolding before the tourist so long as he continues his sightseeing. The touristic value of a modern community lies in the way it organizes social, historical, cultural and natural elements into a stream of impressions. Guidebooks contain references to all types of attractions, but the lively descriptions tend to be of the social materials. Modern society makes of itself its principal attraction in which the other attractions are embedded. Baedeker wrote of Paris:

> Paris is not only the political metropolis of France, but also the center of the artistic, scientific, commercial, and industrial life of the nation. Almost every branch of French industry is represented here, from the fine-art handicrafts to the construction of powerful machinery. . . .
>
> The central quarters of the city are remarkably bustling and animated, but owing to the ample breadth of the new streets and boulevards and the fact that many of them are paved with asphalt or wood, Paris is a far less noisy place than many other large cities. Its comparative tranquility, however, is often rudely interrupted by the discordant cries of the itinerant hawkers of wares of every kind, such as "old clothes" men, the vendors of various kinds of comestibles, the crockery-menders, the "fontaniers" (who clean and repair filters, etc.), the dog barbers, and newspaper-sellers. As a rule, however, they are clean and tidy in their dress, polite in manner, self-respecting, and devoid of the squalor and ruffianism which too often characterise their class. [9]

Georg Simmel began the analysis of this modern form of social consciousness which takes as its point of departure social structure itself. Simmel wrote:

> Man is a differentiating creature. His mind is stimulated by the differences between a momentary impression and the one which preceded it. Lasting impressions, impressions which differ only slightly from one another, impressions which

take a regular and habitual course and show regular and habitual contrasts—all these use up, so to speak, less consciousness than does the rapid crowding of changing images, the sharp discontinuity in the grasp of a single glance, and the unexpectedness of onrushing impressions. These are the psychological conditions which the metropolis creates. With each crossing of the street, with the tempo and multiplicity of the economic, occupational and social life, the city sets up a deep contrast with the small town and rural life with reference to the sensory foundations of psychic life.[10]

Simmel claims to be working out an aspect of the *Gemeinschaft-Gesellschaft* distinction. It would be more accurate to say that he is describing the difference between everyday life impressions, be they rural *or* urban, and the impressions of a strange place formed by a tourist on a visit, a vantage point Simmel knew well.[11]

Baedeker's and Simmel's stress on the work dimension of society is also found in touristic descriptions of New York City, which is always in the process of being rebuilt, and the waterfront areas of any city that has them. Similarly, Mideastern and North African peoples have traditionally made much use of their streets as places of work, and tourists from the Christian West seem to have inexhaustible fascination for places such as Istanbul, Tangiers, Damascus and Casablanca, where they can see factories without walls.

Primitive social life is nearly totally exposed to outsiders who happen to be present. Perhaps some of our love for primitives is attached to this innocent openness.

Modern society, originally quite closed up, is rapidly restructuring or institutionalizing the rights of outsiders (that is, of individuals not functionally connected to the operation) to look into its diverse aspects. Institutions are fitted with arenas, platforms and chambers set aside for the exclusive use of tourists. The courtroom is the most important institution in a democratic society. It was among the first to open to the outside and, I think, it will be among the first to close as the workings of society are increasingly revealed through the opening of other institutions to tourists. The New York Stock Exchange and the Corning Glass factory have specially designated visitors' hours, entrances and galleries. Mental hospitals, army bases and grade schools stage periodic open houses where not mere work but Good Work is displayed. The men who make pizza crusts by tossing the dough in the air often work in windows where they can be watched from the sidewalk. Construction companies cut peepholes into the fences around their work, nicely arranging the holes for sightseers of different heights. The becoming public of almost everything—a process that makes all men equal before the attraction—is a necessary part of the integrity of the modern social world.

TOURIST DISTRICTS

Distinctive local attractions contain (just behind, beside or embedded in the parts presented to the tourists) working offices, shops, services and facilities: often an entire urban structure is operating behind its touristic front. Some of these touristic urban areas are composed of touristic *districts*. Paris is "made up" of the Latin Quarter, Pigalle, Montparnasse, Montmartre; San Francisco is made up of the Haight Ashbury, the Barbary Coast and Chinatown; and London, of Soho, Piccadilly Circus, Blackfriars, Covent Gardens, the Strand. Less touristically developed areas have only one tourist district and are, therefore, sometimes upstaged by it: the Casbah, Beverly Hills, Greenwich Village. An urban sociologist or an ethnographer might point out that cities are composed of much more than their tourist areas, but this is obvious. Even tourists are aware of this. More important is the way the tourist attractions appear on a regional base as a model of social structure, beginning with "suggested" or "recommended" *communities, regions* and *neighborhoods*, and extending to matters of detail, setting the tourist up with a matrix he can fill in (if he wishes) with his own discoveries of his own typical little *markets, towns, restaurants* and *people*. This touristic matrix assures that the social structure that is recomposed via the tour, while always partial, is nevertheless not a skewed or warped representation of reality. Once on tour, only the individual imagination can modify reality, and so long as the faculty of imagination is at rest, society appears such as it is.

The taxonomy of structural elements provided by the attractions is universal, not because it *already* contains everything it might contain but rather, because the logic behind it is potentially inclusive. It sets up relationships between elements (as between neighborhoods and their cities) which cross the artificial boundaries between levels of social organization, society and culture, and culture and nature. Still, the resulting itineraries rarely penetrate lovingly into the precious details of a society as a Southern novelist might, peeling back layer after layer of local historical, cultural and social facts, although this is the ideal of a certain type of snobbish tourism. Such potential exists in the structure of the tour, but it goes for the most part untapped. Attractions are usually organized more on the model of the filing system of a disinterested observer, like a scientist who separates his passions from their object, reserving them entirely for matters of method; or like a carpetbagging politician who calculates his rhetoric while reading a printout of the demographic characteristics of the region he wants to represent. In short, the tourist world is complete in its way, but it is constructed after the fashion of all worlds that are filled with people who are just passing through and know it.

THE DIFFERENTIATIONS OF THE TOURIST WORLD

Functioning *establishments* figure prominently as tourist attractions. Commercial, industrial and business establishments are also basic features of social regions, or they are first among the elements from which regions are composed. Some, such as the Empire State Building, the now-defunct Les Halles in Paris, and Fisherman's Wharf in San Francisco, overwhelm their districts. Others fit together in a neat structural arrangement of little establishments that contribute to their district's special local character: flower shops, meat and vegetable markets, shoe repair shops, neighborhood churches. Unlike the Empire State Building, with its elevators expressly for sightseers, these little establishments may not be prepared for the outside visitors they attract. A priest who made his parish famous had this problem, but apparently he is adjusting to the presence of tourists:

> For a time, in fact, St. Boniface became an attraction for tourists and white liberals from the suburbs. Father Groppi recalled that he had sometimes been critical of the whites who overflowed the Sunday masses at St. Boniface and then returned to their suburban homes.
>
> "But now I can understand their problems," he said. "They come from conservative parishes and were tired of their parish organizations, the Holy Name Society and that sort of nonsense."[12]

Under normal conditions of touristic development, no social establishment ultimately resists conversion into an attraction, not even *domestic establishments*. Selected homes in the "Society Hill" section of downtown Philadelphia are opened annually for touristic visitation. Visitors to Japan are routinely offered the chance to enter, observe and—to a limited degree—even participate in the households of middle-class families. Individual arrangements can be made with the French Ministry of Tourism to have coffee in a French home, and even to go for an afternoon drive in the country with a Frenchman of "approximately one's own social station."[13]

A version of sociology suggests that society is composed not of individuals but *groups*, and groups, too, figure as tourist attractions. Certain groups work up a show of their group characteristics (their ceremonies, settlement patterns, costumes, etc.) especially for the benefit of sightseers:

At an open meeting yesterday of Indian businessmen, government officials and airline representatives, Dallas Chief Eagle, spokesman and director of the new United States Indian International Travel agency, said the cooperative hoped to be able to offer low-cost group tours to German tourists by June.[14]

Other groups, even other Indian groups, militantly resist such showmanship, even though their leaders are aware of their touristic potential, because this kind of behavior *for* tourists is widely felt to be degrading.[15] Given the multichanneled nature of human communication, these two versions of the group (the proud and the practical) need not be mutually exclusive. The following account suggests that a member of one of our recently emergent self-conscious minorities can do his own thing and do a thing for the tourists at the same time:

New Jersey, Connecticut and even Pennsylvania license plates were conspicuous around Tompkins Square yesterday, indicating that the Lower East Side's new hippie haven is beginning to draw out-of-state tourists.

"You go to where the action is," a blond girl in shorts said through a thick layer of white lipstick. The girl, who said her name was Lisa Stern, and that she was a Freshman at Rutgers University, added: "I used to spend weekends in Greenwich Village, but no longer." However, Lisa didn't find much action in Tompkins Square Park, the scene of a Memorial Day clash between about 200 hippies and the police. . . . Yesterday there was no question any more as to a hippie's right to sit on the grass or to stretch out on it.

Some tourists from New Jersey were leaning over the guardrail enclosing a patch of lawn, much as if they were visiting a zoo, and stared at a man with tattooed arms and blue-painted face who gently waved at them while the bongo drums were throbbing.[16]

Other groups—the Pennsylvania "Dutch," The Amanas, Basques, and peasants everywhere—probably fall somewhere in between resistance and acquiescence to tourism, or they vacillate from self-conscious showiness to grudging acceptance of it.

Perhaps because they have a man inside, *occupations* are popular tourist attractions. In some areas, local handicrafts would have passed into extinction except for the intervention of mass tourism and the souvenir market:

Palekh boxes are formed from papier-mâché and molded in the desired shape on a wood form. A single artist makes the box, coats it with layers of black lacquer, paints his miniature picture, adds final coats of clear lacquer and signs his name and the date. Each box represents two to three days' work. Some of Palekh's 150 artists work at home. . . . I watched Constantine Bilayev, an artist in his 50's, paint a fairytale scene he might have been doing for his grandchildren. It illustrated the story of a wicked old woman with a daughter she favored and a stepdaughter she hated. She sent the stepdaughter into the woods to gather firewood, hoping harm would befall the Girl. Instead, the stepdaughter triumphed over every adversity.[17]

In addition to this cute side of occupational sightseeing, there is a heavy, modern workaday aspect. In the same community with the box makers, there are *real* young ladies triumphing over adversity while serving as tourist attractions. The report continues:

> But the main attraction of this city of 400,000 people is the Ivanovo Textile Factory, an industrial enormity that produces some 25,000,000 yards of wool cloth a year. The factory represents an investment of $55 million. The factory's machinery makes an ear-shattering din. Ranks of machines take the raw wool and convert it into coarse thread, and successive ranks of devices extrude the thread into ever-finer filaments. The weaving machines clang in unison like a brigade on the march—Raz, Dva, Raz, Dva, Raz, Dva as an unseen Russian sergeant would count it out. The 7,500 workers are mostly young and mostly female. A bulletin board exhorts them to greater production in honor of the Lenin centenary.

Along with handicraft and specialized industrial work, there are other occupational attractions including glass blowers, Japanese pearl divers, cowboys, fishermen, Geisha girls, London chimney sweeps, gondoliers and sidewalk artists. Potentially, the entire division of labor in society can be transformed into a tourist attraction. In some districts of Manhattan, even the men in gray flannel suits have been marked off for touristic attention.

Connecting the urban areas of society are *transportation networks*, segments and intersections of which are tourist attractions. Examples are: the London Bridge, the Champs Elysées, Hollywood and Vine, Ponte Vecchio, the Golden Gate, Red Square, the canals of Venice and Amsterdam, Broadway, the Gate of Heavenly Peace, the rue de Rivoli, the Spanish Steps, Telegraph Avenue, the Atlantic City Boardwalk, the Mont Blanc tunnel, Union Square and New England's covered bridges. Along these lines is the following comment on an attraction that is not well known but for which some hopes have been raised:

> The city of Birmingham recently opened its first expressway. To do so it had to slice a gash through famed Red Mountain in order to complete construction and get people in and out of the city in a hurry. To the drivers of Birmingham the freeway means a new convenience, but to the thousands of visitors the giant cut at the crest of the mountain has become a fascinating stopping place . . . a new and exciting tourist attraction.[18]

In addition to roads, squares, intersections, and bridges, *vehicles* that are re-stricted to one part of the worldwide transportation network also figure as attractions: rickshaws, gondolas, San Francisco's cable cars and animal-powered carts everywhere.

Finally, the system of attractions extends as far as society has extended its *public works*, not avoiding things that might well have been avoided:

> A London sightseeing company has added a tour of London's public lavatories to its schedule. The firm, See Britain, said the lavatories tour will begin Sunday and cost five shillings (60 cents). It will include lavatories in the City and the West End. A spokesman said visitors will see the best Victorian and Edwardian lavatories in the areas with a guide discussing the style of the interiors, architecture, hours of opening and history.[19]

The presentation of the inner workings of society's nether side is, of course, the Paris sewer tour.

Although the tourist need not be consciously aware of this, the thing he goes to see is society and its works. The societal aspect of tourist attractions is hidden behind their fame, but this fame cannot change their origin in so-cial structure. Given the present sociohistorical epoch, it is not a surprise to find that tourists believe sightseeing is leisure activity, and fun, even when it requires more effort and organization than many jobs. In a marked contrast to the grudging acquiescence that may characterize the relation of the indi-vidual to his industrial work, individuals happily embrace the attitudes and norms that lead them into a relationship with society through the sightsee-ing act. In being presented as a valued object through a so-called "leisure" ac-tivity that is thought to be "fun," society is renewed in the heart of the individual through warm, open, unquestioned relations, characterized by a near absence of alienation when compared with other contemporary rela-tionships. This is, of course, the kind of relationship of individual and society that social scientists and politicians think is necessary for a strong society, and they are probably correct in their belief.

Tourist attractions in their natural, unanalyzed state may not appear to have any coherent infrastructure uniting them, and insofar as it is through the attraction that the tourist apprehends society, society may not appear to have coherent structure, either. It is not my intention here to overorganize the touristic consciousness. It exhibits the deep structure, which is social structure, that I am describing here, but this order need never be perceived as such in its totality. Consciousness and the integration of the individual into the modern world require only that one attraction be linked to one other: a district to a community, or an establishment to a district, or a role to an establishment. Even if only a single linkage is grasped in the immediate present, this solitary link is the starting point for an endless spherical system of connections which is society and the world, with the individual at one point on its surface.

NOTES

1. Detailed microstudies of social structure are provided by Edward T. Hall, *The Hidden Dimension* (Garden City, N.Y.: Anchor Books, 1969), and Robert Sommer, *Personal Space: The Behavioral Basis of Design* (Englewood Cliffs, N.J.: Prentice-Hall, 1969).

2. See Erving Goffman, *Relations in Public: Microstudies of the Public Order* (New York: Basic Books, 1971) and *Behavior in Public Places: Notes on the Social Organization of Gatherings* (New York: Free Press, 1963).

3. *The New York Times*, June 30, 1969, p. 1.

4. Ibid., May 22, 1967, p. 39.

5. Goffman, *Relations in Public*, p. 62.

6. Ibid., p. 63.

7. Emile Durkheim, *The Rules of Sociological Method.* trans. S. A. Solovay and J. H. Mueller (New York: Free Press, 1938), p. 30.

8. Walter Benjamin, *Illuminations*, ed. Hannah Arendt, trans. Harry Zohn (New York: Schocken, 1969), pp. 223–24.

9. Karl Baedeker, *Paris and Environs*, 14th rev. ed. (Leipzig: Karl Baedeker, Publisher, 1900), pp.xxix–xxx.

10. *The Sociology of Georg Simmel*, ed. and trans. Kurt H. Wolff (Glencoe, Ill.: Free Press, 1950), p. 410.

11. See Simmel's essay on "The Stranger," ibid. pp. 402–8.

12. *The New York Times*, April 12, 1970, p. 34.

13. From my field notes.

14. Paris: *International Herald Tribune*, March 26, 1971, p. 7.

15. Interestingly, behavior *for* tourists is only felt to be degrading by members of already exploited minorities. Middle- class hippies and radicals seem to enjoy working in front of the camera. Perhaps the leaders of exploited minorities teach noncooperation with tourists because this is one of the only areas in which members of these minorities can dramatize self-determination.

16. Paul Hoffman. "Hippie's Hangout Draws Tourists," *The New York Times*, June 5, 1967, p. 43.

17. Irwin M. Chapman. "Visit to Two Russian Towns," *The New York Times*, February 23, 1969, sect. 10, p. 29.

18. News release dated April 27, 1970 from "Operation New Birmingham," a civic group, quoted in "Images of America: Racial Feeling Remains Strong in the Cities," *The New York Times*, May 24, 1970, p. 64.

19. "For Tourists Who Want to See All," *International Herald Tribune*, November 4, 1970.

PHENOMENOLOGY OF TOURIST EXPERIENCES

Erik Cohen[1]

Abstract Contemporary studies of tourism see the tourist experience as either something essentially spurious and superficial, an extension of an alienated world, or as a serious search for authenticity, an effort to escape from an alienated world. It is argued that neither of these views is universally valid. A more discriminating distinction between five types of tourist experiences is proposed, based on the place and significance of tourist experience in the total world-view of tourists, their relationship to a perceived 'centre' and the location of that centre in relation to the society in which the tourist lives. It is proposed that the resulting continuum of types of tourist experience is both more comprehensive than alternative conceptual frameworks and capable of reconciling and integrating the conflicting interpretations arising from earlier studies.

INTRODUCTION

What is the nature of the tourist experience? Is it a trivial, superficial, frivolous pursuit of vicarious, contrived experiences, a 'pseudo-event' as Boorstin (1964: 77–117) would have it, or is it an earnest quest for the authentic, the pilgrimage of modern man, as MacCannell (1973: 593) believes it to be?

Tourists are often seen as 'travellers for pleasure';[2] however, though sufficient for some purposes, this is a very superficial view of the tourist. The more precise quality and meaning of the touristic experience have seldom been given serious consideration either in theoretical analysis or in empirical research. Not that we lack controversy—indeed, recently, the nature and meaning of tourism in modern society became the subject of a lively polemic among sociologists and social critics. In one camp of the polemic we find those, like Boorstin (1964) and lately Turner and Ash (1975), for whom tourism is essentially an abberation, a symptom of the *malaise* of the age. Boorstin bemoans the disappearance of the traveller of old, who was in search of authentic experiences, and despises the shallow modern mass tourist savoring 'pseudo-events'. The opposing, newer camp is represented by Mac-Cannell; he criticizes the critics, claiming that '. . . Boorstin only expresses a long-standing touristic attitude, a pronounced dislike . . . for other tourists, an attitude that turns man against man in a they-are-the-tourists-I-am-not equation' (MacCannell, 1973: 602). He argues that Boorstin's approach, '. . . is so prevalent, in fact, (among the tourists themselves as well as among travel writers) that it is a part of the problem of mass tourism, not an analytical re-flection on it' (MacCannell, 1973: 600). As in every polemic, however, the protagonists of the opposing views tend to overstate their case. Thus Mac-Cannell, claiming to confute Boorstin's view with empirical evidence, states that 'None of the accounts in my collection (of observations of tourists) sup-port Boorstin's contention that tourists want superficial, contrived experi-ences. Rather, tourists demand authenticity, just as Boorstin does' (*ibid.* p. 600). But, MacCannell himself is very selective in the choice of his obser-vations: his accounts are mostly of young, 'post-modern' (Kavolis, 1970) tourists; Boorstin's thesis may well find more support in a different sample, composed primarily of sedate, middle-class, middle-aged tourists. Hence, even if one admits that Boorstin's claims may be too extreme and that some tourists may indeed be in search of 'authenticity', it nevertheless appears too far-fetched to accept MacCannell's argument that all tourists single-mind-edly pursue 'real' authentic experiences, but are denied them by the machi-nations of a tourist establishment which presents them with staged tourist settings and 'false backs'. The conflict between these contrasting concep-tions of tourists remains thus unresolved as the proponents of each claim to describe '*the* tourist' as a general type, while implicitly or explicitly denying the adequacy of the alternative conception.

In my view, neither of the opposing conceptions is universally valid, though each has contributed valuable insights into the motives, behaviour and experiences of *some* tourists. Different kinds of people may desire differ-ent modes of touristic experiences; hence '*the* tourist' does not exist as a type. The important point, however, is not merely to prove that both concep-tions enjoy some empirical support, though neither is absolutely correct; rather it is to account for the differences within a more general theoretical framework, through which they will be related to, and in turn illuminated by, some broader views of the relationship of modern man to his society and culture. In this paper I shall attempt to do so by examining the place and significance of tourism in a modern person's life; I shall argue that these are derived from his total world-view, and depend especially on the question of whether or not he adheres to a 'centre', and on the location of this 'centre' in relation to the society in which he lives. Phenomenologically distinct modes of touristic experiences are related to different types of relationships which obtain between a person and a variety of 'centres'.

TOURISM AND THE QUEST FOR THE CENTRE

The concept of the 'centre' entered sociological discourse in several overlapping, but not identical fashions. M. Eliade (1971: 12–17) pointed out that every religious 'cosmos' possesses a centre; this is ' . . . pre-eminently the zone of the sacred, the zone of absolute reality' (ibid., 17). In traditional cosmological images it is the point where the *axis mundi* penetrates the earthly sphere, ' . . . the meeting point of heaven, earth and hell' (ibid., 12).

However, the centre is not necessarily geographically central to the life-space of the community of believers; indeed, as Victor Turner has pointed out, its ex-centric location may be meaningful in that it gives direction and structure to the pilgrimage as a sacred journey of spiritual ascension to 'The Center Out There' (Turner, 1973). The 'centre', however, should not be conceived in narrowly religious terms. E. Shils (1975) has argued that every society possesses a 'centre', which is the charismatic nexus of its supreme, ultimate moral values. While Shils does not deal explicitly with the location of the symbolic bearers of the charismatic 'centre', there is little doubt that he considers the locus of its paramount symbols e.g. the monarch or the crown (Shils & Young, 1953) to be ordinarily within the geographical confines of the society. Shils' concept of the centre was further developed by S. N. Eisenstadt (1968) who distinguishes between multiple 'centres', e.g. political, religious or cultural; in modern society these centres do not necessarily overlap, and their paramount symbols may be differentially located. The individual's 'spiritual' centre, whether religious or cultural, i.e. the centre which for the individual symbolizes ultimate meanings, is the one with which we are concerned in this paper.

Structural-functionalist theory, particularly in the Parsonian variety, assumes as a matter of course that the spiritual centre of the modern individual will be located within the confines of his society—he will 'conform' with this society's ultimate values. Such conformity may indeed generate tensions and dissatisfactions. These, however, will be taken care of by the mechanisms of 'pattern maintenance' and 'tension management'. The latter will include various types of leisure and recreational activity in which the indi-

vidual finds release and relief. Such activities take place in segregated settings, which are not part of 'real' life; in Schutz's phenomenological terminology, they may be called 'finite provinces of meaning' (Berger & Luckman,
1966: 39). Though consisting of activities representing a reversal of those de-
manded by the central value-nexus (e.g. 'play' as against 'work'), they are
'functional' in relieving the tension built up in the individual and hence reinforce, in the long run, his allegiance to the 'centre'.[3] The individual may
need relief from tension, created by the values, but he is not fundamentally
alienated from them. Tourism, in the Parsonian scheme, is a recreational activity *par excellence*: it is a form of temporary getaway from one's centre, but
in relation to the individual's biography, his life-plan and aspirations, it remains of peripheral significance. Indeed, in terms of a functional theory of
leisure, tourism only remains fuctional, so long as it does not become central
to the individual's life-plan and aspirations—since only so long will it regulate
his tensions and dissatisfactions, refreshing and restoring him, without destroying his motivation to perform the tasks of his everyday life. This means
that tourism is essentially a temporary reversal of everyday activities—it is a
no-work, no-care, no-thrift situation; but it is in itself devoid of deeper meaning: it is a 'vacation', i.e. 'vacant' time. If tourism became central, the individual would become 'deviant', he would be seen as 'retreating', opting-out, or
escaping the duties imposed upon him by his society.

The assumption that modern man is normally a conformist, and that he
will hence generally adhere to the centre of 'his' society is, to say the least,
simplistic. Many moderns are alienated from their society. What about the
'spiritual' centre of such alienated people? Several alternatives can be discerned: (a) some may be so completely alienated as not to look for any centre
at all, i.e. not to seek any ultimate locus of meaning; (b) some, aware of what
to them looks an irretrievable loss of their centre, seek to experience vicariously the authentic participation in the centre of others, who are as yet less
modern and less, in E. Heller's (1961) term, 'disinherited'; (c) some, particularly those whom Kavolis (1970) described as 'post-modern' often possess a
'decentralized personality', and equivocate between different centres, almost
turning the quest into the purpose of their life; (d) finally some may find that
their spiritual centre lies somewhere else, in another society or culture than
their own. I argue that within the context of each of these possible types of
attitude to the centre, tourism will be endowed with a different significance.
In the following I shall develop a phenomenology of modes of touristic experiences and relate them to these alternative forms of relationship between a
modern person and various 'centres'.

THE MODES OF TOURIST EXPERIENCES

Travelling for pleasure (as opposed to necessity) beyond the boundaries life-space assumes that there is some experience available 'out there', which cannot be found within the life-space,[4] and which makes travel worthwhile. A person who finds relief from tensions within his life space, or does not perceive outside its boundaries any attractions the desire for which he cannot also fulfil at home, will not travel for pleasure.

Risking some over-simplification, I argue that primitive society usually entertained an image of a limited 'cosmos', ideally co-terminous with its life-space, surrounded by a dangerous and threatening chaos. Insofar as the sacred centre was geographically located within the life-space, primitive man had no reason or desire to venture beyond its boundaries. It is only when a powerful mythological imagery locates the 'real' centre in another place, beyond the limits of the empirical world, a 'paradise' beyond the surrounding chaos, that 'paradisiac cults' terminating in large scale voyages, develop (Eliade, 1969, 88–111). This is the original, archaic pilgrimage, the quest for the mythical land of pristine existence, of no evil or suffering, the primaeval centre from which man originally emerged, but eventually lost it.[5] The pilgrimage later on becomes the dominant form of non-instrumental travelling in traditional and particularly peasant societies (Turner, 1973). However, the traditional pilgrimage differs from the archaic in that the pilgrim's goal, the centre, is located within his 'world', but beyond the boundaries of the immediate life-space; this contingency is predicated upon a separation between the limited life-space and his 'world': the image of the latter is vastly expanded and embraces a large number of life-spaces of individual communities or societies. Thus, Jerusalem becomes the centre of the Jewish and Christian 'world', Mecca that of the Muslim 'world'. Traditional pilgrimage is essentially a movement from the prophane periphery towards the sacred centre of the religious 'cosmos'.

Modern mass tourism, however, is predicated upon a different development: the gradual abandonment of the traditional, sacred image of the cosmos, and the awakening of interest in the culture, social life and natural environment of others. In its extreme form, modern tourism involves a *generalized* interest in or appreciation of that which is different, strange or novel in comparison with what the traveller is acquainted with in his cultural world (Cohen, 1974: 533, 1972: 165). Hence, it leads to a movement *away* from the spiritual, cultural or even religious centre of one's 'world', into its periphery, toward the centres of other cultures and societies.

Pilgrimages and modern tourism are thus predicated on different social conceptions of space and contrary views concerning the kind of destinations worth visiting and of their location in the socially constructed space; hence they involve movement in opposite directions: in pilgrimage from the periphery toward the cultural centre, in modern tourism, away from the cultural centre into the periphery.

These differences notwithstanding, the *roles* of pilgrim and tourist are often combined, particularly in the modern world (Dupont, 1973, Cohen, 1974: 542). The fusion or the role does not, however, mean a fusion of the divergent cognitive structures. MacCannell, who views the tourist as a modern pilgrim (1973: 593), does not expressly discuss the problem of the cognitive structure of the tourist's 'world,' in contrast to that of the pilgrim.

Here I shall develop a phenomenological typology of tourist experiences by analysing the different meanings which interest in and appreciation of the culture, social life and the natural environment of others has for the individual traveller. The degree to which his journey represents a 'quest for the centre', and the nature of that centre will be at the heart of this analysis. The typology, in turn, relates to different points of continuum of privately constructed 'worlds' of individual travellers (not necessarily identical with those prevalent in their culture), ranging between the opposite poles of the conception of space characteristic of modern tourism on the one hand and that of the pilgrimage on the other. I have distinguished five main modes of touristic experiences:

1. Recreational Mode
2. Diversionary Mode
3. Experiential Mode
4. Experimental Mode
5. Existential Mode.

These modes are ranked here so that they span the spectrum between the experience of the tourist as the traveller in pursuit of 'mere' pleasure in the strange and the novel, to that of the modern pilgrim in quest of meaning at somebody else's centre. Let us now discuss each in some detail.

1. *The Recreational Mode*: this is the mode of touristic experiences which a structural-functionalist analysis of society would lead us to expect as typical for modern man. The trip as a recreational experience is a form of entertainment akin in nature to other forms of entertainment such as the cinema, theatre, or television. The tourist 'enjoys' his trip, because it restores his physical and mental powers and endows him with a general sense of well-being. As the term 'recreation' indicates, even this mode of tourist experi-

ence is ultimately and distantly related to and derived from the religious voyage to the sacred, life-endowing centre, which rejuvenates and 're-creates'.[6] Indeed, one can follow the process of 'secularization' of tourism historically, e.g. in the change from 'thermalists', whose belief in the healing properties of thermal springs was ultimately grounded in mythological images of springs as 'centres' from which supernatural powers penetrate the empirical world, to tourists, who 'take the waters' primarily as a form of high-class socializing (Lowenthal, 1962). Though the belief in the recuperative or restorative power of the tourist trip is preserved, it is a secular, rational belief in the value of leisure activities, change of climate, rest etc.

While the traditional pilgrim is newly born or 're-created' at the centre, the tourist is merely 'recreated'. In the recreational tourist trip, the intent and meaning of the religious voyage is secularized: it loses its deeper, spiritual content. Though the tourist may find his experiences on the trip 'interesting', they are not personally significant. He does not have a deep commitment to travel as a means self-realization or self-expansion. Like other forms of mass-entertainment, recreational tourism appears from the perspective of 'high' culture as a shallow, superficial, trivial and often frivolous activity, and is ridiculed as such by Boorstin and other cultural critics. A correlate of this view is that the tourist travelling in that mode appears often to be gullible to the extreme (Mitford, 1959), easy to be taken in by blatantly inauthentic or outrightly contrived, commercialized displays of the culture, customs, crafts and even landscapes of the host society. His apparent gullibility, however, ought not to be ascribed solely to his ignorance; rather he does not really desire or care for the authentic (Huetz de Lemp, 1964: 23); he is 'no stickler for authenticity' (Desai, 1974: 4). Since he seeks recreation, he is quite eager to accept the make-believe and not to question its authenticity; after all one does not need to be convinced of the authenticity of a TV play or a motion picture in order to enjoy it as a recreative, entertaining or relaxing experience.

The recreation-seeking tourist, hence, thrives on what Boorstin (1964), calls 'pseudo-events'. But the depth of contempt in which he is held on that account by intellectuals and 'serious' travellers is misplaced: the tourist gets what he wants—the pleasure of entertainment, for which authenticity is largely irrelevant. Such recreation-oriented tourists should be looked upon less as shallow, easily gullible simpletons who believe any contraption to be 'real', or as stooges of a prevaricating tourist establishment, but rather as persons who attend a performance or participate in a game; the enjoyability of the occasion is contingent on their willingness to accept the make-believe or half-seriously to delude themselves. In a sense, they are accomplices of the tourist establishment in the production of their own deception.[7] Recreation-oriented tourists like the audience of a play can completely legitimately enjoy themselves despite, or even—as in the case of some of the more outlandish performances of local custom—because, the fact that the experienced is not 'real'; the real thing may be too terrifying or revolting, to be enjoyable. For the recreation-seeking tourist, the people and landscapes he sees and experiences are not part of his 'real' world; like other recreational settings, they are 'finite provinces of meaning' separate from reality, though this is not explicitly admitted by either the tourists or the staff of tourist establishments. Indeed, tourists as well as staff, may be mutually aware of the fact that each is playing a role in order to upkeep an inauthentic, indeed artificial, but nevertheless enjoyable, 'construction of (touristic) reality'. If this is openly admitted, the tourist situation would be homologous to that of mass entertainment. The distinguishing trait of the tourist situation, however, is that such an admission would spoil the game.

Tourism as recreation is, in itself, not a 'serious business'; rather it is an 'idle pleasure' (Lowenthal, 1962: 124), and as such had a hard time in gaining recognition as a legitimate reason for travelling. It achieved such legitimation, indeed, not because it is enjoyable in itself, but rather on the strength of its recuperative powers, as a mechanism which recharges the batteries of weary modern man (Glasser, 1975: 19–20), refreshes and restitutes him so he is able again to return to the wear and tear of 'serious' living. Such tourism serves as a 'pressure-valve' for modern man. When he cannot take the pressures of daily living any more, he goes on vacation. If he overdoes it, or fails to return to serious living, his behaviour becomes 'dysfunctional', in its extreme anomic escapism. But ordinarily it is 'functional' because it manages the tensions generated by modern society and hence helps to preserve the adherence of the individual to it—in a similar way in which the Carnival (e.g. Baroja, 1965: 23–4) and other forms of legitimate debauchery, normatively circumscribed in time and place, served as a 'pressure-valve' of traditional Christian society. In the functionalist view, recreational tourism is chiefly caused by the 'push' of the tourist's own society, not by the particular 'pull' of any place beyond its boundaries. The recreational tourist is primarily 'getting away'. Hence, he is often equanimous as to the choice of possible destinations for his 'holiday', thus providing the advertisement industry with plentiful opportunities to tilt his decision in a variety of competing directions.

Though not serious business in itself, recreation, then performs a serious 'function'—it restitutes the individual to his society and its values, which, despite the pressures they generate, constitute the centre of his world. Insofar as he is aware of this function and values it, it becomes in an oblique sense, the meaning of his trip. If it were not for the pressures generated in his daily life at home, or if the pressures were resolved by alternative mechanisms, as e.g. they are in traditional societies, he may find no need to travel; he would stay at home. Here we have one of the main reasons for the tremendous upsurge in tourism in modern, and particularly in urban society (Dumazdier, 1967: I25-6): this society generates pressure which it has few means to resolve; peasants, even in modern societies travel little.

2. *The Diversionary Mode*: recreational tourism is a movement away from the centre, which serves eventually to reinforce the adherence to the centre. Hence, it may possess a meaning for the person oriented to that centre.

As we pointed out above, however, modern men are often alienated from the centre of their society or culture. Some of them, may not be seeking alternative centres: their life, strictly speaking, is 'meaningless', but they are not looking for meaning, whether in their own society or elsewhere. For such people, travelling in the mode just described, loses its recreational significance: it becomes purely diversionary—a mere escape from the boredom and meaninglessness of routine, everyday existence, into the forgetfulness of a vacation, which may heal the body and sooth the spirit, but does not 'recreate'—i.e. it does not re-establish adherence to a meaningful centre, but only makes alienation endurable. Diversionary tourism is then, in terms of what Glasser calls the 'Therapy School' of sociology of leisure '. . . a healing balm for the robots. . . . It accepts that for most people work will always be emotionally uncommitting and therefore unrewarding, and that they are condemned to seek in their leisure temporary oblivion and comfort for abraded nerve endings . . . the Therapy School . . . [puts] emphasis on immediate diversion . . .' (Glasser, 1975: 21).

The diversionary mode of tourist experience, hence, is similar to the recreational except that it is not 'meaningful', even in an oblique sense. It is the meaningless pleasure of a centre-less person.

The recreational and diversionary modes of touristic experience have been the target of the savage criticism of tourism by culture critics such as Boorstin (1964) and Turner and Ash (1975). They are apparently characteristic of most mass tourists from modern, industrial urban societies. On this point I tend to agree with Boorstin, rather than with MacCannell. Even then, however, an interesting question remains unresolved: which one of these two modes is the prevalent one? One cannot approach this question without first taking a stand on that most basic problem; how deeply is modern man alienated? Even the critics of tourism may not be unanimous on this question. Hence, even the criticisms may differ: if modern man is conceived of as adhering to a central nexus of 'Western values', his prevailing mode of travel is recreational; he may then be criticized for his narrow 'parochialism', his lack of readiness to relate to the values of others except in a superficial, casual manner. If modern man is conceived of as alienated, then his prevailing mode of travel is diversionary; tourism is then criticized primarily as a sympton of the general *malaise* of modern society.

The two modes of tourism discussed above, however, do not exhaust the field; some tourists, primarily the minority of 'post-modern', and other, non-institutionalized types of tourists (Cohen, 1972) indeed derive a deeper meaning from their travels, of the kind MacCannell finds characteristic of tourists in general. The remaining three modes of touristic experience represent different levels of depth of meaning which tourism may possess for the individual.

3. *Experiential Mode*: the recreational tourist adheres to the centre of his society or culture; the diversionary tourist moves in a centre-less space. But what happens when the disenchanted or alienated individuals become growingly aware of their state of alienation, and the meaninglessness and fatuity of their daily life, as many younger members of the middle classes in the 'post-modern' society have become?

One direction which their search for meaning might take is the attempt to transform their society through revolution; another, less radical alternative is to look for meaning in the life of others—tourism (MacCannell, 1976: 3).

The renewed quest for meaning, outside the confines of one's own society is commenced, in whatever embryonic, unarticulated form, by the search for 'experiences':[8] the striving of people who have lost their own centre and are unable to lead an authentic life at home to recapture meaning by a vicarious, essentially aesthetic, experience of the authenticity of the life of others (MacCannell, 1973). This mode of tourism we shall call 'experiential'.

The 'experiential' mode characterizes the tourist as he emerges from MacCannell's description. If Boorstin is among the most outspoken critics of recreational and *a forteriori* diversionary tourism, which in his view encompass all modern tourism, MacCannell attempts to endow tourism with a new dignity by claiming that it is a modern form of the essentially religious quest for authenticity. But though he puts forward his view of the tourist against that of the 'intellectuals' (MacCannell, 1973: 598–601), implying that it holds for 'the tourist' in general, it is clear that his claim is based on a view of modern man who, alienated from the spiritual centre of his own society, actively, though perhaps inarticulately, searches for a new meaning. Indeed,

MacCannell argues that 'The concern of moderns for the shallowness of their lives and inauthenticity of their [everyday] experiences parallels concern for the sacred in primitive society' (MacCannell, 1973: 589–90). Unlike in situations where such shallowness engenders a desire for an internal spiritual revolution, the modern tourist turns elsewhere for authenticity: 'The more the individual sinks into everyday life, the more he is reminded of reality and authenticity elsewhere' (MacCannell, 1976: 160). MacCannell claims that 'Pretension and tackiness generate the belief that somewhere, only not right here, not right now, perhaps just over there someplace, in another country, in another life-style, in another social class, perhaps, there is *genuine* society' (MacCannell, 1976: 155). Therefore 'Authentic experiences are believed to be available only to those moderns who try to break the bonds of their everyday existence and begin to "live"' (MacCannell, 1976: 159). The search for authentic experiences is essentially a religious quest: therefore it follows that ' . . . tourism absorbs some of the social functions of religion in the modern world' (MacCannell, 1973: 589). However, since 'Touristic consciousness is motivated by the desire for authentic experience . . .' (*ibid.*: 597), rather than trivial ones, the chief problem facing the tourist becomes ' . . . to tell for sure if the experience is authentic or not'. (*ibid.*: 597). As against Boorstin and others who maintain that the tourist is content with contrived experiences, or is a mere superficial stooge, MacCannell endeavours to prove that the tourist is in fact a serious victim of a sophisticated deception: the tourist establishment 'stages authenticity', so that tourists are misled to believe that they succeeded in breaking through the contrived 'front' of the inauthentic, and have penetrated into the authentic 'back' regions of the host society, while in fact they were only presented with 'false backs', staged by the tourist establishment, or, in Carter's (1971) term, 'fenced in'. The problem is not the cultural shallowness of the tourists but the sophisticated machinations of the tourist establishment. However, though critical of the tourist establishment as the progenitor of a 'false (touristic) consciousness' (MacCannell, 1973: 89), MacCannell is nevertheless convinced of the 'functional' importance of tourism. Indeed, in an admittedly Durkheimian mode, he claims that tourism ' . . . is a form of ritual respect for society' (MacCannell, 1973: 589) and hence, apparently reinforces social solidarity. But he probably means 'Society' in general (and not necessarily the one of which the tourist is a member), since it was precisely inauthenticity of life in his own society, coupled with the ' . . . reminder (through the availability of souvenirs) of reality and authenticity elsewhere' (MacCannell, 1976: 160) and the ' . . . availability of authentic experiences at other times and other places' (*ibid.*: 148) which motivated the tourist for his quest in the first place. MacCannell likens tourism to the religious pilgrimage: 'The motive behind pilgrimage is similar to that behind a tour: both are quests for authentic experiences' (MacCannell, 1973: 593). But, the similarity he points out notwithstanding, there are some important, and to my mind crucial, differences: first, the pilgrim always undertakes his journey to the spiritual centre of *his* religion, though that centre may be located far beyond the boundaries of his life-space or society. It is true that the tourist, too, may travel to the artistic, national, religious and other centres of his own society or culture and pay them 'ritual respect'. But one of the distinguishing characteristics of modern tourism is precisely the generalized interest in the environment, and the desire for experiences far beyond the limits of the traveller's own cultural realm; indeed, it is often the sheer strangeness and novelty of other landscapes, lifeways and cultures which chiefly attract the tourist (Cohen, 1972).

Secondly, in contrast to the pilgrim, the experience-oriented tourist, even if he observes the authentic life of others, remains aware of their 'otherness', which persists even after his visit; he is not 'converted' to their life, nor does he accept their authentic lifeways. The pilgrim senses spiritual kinship with even a geographically remote centre; the 'experiential' tourist remains a stranger even when living among the people whose 'authentic' life he observes, and learns to appreciate, aesthetically. The pilgrim's experience is 'existential': he participates in, partakes of and is united with his co-religionists in the *communitas* created by the sacredness of the centre (Turner, 1973). He is fully involved in and committed to the beliefs and values symbolized by the centre. MacCannell's tourist, however, experiences only vicariously the authenticity of the life of others, but does not appropriate it for himself. Hence, though his quest may be essentially religious, the actual experience is primarily aesthetic, owing to its vicarious nature. The aesthesis provoked by direct contact with the authenticity of others may reassure and uplift the tourist, but does not provide a new meaning and guidance to his life. This can best be seen where 'experiential' tourists observe pilgrims at a pilgrimage centre: the pilgrims experience the sacredness of the centre; the tourists may experience aesthetically the authenticity of the pilgrims' experience. The 'experiential' mode of tourism though more profound than the 'recreational' or 'diversionary', does not generate 'real' religious experiences.

MacCannell provides the clues for an analysis of the search for new meaning through tourism. But his work falls short of accomplishing that task; an extension of his approach leads to the distinction of still more profound modes of touristic experiences, and to the eventual closure of the gap separating the mode of experience of the modern mass tourist from that of the traditional pilgrim.

4. *Experimental Mode*: this mode of the touristic experience is characteristic of people who do not adhere any more to the spiritual centre of their
own society, but engage in a quest for an alternative in many different directions. It is congenial to the more thoughtful among the disoriented postmodern travellers, particularly the more serious of the 'drifters' (Cohen,
1973), who, endowed with a 'decentralized personality' (Kavolis, 1970:
438–9) and lacking clearly defined priorities and intimate commitments, are
pre-disposed to try out alternative life-ways in their quest for meaning.
Travel is not the only possible form of their quest; mysticism, drugs, etc.,
may serve as alternative paths to the same goal; indeed, Eliade considers that
the internal and external quests for the centre are homologous (Eliade,
1971:18). But for those who do travel in quest of an alternative spiritual centre, travel takes up a new and heightened significance. While the traveller in
the 'experiential' mode derives enjoyment and reassurance from the fact that
others live authentically, while he remains 'disinherited' (Heller, 1961) and
content merely to observe the authentic life of others, the traveller in the 'experimental' mode engages in that authentic life, but refuses fully to commit
himself to it; rather, he samples and compares the different alternatives, hoping eventually to discover one which will suit his particular needs and desires. In a sense, the 'experimental' tourist is in 'search of himself', insofar as
in a trial and error process, he seeks to discover that form of life which elicits
a resonance in himself; he is often not really aware of what he seeks, of his
'real' needs and desires. His is an essentially religious quest, but diffuse and
without a clearly set goal.

Examples of such seekers who experiment with alternative lifeways
abound among the younger, post-modern set of travellers: urban American,
European or Australian youngsters who taste life in farming communities,
the Israeli kibbutzim, the Indian asramas, remote Pacific villages and hippie
communes, engage in the experimental mode of tourism. An enlightening
example is a short story, apparently written by a foreign student, in an Israeli
student paper, entitled 'In search of in search of . . .' (Coven, 1971), which
commences: 'I was in search of religion. I was in the depths, the bitter waters. No future, no meaning, loneliness, and boredom. I wanted religion, any
religion' (*ibid.*: 22); after describing several attempts to find religion in different Christian and Jewish settings in Israel, the story ends inclusively; the
search goes on . . .

Indeed, in extreme cases the search itself may become a way of life, and
the traveller an eternal seeker. Such may be the case with those 'drifters'
who get accustomed to move steadily between different peoples and cultures, who through constant wandering completely lose the faculty of mak-

ing choices, and are unable to commit themselves permanently to anything. If the 'seeker' attitude becomes habitual, it excludes the very possibility of that essentially religious 'leap of faith', which commitment to a new 'spiritual' centre consists of; the habitual seeker cannot be 'converted'.

5. *Existential Mode*: if the preceding mode of touristic experience characterizes the 'seeker', the 'existential' mode in its extreme form is characteristic of the traveller who is fully committed to an 'elective' spiritual centre, i.e. one external to the mainstream of his native society and culture. The acceptance of such a centre comes phenomenologically closest to a religious conversion, to 'switching worlds', in Berger and Luckmann's (1966: 144) terminology, though the content of the symbols and values so accepted need not be 'religious' in the narrow sense of the term. The person who encounters in his visit to an Israeli kibbutz a full realization of his quest for human communion; the seeker who achieved enlightenment in an Indian asrama; the traveller who finds in the life of a remote Pacific atoll the fulfilment of his cravings for simplicity and closeness to nature; all these are examples of 'existential' touristic experiences.

For the person attached to an 'elective' external centre, life away from it is, as it were, living in 'exile'; the only meaningful 'real' life is at the centre.[9] The experience of life at the centre during his visits sustains the traveller in his daily life in 'exile', in the same sense in which the pilgrim derives new spiritual strength, is 're-created', by his pilgrimage.

Those most deeply committed to a new 'spiritual' centre may attach themselves permanently to it and start a new life there by 'submitting'[10] themselves completely to the culture or society based on an orientation to that centre: they will desire to 'go native' and to become, respectively, Hindu recluses, Israeli kibbutz members, Pacific islanders, etc.

However, what makes 'existential' experiences a touristic phenomenon is the fact that there are many people—and their number is increasing in a growingly mobile world—who, for a variety of practical reasons, will not be able or willing to move permanently to their 'elective' centre, but will live in two worlds: the world of their everyday life, where they follow their practical pursuits, but which for them is devoid of deeper meaning; and the world of their 'elective' centre, to which they will depart on periodical pilgrimages to derive spiritual sustenance. Thus, e.g. there are some non-Jewish tourists who every year return to live for a few months on a kibbutz, while spending the rest of the year in their home country.

The visit to his centre of the tourist travelling in the existential mode is phenomenologically analogous to a pilgrimage. Indeed, Turner (1973: 193-4) refers to the community of pilgrims as an 'existential *communitas'*. In terms of the relationship of their existential quest to the culture of their society of origin, traditional pilgrimage and 'existential' tourism represent two extreme configurations: the traditional religious pilgrimage is a sacred journey to a centre which, though geographically 'ex-centric' is still the centre of the pilgrim's religion; it is the charismatic centre from which the pilgrim's life derives meaning, the spiritual centre of his society. Hence, though living away from the centre, the pilgrim is not living in 'exile'. His world and daily abode is hallowed, or given meaning through the centre. The centre, however, is *given*; it is not elective, not a matter of choice.

The centre of the 'existential' tourist, however, is not the centre of his culture of origin; it is an 'elective' centre, one which he chose and 'converted' to. Hence, it is not only ex-centric to his daily abode, but beyond the boundaries of the world of his daily existence; it does not hallow his world; hence, he lives in 'exile'. His pilgrimage is not one from the mere periphery of a religious world toward its centre; it is a journey from chaos into another cosmos, from meaninglessness to authentic existence.

Between these two extremes, the pilgrimage to a traditionally given centre and to an 'elective' one, different intermediate types can be discerned. There exist other than purely *religious* traditional centres of pilgrimage— such as cultural, aesthetic (artistic or natural) or national ones. Visits to the great artistic centres of the past, the heritage of one's own culture, such as were included, e.g. in the Grand Tour (Lambert (ed.), 1935, Trease, 1967), or any visit by people of 'Western' culture to the sites of classical antiquity may take on the quality of *cultural* pilgrimages. Visits to the shrines of the civil religion (Bellah, 1967) such as the Capitol or the Lincoln Monument by U.S. citizens, or those of the official state religion, e.g. Lenin's Tomb by Soviet citizens (MacCannell, 1976: 85) are forms of *political* pilgrimage. A person's culture may include, in addition to the religious any number of primary and secondary cultural, aesthetic and national centres, visits to which may be conducted in the existential mode of pilgrimages. Indeed, in the complexities of the modern world, the 'world' of any given culture and society is not clearly bounded; the cultural inheritance of one society is often appropriated by, and made part of other cultures. Many Westerners consider the centres of the ancient Greek or Hebrew cultures as part of 'their' tradition. Hence, what is today an 'elective' centre of a few individuals, outside the confines of their culture of origin, may tomorrow be appropriated by that culture; centres are 'traditional' or 'elective' only relatively to a given point in history.

We spoke of the 'existential' tourist as one who adheres to an 'elective' centre. Such a centre may be completely extraneous to his culture of origin, the history of his society or his biography. But it may also be a traditional centre to which he, his forebears or his 'people' had been attached in the past, but become alienated from. In this case, the desire for a visit to such a centre derives from a desire to find one's spiritual roots. The visit takes on the quality of a home-coming to a historical home. Such travellers, so to speak, re-elect their traditional centre. This conception is perhaps most clearly articulated in the ideology of Zionism. The full realization of the Zionist ideal is 'aliyah', literally 'ascension', the essentially religious term used to describe the act of permanent migration of a Zionist Jew to Israel.

Many Zionists, however, though Israel is their centre, do not take the ultimate step of 'Aliyah'. Their commitment to the 'centre' is expressed in a variety of less radical forms of behaviour, one of which are repeated sojourns in Israel, differing in content, frequency and length: periods of study and volunteer work on kibbutz settlements, yearly visits as private persons or in groups organized by different Zionist organizations, or eventual retirement to Israel, etc.[11] All of these are, in various degrees, forms of 'tourism' (Cohen, 1974). Particularly those who return yearly for relatively short visits for no other reason but to live for a while in Israel, exemplify the 'existential' mode of tourism, in the form of a renewed relationship to a historical centre.

It is interesting to note that recently, the motivation for 'existential' tourism to Israel has apparently widened to include not only Zionists in the narrow sense, but also Diaspora Jews who desire to taste 'genuine' Jewish communal life, the borderline between these and Jews who come for religious reasons, i.e. pilgrims in the narrower traditional religious sense has thus become blurred. Even people who are not pilgrims in any sense, may be overcome by an 'existential' experience at the centre. This comes through powerfully from a recent review of S. Bellow's book *To Jerusalem and Back*: 'The most saline of American writers finds himself unable to escape the tenebrous undertow of Jewish mysticism. "My inclination is to resist imagination when it operates in this way," he writes. "Yet I, too, feel that the light of Jerusalem has purifying powers and filters the blood and the thought. I don't forbid myself the reflection that light might be the outer garment of God"' (*Time*, 1976: 62).

A craving for an existential experience at one's historical sources probably motivates many old-time immigrants—and their progeny—who travel from their country of abode to visit the 'old country', from which they or their parents once departed: e.g. the American Italians or Irish visiting Italy or Ireland, the Corsicans in France visiting Corsica, the American Chinese visiting pre-Communist China etc. Perhaps the most interesting recent example of the sudden awakening of such cravings among a long-exiled people is the renewed interest of American blacks in Africa as the land of their fathers (*Spiegel*, 1973). Though I have to add a point to be discussed more fully below, that the mere desire for such an experience is not a guarantee for its fulfilment as many American blacks who visited Africa and for that matter Jews who visited Israel, learned to their sorrow.

The various modes of tourist experience were here presented in an ascending order from the most 'superficial' one motivated by the desire for mere 'pleasure', to that most 'profound', motivated by the quest for meaning. The modes were separated for analytic purposes; any individual tourist may experience several modes on a single trip; a change from one mode to another may also occur in the 'touristic biography' of any individual traveller. The mix of modes characteristic of different types of trips and the changes in the desired modes of experiences during a person's 'touristic biography' are empirical problems for further investigation.

One particular conceptual problem, however, remains to be clarified: the problem of 'multiple centres'. We have throughout proceeded on the tacit assumption that the individual adheres to only one principal 'spiritual' centre. If he is alienated from the centre of his society or culture, he may look for it elsewhere.

This, however, is an over-simplification, which needs two qualifications: first, some people, we may call them 'humanists', entertain extremely broad conceptions of 'their' culture and are willing to subsume under it everything, or almost everything human, on the principle of Goethe's famous statement 'Nichts Menschlichesist mir fern' ('Nothing human is alien to me'). For such people, there is no single principal 'spiritual' centre: every culture is a form in which the human spirit is manifested. They may thus travel in the experiential, or even existential modes, without being alienated from their culture of origin; for them, the culture they happen to have been reared in, is just one of the many equally valid cultures. The narrower the scope of cultures given equal status, the closer the 'humanist' comes to a 'cultural' tourist. The more important an external centre becomes relative to his culture of origin, the closer he approximates the 'existential' tourist. Secondly, there are people, we may call them 'dualists' or more broadly 'pluralists', who adhere simultaneously to two or more heterogeneous 'spiritual' centres, each giving rise to equally authentic, though different, forms of life. Such persons may feel equally at home in two or more 'worlds', and even enjoy 'existential' experiences from their sojourn at another centre or centres, without being alienated from their own. American Zionists, for example, must not necessarily feel in 'exile' in the United States, but may adhere simultaneously to the 'American Dream' and to Israel as the Zionist centre, and be equally committed to both.

'Humanists' and 'dualists' or 'pluralists' qualify the underlying hypothesis of this paper that a person seeks and ultimately adheres to 'spiritual' centres of others only after he realizes the discomfort of his alienation to the centre of his own culture and society. They indicate the necessity for a more thorough phenomenological investigation of the variety of complex world-views which developed in the modern world, for the analysis of which Eliade's or Shils' basic models do not suffice any more.

CONCLUSIONS

The typology of modes of tourist experience presented above reconciles the opposing views of '*the* tourist' in the current polemic on tourism and thereby prepares the way for a more systematic comparative study of touristic phenomena. Our discussion shows that, depending on the mode of the touristic experience, tourism spans the range of motivations between the desire for mere pleasure characteristic of the sphere of 'leisure' and the quest for meaning and authenticity characteristic of the sphere of 'religion'; it can hence be approached from both, the perspective of the 'sociology of leisure' as well as that of the 'sociology of religion'. But neither of these approaches will exhaust the whole phenomenon, owing to the differences in the modes of experiences desired by different tourists. The context within which the typology has been developed was borrowed from the sociology of religion: my point of departure was a tourist's fundamental world-view, and specifically, his adherence to, or quest for a 'spiritual' centre. I assumed that different world-views are conducive to different modes of the touristic experience. In fact I tackled the same problem which MacCannell addressed himself to, but, instead of assuming that all tourists are 'pilgrims', I attempted to answer the question, under what conditions and in what sense tourism becomes a form of pilgrimage? It now remains to work out some of the implications of the typology developed in response to this question.

By claiming that tourists pursue different modes of experience, we did not imply that these are invariably realized in their trip. Two problems can be discerned here: first, from the viewpoint of the tourist, what are the chances of *realization* of the different modes of touristic experience? Second, from the point of view of the external observer, what are the possibilities of *falsification* of such experiences by the tourist establishment? Again, I raise questions which MacCannell has been concerned with, but my answers are somewhat different.

While MacCannell takes a lofty view of the desires of the tourists, and a pessimistic view of their realizability, I claim that the various modes of touristic experiences differ in the ease of their realization; generally speaking, the more 'profound' the mode of experience, the harder it becomes to realize it. The 'diversionary' mode is the easiest to realize: as with any kind of entertainment, it suffices if the travel experience has been pleasurable. The realization of the 'recreational' mode demands, in addition, that the experience perform a restorative function for the individual. Since the traveller in these two modes has no pretensions for authenticity, his experience cannot be falsified. He can achieve his aim even when he is fully aware that his experience was staged in a 'tourist space'. As in other forms of entertainment, there is no need fully to camouflage the staging. The art of the tourist 'producer' is to create in the tourist a semi-conscious illusion and to engage his imagination until he is turned into a willing accomplice, rather than a stooge, of the game of touristic make-believe. The tourist and the touristic entrepreneur may agree that they deal in contrivances; indeed, the fact that these are contrivances often ensures their enjoyability. Insofar as much of what tourists around the world come in touch with in their sightseeing tours, e.g. on visits to 'native villages', or at performances of 'folkloristic dances and ceremonies' becomes explicitly defined as entertainment, rather than authentic culture, no falsification of the experience of the unpretentious 'diversionary' or 'recreational' tourist is involved.

The situation is completely different for tourists travelling in the other modes of touristic experience; for them, the authenticity of the experience is crucial for its meaning. This is true not only for the 'experiential' tourist, who is reassured by the authentic life of others, and for whom authenticity is obviously a *sine qua non* for the realization of his experience. It is equally true for the 'experimental' and 'experiential' tourist: one can hardly experiment with alternative ways of life if these are merely contrived for one's convenience, nor can one derive existential meaning from a 'spiritual centre' outside one's society or culture, if such a centre is only a chimera, advertised to lure tourists in quest of existential experiences. No wonder that MacCannell, who discusses mainly what we termed 'experiential' tourism, emphasises that the tourist constantly faces the danger of a 'false' (touristic) consciousness, by becoming the victim of the machinations of the tourist establishment, which presents him with a '. . . false back [which] is more insidious and dangerous than a false front; [hence] an inauthentic demystification of social life [of the hosts] is not merely a lie but a superlie, the kind that drips with sincerity' (MacCannell, 1973: 599). In MacCannell's view, the prevalent fate of tourists is to become entrapped in 'tourist space', never able to realize their craving for authenticity: '. . . there is no way out for them so long as they press their search for authenticity' (MacCannell, 1973: 601). This claim attains with MacCannell almost the status of a 'touristic condition' reflecting a generally absurd human condition captured in works of existentialist philosophers. If for Sartre, there is 'No Exit' from the human existence and no way to penetrate the subjectivity of others, for MacCannell there is no way for the tourist to penetrate the others' authenticity. Taken to its extreme, the quest of MacCannell's tourist, like that of Camus's or Sartre's heroes, is absurd.

I do not subscribe to this view and believe that at least some modern tourists, particularly the explorer and the original drifter (Cohen, 1972, 1973) are capable of penetrating beyond the staged 'tourist space' and its false backs and observe other people's life 'as it really is'. But this demands an effort and application, and a degree of sophistication which most tourists do not possess. There is hence a high chance that any of those tourists who desire authenticity, will be misled by the tourist establishment, and their experience will be falsified; as long as they do not grasp the falsification, they may labour under the illusion that they have realized their aim; if and when they penetrate the deception, they will be both enlightened and disenchanted; their resentment will give rise to demands for 'honesty in tourism'.

The mechanisms which support the constitution of the touristic illusion and the processes of its denouement have yet to be studied in detail. Such a study would, in MacCannell's neo-Marxist terminology, represent the examination of the processes through which 'false (touristic) consciousness' is created and those through which '(touristic) class consciousness' emerges. MacCannell has done some pioneering work in this field, but much more systematic study is needed.

The tourist travelling in the experimental mode also faces the problem of authenticity. The danger of delusion will be less serious in his case, since his desire to experiment with other forms of life and not just experience them, leads him off the beaten track and sharpens his critical faculties. Being inquisitive and uncommitted, he is tuned to discover deception. His major problem, however, is to achieve commitment to any of the life ways with which he experiments. What originally appears as experimentation with a view to an ultimate commitment to one of the alternatives, may turn into a predicament. An 'experimental' tourist with a decentralized personality, may easily become an 'eternal seeker'. If false consciousness is the danger faced by the 'experiential' tourist, total disorientation, and ultimate alienation from all human society, is the threat to the 'experimental' tourist. The fate of some modern drifters strongly supports this argument.

The tourist travelling in the existential mode faces the most serious problem of realization. Commitment to and authenticity of the experience of the 'elective' centre are not enough; the ultimate problem is that of 'commensurability': is the 'true' life at the centre indeed commensurable to his high hopes and expectations? Does it enable the traveller to live authentically, to achieve self-realization? This is a problem which existential tourists share with pilgrims. The centre, of course, symbolises an ideal. Ideals are not fully realizable, but can only be approached 'asymptotically'.[12] The geographical centre symbolizes the ideal one; between the two, however, there is necessarily a discrepancy: Jerusalem may be the Holy City, but ordinary human life in Jerusalem is far from holy. The pilgrim or the existential tourist 'ascends' spiritually to the ideal centre, but he necessarily arrives at the geographical one. How does he handle the discrepancy? For example: a person adhering to the ideal of voluntary collectivism, may go to live on a kibbutz, as an 'elective' centre embodying his ideals; soon, however, he will realize that life on the kibbutz is far from ideal. He will thus encounter a discrepancy between the ideal conception and actual life, which, if not dealt with satisfactorily, may provoke a personal crisis of meaninglessness, futility and disenchantment.

I distinguish three kinds of 'existential' tourists in terms of the manner in which they deal with the perceived discrepancy:

(a) 'Realistic idealists', who are willing to concede that even the most ideal place, society or culture have shortcomings, and are thus able to achieve self-realization at the centre without deluding themselves of its faultlessness. I suggest that these are often people who became committed to their 'elective' centre after a prolonged quest and experimentation, and are thus bereft of illusions.

(b) 'Starry-eyed idealists', those 'true believers' (Hoffer, 1952) who will see perfection in whatever they find at the centre and refuse to face the reality of life in it, inclusive of its shortcomings. From the point of view of the external observer, their self-realization will be based on self-delusion. I suggest that these are often people whose commitment to an 'elective' centre was a result of a sudden conversion, of a precipitous 'switching of worlds' in the certainty of discovery of a panacea.

(c) Finally, there are the 'critical idealists' who oscillate between a craving for the centre from afar, and a disenchantment when they visit it. They are attached to the ideal which the centre is meant to represent, but reject the re-

ality they found at it. For these, the centre has meaning when they are remote, but tends to lose it when they approach it. Their attitude has been
forcefully expressed by the Jewish writer Elie Wiesel, at a Conference on
Jewish Intellectuals in New York in 1971: 'I am at home in Jerusalem when I
am not there'.[13] I suggest that the 'critical idealists' tend to be people who ad-
hered to the centre for a long time from afar, and for whom the trip was a realization of a long-cherished dream. They may preserve their dream, while
denying the adequacy of its earthly embodiment, and advocating a reform of
the actual centre to bring it closer to the ideal.

The problem of discrepancies, however, can be 'resolved' in another
way—at the expense of the authenticity of the tourist's experience, i.e. by
straightforward falsification. As demand for existential experiences increases, the tourist establishment and other bodies may set out to supply it.
The existential mode of the tourist experience, based as it often is on a prior
commitment, is particularly amenable to falsification. The tourist, expecting
the ideal life at the centre, is easily taken in; he is helped, as it were, to become a 'starry-eyed idealist'. Like traditional pilgrimage centres, centres of
'existential' tourism are advertised and embellished; tours through 'existential tourist space', like traditional pilgrimages, are staged. New centres may
even be straightforwardly invented. The purveyance of existential experiences becomes big business. Tourist-oriented centres of Eastern religion,
catering for 'instant enlightenment' may be one example.[14] Another are the
massive 'Zionist pilgrimages' staged by the Israeli governmental and national institutions, in which the visitors are brought to a pitch of Zionist ec-
stasy at the height of a well-planned and organized tour through staged
'Zionist tourist space'. The largest of these pilgrimages, equal in everything
to its religious counterpart, was the massive United Jewish Appeal 'This Year
in Jerusalem' tour of 1976, which brought several thousand people to the
country and large contributions to the U.J.A. The study of staging the 'existential' touristic sites and tours, such, as the U.J.A. pilgrimages, is just com-
mencing, but promises rich and interesting data for comparison with
traditional religious pilgrimages.[15]

One last word on the relationship between the modes of touristic experiences and the problem of strangeness. It is generally assumed that tourists,
when leaving their familiar environment, expose themselves to increasing
degrees of strangeness, against which the more routine, less adventurous
mass tourists are protected by an 'ecological bubble of their home environment' (Cohen, 1972: 171), so as not to suffer a disorienting culture shock
which would spoil the pleasure of their trip. This argument is based on a
tacit assumption that the tourist, adhering to the 'spiritual centre' of his own

society or culture, prefers its lifeways and thought-patterns, and feels threatened and incommoded when presented with the different, unfamiliar ones of the host country. Strangeness, however, may be not only a threat, but also a lure and challenge (Cohen, in preparation (a)). This seems particularly true for those travellers for whom the above assumption does not hold and who have either lost their 'centre' and travel in the experiential or experimental mode, or adhere to a new 'elective' one outside their society (existential mode). Such travellers may well desire exposure to strangeness and not shun it, but rather seek to 'submit' to it. Unlike the mass tourist, they will not suffer from a culture shock when exposed to the host environment, but may rather experience what Meintel (1973: 52) calls a 'reverse culture shock' upon return home. Talking of the personal experience of (particularly post-modern) anthropologists, Meintel observes: 'Desirable values, . . . which were not experienced before and which may have been attained as a stranger in a foreign setting may appear unrealizable in the home situation. Nash attributes the fact that "many anthropologists come alive only when a field trip is in prospect for them" to the attractions of the stranger role (Nash, 1963: 163), but perhaps, desirable personal ends attained to a significant degree elsewhere are actually unattainable in the situations to which these individuals return'. (Meintel, 1973: 53). Her observation may well apply to 'existential' tourists as well, provided that they succeeded in realizing the desired experiences. The problem of such travellers is, however, that being the most committed and nurturing the highest expectations, they may indeed experience a 'shock' upon arrival at their 'elective' centre—but not one emanating from the contrast between home and their 'elected' external centre, but rather from the fact that this 'centre' is too much like home and hence does not correspond to their idealized image.

The phenomenological analysis of tourist experiences in this paper has been highly speculative; contrary to other areas in the study of tourism, the in-depth study of tourist experiences is not yet much developed, though an endless number of surveys of tourist 'motivations' has been conducted. I hope that the conceptual framework and the typology here proposed, will serve as the theoretical baseline for more profound, empirical studies of tourist experiences.[16]

NOTES

1. The collection of material on which this paper is based was facilitated by a grant of the Basic Research Unit of the Israel National Academy of Sciences and Humanities. Thanks are due to the Academy for its support and to Dr. J. Dolgin and J. Michalowicz for their comments on an earlier draft of this paper.

2. Definitions of the concept 'tourist' abound in the literature. 'Travelling for plea-sure' is the most commonly evoked dimension of the phenomenon; for additional di-mensions necessary for a systematic definition of the tourist as a traveller role, see Cohen, 1974. The present paper departs on a different track—it does not deal with the tourist's role, but with the precise nature of his supposedly 'pleasurable' experience.

3. Cf. e.g. Gross, 1961L: 5: 'in the area of tension management, the cathartic and restorative functions of leisure are pre-eminent, . . .'

4. If the experience were available within the life-space, there would be no need take the trouble to travel: cf. Stouffer, 1950.

5. 'Paradisiac cults' are predicated on the belief that paradise, i.e. the centre, is a place which can be approached by an actual voyage, though that voyage may include miraculous elements (e.g. men flying over the sea, Eliade,1969: 101–104); if it is be-lieved that the centre is located on a wholly different sphere, it will be approachable by a 'spiritual journey', such as that of the shaman (Rasmussen, 1972), in which a man is miraculously transported to other spheres without actual physical movement through empirical space.

6. This is evidenced by the recurrent use of paradisiac imagery in modern mass tourism (see e.g. Turner and Ash, 1975: 149 ff). But the 'paradise' these tourists seek is of a stereotyped, commercialized kind—it is an idyllic place equipped with all modern amenities. For a discussion of 'paradise' as a 'type of touristic community' see MacCannell, 1976: 183. For an example of the process of debasement of the paradisiac image, see Cohen (in preparation, (b)).

7. An excellent example, in which the game of make-believe has been brought al-most to the level of a fine art is mass tourism in Hawaii. Thus Crampon describes a three-stage game through which the 'royal visitor to the Islands' (i.e. the tourist) be-comes a Hawaiian; at the end of this process, the tourist comes to like Hawaii, since the Hawaiian kama'aina likes Hawaii. Crampon claims that 'Probably . . . this visitor is not 'acting'. He does like Hawaii. He is convinced that Hawaii is a Paradise' (Crampon, n.d.: 54). The game has terminated in successful self-delusion, with the full cooperation of the tourist.

8. For MacCannell's definition of 'experience' in the sense here used, see Mac-Cannell, 1976: 23; for some concrete examples of touristic 'experiences' see ibid.: 97.

9. This point is admirably illustrated in an anecdote told by Eliade of the famous German historian Th. Mommsen. After a lecture in which Mommsen gave by heart a detailed account of the topography of ancient Athens, a valet had to take him home, since, ' . . . the famous historian did not know how to go home alone. The greatest liv-ing authority on fifth-century Athens was completely lost in his own city of Wilhelminian Berlin' (Eliade, 1976: 19). Eliade continues: 'Mommsen admirably illus-trates the existential meaning of "living in one's own world". His real world, the only one which was relevant and meaningful was the classical Greco-Roman world. For Mommsen, the world of the Greeks and Romans was not simple history . . . ; it was his world—that place where he could move, think and enjoy the beatitude of being alive and creative. . . . Like most creative scholars, he probably lived in two worlds: the uni-verse of forms and values, to the understanding of which he dedicated his life and which corresponds somehow to the "cosmicized" and therefore "sacred" world of the primitives, and the everyday "profane" world into which he was "thrown" as Hei-degger would say. Mommsen obviously felt detached from the profane, non-essential, and for him meaningless and ultimately chaotic space of modern Berlin' (ibid. 19). While the historian Mommsen's 'real' world was remote in time, the existential tourist's real world is remote in space; but the cognitive structure of their respective worlds is otherwise identical.

10. On the concept of 'submission', as a voluntary form of transition from strangeness to familiarity, see Cohen (in preparation (a)).

11. I intend to deal in a separate paper with the different forms of temporary migration of Jews to Israel which recently proliferated, and through which the boundary between Israeli Jews and Jews of the Diaspora became progressively blurred.

12. This idea has been mostly fully developed in the work of the philosopher E. Bloch; most pertinent for our purposes is his discussion of 'geographical utopias' (Bloch, 1959: 873–929). I am grateful to Dr. Paul Mendes-Flohr who introduced me to Bloch's ideas.

13. Reported to me by Paul Mendes-Flohr.

14. An excellent example is the Bhagwan Shree Rajneesb Ashram in Poona, visited primarily by Westerners. Rajneesh, who '. . . speeds up the usually slow Hindu attainment of meditation and bliss with a sort of pop-Hinduism . . .', argues that 'Westerners want things quickly, so we give it to them right away . . .' (Bangkok Post, 1978: 7).

15. I am obliged for the information on the U.J.A. to Dr. Janet O'Dea, who currently studies the U.J.A. 'pilgrimages' to Israel.

16. Accepted 10.1.78.

REFERENCES

Bangkok Post (1978): Sex Guru Challenges Desai, Bangkok Post, 23.8–1978: 7.

Baroja, E. J. C. (1965). El Carnaval, Madrid: Taurus.

Bellah, R. N. (1967). 'Civil Religion in America', Daedalus, Winter, 1967, 1–21.

Berger, P. and Luckmann, Th. (1966). The Social Construction of Reality, Harmondsworth: Penguin.

Bloch, E. (1959). Das Prinzip Hoffnung, Frankfurt am Main: Suhrkamp Verlag, Vol. II.

Boorstin, D. J. (1964). The Image: A Guide to Pseudo-Events in America, New York: Harper & Row.

Carter, J. (1971). 'Do Fence Them In!', Pacific Islands Monthly, 42 (6): 49–53.

Cohen, E. (1972). 'Towards a Sociology of International Tourism', Social Research, 39 (I), 164–89.

———. (1973). 'Nomads from Affluence: Notes on the Phenomenon of Drifter-Tourism', Internat. J. of Comparative Sociology, 14 (1–2), 89–103.

———. (1974). 'Who Is a Tourist? A Conceptual Clarification', Sociological Review, 22 (4), 527–55.

———. (in preparation (a)). Strangeness and Familiarity: The Sociology of Temporary Migration.

———. (in preparation (b)). The Pacific Islands from Utopia to Consumer Product: The Transformation of Paradise.

Coven, I. (1971). 'In search of in search of . . .' , Lilit, No. 7: 22–23.

Crampon, L. J. (n.d.). 'The Impact of Aloha', in: Crampon, L. J., Tourist Development Notes, Boulder, Colo.: Univ. of Colorado, Graduate School of Business Admin., Business Research Divison, Vol. III, 51–60 (Mimeo).

Desai, A. V. (1974). 'Tourism—Economic Possibilities and Policies', in Tourism in Fiji Suva: University of the South Pacific, 1–12.

Dumazdier, J. (1967). *Toward a Society of Leisure*, New York: Free Press.

Dupont, G. (1973). 'Lourdes: Pilgrims or Tourists?', *Manchester Guardian Weekly* 108 (20), 10.5.1973:16.

Eisenstadt, S. N. (1968). 'Transformation of Social, Political and Cultural Orders in Modernisation', in Eisenstadt, S. N. (ed.), *Comparative Perspectives on Social Change* Boston: Little, Brown and Co., 256–279.

Eliade, M. (1969). *The Quest; History and Meaning in Religion*, Univ. of Chicago Press, Chicago and London.

———. (1971). *The Myth of Eternal Return*, Princeton, N.J., Princeton Univ. Press.

———. (1976). *Occultism, Witchcraft and Cultural Fashions*, Chicago: Univ. of Chicago Press.

Glasser, R. (1975). 'Life Force or Tranquilizer', *Society and Leisure*, 7(3), 17–26.

Gross, E. (1961). 'A Functional Approach to Leisure Analysis', *Social Problems*, 9(1), 2–8.

Heller, E. (1961). *The Disinherited Mind*, Harmondsworth: Penguin Books.

Hoffer, E. (1952). *The True Believer: Thoughts on the Nature of Mass Movements*, London: Seeker & Warburg.

Huetz De Lemps, Ch. (1964). 'Le Tourisme dans l'Archipel des Hawaii', *Cahiers d'Outre-Mer*, 17 (65), 9–57.

Kavolis, V. (1970). 'Post Modern Man: Psychocultural Responses to Social Trends', *Social Problems*, 17 (4), 435–48.

Lambert, R. S. (ed) (1935). *Grand Tour: A Journey in the Tracks of the Age of Aristocracy*, London: Faber & Faber.

Lowenthal, D. (1962). 'Tourists and Thermalists', *Geographical Review*, 52 (l), 124–27.

MacCannell, D. (1973). 'Staged Authenticity: Arrangements of Social Space in Tourist Settings', *American Journal Of Sociology*, 79 (3): 589–603.

———. (1976). *The Tourist: A New Theory of the Leisure Class*, New York: Schocken Books.

Meintel, D. A. (1973). 'Strangers, Homecomers and Ordinary Men', *Anthropological Quarterly*, 46 (1), 47–58.

Mitford, N. (1959). 'The Tourist', *Encounter*, 13 (4), 3–7.

Nash, D. (1963). 'The Ethnologist as Stranger: as Essay in the Sociology of Knowledge', *Southwestern J. of Anthropology*, 19, 149–67.

Rasmussen, K. (1972). 'A Shaman's Journey to the Sea Spirit', in W. A. Lessa and E. Z. Vogt (eds.), *Reader in Comparative Religion*, New York, Harper & Row, 388–91.

Shils, E. (1975). 'Center and Periphery', in E. Shils: *Center and Periphery: Essays in Macrosociology*, Chicago & London: Univ. of Chicago Press, 3–16

Shils, E., and Young, M. (1953). 'The Meaning of the Coronation', *Sociological Review* 1(2), 63–82.

Spiegel, Der, (1973). 'Enge Bindung', *Der Spiegel*, 27 (4); 22.1.197 3: 111.

Stouffer, S. A. (1940). 'Intervening Opportunities: A Theory Relating Mobility and Distance', *American Sociological Review*, 5: 845–67.

Time. (1976). 'Review of S. Bellow's *To Jerusalem and Back'*, *Time*, 8.11–1976: 62.

Trease, G. (1967). *The Grand Tour*, Heinemann, London.

Turner, L. and Ash, J. (1975). *The Golden Hordes*, London: Constable.

Turner, V. (1973). 'The Center Out There: The Pilgrim's Goal', *History of Religions*, 12 (3), 191–230.

AMERICA

Jean Baudrillard

I went in search of *astral* America,[1] not social and cultural America, but the America of the empty, absolute freedom of the freeways, not the deep America of mores and mentalities, but the America of desert speed, of motels and mineral surfaces. I looked for it in the speed of the screenplay, in the indifferent reflex of television, in the film of days and nights projected across an empty space, in the marvellously affectless succession of signs, images, faces, and ritual acts on the road; looked for what was nearest to the nuclear and enucleated universe, a universe which is virtually our own, right down to its European cottages.

I sought the finished form of the future catastrophe of the social in geology, in that upturning of depth that can be seen in the striated spaces, the reliefs of salt and stone, the canyons where the fossil river flows down, the immemorial abyss of slowness that shows itself in erosion and geology. I even looked for it in the verticality of the great cities.

I knew all about this nuclear form, this future catastrophe when I was still in Paris, of course. But to understand it, you have to take to the road, to that travelling which achieves what Virilio calls the aesthetics of disappearance.

For the mental desert form expands before your very eyes, and this is the purified form of social desertification. Disaffection finds its pure form in the barrenness of speed. All that is cold and dead in desertification or social enucleation rediscovers its contemplative form here in the heat of the desert. Here in the transversality of the desert and the irony of geology, the transpolitical finds its generic, mental space. The inhumanity of our ulterior, asocial, superficial world immediately finds its aesthetic form here, its ecstatic

---

[1] '*l'Amérique sidérale*': this term and its variant forms have been rendered throughout by 'astral' or the less familiar 'sidereal,' according to context. [Tr.]

form. For the desert is simply that: an ecstatic critique of culture, an ecstatic form of disappearance.

The grandeur of deserts derives from their being, in their aridity, the negative of the earth's surface and of our civilized humours. They are places where humours and fluids become rarefied, where the air is so pure that the influence of the stars descends direct from the constellations. And, with the extermination of the desert Indians, an even earlier stage than that of anthropology became visible: a mineralogy, a geology, a sidereality, an inhuman facticity, an aridity that drives out the artificial scruples of culture, a silence that exists nowhere else.

The silence of the desert is a visual thing, too. A product of the gaze that stares out and finds nothing to reflect it. There can be no silence up in the mountains, since their very contours roar. And for there to be silence, time itself has to attain a sort of horizontality; there has to be no echo of time in the future, but simply a sliding of geological strata one upon the other giving out nothing more than a fossil murmur.

Desert: luminous, fossilized network of an inhuman intelligence, of a radical indifference—the indifference not merely of the sky, but of the geological undulations, where the metaphysical passions of space and time alone crystallize. Here the terms of desire are turned upside down each day, and night annihilates them. But wait for the dawn to rise, with the awakening of the fossil sounds, the animal silence.

Speed creates pure objects. It is itself a pure object, since it cancels out the ground and territorial reference-points, since it runs ahead of time to annul time itself, since it moves more quickly than its own cause and obliterates that cause by outstripping it. Speed is the triumph of effect over cause, the triumph of instantaneity over time as depth, the triumph of the surface and pure objectality over the profundity of desire. Speed creates a space of initiation, which may be lethal; its only rule is to leave no trace behind. Triumph of forgetting over memory, an uncultivated, amnesic intoxication. The superficiality and reversibility of a pure object in the pure geometry of the desert. Driving like this produces a kind of invisibility, transparency, or transversality in things, simply by emptying them out. It is a sort of slow-motion suicide, death by an extenuation of forms—the delectable form of their disappearance. Speed is not a vegetal thing. It is nearer to the mineral, to refraction through a crystal, and it is already the site of a catastrophe, of a squandering of time. Perhaps, though, its fascination is simply that of the void. There is no seduction here, for seduction requires a secret. Speed is sim-

ply the rite that initiates us into emptiness: a nostalgic desire for forms to re-
vert to immobility, concealed beneath the very intensification of their mobility. Akin to the nostalgia for living forms that haunts geometry.

Still, there is a violent contrast here, in this country, between the growing
abstractness of a nuclear universe and a primary, visceral, unbounded vitality, springing not from rootedness, but from the lack of roots, a metabolic
vitality, in sex and bodies, as well as in work and in buying and selling. Deep
down, the U.S., with its space, its technological refinement, its bluff good
conscience, even in those spaces which it opens up for simulation, is the *only
remaining primitive society*. The fascinating thing is to travel through it as
though it were the primitive society of the future, a society of complexity,
hybridity, and the greatest intermingling, of a ritualism that is ferocious but
whose superficial diversity lends it beauty, a society inhabited by a total
metasocial fact with unforeseeable consequences, whose immanence is breath-
taking, yet lacking a past through which to reflect on this, and therefore fundamentally primitive.... Its primitivism has passed into the hyperbolic,
inhuman character of a universe that is beyond us, that far outstrips its own
moral, social, or ecological rationale.

Only Puritans could have invented and developed this ecological and biological morality based on preservation—and therefore on discrimination—
which is profoundly racial in nature. Everything becomes an overprotected
nature reserve, so protected indeed that there is talk today of denaturalizing
Yosemite to give it back to Nature, as has happened with the Tasaday in the
Philippines. A Puritan obsession with origins in the very place where the
ground itself has already gone. An obsession with finding a niche, a contact,
precisely at the point where everything unfolds in an astral indifference.

There is a sort of miracle in the insipidity of *artificial paradises*, so long as
they achieve the greatness of an entire (un)culture. In America, space lends a
sense of grandeur even to the insipidity of the suburbs and 'funky towns'.
The desert is everywhere, preserving insignificance. A desert where the miracle of the car, of ice and whisky is daily re-enacted: a marvel of easy living
mixed with the fatality of the desert. A miracle of obscenity that is genuinely
American: a miracle of total availability, of the transparency of all functions
in space, though this latter nonetheless remains unfathomable in its vastness
and can only be exercised by speed.

The Italian miracle: that of stage and scene.

The American miracle: that of the obscene.

The profusion of sense, as against the deserts of meaninglessness.

It is metamorphic forms that are magical. Not the sylvan, vegetal forest, but the petrified, mineralized forest. The salt desert, whiter than snow, flatter than the sea. The effect of monumentality, geometry, and architecture where nothing has been designed or planned. Canyonsland, Split Mountain. Or the opposite: the amorphous reliefless relief of Mud Hills, the voluptuous, fossilized, monotonously undulating lunar relief of ancient lake beds. The white swell of White Sands.... It takes this surreality of the elements to eliminate nature's picturesque qualities, just as it takes the metaphysics of speed to eliminate the natural picturesqueness of travel.

In fact the conception of a trip without any objective and which is, as a result, endless, only develops gradually for me. I reject the picturesque tourist round, the sights, even the landscapes (only their abstraction remains, in the prism of the scorching heat). Nothing is further from pure travelling than tourism or holiday travel. That is why it is best done in the extensive banality of deserts, or in the equally desert-like banality of a metropolis—not at any stage regarded as places of pleasure or culture, but seen televisually as scenery, as scenarios. That is why it is best done in extreme heat, the orgasmic form of bodily deterritorialization. The acceleration of molecules in the heat contributes to a barely perceptible evaporation of meaning.

It is not the discovery of local customs that counts, but discovering the immorality of the space you have to travel through, and this is on a quite different plane. It is this, together with the sheer distance, and the deliverance from the social, that count. Here in the most moral society there is, space is truly immoral. Here in the most conformist society, the dimensions are immoral. It is this immorality that makes distance light and the journey infinite, that cleanses the muscles of their tiredness.

Driving is a spectacular form of amnesia. Everything is to be discovered, everything to be obliterated. Admittedly, there is the primal shock of the deserts and the dazzle of California, but when this is gone, the secondary brilliance of the journey begins, that of the excessive, pitiless distance, the infinity of anonymous faces and distances, or of certain miraculous geological formations, which ultimately testify to no human will, while keeping intact an image of upheaval. This form of travel admits of no exceptions: when it runs up against a known face, a familiar landscape, or some decipherable message, the spell is broken: the amnesic, ascetic, asymptotic charm of disappearance succumbs to affect and worldly semiology.

This sort of travel creates its own peculiar type of event and innervation, so it also has its own special form of fatigue. Like a fibrillation of muscles, striated by the excess of heat and speed, by the excess of things seen or read, of places passed through and forgotten. The defibrillation of the body over-loaded with empty signs, functional gestures, the blinding brilliance of the sky, and somnabulistic distances, is a very slow process. Things suddenly be-come lighter, as culture, our culture, becomes more rarefied. And this spec-tral form of civilization which the Americans have invented, an ephemeral form so close to vanishing point, suddenly seems the best adapted to the probability—the probability only—of the life that lies in store for us. The form that dominates the American West, and doubtless all of American cul-ture, is a seismic form: a fractal, interstitial culture, born of a rift with the Old World, a tactile, fragile, mobile, superficial culture—you have to follow its own rules to grasp how it works: seismic shifting, soft technologies.

The only question in this journey is: how far can we go in the extermination of meaning, how far can we go in the non-referential desert form without cracking up and, of course, still keep alive the esoteric charm of disappear-ance? A theoretical question here materialized in the objective conditions of a journey which is no longer a journey and therefore carries with it a funda-mental rule: aim for the point of no return. This is the key. And the crucial moment is that brutal instant which reveals that the journey has no end, that there is no longer any reason for it to come to an end. Beyond a certain point, it is movement itself that changes. Movement which moves through space of its own volition changes into an absorption by space itself—end of resis-tance, end of the scene of the journey as such (exactly as the jet engine is no longer an energy of space-penetration, but propels itself by creating a vacuum in front of it that sucks it forward, instead of supporting itself, as in the tra-ditional model, upon the air's resistance). In this way, the centrifugal, eccen-tric point is reached where movement produces the vacuum that sucks you in. This moment of vertigo is also the moment of potential collapse. Not so much from the tiredness generated by the distance and the heat, as from the irreversible advance into the desert of time.

Tomorrow is the first day of the rest of your life.

READING AND WRITING TRAVEL

The essays in this section demonstrate how the experience of travel is multiplied and manipulated, invented even, by reading and writing. From the literary travelogue to narratives of political conquest, writing makes sense of the travel experience, manipulating it by the play of memory and imagination, literary and linguistic tradition, ideology and politics. While travel writing is usually categorized as "nonfiction," this play of memory, ideology, and imagination suggests that it is also "creative" writing. Not only does the word make sense of travel, authorizing the agenda of the visitor and claiming authority over indigenous peoples and newly "discovered" lands, but it orders a multifarious experience and project into a manageable document. And in many ways, the word *is* the journey. Traveling back to European readers, narratives of discovery complete and mimic the route of the physical journey, demonstrating that the circular route between journey, reading, and writing is itself a kind of voyage.

This section begins with a short piece from Hélène Cixous's "The School of Dreams" in *Three Steps on the Ladder of Writing* that transports us to the secret places under the bed where dreams and imagination await. Here Cixous demonstrates the importance of travel, "the wearing out of the shoes," the journey, and movement to the imaginative writer. She says that "the true poet is a traveler," and she speaks of the physicality of using "your own body as a form of transport," in the sense both of movement and of being transported to a different place. Writing, she says, has to do with displacement, with leaving the self even if only in dreams.

First appearing in *Mosaic*, Butor's essay "Travel and Writing" further demonstrates the ways in which reading and travel are connected, from moving the eyes across the page, to reading while traveling, to reading the signs of different places. The essay breaks down the different kinds of travel and the types of reading of tracks, signs, customs, and texts that accompany them. Each has its own semiotics of reading and inscription as well as its own logic of movement, which he quickly and brilliantly sketches. He then explores the role of writing in the experience of travel—as a reason for travel, as travel itself—and how we mark our travels with naming, mapping, and writing. He suggests that travel, like writing, has a grammar, a narrative structure, and (literary) traditions that give it order and meaning. By going beyond traditional discussions of travel literature as narrative, autobiography, and ethnography, Butor asks us to redefine what we mean by travel and the place of reading and writing in relation to movement and place.

Similarly, Michel de Certeau redefines travel—to include everyday journeys around town or through rooms. "Spatial Stories," from his important *The Practice of Everyday*, turns stories into travel events of spatial movement and mapping, arguing that "Every story is a travel story—a spatial practice." De Certeau's essay breaks down the elements of story, movement, place, and space and defines stories as events that traverse and organize places, that select and link places together by means of sentences or itineraries of them. He also distinguishes between space (*espace*) and place (*lieu*). A place is the order by which things are distributed in relationships of coexistence; it represents stability and position. Space is composed of intersections of mobile elements and considers vectors of direction, velocity, and time. Space is a "practiced place" that derives from the operations that orient, situate, temporalize it. In stories, place is determined by objects that are static, while space is determined by operations, the actions of historical subjects in a place. Stories thus carry out the labor that transforms places into spaces and spaces into places. In addition to delineating between maps (that describe places) and tours (that delineate action or operations through space), de Certeau points out the role of frontiers and bridges in storytelling and spatiality. Frontiers represent borders, place and displacement, and the establishment, displacement, or transcendence of limits. Bridges represent the relationships with the frontier, the border crossings between legitimate space and its alien exterior. Just as stories are frontiers for their cultures, for they go ahead of social practices, they are also bridges that connect and oppose differences.

From his classic study of travel writing, *Abroad: British Literary Traveling Between the Wars*, Paul Fussell's essay focuses on the travel writing between the two "great" wars. He examines the hybrid nature of travel literature and its affinity to other genres, like the essay, the war memoir, comic novel, romance, myth, pastoral romance, allegory, and quest romance. The reader of travel narratives, Fussell asserts, follows imaginatively in the exotic adventures of the traveler, whose activity—and hence the travel book itself—is "an implicit celebration of freedom." Of course, Fussell has in mind the adventures of the men of privilege who can afford freedom, adventure, and the education to write perspicaciously about them. Invoking Butor's thesis that reading and writing are a kind of travel, Fussell argues that the ideal travel book invites the reader "abroad, into the author's brain, and into his own." For the writers of the 1930s, the subjects of his book, travel books became "the basic trope of the generation."

While Butor and Fussell see the close connections between writing and travel, Wayne Franklin and Mary Louise Pratt demonstrate connections between writing and power, especially in the discourses of explorers and colonizers. Wayne Franklin, in the selection taken from the introduction to his *Discoverers, Explorers, Settlers: Diligent Writers of Early America*, maps out the strain on language, knowledge, and self-identity for early explorers of the New World who did not have an adequate vocabulary to describe their new experiences. For early explorers like Christopher Columbus and Hernán Cortés, who experienced contact with Native Americans and the New World, with its profusion of natural objects, as "a form of culture shock," European languages were inadequate to describe or name what they saw. Turning to writing to try to make sense of their experiences, to bring some order to their life, and as a means of self-understanding, Franklin claims, these early explorers were handicapped by the disjuncture between European knowledges and the challenges the New World presented to them. Disclosing the imperialism of language and writing, Franklin also argues that despite the strain, discourse was a tool of domesticating, colonizing, and mythologizing America.

Mary Louise Pratt considers in more detail the role of travel writing in the imperialistic project in her essay, "Scratches on the Face of the Country; or, What Mr. Barrow Saw in the Land of the Bushmen." Looking primarily at travel writing about Africa, Pratt considers how discourses of the imperial frontier work in the service of ideology to normalize, codify, and reify the "native" Other and to validate European expansionist projects. By examining a number of the discourses available to European travel and exploration writers, Pratt demonstrates the polyphony of voices and variety of ways of codifying the Other. The first discourse she discusses is what she terms manners-and-customs descriptions. Typically the writer homogenizes the indigenous people into a collective "they" or "he" that fixes the Other in a timeless present without reference to the observing self or encounters with the writer. Thus individualities and differences are subsumed under a normalizing portrait that is often separated from the main narrative. The next type of discourse Pratt examines is the presentation of landscape. In imperialistic travel writing what is often narrated is a descriptive sequence of sights with the traveler as a kind of moving eye that registers these sights. This kind of discourse "centers landscape, separates people from place, and effaces the speaking self" into an imperial eye that commands the panorama before him. Another type of writing focuses on information and incorporates a particular reality into an information system of European make and for the purposes of European colonial, capitalist expansion. When this eye surveys the landscape, it does so with the prospects for future use, often erasing indigenous populations from their habitat. While the writer presents himself as an invisible, passive, and innocent conduit of information, he does so knowing that the power of the European state lies behind him. Finally, Pratt discusses sentimental, experiential travel writing. Unlike the other discourses, this one does show encounters and relations with the indigenous people (often erotic) and positions the writer as hero of the adventures narrated. But even as it narrates encounters with the people, it situates the "European as the center of a stage—someone else's stage." While the narrative voice is associated with the private sphere of the bourgeois world, it too serves European expansion even as it mystifies it with internal critiques. Pratt ends by reminding her reader of the polyphonous quality of travel writing and how the multiplicity of voices is itself an instrument of an ideology that seeks to legitimize European expansion.

As many writers in addition to those collected here point out, travel literature is a hybrid, multi-tasked undertaking that borrows from various literary genres, academic disciplines, and discourses. While the focus of travel writing is usually on place, the environment experienced by the traveler, Jonathan Raban, himself a traveling writer, argues that travel writing is more about time than place, for the author reconstructs the past of the journey in the book. Michael Kowalewski in his review of modern travel literature points to travel writing's "dauntingly heterogeneous character" as well as to the efforts of modern writers to avoid the imperialistic attitudes of previous narratives. This imperialistic position is ably described by J. B. Harley, who looks at maps as texts that promote colonial expansion and power. Building on the work of Pratt and other colonialist and postcolonialist scholars, Patrick Holland and Graham Huggan find that contemporary travel writing continues to perpetuate an ethnocentric view of "other" cultures, peoples, and places. For all, writing about the travel experience manages, defines, and manipulates it.

FOR FURTHER READING

Harley, J. B. "Maps, Knowledge, and Power." *Iconography of Landscape: Essays on the Symbolic Representation, Design and Use of Past Environment*. Ed. Denis Cosgrove and Stephen Daniels. Cambridge: Cambridge UP, 1988. 277–312.

Holland, Patrick, and Graham Huggan. *Tourists with Typewriters: Critical Reflections on Contemporary Travel Writing*. Ann Arbor: U of Michigan P, 1998.

Kowalewski, Michael. "Introduction: The Modern Literature of Travel." *Temperamental Journeys: Essays on the Modern Literature of Travel*. Athens, Ga.: U of Georgia P, 1992. 1–16.

Pratt, Mary Louise. *Imperial Eyes: Travel Writing and Transculturation*. New York: Routledge, 1992.

Raban, Jonathan. "The Journey and the Book." *For Love and Money: Writing, Reading, Travelling, 1969–1987*. London: Collins Harvill, 1987. 253–60.

THE SCHOOL OF DREAMS IS LOCATED UNDER THE BED

Hélène Cixous

I have a faint recollection from an apparently naïve *Grimm's Tale* of a king whose daughters were ruining him. He kept them carefully locked in, as is proper, and didn't know why each day they needed to change their shoes. The daughters mysteriously wore out their shoes. Up until the day the king planted a spy to throw light on this matter. At nightfall the daughters pulled the bed aside, lifted up the trap door, climbed down the ladder beneath the palace, and went out into the forest and danced all night. Perhaps my version is not completely accurate, but that is of no importance, since it's the perfect metaphor for the School of Dreams, bringing together all the elements, including jouissance. It's about doing what is forbidden: sexual pleasure. There is also the wearing out of the shoes, which gave me particular pleasure when I was little without my knowing why. Now I know much better why and I dedicate this tale to Mandelstam.

Mandelstam asks very seriously in his "Conversation about Dante": how many pairs of shoes Dante must have worn out in order to write *The Divine Comedy*, because, he tells us, that could only have been written on foot, walking without stopping, which is also how Mandelstam wrote.[1] Mandelstam's whole body was in action, taking part, searching. Walking, dancing, pleasure: these accompany the poetic act. I wonder what kind of poet doesn't wear out their shoes, writes with their head. The true poet is a traveler. Poetry is about traveling on foot and all its substitutes, all forms of transportation.

Mandelstam wore out hundreds of pairs of shoes. You cannot write such intense, dense poetry without the kind of a dance that dances you round the world. Mandelstam himself could not write without walking round and round. When he was prevented from walking he died.

So perhaps dreaming and writing do have to do with traversing the forest, journeying through the world, using all the available means of transport, using your own body as a form of transport. *The Wanderer*, a beautiful text by Hofmannsthal, tells the story of a journey through Greek and Turkish lands in which the narrator meets a strange traveler.[2] This man has apparently been walking for centuries, he is never named, but when you have lived in the country of poets, you immediately recognize who he is: he is Rimbaud. To meet Rimbaud we have to walk to Austria, to the Greece that is hidden within Austria; we have to travel to the heart of the country of the unconscious, where we may again find those countries we have lost, including Algeria and the Jardin d'Essais. But for this we have to walk, to use our whole body to enable the world to become flesh, exactly as this happens in our dreams. In dreams and writing our body is alive: we either use the whole of it or depending on the dream, a part. We must embark on a body-to-body journey to discover the body.

In *"Love"* the event is inscribed by means of transport. Ana is transported, she is on the tracks, in a tram, and this means of transport is an element of immobility: the tram carries her, she doesn't move, and in front of her she sees the perfectly immobile blindman. It has to do with displacement.

In order to go to the School of Dreams, something must be displaced, starting with the bed. One has to get going. This is what writing is, starting off. It has to do with activity and passivity. This does not mean one will get there. Writing is not arriving; most of the time it's *not arriving*. One must go on foot, with the body. One has to go away, leave the self. How far must one not arrive in order to write, how far must one wander and wear out and have pleasure? One must walk as far as the night. One's own night. Walking through the self toward the dark.

NOTES

1. Ossip Mandelstam, "Conversation About Dante," in *Mandelstam*, p. 7.
2. Hugo Von Hofmannstal [sic], "The Wanderer," in *Selected Prose*, tr. Mary Hottinger and Tania and James Stern (New York: Pantheon, 1963).

TRAVEL AND WRITING

Michel Butor

For Ross Chambers, in Australia

PREFACE

I have travelled a lot, it is said; yet, certainly not enough to satisfy me; I need merely glance at a globe and see those innumerable regions where I have never been to be seized once again by a violent desire, the opposite of nostalgia for which French has no name (there must be a reason for this lack), and to which I myself cannot give a name at the moment.[1] Recently I have travelled less; I am growing wiser it seems to me, and more settled and I have problems of all sorts, it is true: I need to feel my surroundings secure (children grow up, objects accumulate and need to be ordered). But above all, I need to digest my previous travels which I haven't yet quite finished, which I never shall feel completely finished; for me, it is a question of finding a *modus vivendi* with them through writing before being able to truly set forth again; so, in order to travel better, I actually travel less.

And I write. I have always felt the intense bond that exists between my travels and my writing; I travel in order to write—not only to find subject matter, topics or events, like those who go to Peru or China to return with lecture notes and newspaper articles (I also do this, although, unfortunately, not yet in those two particular countries; that will come in time)—but because to travel, at least in a certain manner, is to write (first of all because to travel is to read), and to write is to travel. It is this relationship that I would like to explore somewhat in this text.

If this kinship between travel and writing has always been (more or less) sensed (one need only think of the Roman journeys of Rabelais and Montaigne), it is certain that this feeling was the most evident in the Romantic era, notably in Germany and France. All our writers set out on the road. They

69

made their journey to Italy or the Orient, published their accounts of it, and furnished us, in consequence, with an inestimable collection of documents and reflections upon this question.

I. READING AS TRAVEL
1. Escape

Let us enter the *métro parisien* (that of Moscow, Tokyo or New York would serve equally well) at the end of a work day, during the evening rush-hour. Examine the harassed, closed faces, exhaustion and boredom graying their skin. They wish to see nothing around them, they pay no attention to one another; their eyes constantly avoid resting on anything, or fix themselves on an insignificant detail, a raincoat button or a door handle; it is as if they were clinging to a buoy; they close from time to time, thinking of their over-crowded apartment, often hiding behind newspapers from which they glean a tidbit of news or some other distraction. But, among them, here is one who is reading a book. His eyes never leave the volume he fingers slowly, running along line after line, penetrating page after page. He smiles, beams in expectation. He has found an outlet, he is elsewhere: in the London fog, on the mesas of the Wild West, searching medieval forests, or even in the sound-proofed room, the laboratory of the "writer."

There is travel, therefore, even if the work is not (at least outwardly) a *récit de voyage*;[2] this is for two reasons: first, because there is (at least) the path of the eye from sign to sign, like all sorts of itineraries which can often, but not always, be grossly simplified as the progression along a line from a point of departure to a point of arrival (a path which can become that of the head turning to decipher the inscription[3] wound around the cupolas of *Saint-Marc*; or that of the entire body: such is the line read in a guidebook or a railway timetable: Fontainebleau, Sens, Dijon, Lyons—I can reread it from station to station while taking the train from Paris to Lyons, each word separated by kilometers) and then because there is this outlet, this flight, this retreat; because through the skylight of the page I find myself elsewhere, whether it be in the writer's study or on his page (but wretched magician who leaves us on the page, poor master who cannot lead us elsewhere).

Notice immediately how often the stages of this last journey, perpendicular to the other one, obscure the others. Impatient, we wish to be immediately in Chicago, in Mexico, in Brocéliande; we scarcely consider all the intermediaries which permit our transportation: the creation of the work, the efforts of the author, his "ins and outs." We jump ahead to the point of arrival.

2. *The Mythology of Whiteness*

The escape which it provides from the wounding, pressing, hateful, obscure daily world makes reading a ceremony of purification, a ceremony often reinforced by a complete ritual. To discern this ritualized behavior is to clarify the role played, in our society, by that which might be called the vestment of whiteness. It is not happenstance that the paper in our books is white, always as white as possible, or that one of the most disturbing innovations of the Surrealists was their experimentation with printing on colored paper, experimentation which was, unfortunately, too rare and too disorganized. The "elsewhere" the book gives us appears, as we cross the page, to be penetrated with whiteness, baptized. Sometimes the refusal of the world as it is, the discouragement before the difficulties of transforming it, become so powerful that the reader prefers to remain suspended in the whiteness, calm at last. The "elsewhere" which appears thanks to textual signs may now be considered only as an inundation of white light; the signs themselves—a stain, the imprint of the real on this ingenuousness like a finger soiled with grease or ink—must deny themselves, efface themselves insofar as we read them. Just as in a detective story a second murder, that of the criminal by the detective, must erase the first, so in the mythology of the "pure-white writing"—so verbose, constantly lapping back upon itself like water in a washing machine—the second line must efface the first to leave us in this ocean of nowhere, frontispiece of the *Snark Hunt*.

But, just as the text can only create itself by creating something else, similarly it can only destroy itself by destroying something else as well.

II. TRAVEL AS READING
1. Traveller-Readers

The *récit de voyage* effects and demonstrates this double journey that is all reading; it can carry the perpendicular path along with it to effect a displacement of the reader, to change his mental location, and finally, it can change his physical location.

This explains why a trip is, for our contemporaries, a privileged place for reading; how many read only in the subway, the train, the plane? These moving locations furnish the necessary retreat from the enchainments of daily life, the motion I see through the portholes and windows reinforces the movement of the *récit*, of the reading itself.

Beyond these two fundamental types of travel, reading may also superimpose at least three others:

that of the reader in the vehicle which permits him this leisure; this, in turn, can be doubly reflected: within the moving train, I can change cars between two chapters; furthermore, all the immobility upon the earth's surface is always only an illusion: we need enlarge only slightly our frame of reference to perceive that we are always moving in relation to other celestial bodies; we need merely apply time to space (travel is an illustration of this) to arrive at that traditional, and inexhaustible, metaphor of the individual life, or even all of history, as a journey from birth to death,

that of the author—independently of the path of the writing on the paper—an author who can transport himself by writing (for example, if he keeps a diary of his journey),

that of the *récit* itself—which may or may not have characters (it may only have a succession of views or a montage of sequences)[4]—with all the reflections which can intervene between the author or authors (a travelling critic speaking to us about a travelling writer) and the character or characters, with the superimposition of narrators or pseudonyms more or less fluid with respect to one another, who themselves can be reading *récits de voyages*, etc.

If there is a solidarity between perpendicular journeys (that is, if the path from the place "read about" to the place of reading sweeps along—or is swept along by—the movement of reading, in an effective oblique line which moves the reader himself, refreshing the world for him), it follows that the very form of the described trip cannot be completely separated from the form of its description or the effect it produces: its transforming power. An analysis of different types of travel will give us, in consequence, a new key for distinguishing between the literary genres in action, this emerging above all in the very "physics" of the book or writing.

2. Elementary Considerations of a Portable Iterology

I propose, therefore, a new science (they are springing up like mushrooms these days; they can be gathered in the shade of all Sorbonnes; some among the crop will even end by bearing fruit), strictly tied to literature, concerned with human travel; I amuse myself by naming this science "Iterology." Naturally, I cannot actually found this science, but for those who will be employed therein, here are some preliminary ideas, packaged loosely.

Travel: a word repeated a thousand times in the streets, in advertising; it is seduction itself. It draws us to travel agencies. But, by this very fact, its popular meaning has become considerably restricted. We have the impression that there is only one type of travel, the "round trip." Given the fundamental metaphorical function of travel in all reading (and, correlatively, writing) and, in consequence, in our knowledge of the real and our action upon it, it is certain that the above mentioned reduction will develop mytho- logical powers all the more deceitful the less we notice it. It is easy to see that many human movements are one-way trips. But, in our charted regions, the railroad notion of a one-way trip itself implies a point of departure and a point of arrival (terms or termini)[5], necessary because our society obliges us to have a fixed residence, the address inscribed on our identification cards. This rootage has not always existed, and in many places is, even today, not the case.

3. Travel Without Specific Limits: Wandering, Nomadism

We come from nowhere in particular, we go nowhere in particular; carrying along all our belongings, we set up a tent or shelter of branches, and leave no trace behind on departing.

A space so visited—even if it is not opposed to any forbidden exterior, to any domain possessed by another which can only be entered under certain conditions (like the Roman Empire behind its fixed borders, as opposed to limitless barbaric wandering)—can, nevertheless, be perfectly defined; and it is easy to show that it is already a reading space.[6] Hunter tribes: animals are "tracked," a matter of reading their marks and the signs which betray them. Shepherd tribes: a matter of following the signs of vegetation and the sea- sons, in order to pass from one location to another at the proper time. There is quickly an (at least) provisional marking of the domains of these herds; it is necessary to read the signs of the defiant presence of some other herd or tribe. Points of reference become increasingly important. At the time of the tran- shumance, from one year to the next, we wish to enjoy once again the good trees, the pastures, the points of shade or water (Rousseau has already noted the importance of water sources in his *Essai sur l'origine des langues*). From this time on, a few recognizable sites, a few natural landmarks, are isolated, then named and consecrated; they are retained, preserved, in *récits*; the sur- face of the earth becomes a page and an imprint is left upon it. Wandering, then, is staked out with signs, with characters.

Death halts wandering abruptly. The individual journey has a limit. Birth, on the other hand, is produced in movement itself; the child moves in his mother's womb even as she herself moves; the child can be born anywhere. On the other hand, he who dies is abandoned on the spot; even if he is burned and his ashes (or some relics) are carried along, his path stops there. The tomb is the mark *par excellence* for this very reason. Even today we see an equivalence between the sepulcher and the monument. In burial, the wan- derer becomes a tree, a signifying sprout. This liaison between writing and death comes to us from the subsoil of history; cities will be founded upon such sacrifices.

So, for the Australian aborigine to move in what appears to us a desert is, in fact, to move within his own history.

4. Travel with a Specific Goal: Settlement, Exodus

This millennial writing transforms the desert, bit by bit, into a text, a thick tissue of traces and marks. Different factors may drive these wanderers from one such marked-out area to another, almost virgin (at least for them) region, may provoke a migration which itself may be stopped by natural or political obstacles: the seashore, the boundary of an empire; or, perhaps, the cultural tissue becomes so strong, so powerful, that it becomes necessary to protect the borders, to maintain the tombs; a settlement, then, is established. The path of indefinite wandering "arrives" at some spot. This is particularly the case when a wandering civilization encounters another, long-settled, whose especially imposing and unavoidable monuments are automatically adopted as landmarks by the newly arrived.

This settling may be only partially complete. We find, then, an opposition between the "strong places"—cities, monuments—and a far less established countryside. It was not long ago that in many European countries a journey to a city was like passing from a mode of wandering to a settled state; this is true in many regions of Africa to this day.

If, in the wandering civilization, the end of an individual's journey is equivalent to his death, the settling of an entire people—even if it permits the enjoyment of an economic affluence immeasurably greater than that to which it was accustomed, or the attainment of an incomparably more solid and efficient language—is always lived (in a certain fashion) rather like a death, an overcome death, ostentatious; a sort of life beyond death. We each keep, more or less hidden within us, a nostalgia for wandering. To travel is to live once again.

Inversely, a settled population can be driven from its habitation by an invasion or natural catastrophe. It carries off all the possessions possible, no longer having hopes of returning one day to its ravaged, destroyed "home." This is exodus. The previous language and the minute acquaintance with the terrain are no longer of any use; an immense nostalgia develops. There is a search for another place for settlement, a promised land.

As long as all possibility of return is not eliminated, as long as the lost language is still felt to be partially functional, it is exile, one of the conditions for the predilection toward poetic inventions: to preserve the ancient language, to re-actualize it, to refresh it.

5. Travel between Two Definite Terms: Changing House, Emigration

Although settled, we abandon one specific place in order to go to another specific place, carrying all our possessions, abandoning all rights to the former place. There will be no return. Someone else will live in the former home, without (in general) the previous occupant resenting any contact with the newcomer. This is changing houses, "moving."[7] In this case, the precise point of arrival is well known in advance: it has been visited, chosen. But such a term can also be quite vague: there is emigration. We know that we are going to America or Australia. We are resigned—having applied for and received our travelling papers—but we have, in reality, few pieces of specific information about these promised lands; we carry our few possessions, we know that we will settle ourselves, but we don't know quite where.

When the point of arrival is settled in advance, it exercises a general attraction, we desire it, it emits signs. Thus, in the countryside, the city glows, even if the population is settled to the point of serfdom, bound to a soil lined with the furrows of labor or terraces like long lines of writing. In similar fashion, the horizon gleams for the emigrant with the lights of an El Dorado.

6. Travel with a Double Term: Round-Trips

In this case, the final point of arrival coincides with the point of departure. We are truly settled. We depart, but leave behind our possessions, our roots; we keep our rights. It is well understood from the beginning that we will return. If we suppose momentarily that this place of rootage (of attachment) is simple, we can distinguish a linear and a circular form, regardless of how they may appear when we follow them on a map. I call "linear" those trips in which the return trip is the exact reverse of the original outward journey; a "circular" trip is one in which we desire to see more countries and choose a different return route. The latter, generally, is filled with stopping-places, while the former is impatient, stretching as much toward the intermediate destination as to the home to which we return.[8]

7. Business, Vacations

The linear journey, in its pure state, is the business trip. We do not leave our preoccupations; we pay no attention to the travelling itself. The sooner we can arrive the better, for the sooner we will be back again. But, the linear trip is mongrelized by "vacation," a trip in which time opens up, a perfect equivalent to that refuge offered by reading in the *métro* car. We need merely study vacation publicity to find once again the mythological whiteness of the page: it's to the beach, then, or the ski resort. Leave your worries! Escape!

In this vacation, travel can become theater. We mimic another trip, change houses for a while, settle elsewhere briefly, seek a new region to live, play at emigrating, at wandering; thus, we go camping and return to a tent or the open, starry skies; for a short time we have no fixed residence. We generally have a second point of departure (we take the train to such and such a station, it usually being too difficult to set out camping from our very house), a second point of arrival (our "forwarding address"); we wander between the two, taking advantage of the landmarks, trying to recapture the reading of natural signs. Bathing ourselves in original wandering, we exorcise the terror of exodus.

8. The Alien

Upon arriving in a new place—and this is particularly true for the trip abroad, where another language is spoken—with the freedom of vacationing, I will need to begin learning to read once more. The gestures will not be the same: other manners, other laws, other traffic rules. I will decipher the billboards, the newspaper headlines, the street signs (sometimes in another alphabet which, in China or Japan for example, can offer enormous resistance). My temporary lodging, my adaptation, my rest, my interest all depend in large part upon my ability to read. My own tongue will find itself refreshed, I will discover unsuspected aspects of it and my behavior as well; my departed home and country will soon become as seductive as the finally visited country of my dreams. I used to desire Venice; Venice made me desire Paris, Nevers, Maubeuge; it illuminates them.

Not all places have the same power, certainly; they are more or less difficult to read, more or less fascinating, more or less efficacious; above all, they form systems with respect to each other and to the original spot where we will return. Vacations are, then, organized in tours, in tourism.

9. Return to the Native Land

This is an essential Romantic theme; the notion expressed in this subtitle does not refer to a definitive return, but quite the reverse. It is well understood that the young man who left his village for Paris has adopted this village as his home. He wants to return to it. It is there he has left his possessions, his rights. He swears that he belongs to Paris. But, one day he leaves in search of himself, of that former face abandoned, travestied, hidden, betrayed; moreover, this return to the native land is often involuntary: through a chance occurrence during a business trip or ordinary vacation he stumbles upon his past (in some manner); and that is the shock. A wall crumbles within him. He bursts into tears and returns to the capital another man.

The native land may be so thoroughly repressed at the time of emigration that the emigrant himself cannot return, nor even his children or grandchildren who will do everything possible to conceal their origin in Italy, Poland or Ireland; they will even change their name. This is the phenomenon so well studied in the United States: the "third generation." Only when the family finally feels that it belongs, that it is well adopted by the new country, that it is first and foremost "American," will the descendants wish to visit their country of origin, to renew those ties so painfully cut. This, then, is travel in the history of one's family.

10. Pilgrimages

The word designates, first of all, the journey to the tomb of a saint, next to the spot of a vision, an oracular site; one carries his question there and expects a response, a curing of the body or soul. The sanctified spot detaches itself from the midst of profane regions; it is the skylight onto paradise. Later, the pilgrimage becomes a journey to those places which speak,[9] which tell us of our history and ourselves. Such are the Roman pilgrimages in the Renaissance. Just as the town diffuses its semantic power onto the countryside, so certain sites carry, to this very day, the speech of a fundamental historical moment which detaches itself from the more vague epochs that it clarifies.

All the great Romantic tours are round-trip and are pilgrimages of the latter type. It seems to me that Chateaubriand's *L'Itinéraire de Paris à Jérusalem* is a particularly clear illustration of this, beyond the fact that the trip itself was part of a design which was clearly conscious of writing (and, even then, not the design of that book but another: *Les Martyrs*), beyond the fact that it gives Nineteenth Century French literature a prototype which numerous later writers will strive to imitate:

> I had stopped the plan of *Les Martyrs*: most of the books of this work were outlined; I did not believe that I had to write the last word in it before having seen the scene of the countries where my scene was set; others have their resources in themselves; for myself, I need to compensate for such a lack with all types of work. Also, when one does not find the description of such and such famous place in this *Itinéraire*, it is necessary to look for it in *Les Martyrs*.

This principal motive which caused me to leave France again after so many years was joined by other considerations: a trip to the Orient completed the circle of studies that I had promised myself to finish. I had contemplated in the American deserts the monuments of nature; among the monuments of man I knew only two kinds of antiquities: Celtic and Roman; I still had to travel through the ruins of Athens, of Memphis, and of Carthage. I also wished to accomplish the pilgrimage to Jerusalem:

> *Il gran sepolcro adora, e cioglie il voto*
> . . . . *Qui devoto*[10]

It may seem strange to speak of vows and pilgrimages today, but on this point I am unashamed, and I set myself long ago in the class of superstitious and weak people. I will be perhaps the last Frenchman to set out from my country to the Holy Land with the ideas, the goal and the sentiments of an ancient pilgrim.

In each of these places a great tomb. The whole *Itinéraire* is a "long pilgrimage to the tombs of great men." What reading of inscriptions!

Three fundamental stations, three ideogrammatic cities mark the way for the ideal Romantic journey, a journey never completely realized: Rome, Athens, Jerusalem, each accompanied by such and such a satellite, such and such a complement. Just as the emigrant's descendent breaks his parents' repression in his return to the native land, Chateaubriand, in his reading of ancestral cities, shatters the false antiquity and Christianity inherited from the Eighteenth Century. The horizon which separates Paris from Greece or Jerusalem is also a mental horizon.

11. Exploration

To those travels in our history that are the Romantic pilgrimages—which allow us to reread (in another fashion) those messages historically transmitted to us—we must oppose others, equally "round trip" in their nature: voyages of exploration.

In this case, we set off for an unknown region (rather: a poorly known, or foreshadowed, one); only rarely can we trust *récits* or our own plans; by going to the other side of the physical or mental horizon we stretch this horizon. Such a miracle was Magellan's voyage when, without retracing his path, he returned to the point of departure.

The exploratory voyage allows us to rediscover primitive wandering in the parentheses of fixed residence; we must know how to read natural signs. The *récits* of the great navigators or explorers show that this reading generally requires a teacher. Usually, it is a (more or less) settled native who teaches the explorer to recognize the trails, to identify landmarks, to perceive the dangers. The unknown land is already elaborated like a text, even if the native translator is often eliminated in the end by his dangerous pupil.

Truly uninhabited lands always take the longest to penetrate; the most recent scientific instruments are necessary to aid us in our surveying. Even on our planet, uninhabited lands (Antarctica, for example) often remain unexplored to this day.

The voyage of discovery demonstrates most strikingly the phenomena of marking and writing. Crosses, monuments, tombs are erected and inscribed. The first thing that Americans do upon walking on the moon is to raise a flag, and no one even dreams of being surprised.

Where the textual fabric of the new land is already quite dense, the explorer will bring home the names taught him by native instructors, but even more often, he, the new Adam, will untiringly name each identifiable site; so, world maps will become covered with names, the tracing of the coastlines will be practically outlined by this throng of vocables. Even before the conqueror, the explorer seizes with his language the land he crosses.

12. The Animation of Terms

Our society has affixed us, it wishes to know us only with a single address; this organizes, still more, our representation of space—except in the vacation intervals which are (more or less) studious or laborious; but a more rigorous examination shows us that this prevalent notion of domicile (or rootage) is, today, more and more complex. In fact, these terms of which we speak are themselves constantly enlivened by movement. At the beginning of this text, I evoked the image of the *métro parisien*. When the traveller departs for the *club Méditerranée*, he not only leaves behind his apartment on the *boulevard Barbès*, but an entire ensemble of terms: the factory where he is foreman or the bank where he is employed, the path he treads (at least) every morning and evening. Similarly, the towns he is going to visit are not merely single hotel rooms, but a number of museums, churches, restaurants, landmarks, streets and squares he will tour, a number of trains, taxis and buses he will ride. Travel makes us pass from a first ensemble of pathways to a second.

13. Multiplication of Residences

There are degrees of residency as of settlement. If I have my address in Paris, I can go to Rome so habitually that I find myself perfectly at home there; I may have an established room at a friend's house. We are seeing the multiplication of secondary residences. With a certain amount of fortune (at once

monetary affluence and luck), it becomes impossible to distinguish the principal one among them. This is a higher form of nomadism, the union of residency and wandering.

This truly was the case with the kings and great lords of the Middle Ages.
The knights were wanderers in comparison with the serfs bound to their
fields. Kings promenaded from château to château. The monarchy's settlement at Versailles was the triumph of the Parisian bourgeoisie, which succeeded in mimicking, in its town, the semantic absolutism of the Rome of
yesteryear.

14. Vehicles

This becomes even more important as the diverse fixed residences are able to
be connected by mobile ones. Kings between two châteaux simply set up
tents. We are evoking here, in the distance, the portable palaces of Kubla
Khan in Marco Polo.

And, at this point it becomes absolutely necessary to let the consideration
of inherent vehicles intervene in our typology of travels. Some vehicles, in
fact, are themselves domiciles; this was formerly the case with boats (micro-
cosms of the world) or gypsy caravans which the sedentary folk watched pass
with a fright mingled with no little envy. Today, the domicile of each town
dweller is augmented by that rolling room which is his car, in which he feels
at home, and where he transports, at his pleasure, a number of objects by
no means insignificant in comparison with those a knight of old might have
carried.

And if we succeed in loosening somewhat this notion of personal possession, we can imagine the extent to which the notion of a fixed residence—
with all the legislation attached to it—can become outdated.

15. Suggestions

To these first distinctions, we must add many others. Here are some examples: to study travels according to

their scansion: is the journey composed of stopping-places, and how far
apart? within these stages is there a change of vehicle or method of movement? we notice that almost all of our trips mix vehicles or modes of travel
and that their scansion is (in general form) strictly tied to these in intention;

their speed;

their equipage;

their company: solitary journeys (that of the knight errant in the romances of the Middle Ages), family trips, group trips, societal exoduses, hitch-hiking, family reunions, travels whose stages are marked by "acquaintances," "relatives," or "hosts."

16. Verticals

But even from the point of view of the geometry of the route another dimension must be introduced. So far we have considered motion only on a single plane on a surface. Let's occupy ourselves a bit with thicknesses:

travels of ascent: to climb a mountain (Dante's *Purgatorio*), to be lifted in a balloon, an airplane, a rocket; they are characterized by a progressive enlargement of the horizon or system of reference: we situate the point of departure from the point of arrival: the path of reading is accomplished naturally in the discovery of this ascensional vector, which needs to be completed, equilibrated by its opposite;

travels of descent (Dante's *Inferno*, so many pages of Hugo, *Le Voyage au centre de la Terre*), in which a provisional shrinking of the horizon leads to the opening up of immense caverns, makes us climb to the surface of the other side of the normal horizon and denounce this surface as a lie. It is a matter of reversed—and reversing—ascent, where the point of arrival situates the point of departure by making it undergo a reorientation (this is why this point of arrival is so often conceived of as a center), by forcing it to an avowal.

17. Nerval and Chateaubriand

Let's examine, for example, *Le Voyage en Orient* by Gérard de Nerval in comparison with *L'Itinéraire de Paris à Jérusalem*. The author of *Aurélia* carefully avoids the three essential stopping-places, the three key words, of the author of *Les Martyrs*: Rome, Athens, Jerusalem. He chooses, instead, three intermediary towns on his route as principal stations, and he takes them in reverse order: Cairo, Beirut, Constantinople.

Constantinople, the capital of an empire, will take the place of Rome; Cairo, with its Egyptian science, that of Athens; Beirut, with its proximity to the Druses and Hakem their messiah, that of Jerusalem. It is not that Nerval feels that these three towns can (in any sense) replace the three traditional ones of the West, but that travelling there permits him to test the elements of untruth in the "statement" offered us by the traditional towns.

Whereas Chateaubriand leaves France to allow his book to be veracious (this does not only concern the scenery, since the speech of these three places was deformed by eighteenth century French), believing that in refinding a

place one becomes capable of understanding it in all its glory, Nerval esti-
mates that it is not sufficient to go to Rome to eliminate the deformations of
the Roman text, that this alteration is not only situated between Rome and
Paris, but is already *in* the imperial and papal city. It is necessary, therefore,
to post oneself in an exterior monitoring position in order to reveal the fissures of the Roman surface, to seize the text from below.

To Nerval's eyes, Chateaubriand's journey remains a voyage along the surface, while his own is calculated, utilizing annex centers, lobbies of ellipses
englobing the principal centers; this allows him to place in evidence, by par-
allax, all the dimension of the snare harbored by the normal centers. Wandering the streets or environs of Cairo, Beirut, or Constantinople, Nerval is
always lying in wait for anything that will allow him to sense a cavern extending beneath Rome, Athens, and Jerusalem.

This is always achieved through the roundabout way of a *récit*, a fiction;
the only true descent—prelude, in fact, to a *récit*, serving as a metaphor or
sacrament to all the others—is that of the pyramid.

The science of the pyramid, masonic wisdom, is presented as the foundation for Athens' wisdom and science. The passion of Hakem, his sojourn in
the *maristan*, the insane asylum, is the equivalent of an underground trip; it
opposes another incarnation to that of the dead Christ at Jerusalem. And finally, in the nights of Ramadan, the storyteller leads us with Adoniram
through the subterranean world where, not only the emperor Solomon, but
also the same Jehovah from whom he draws his so clumsily apparent power,
reveal themselves as usurpers.

Just as the three cities of Chateaubriand are in communication—Rome,
with its emperors and popes, reassembling the heritage, the testament, of
Athens and Jerusalem—the caverns of Nerval, by scrambling them slightly,
become engaged in intercourse: the Drusian messiah lived his passion in
Cairo; because it extends below Jerusalem, the underground world of Adoniram ends by mining the very soil of Rome.

There is, certainly, a subterranean presence in *L'Itinéraire*, due to the fundamental theme of the tombs, but Chateaubriand finds it sufficient to raise
once again the monuments and inscriptions, to accept what his been retained
of the dead person at the moment of his burial, his transformation in character; Nerval, in contrast, wishes to wrest from the dead the secret of what we
have justly wished not to retain. For this reason, he is obliged to discover
those oblique paths which allow him to sneak under the cobblestones.

Chateaubriand's pilgrimage is a journey in history, Nerval's is the false-
ness of history.

III. TRAVEL AS WRITING
1. The Library of Travel

Since our over-all purpose is to place in evidence the ties between travel and the book, we must study different journeys according to their degree of "literariness."

All the Romantic voyages are bookish. Lamartine, Gautier, Nerval, Flaubert, and others correct, complete, vary the theme set by Chateaubriand.

In all cases, books are at the origin of the trip; books read (in particular, *L'Itinéraire*), projected books (starting with *Les Martyrs*);

the travellers read books during their journeys,

they write them, usually keeping a journal,

and they always produce a book upon their return, otherwise we would not talk about them.

They travel in order to write, they travel while writing, because, for them, travel is writing.

2. Signatures

It has been like this since primeval wandering. While travelling, the horde clears a path, isolates landmarks, stakes out its territory and inscribes its tombs therein. The explorer marks the earth on which he lands. Our travellers will leave their traces in the towns of their pilgrimage: so many registers signed, checks cashed, mementos inscribed. And, in these books, what emotion is created when the traveller discovers the trace of a previous traveller!

To leave a trace of our passing is to belong to a spot, to become ourselves a Roman, Athenian, Cairote; therefore, we do it not only to return home with the light of these place-ideograms within us, but also to make our very existence a hopefully indelible "stroke" on a visited spot. For later travellers, it is certain that going to Athens is also—in a very slim measure by comparison with other reasons, but nonetheless surely—to go see the city visited by Chateaubriand, his visit being tied to certain other acts and illuminating them in a particular way.

Although we may understand perfectly well that the soldiers of the Napoleonic army wished absolutely to mark their passage by signing, with vigorous slashes, the upper casements of the first pylon of the grand temple of Karnak, and although it truly moves us to find them there, from the moment an exceptionally dense textual tissue re-covers the soil or the landscape, the modern traveller develops scruples about leaving a disturbing mark which he judges too uninteresting by comparison with what he would destroy in the process. Thus, the early tourist is succeeded by one who, conscious of the troubles he brings to the refreshing and educational place, dreams of leaving it intact, who wishes not simply to be the only outsider, but also to be a kind of invisible intruder, without weight, without tainting effect: a sort of phantom who leaves no trace, like the man who wants to walk in snow without leaving footprints.[11] Under another guise, we find once again our mythology of the white page.

3. The Book as Mark

Instead of the direct mark which risks destroying the previous signs (or even their absence), we often prefer a more respectful and elegant one (which often proves ultimately more conclusive): the creation of representative objects, an eminent example being the book. We have already mentioned the essential role of nomination in exploratory travel, an act whose product frequently is inscribed upon the piece itself, first of all on maps and in *récits*; sometimes this occurs after a long time: thus, the names the first Portuguese navigators give to their moorings up and down the coast of Brazil are today inscribed on train stations, intersections, street signs.

It is travel itself which names places, but once these places are named successive voyages will repeat them in some order. The very complex "words" which are the great sites will be linked by the travellers in a sentence. Because he travels there by way of Venice, Athens or Constantinople, Chateaubriand approaches the "term" Jerusalem in a certain way. One stopping-place produces the effect of a parenthesis or a digression, while another is, on the contrary, an essential stage of an argument. The grammar of the book will strive to restore the "grammar" of the path of travel.

IV. WRITING AS TRAVEL

It is not necessary, however, that there be a book; it suffices that there is a trace (whatever it may be), a recording of the travel; this is precisely what is difficult to avoid today. The mere fact that I create an itinerary, that I set towns or spots in a certain order, marks a stable sign on the surface, or even the thickness, of the world. Since I have already proposed a science, I can also propose an art: it would consist, quite simply, in travelling, and perhaps leaving a few traces here and there; but, these would be purely subordinate to the general effect: such and such an innovation in the itinerary, such and such a change of vehicle, such and such a prolongation of stay being able to arouse as much admiration, or commentary, as a beautiful image in a great poem.

But, note those resources possessed by the book, all the guises in which it may dress itself these days (and let us dream for a moment about all the intermediaries between this travel of pure execution, prepared improvisation, and its bookish division); from the moment the book becomes the principal means of marking his passage, the writer is allowed, in working on his book, to work considerably upon this mark.

If Romantic travel leads to the composition of a book, this is because in writing a book one is engaged in the act of travelling. If reading is a crossing—even if it often pretends to be only an erased passage through the cloud of whiteness—writing, always the transformation of reading, is necessarily even more so.

The terms Rome, Athens, Jerusalem are arranged in a particular order by the sentence which is my journey, and they can be varied at the instruction of my travelling-writing; in the *récit* I propose, how many undergrounds and oblique views it becomes possible for me to discover.

V. ENVOI

I seldom write "on the spot." I do not keep a travel diary. I speak of one place in another place, for another place. I need to make my travels travel. Between two terms of one of my sentences, between the verbal sites which I detach and mark, the earth turns.

I have created for myself an entire system of nations that I improve little by little,

or rather:

I have created for myself a system of nations which improves itself little by little,

or rather:

an entire system of countries which improves itself in creating me little by little.

And I send this text, all the way from the Maritime Alps, simultaneously to Paris, to Australia, and to California that it may be diffused in many other places.

Tours, France

Translated by John Powers and K. Lisker

NOTES

1. On 16 November, 1973, Michel Butor gave a lecture entitled "Travel and Creative Writing" before a crowded auditorium at Stanford University. This lecture was an abridged version of a longer text entitled *"Le voyage et l'ecriture,"* originally published in French by the journal *Romantisme* (No. 4, 1972), pp. 4–19. At M. Butor's generous request, we are presenting, for the first time in English this longer more fully articulated original text. (All notes are by the translators.)

M. Butor's texts have, of course, consistently "tested" traditional conceptions of language (his most recent book, a typesetter's nightmare, crosses the *accent grave* and the *accent aigu* in the word *"ou,"* producing a hybrid title meaning either/both "or" and "where"), genre (in *L'Emploi du Temps* for example) and the book (*Mobile*). While this particular essay is in a less rigorous vein than his longer texts, it is written in a graceful, flowing style which seems to capture, in prose, the wanderlust he so freely admits. In translating this text, therefore, we have attempted insofar as possible to preserve its smoothness and carefully managed wandering quality. We have been obliged, unfortunately, occasionally to sacrifice the smoothness of the original for the sake of clarity, often substituting the more definitive "stopping-place" of the semicolon for the French comma, which in the writing of M. Butor far outdistances its English relative in serviceability.

2. We have consistently left the term *"récit"* untranslated, feeling that its polysemic character (narrative, tale, story, account, etc., depending on context) would be in no way clarified by translation into its numerous English counterparts which are equally polyvocal and even more definitionally controversial in the English-speaking world. (This is particularly true of the term "narrative," the most rough-and-ready translation of *"récit,"* since much recent literature has so broadened the narrative horizon that most definitions have—or are about to be—exploded.) The phrase *"récit de voyage"* has no precise English equivalent. There is a certain inelegance, and inaccuracy, to "travel narrative," or "travel account," and the term "travelogue" carries with it invidious connotations of cinema short subjects: "Welcome to Corcovado" ("See the smiling Brazilians . . .").

3. The verb "inscrire" (to inscribe), and its numerous nominal and adjectival transformations, have become privileged terms in recent French (particularly "structuralist") thought. Such diverse thinkers is Jacques Monod, Jacques Derrida and Claude Lévi-Strauss have used these terms to designate not only a "writing upon" (as the epitaph on a tombstone) but also a "writing within the very structure" of the system or object under consideration. While M. Butor usually uses this term in the former sense in this essay, his French audience would be immediately aware of the implications, and resonances, of his choice of words.

4. Such a definition of a potential *récit* exemplifies the semantic breadth of the term described above (note 2), and finds an excellent illustration in M. Butor's own text *Mobile*, a sequence of clippings, phrases, block capitals, quotations and more, presenting the United States alphabetically, state by state.

5. Originally *"termes, ou terminus."* M. Butor uses these words to designate a stopping-point, an end. While the word "terminus" more commonly designates such an end in English, we have consistently translated both words as "term," just as M.

Butor has privileged the word *"terme"* in his essay. As the essay develops, it becomes increasingly evident that he is employing this word in a double-edged way, utilizing its bivocality to signify both a stopping-point and a place (or word) bearing a semantic character. That is: the city Rome is simultaneously an arrival point in a journey and itself a sign with certain denotations and connotations. The play of these two senses of "term" will become increasingly apparent as the essay progresses. Further: along with the use of terms "inscribe," "inscription, etc. this double sense of "term" reflects the profoundly linguistic nature of recent French thought.

6. The inelegant "reading space" has been chosen as a less confusing term than "space of reading" as a translation of *"espace de lecture."*

7. While the American term "moving" is the most appropriate transition for *"le déménagement,"* we have preferred "changing houses," since the setting forth of a word like "moving" in an essay on travel cannot help but be extraordinarily confusing.

8. This is most clearly exemplified in the notion of the "non-stop flight."

9. This is a third example of the language metaphor in the essay, and we need merely mention that M. Butor's use of "parler" (to speak) can be understood as "to give information (about)."

10. *"He adores the great sepulcher, and fulfills the vow*
. . . . *Here made"*

11. We have taken the liberty of adding this final simile, which is from M. Butor's lecture, to the original text, finding it both illuminating and charming.

SPATIAL STORIES

Michel de Certeau

"Narration created humanity."
Pierre Janet, L'Evolution de la mémoire el la notion de temps,
1928, p. 261.

In modern Athens, the vehicles of mass transportation are called *metaphorai.*
To go to work or come home, one takes a "metaphor"—a bus or a train. Stories
could also take this noble name: every day, they traverse and organize places;
they select and link them together; they make sentences and itineraries out
of them. They are spatial trajectories.

In this respect, narrative structures have the status of spatial syntaxes. By
means of a whole panoply of codes, ordered ways of proceeding and constraints, they regulate changes in space (or moves from one place to another)
made by stories in the form of places put in linear or interlaced series: from
here (Paris), one goes there (Montargis); this place (a room) includes another
(a dream or a memory); etc. More than that, when they are represented in descriptions or acted out by actors (a foreigner, a city-dweller, a ghost), these
places are linked together more or less tightly or easily by "modalities" that
specify the kind of passage leading from the one to the other: the transition
can be given an "epistemological" modality concerning knowledge (for example: "it's not certain that this is the Place de la République"), an "alethic"
one concerning existence (for example, "the land of milk and honey is an improbable end-point"), or a deontic one concerning obligation (for example:
"from this point, you have to go over to that one"). . . . These are only a few
notations among many others, and serve only to indicate with what subtle
complexity stories, whether everyday or literary, serve us as means of mass
transportation, as *metaphorai.*

Every story is a travel story—a spatial practice. For this reason, spatial practices concern everyday tactics, are part of them, from the alphabet of spatial indication ("It's to the right," "Take a left"), the beginning of a story the rest of which is written by footsteps, to the daily "news" ("Guess who I met at the bakery?"), television news reports ("Teheran: Khomeini is becoming increasingly isolated . . ."), legends (Cinderellas living in hovels), and stories that are told (memories and fiction of foreign lands or more or less distant times in the past). These narrated adventures, simultaneously producing geographies of actions and drifting into the commonplaces of an order, do not merely constitute a "supplement" to pedestrian enunciations and rhetorics. They are not satisfied with displacing the latter and transposing them into the field of language. In reality, they organize walks. They make the journey, before or during the time the feet perform it.

These proliferating metaphors—sayings and stories that organize places through the displacements they "describe" (as a mobile point "describes" a curve)—what kind of analysis can be applied to *them*? To mention only the studies concerning spatializing *operations* (and not spatial systems), there are numerous works that provide methods and categories for such an analysis. Among the most recent, particular attention can be drawn to those referring to a semantics of space (John Lyons on "Locative Subjects" and "Spatial Expressions"),[1] a psycholinguistics of perception (Miller and Johnson-Laird on "the hypothesis of localization"),[2] a sociolinguistics of descriptions of places (for example, William Labov's),[3] a phenomenology of the behavior that organizes "territories" (for example, the work of Albert E. Scheflen and Norman Ashcraft),[4] an "ethnomethodology" of the indices of localization in conversation (for example, by Emanuel A. Schegloff),[5] or a semiotics viewing culture as a spatial metalanguage (for example, the work of the Tartu School, especially Y. M. Lotman, B. A. Ouspenski),[6] etc. Just as signifying practices, which concern the ways of putting language into effect, were taken into consideration after linguistic systems had been investigated, today spatializing practices are attracting attention now that the codes and taxonomies of the spatial order have been examined. Our investigation belongs to this "second" moment of the analysis, which moves from structures to actions. But in this vast ensemble, I shall consider only *narrative actions*; this will allow us to specify a few elementary forms of practices organizing space: the bipolar distinction between "map" and "itinerary," the procedures of delimitation or "marking boundaries" (*"bornage"*) and "enunciative focalizations" (that is, the indication of the body within discourse).

"SPACES" AND "PLACES"

At the outset, I shall make a distinction between space (*espace*) and place (*lieu*) that delimits a field. A place (*lieu*) is the order (of whatever kind) in accord with which elements are distributed in relationships of coexistence. It thus excludes the possibility of two things being in the same location (*place*). The law of the "proper" rules in the place: the elements taken into consideration are *beside* one another, each situated in its own "proper" and distinct location, a location it defines. A place is thus an instantaneous configuration of positions. It implies an indication of stability.

A *space* exists when one takes into consideration vectors of direction, velocities, and time variables. Thus space is composed of intersections of mobile elements. It is in a sense actuated by the ensemble of movements deployed within it. Space occurs as the effect produced by the operations that orient it, situate it, temporalize it, and make it function in a polyvalent unity of conflictual programs or contractual proximities. On this view, in relation to place, space is like the word when it is spoken, that is, when it is caught in the ambiguity of an actualization, transformed into a term dependent upon many different conventions, situated as the act of a present (or of a time), and modified by the transformations caused by successive contexts. In contradistinction to the place, it has thus none of the univocity or stability of a "proper."

In short, *space is a practiced place.* Thus the street geometrically defined by urban planning is transformed into a space by walkers. In the same way, an act of reading is the space produced by the practice of a particular place: a written text, i.e., a place constituted by a system of signs.

Merleau-Ponty distinguished a "geometrical" space ("a homogeneous and isotropic spatiality," analogous to our "place") from another "spatiality" which he called an "anthropological space." This distinction depended on a distinct problematic, which sought to distinguish from "geometrical" univocity the experience of an "outside" given in the form of space, and for which "space is existential" and "existence is spatial." This experience is a relation to the world; in dreams and in perception, and because it probably precedes their differentiation, it expresses "the same essential structure of our being as a being situated in relationship to a milieu"—being situated by a desire, indissociable from a "direction of existence" and implanted in the space of a landscape. From this point of view "there are as many spaces as there are distinct spatial experiences."[7] The perspective is determined by a "phenomenology" of existing in the world.

In our examination of the daily practices that articulate that experience, the opposition between "place" and "space" will rather refer to two sorts of determinations in stories: the first, a determination through objects that are ultimately reducible to the *being-there* of something dead, the law of a "place" (from the pebble to the cadaver, an inert body always seems, in the West, to found a place and give it the appearance of it tomb); the second, a determination through *operations* which, when they are attributed to a stone, tree, or human being, specify "spaces" by the actions of historical *subjects* (a movement always seems to condition the production of a space and to associate it with a history). Between these two determinations, there are passages back and forth, such as the putting to death (or putting into a landscape) of heroes who transgress frontiers and who, guilty of an offense against the law of the place, best provide its restoration with their tombs; or again, on the contrary, the awakening of inert objects (a table, a forest, a person that plays a certain role in the environment) which, emerging from their stability, transform the place where they lay motionless into the foreignness of their own space.

Stories thus carry out a labor that constantly transforms places into spaces or spaces into places. They also organize the play of changing relationships between places and spaces. The forms of this play are numberless, fanning out in a spectrum reaching from the putting in place of an immobile and stone-like order (in it, nothing moves except discourse itself, which, like a camera panning over a scene, moves over the whole panorama), to the accelerated succession of actions that multiply spaces (as in the detective novel or certain folktales, though this spatializing frenzy nevertheless remains circumscribed by the textual place). It would be possible to construct a typology of all these stories in terms of identification of places and actualization of spaces. But in order to discern in them the modes in which these distinct operations are combined, we need criteria and analytical categories—a necessity that leads us back to travel stories of the most elementary kind.

TOURS AND MAPS

Oral descriptions of places, narrations concerning the home, stories about the streets, represent a first and enormous corpus. In a very precise analysis of descriptions New York residents gave of their apartments, C. Linde and W. Labov recognize two distinct types, which they call the "map" and the "tour." The first is of the type: "The girls' room is next to the kitchen." The second: "You turn right and come into the living room." Now, in the New York corpus, only three percent of the descriptions are of the "map" type. All the rest, that is, virtually the whole corpus, are of the "tour" type: "You come in through a low door," etc. These descriptions are made for the most part in terms of *operations* and show "how to enter each room." Concerning this second type, the authors point out that a circuit or "tour" is a speech-act (an act of enunciation) that "furnishes a minimal series of paths by which to go into each room"; and that the "path" is a series of units that have the form of vectors that are either "static" ("to the right," "in front of you," etc.) or "mobile" ("if you turn to the left," etc.).[8]

In other words, description oscillates between the terms of an alternative: either *seeing* (the knowledge of an order of places) or *going* (spatializing actions). Either it presents a *tableau* ("there are . . ."), or it organizes *movements* ("you enter, you go across, you turn . . ."). Of these two hypotheses, the choices made by the New York narrators overwhelmingly favored the second.

Leaving Linde and Labov's study aside (it is primarily concerned with the rules of the social interactions and conventions that govern "natural language," a problem we will come back to later), I would like to make use of these New York stories—and other similar stories[9]—to try to specify the relationships between the indicators of "tours" and those of "maps," where they coexist in a single description. How are *acting* and *seeing* coordinated in this realm of ordinary language in which the former is so obviously dominant? The question ultimately concerns the basis of the everyday narrations, the relation between the itinerary (a discursive series of operations) and the map (a plane projection totalizing observations), that is, between two symbolic and anthropological languages of space. Two poles of experience. It seems that in passing from "ordinary" culture to scientific discourse, one passes from one pole to the other.

In narrations concerning apartments or streets, manipulations of space or "tours" are dominant. This form of description usually determines the whole style of the narration. When the other form intervenes, it has the characteristic of being *conditioned* or *presupposed* by the first. Examples of tours conditioning a map: "if you turn to the right, there is . . ." or the closely related form, "if you go straight ahead, you'll see . . ." In both cases, an action permits one to see something. But there are also cases in which a tour assumes a place indication: "There, there's a door, you take the next one"— an element of mapping is the presupposition of a certain itinerary. The narrative fabric in which describers (*descripteurs*) of itineraries predominate is thus punctuated by describers of the map type which have the function of indicating either an *effect* obtained by the tour ("you see . . .") or a *given* that it postulates as its limit ("there is a wall"), its possibility ("there's a door"), or an obligation ("there's a one-way street"), etc. The chain of spatializing operations seems to be marked by references to what it produces (a representation of places) or to what it implies (a local order). We thus have the structure of the travel story: stories of journeys and actions are marked out by the "citation" of the places that result from them or authorize them.

From this angle, we can compare the combination of "tours" and "maps" in everyday stories with the manner in which, over the past five centuries, they have been interlaced and then slowly dissociated in literary and scientific representations of space. In particular, if one takes the "map" in its current geographical form, we can see that in the course of the period marked by the birth of modern scientific discourse (i.e., from the fifteenth to the seventeenth century) the map has slowly disengaged itself from the itineraries that were the condition of its possibility. The first medieval maps included only the rectilinear marking out of itineraries (performative indications chiefly concerning pilgrimages), along with the stops one was to make (cities which one was to pass through, spend the night in, pray at, etc.) and distances calculated in hours or in days, that is, in terms of the time it would take to cover them on foot.[10] Each of these maps is a memorandum prescribing actions. The tour to be made is predominant in them. It includes the map elements, just as today the description of a route to be taken accompanies a hasty sketch already on paper, in the form of citations of places, a sort of dance through the city: "20 paces straight ahead, then turn to the left, then another 40 paces. . . ." The drawing articulates spatializing practices, like the maps of urban routes, arts of actions and stories of paces, that serve the Japanese as "address books,"[11] or the wonderful fifteenth-century Aztec map describing the exodus of the Totomihuacas. This drawing outlines not the "route" (there wasn't one) but the "log" of their journey on foot—an outline marked out by footprints with regular gaps between them and by pictures of the successive events that took place in the course of the journey (meals, battles, crossings of rivers or mountains, etc.): not a "geographical map" but "history book."[12]

Between the fifteenth and the seventeenth centuries, the map became more autonomous. No doubt the proliferation of the "narrative" figures that have long been its stock-in-trade (ships, animals, and characters of all kinds) still had the function of indicating the operations—travelling, military, architectural, political or commercial—that make possible the fabrication of a geographical plan.[13] Far from being "illustrations," iconic glosses on the text, these figurations, like fragments of stories, mark on the map the historical operations from which it resulted. Thus the sailing ship painted on the sea indicates the maritime expedition that made it possible to represent the coastlines. It is equivalent to a describer of the "tour" type. But the map gradually wins out over these figures; it colonizes space; it eliminates little by little the pictural figurations of the practices that produce it. Transformed first by Euclidean geometry and then by descriptive geometry, constituted as a formal ensemble of abstract places, it is a "theater" (as one used to call atlases) in which the same system of projection nevertheless juxtaposes two very different elements: the data furnished by a tradition (Ptolemy's *Geography*, for instance) and those that came from navigators (portulans, for example). The map thus collates on the same plane heterogeneous places, some *received* from a tradition and others *produced* by observation. But the important thing here is the erasure of the itineraries which, presupposing the first category of places and conditioning the second, makes it possible to move from one to the other. The map, a totalizing stage on which elements of diverse origin are brought together to form the tableau of a "state" of geographical knowledge, pushes away into its prehistory or into its posterity, as if into the wings, the operations of which it is the result or the necessary condition. It remains alone on the stage. The tour describers have disappeared.

The organization that can be discerned in stories about space in everyday culture is inverted by the process that has isolated a system of geographical places. The difference between the two modes of description obviously does not consist in the presence or absence of practices (they are at work everywhere), but in the fact that maps, constituted as proper places in which to *exhibit the products* of knowledge, form tables of *legible* results. Stories about space exhibit on the contrary the operations that allow it, within a constraining and non-"proper" place, to mingle its elements anyway, as one apartment-dweller put it concerning the rooms in his flat: "One can mix them up" (*"On peut les triturer"*).[14] From the folktale to descriptions of residences, an exacerbation of "practice" (*"faire"*) (and thus of enunciation), actuates the stories narrating tours in places that, from the ancient cosmos to contemporary public housing developments, are all forms of an imposed order.

In a pre-established geography, which extends (if we limit ourselves to the home) from bedrooms so small that "one can't do anything in them" to the legendary, long-lost attic that "could be used for everything,"[15] everyday stories tell us what one can do in it and make out of it. They are treatments of space.

MARKING OUT BOUNDARIES

As operations on places, stories also play the everyday role of a mobile and magisterial tribunal in cases concerning their delimitation. As always, this role appears more clearly at the second degree, when it is made explicit and duplicated by juridical discourse. In the traditional language of court proceedings, magistrates formerly "visited the scene of the case at issue" ("*se transportaient sur les lieux*") (transports and juridical metaphors), in order to "hear" the contradictory *statements* (*dits*) made by the parties to a dispute concerning debatable boundaries. Their "interlocutory judgment," as it was called, was an "operation of marking out boundaries" (*bornage*). Written in a beautiful hand by the court clerk on parchments where the writing sometimes flowed into (or was inaugurated by?) drawings outlining the boundaries, these interlocutory judgments were in sum nothing other than meta-stories. They combined together (the work of a scribe collating variants) the opposing stories of the parties involved: "Mr. Mulatier declares that his grandfather planted this apple tree on the edge of his field. . . . Jeanpierre reminds us that Mr. Bouvet maintains a dungheap on a piece of land of which he is supposed to be the joint owner with his brother André. . . ." Genealogies of places, legends about territories. Like a critical edition, the judge's narration reconciles these versions. The narration is "established" on the basis of "primary" stories (those of Mr. Mulatier, Jeanpierre, and so many others), stories that already have the function of *spatial legislation* since they determine rights and divide up lands by "acts" or discourses about actions (planting a tree, maintaining a dungheap, etc.).

These "operations of marking out boundaries," consisting in narrative contracts and compilations of stories, are composed of fragments drawn from earlier stories and fitted together in makeshift fashion (*bricolés*). In this sense, they shed light on the formation of myths, since they also have the function of founding and articulating spaces. Preserved in the court records, they constitute an immense travel literature, that is, a literature concerned with actions organizing more or less extensive social cultural areas. But this literature itself represents only a tiny part (the part that is written about disputed points) of the oral narration that interminably labors to compose spaces, to verify, collate, and displace their frontiers.

The ways of "conducting" a story offer, as Pierre Janet pointed out,[16] a very rich field for the analysis of spatiality. Among the questions that depend on it, we should distinguish those that concern dimensions (extensionality), orientation (vectorality), affinity (homographies), etc. I shall stress only a few of its aspects that have to do with delimitation itself, the primary and literally "fundamental" question: it is the partition of space that structures it. Everything refers in fact to this differentiation which makes possible the isolation and interplay of distinct spaces. From the distinction that separates a subject from its exteriority to the distinctions that localize objects, from the home (constituted on the basis of the wall) to the journey (constituted on the basis of a geographical "elsewhere" or a cosmological "beyond"), from the functioning of the urban network to that of the rural landscape, there is no spatiality that is not organized by the determination of frontiers.

In this organization, the story plays a decisive role. It "describes," to be sure. But "every description is more than a fixation," it is "a culturally creative act."[17] It even has distributive power and performative force (it does what it says) when an ensemble of circumstances is brought together. Then it founds spaces. Reciprocally, where stories are disappearing (or else are being reduced to museographical objects), there is a loss of space: deprived of narrations (as one sees it happen in both the city and the countryside), the group or the individual regresses toward the disquieting, fatalistic experience of a formless, indistinct, and nocturnal totality. By considering the role of stories in delimitation, one can see that the primary function is to *authorize* the establishment, displacement or transcendence of limits, and as a consequence, to set in opposition, within the closed field of discourse, two movements that intersect (setting and transgressing limits) in such a way as to make the story a sort of "crossword" decoding stencil (a dynamic partitioning of space) whose essential narrative figures seem to be the *frontier* and the *bridge*.

1. *Creating a theater of actions*. The story's first function is to authorize, or more exactly, to *found*. Strictly speaking, this function is not juridical, that is, related to laws or judgments. It depends rather on what Georges Dumézil analyzes in connection with the Indo-European root *dhē* "to set in place," and its derivatives in Sanskrit (*dhātu*) and Latin (*fās*). The Latin noun "*fās*," he writes, "is properly speaking the mystical foundation, which is in the invisible world, and without which all forms of conduct that are enjoined or authorized by *ius* (human law) and, more generally speaking, all human conduct, are doubtful, perilous, and even fatal. *Fās* cannot be subjected to analysis or casuistry, as *ius* can: *fās* can no more be broken up into parts than its name can be declined." A *foundation* either exists or it doesn't: *fās est* or *fās non est*. "A time or a place are said to be *fasti* or *nefasti* [auspacious or inauspacious] depending on whether they provide or fail to provide human action with this necessary foundation."[18]

In the Western parts of the Indo-European world, this function has been divided in a particular way among different institutions—in contrast to what happened in ancient India, where different roles were played in turn by the same characters. Occidental culture created its own ritual concerning *fās*, which was carried out in Rome by specialized priests called *fētiāles*. It was

practiced "before Rome undertook any action with regard to a foreign nation," such as a declaration of war, a military expedition, or an alliance. The
ritual was a procession with three centrifugal stages, the first within Roman
territory but near the frontier, the second on the frontier, the third in foreign
territory. The ritual action was carried out before every civil or military
action because it is designed to *create the field* necessary for political or military activities. It is thus also a *repetitio rerum*: both a renewal and a repetition of the originary founding acts, a *recitation* and a *citation* of the
genealogies that could legitimate the new enterprise, and a *prediction* and a
promise of success at the beginning of battles, contracts, or conquests. As a
general repetition before the actual representation, the rite, a narration in
acts, precedes the historical realization. The tour or procession of the *fētiālēs*
opens a space and provides a foundation for the operations of the military
men, diplomats, or merchants who dare to cross the frontiers. Similarly in
the *Vedas*, Visnu, "by his footsteps, opens the zone of space in which Indra's
military action must take place." The *fās* ritual is a foundation. It "provides
space" for the actions that will be undertaken; it "creates a field" which
serves as their "base" and their "theater."[19]

This founding is precisely the primary role of the story. It opens a legitimate *theater* for practical *actions*. It creates a field that authorizes dangerous
and contingent social actions. But it differs in three ways from the function
the Roman ritual so carefully isolated: the story founds *fās* in a form that is
fragmented (not unique and whole), miniaturized (not on a national scale),
and polyvalent (not specialized). It is *fragmented*, not only because of the di-
versification of social milieus, but especially because of the increasing heterogeneity (or because of a heterogeneity that is increasingly obvious) of the
authorizing "references": the excommunication of territorial "divinities,"
the deconsecration of places haunted by the story-spirit, and the extension of
neutral areas deprived of legitimacy have marked the disappearance and fragmentation of the narrations that organized frontiers and appropriations.
(Official historiography—history books, television news reports, etc.—nevertheless tries to make everyone believe in the existence of a national space.) It
is *miniaturized*, because socioeconomic technocratization confines the significance of *fās* and *nefas* to the level of the family unit or the individual, and
leads to the multiplication of "family stories," "life stories," and psychoana-
lytical narrations. (Gradually cut loose from these particular stories, public
justifications nevertheless continue to exist in the form of blind rumors, or
resurface savagely in class or race conflicts). It is finally *polyvalent*, because
the mixing together of so many micro-stories gives them functions that
change according to the groups in which they circulate. This polyvalence

does not affect the relational origins of narrativity, however: the ancient ritual that creates fields of action is recognizable in the "fragments" of narration planted around the obscure thresholds of our existence; these buried fragments articulate without its knowing it the "biographical" story whose space they found.

A narrative activity, even if it is multiform and no longer unitary, thus continues to develop where frontiers and relations with space abroad are concerned. Fragmented and disseminated, it is continually concerned with marking out boundaries. What it puts in action is once more the *fās* that "authorizes" enterprises and precedes them. Like the Roman *fētiāles*, stories "go in a procession" ahead of social practices in order to open a field for them. Decisions and juridical combinations themselves come only afterwards, like the statements and acts of Roman law (*iūs*), arbitrating the areas of action granted to each party,[20] participating themselves in the activities for which *fās* provided a "foundation." According to the rules that are proper to them, the magistrates' "interlocutory judgments" operate within the aggregate of heterogeneous spaces that have already been created and established by the innumerable forms of an oral narrativity composed of family or local stories, customary or professional "poems" and "recitations" of paths taken or countrysides traversed. The magistrates' judgments do not create these theaters of action, they articulate and manipulate them. They presuppose the narrative authorities that the magistrates "hear" compare, and put into hierarchies. Preceding the judgment that regulates and settles, there is a founding narration.

2. *Frontiers and bridges.* Stories are actuated by a contradiction that is represented in them by the relationship between the frontier and the bridge, that is, between a (legitimate) space and its (alien) exteriority. In order to account for contradiction, it is helpful to go back to the elementary units. Leaving aside morphology (which is not our concern here) and situating ourselves in the perspective of a pragmatics and, more precisely, a syntax aimed at determining "programs" or series of practices through which space is appropriated, we can take as our point of departure the "region," which Miller and Johnson-Laird define as a basic unit: the place where programs and actions interact. A "region" is thus the space created by an interaction.[21] It follows that in the same place there are as many "regions" as there are interactions or intersections of programs. And also that the determination of space is dual and operational, and, in a problematics of enunciation, related to an "interlocutory" process.

In this way a dynamic contradiction between each delimitation and its mobility is introduced. On the one hand, the story tirelessly marks out frontiers. It multiplies them, but in terms of interactions among the characters—things, animals, human beings: the acting subjects (*actants*) divide up among themselves places as well as predicates (simple, crafty, ambitious, silly, etc.) and movements (advancing, withdrawing, going into exile, returning, etc.). Limits are drawn by the points at which the progressive appropriations (the acquisition of predicates in the course of the story) and the successive displacements (internal or external movements) of the acting subjects meet. Both appropriations and displacements depend on a dynamic distribution of possible goods and functions in order to constitute an increasingly complex network of differentiations, a combinative system of spaces. They result from the operation of distinctions resulting from encounters. Thus, in the obscurity of their unlimitedness, bodies can be distinguished only where the "contacts" (*"touches"*) of amorous or hostile struggles are inscribed on them. This is a paradox of the frontier: created by contacts, the points of differentiation between two bodies are also their common points. Conjunction and disjunction are inseparable in them. Of two bodies in contact, which one possesses the frontier that distinguishes them? Neither. Does that amount to saying: no one?

The theoretical and practical problem of the frontier: to whom does it belong? The river, wall or tree *makes* a frontier. It does not have the character of a nowhere that cartographical representation ultimately presupposes. It has a mediating role. So does the story that gives it voice: "Stop," says the forest the wolf comes out of. "Stop!" says the river, revealing its crocodile. But this actor, by virtue of the very fact that he is the mouthpiece of the limit, creates communication as well as separation; more than that, he establishes a border only by saying what crosses it, having come from the other side. He articulates it. He is *also* a passing through or over. In the story, the frontier functions as a third element. It is an "in-between"—a "space between," *Zwischenraum*, as Morgenstern puts it in a marvelous and ironic poem on "closure" (*Zaun*), which rhymes with "space" (*Raum*) and "to see through" (*hindurchzuschaun*).[22] It is the story of a picket fence (*Lattenzaun*):

Es war einmal ein Lattenzaun	One time there was a picket fence
mit Zwischenraum, hindurchzuschaun.	with space to gaze
	from hence to thence.

A middle place, composed of interactions and inter-views, the frontier is a sort of void, a narrative symbol of exchanges and encounters. Passing by, an architect suddenly appropriates this "in-between space" and builds a great edifice on it:

Ein Architekt, der dieses sah,	An architect who saw this sight
stand eines Abends plötzlich da-	approached it suddenly one night,
und nahm den Zwischenraum heraus	removed the spaces from the fence
und baute draus ein grosses	
Haus.	and built of them a residence.

Transformation of the void into a plenitude, of the in- between into an established place. The rest goes without saying. The Senate "takes on" the monument—the Law establishes itself in it—and the architect escapes to Afri- or-America:

Drum zog ihn der Senat auch ein.	the senate had to intervene
Der Architekt jedoch entfloh	The architect, however, flew
nach Afri-od-Ameriko	to Afri- or Americoo.
	(Max Knight, trans.)

The Architect's drive to cement up the picket fence, to fill in and build up "the space in-between," is also his illusion, for without knowing it he is working toward the political freezing of the place and there is nothing left for him to do, when he sees his work finished, but to flee far away from the blocs of the law.

In contrast, the story privileges a "logic of ambiguity" through its accounts of interaction. It "turns" the frontier into a crossing, and the river into a bridge. It recounts inversions and displacements: the door that closes is precisely what may be opened; the river is what makes passage possible; the tree is what marks the stages of advance; the picket fence is an ensemble of interstices through which one's glances pass.

The *bridge* is ambiguous everywhere: it alternately welds together and opposes insularities. It distinguishes them and threatens them. It liberates from enclosure and destroys autonomy. Thus, for example, it occurs as a central and ambivalent character in the stories of the Noirmoutrins, before, during, and after the construction of a bridge between La Fosse and Fromentine in Vendée in 1972.[23] It carries on a double life in innumerable memories of places and everyday legends, often summed up in proper names, hidden paradoxes, ellipses in stories, riddles to be solved: Bridgehead, Bridgenorth, Bridgetown, Bridgewater, Bridgman, Cambridge, Trowbridge, etc.

Justifiably, the bridge is the index of the diabolic in the paintings where Bosch invents his modifications of spaces.[24] As a transgression of the limit, a disobedience of the law of the place, it represents a departure, an attack on a state, the ambition of a conquering power, or the flight of an exile; in any case, the "betrayal" of an order. But at the same time as it offers the possibility of a bewildering exteriority, it allows or causes the re-emergence beyond the frontiers of the alien element that was controlled in the interior, and gives ob-jectivity (that is, expression and re-presentation) to the alterity which was hidden inside the limits, so that in recrossing the bridge and coming back within the enclosure the traveler henceforth finds there the exteriority that he had first sought by going outside and then fled by returning. Within the frontiers, the alien is already there, an exoticism or sabbath of the memory, a disquieting familiarity. It is as though delimitation itself were the bridge that opens the inside to its other.

DELINQUENCIES?

What the map cuts up, the story cuts across. In Greek, narration is called "diegesis": it establishes an itinerary (it "guides") and it passes through (it "transgresses"). The space of operations it travels in is made of movements: it is *topological*, concerning the deformations of figures, rather than *topical*, defining places. It is only ambivalently that the limit circumscribes in this space. It plays a double game. It does the opposite of what it says. It hands the place over to the foreigner that it gives the impression of throwing out. Or rather, when it marks a stopping place, the latter is not stable but follows the variations of encounters between programs. Boundaries are transportable limits and transportations of limits; they are also *metaphorai.*

In the narrations that organize spaces, boundaries seem to play the role of the Greek *xoana*, statuettes whose invention is attributed to the clever Daedalus: they are crafty like Daedalus and mark out limits only by moving themselves (and the limits). These straight-line indicators put emphasis on the curves and movements of space. Their distributive work is thus completely different from that of the divisions established by poles, pickets or stable columns which, planted in the earth, cut up and compose an order of places.[25] They are also transportable limits.

Today, narrative operations of boundary-setting take the place of these enigmatic describers of earlier times when they bring movement in through the very act of fixing, in the name of delimitation. Michelet already said it: when the aristocracy of the great Olympian gods collapsed at the end of Antiquity, it did not take down with it "the mass of indigenous gods, the populace of gods that still possessed the immensity of fields, forests, woods, mountains, springs, intimately associated with the life of the country. These gods lived in the hearts of oaks, in the swift, deep waters, and could not be driven out of them. . . . Where are they? In the desert, on the heath, in the forest? Yes, but also and especially in the home. They live on in the most intimate of domestic habits."[26] But they also live on in our streets and in our apartments. They were perhaps after all only the agile representatives of narrativity, and of narrativity in its most *delinquent* form. The fact that they have changed their names (every power is toponymical and initiates its order of places by naming them) takes nothing away from the multiple, insidious, moving force. It survives the avatars of the great history that debaptises and rebaptises them.

If the delinquent exists only by displacing itself, if its specific mark is to live not on the margins but in the interstices of the codes that it undoes and displaces, if it is characterized by the privilege of the *tour* over the *state*, then the story is delinquent. Social delinquency consists in taking the story literally, in making it the principle of physical existence where a society no longer offers to subjects or groups symbolic outlets and expectations of spaces, where there is no longer any alternative to disciplinary falling-into-line or illegal drifting away, that is, one form or another of prison and wandering outside the pale. Inversely, the story is a sort of delinquency in reserve, maintained, but itself displaced and consistent, in traditional societies (ancient, medieval, etc.), with an order that is firmly established but flexible enough to allow the proliferation of this challenging mobility that does not respect places, is alternately playful and threatening, and extends from the microbe-like forms of everyday narration to the carnivalesque celebrations of earlier days.[27]

It remains to be discovered, of course, what actual changes produce this delinquent narrativity in a society. In any event, one can already say that in matters concerning space, this delinquency begins with the inscription of the body in the order's text. The opacity of the body in movement, gesticulating, walking, taking its pleasure, is what indefinitely organizes a *here* in relation to an *abroad*, a "familiarity" in relation to a "foreignness." A spatial story is in its minimal degree, a *spoken* language, that is, a linguistic system that distributes places insofar as it is *articulated* by an "enunciatory focalization," by an act of practicing it. It is the object of "proxemics."[28] Before we return to its manifestations in the organization of memory, it will suffice here to recall that, in this focalizing enunciation, space appears once more as a *practiced* place.

NOTES

1. John Lyons, *Semantics* (Cambridge: Cambridge University Press, 1977), II, 475–81, 690–703.

2. George A. Miller and Philip N. Johnson-Laird, *Language and Perception* (Cambridge, Mass.: Harvard University Press, 1976).

3. See below, p.118.

4. Albert E. Scheflen and Norman Ashcraft, *Human Territories: How We Behave in Space-Time* (Englewood Cliffs, N.J.: Prentice-Hall, 1976).

5. E. A. Schegloff, "Notes on a Conversational Practice: Formulating Place," in *Studies in Social Interaction*, ed. David Sudnow (New York: The Free Press, 1972), pp. 75–119.

6. See, for example, *École de Tartu, Travaux sur les systèmes de signes*, ed. Y. M. Lotman and B. A. Ouspenski (Paris: PUF; Bruxelles: Complexe, 1976), 18–39, 77–93, etc; Jüri Lotman, *La Structure du texte artistique* (Paris: Gallimard, 1973), 309, etc; Jüri Lotman, *The Structure of the Artistic Text*, trans. R. Vroon (Ann Arbor: Department of Slavic Languages and Literatures, The University of Michigan, 1977); B. A. Uspenskii, *A Poetics of Composition*, trans. V. Zavarin and S. Witting (Berkeley: University of California Press, 1973).

7. M. Merleau-Ponty, *Phénoménologie de la perception* (Paris: Gallimard Tel, 1976), 324–44.

8. Charlotte Linde and William Labov, "Spatial Networks as a Site for the Study of Language and Thought," *Language*, 51 (1975), 924–39. On the relation between practice (le faire) and space, see also *Groupe 107* (M. Hammad et al.), *Sémiotique de l'espace* (Paris: DGRST, 1973), 28.

9. See, for example, Catherine Bidou and Francis Ho Tham Kouie, *Le Vecu des habitants dans leur logement à travers soixante entretiens libres* (Paris: CEREBE, 1974); Alain Médam and Jean-François Augoyard, *Situations d'habitat et façons d'habiter* (Paris: ESA, 1976); etc.

10. See George H. T. Kimble, *Geography in the Middle Ages* (London: Methuen, 1938); etc.

11. Roland Barthes, *L'Empire des signes* (Genève: Skira, 1970), pp. 47–51.

12. The map is reproduced and analyzed by Pierre Janet, *L'Evolution de la mémoire et la notion du temps* (Paris: Chahine, 1928), 284–87. The original is in Cuauhtinchan (Puebla, Mexico).

13. See, for example, Louis Marin, *Utopiques: Jeux d'espaces* (Paris: Minuit, 1973), 257–90, on the relation between figures (a "discourse-tour") and the map (a "system-text") in three representations of the city in the seventeenth century: a relation between a "narrative" and a "geometric."

14. Quoted in Bidou and Ho Tham Kouie, *Le Vécu des habitants*, 55.

15. Ibid., 57 and 59.

16. Janet, *L'Evolution de la mémoire*, particularly the lectures on "the procedures of narrative" and "fabrication" (249–94). Médam and Augoyard have used this unit to define the subject matter of their investigation (*Situations d'habitat*, 90–95).

17. Lotman, in *École de Tartu, Travaux sur les systèmes de signes*, 89.

18. Georges Dumézil, *Idées romaines* (Paris: Gallimard, 1969), 61–78, on "Ius fetiale."

19. Ibid.

20. Ibid., 31–45.

21. Miller and Johnson-Laird, *Language and Perception*, 57–66, 385–90, 564, etc.

22. Christian Morgenstern, "Der Lattenzaun" (the picket fence), in *Gesammelte Werke* (München: Piper, 1965), 229.

23. See Nicole Brunet, "Un Pont vers l'acculturation. Ile de Noirmoutiers," Diss. (DEA Ethnologie) Université de Paris VII, 1979.

24. See M. de Certeau, "Délires et délices de Jérôme Bosch," *Traverses*, No. 5–6 (1976), 37–54.

25. See Françoise Frontisi-Ducroux, *Dédale. Mythologie de l'artisan en Grèce ancienne* (Paris: Maspero, 1975), 104, 100–101, 117, etc., on the mobility of these rigid statues.

26. Jules Michelet, *La Sorcière* (Paris: Calmann-Lévy, n.d.), 23–24.

27. See, for example, on the subject of this ambiguity, Emmanuel Le Roy Ladurie, *Le Carnaval de Romans* (Paris: Gallimard, 1979); *The Carnival at Romans*, trans. M. Fenney (New York: George Braziller, 1979).

28. See Paolo Fabbri, "Considérations sur la proxémique," *Langages*, No. 10 (June 1968), 65–75. E. T. Hall defined proxemics as "the study of how man unconsciously structures spaces—the distance between men in the conduct of daily transactions, the organization of space in his houses and buildings, and ultimately the lay out of his towns" ("Proxemics: The Study of Man's Spatial Relations," in *Man's Image in Medicine and Anthropology*, ed. I. Gladston (New York: International Universities Press, 1963)).

TRAVEL BOOKS AS LITERARY PHENOMENA

Paul Fussell

After encountering a number of these books, it's time to inquire what they are. Perhaps it is when we cannot satisfactorily designate a kind of work with a single word (*epic, novel, romance, story, novella, memoir, sonnet, sermon, essay*) but must invoke two (*war memoir, Black autobiography, first novel, picture book, travel book*) that we sense we're entering complicated territory, where description, let alone definition, is hazardous, an act closer to exploration than to travel. Criticism has never quite known what to call books like these. Some commentators, perhaps recalling the illustrated travel lectures of their youth or the travel films that used to be shown as "short subjects," call them *travelogues*. Others, more literary, render that term *travel logs*, apparently thinking of literal, responsible daily diaries, like ships' logs. This latter usage is the one preferred by David Lodge, who says of 30's writing that "it tended to model itself on historical kinds of discourse—the autobiography, the eye-witness account, the travel log: *Journey to a War, Letters from Iceland, The Road to Wigan Pier, Journey without Maps, Autumn Journal,* 'Berlin Diary,' are some characteristic titles." Even Forster is uncertain what to call these things. In 1941 he calls them *travelogues*, in 1949 *travel books*.

Let's call them travel books, and distinguish them initially from guide books, which are not autobiographical and are not sustained by a narrative exploiting the devices of fiction. A guide book is addressed to those who plan to follow the traveler, doing what he has done, but more selectively. A travel book, at its purest, is addressed to those who do not plan to follow the traveler at all, but who require the exotic or comic anomalies, wonders, and scandals of the literary form *romance* which their own place or time cannot entirely supply. Travel books are a sub-species of memoir in which the auto-

biographical narrative arises from the speaker's encounter with distant or unfamiliar data, and in which the narrative—unlike that in a novel or a romance—claims literal validity by constant reference to actuality. The speaker
in any travel book exhibits himself as physically more free than the reader,
and thus every such book, even when it depicts its speaker trapped in Boa
Vista, is an implicit celebration of freedom. It resembles a poetic ode, an Ode
to Freedom. The illusion of freedom is a precious thing in the 20's and 30's,
when the shades of the modern prison-house are closing in, when the passports and queues and guided tours and social security numbers and customs
regulations and currency controls are beginning gradually to constrict life.
What makes travel books seem so necessary between the wars is what
Fleming pointed to in *One's Company*, "that lamb-like subservience to red
tape which is perhaps the most striking characteristic of modern man."
Intellectual and moral pusillanimity is another characteristic of modern
man. Hence Douglas's emphasis on the exemplary function of the travel
writer's internal freedom and philosophic courage:

> It seems to me that the reader of a good travel-book. is entitled not only to an ex-
> terior voyage, to descriptions of scenery and so forth, but to an interior, a senti-
> mental or temperamental voyage, which takes place side by side with the outer
> one.

Thus "the ideal book of this kind" invites the reader to undertake three tours
simultaneously: "abroad, into the author's brain, and into his own." It
follows that "the writer should . . . possess a brain worth exploring; some
philosophy of life—not necessarily, though by preference, of his own forg-
ing—and the courage to proclaim it and put it to the test; be must be naif and
profound, both child and sage." And if the enterprise succeeds, the reader's
"brain" will instinctively adjust itself to accord in some degree with the pattern established by the author's travel, both external and internal: that is, it
will experience an access of moral freedom. It is thus possible to consider the
between-the-wars travel books as a subtle instrument of ethics, replacing
such former vehicles as sermons and essays.

A fact of modern publishing history is the virtual disappearance of the
essay as a salable commodity (I mean the essay, not the "article"). If you
want to raise a laugh in a publisher's office, enter with a manuscript collection of essays on all sorts of subjects. And if you want to raise an even louder
laugh, contrive that your essays have a moral tendency, even if they stop
short of aspiring to promulgate wisdom. The more we attend to what's going
on in the travel book between the wars, the more we perceive that the genre
is a device for getting published essays which, without the travel "men-

struum" (as Coleridge would say), would appear too old-fashioned for generic credit, too reminiscent of Lamb and Stevenson and Chesterton. Thus the travel books of Aldous Huxley, a way of presenting learned essays which without exotic narrative support would find no audience. Thus also the performances of Douglas and of Osbert Sitwell, who, for all his defects, has thought long and hard about the essayistic element in the travel book and has coined for it the eccentric term *discursion,* as in his titles *Discursions on Travel, Art and Life* (1925) and *Winters of Content and Other Discursions on Mediterranean Art and Travel* (1950). "Discursions," he says, is "a word of my own minting, coined from *discourse* and *discursive,* and designed to epitomize the manner in which a traveler formulates his loose impressions, as, for example, he sits in a train, looking out [the] window, and allows the sights he so rapidly glimpses, one after another, to break in upon the thread of his . . . thoughts." *Discursions,* he goes on, "is an attempt . . . to find a new name for a particular kind of essay, that unites in the stream of travel . . . many very personal random reflections and sentiments. . . ." Thus in Sitwell's "travel books" we find a general essay on cabs, prompted by the cabs of Lecce, and one on the theory of bourgeois domestic architecture triggered by the sights of southern Germany. Neither essay could achieve a wide audience if detached from the sense data of the place abroad which has justified it. Alan Pryce-Jones's *The Spring Journey* (1931) is a good example of a travel book which functions as a mere framework for essays. The travel is to Egypt, Palestine, Syria, and Greece, but it is only a medium for inset Carlylean essays and discursive flourishes on the follies of modern education, the difference between Imagination and Fancy, the decay of contemporary civilization, and the superiority of music to "the other arts." An American counterpart is Hemingway's *Green Hills of Africa* (1935). Because of the public persona he has chosen, Hemingway can't plausibly write "essays" in the old schoolmasterly sense. He can get away with essays on bullfighting if he connects his learned comments with memories of toreros he has known, and thus validates his remarks as memoir. But for him to discourse professorially about history and literature would seem unnatural— stuffy, pompous, very un-outdoors. He thus lodges his major essay on the character and history of American literature, his version of Lawrence's *Studies in Classic American Literature,* in a travel book, and presents it there as a conversation with a person encountered by chance, the character Kandinsky, an Austrian who is made to ask who the great writers are. "Tell me. Please tell me," he says, not very credibly. Hemingway responds with an essay of 1200 words, presented as dialogue, considering the merits of Poe, Melville, Emerson, Hawthorne, Whittier, James, Crane, and Twain. We easily remember his brilliant remark, one of the most acute critical perceptions any scholar or critic has uttered, that "all modern American literature comes from one book by Mark Twain called *Huckleberry Finn*," but we may forget that it gets uttered at all because on the African veldt "under the dining tent fly" an Austrian has asked him about American writers. It is an open-air remark, a travel, not a library, remark.

Similarly, if one approached a publisher in 1940 with a collection of assorted ethical and historical essays one would have less chance of success than if one arranged them as "A journey through Yugoslavia" and titled the whole immense work *Black Lamb and Grey Falcon*, as Rebecca West did. We recognize Lawrence's *Aaron's Rod* as akin to a travel book less, perhaps, because it goes to some lengths to describe abroad than because it provides a medium for promulgating essays. Lawrence will suddenly cast away his narrative pretences entirely, face his audience directly, and issue what we perceive is the "topic sentence" of an old-fashioned moral essay. On some of these occasions he sounds like a sort of Hilaire Belloc turned inside out: "The *idée fixe* of today," he will proclaim, "is that every individual shall not only give himself, but shall achieve the last glory of giving himself away." Or "The David in the Piazza della Signoria, there under the dark great Palace, in the position Michelangelo chose for him, there, standing forward stripped and exposed and eternally half-shrinking, half-wishing to expose himself, he is the genius of Florence."

But to emphasize the presence of the essay element in the travel book is to risk not noticing sufficiently this genre's complex relation to adjacent forms which also require two words to designate them: *war memoir, comic novel, quest romance, picaresque romance, pastoral romance.* The memorable war memoirs of the late 20's and early 30's, by Graves and Blunden and Sassoon, are very like travel books and would doubtless show different characteristics if they'd not been written in the travel context of the period between the wars. They are ironic or parodic or nightmare travels, to France and Belgium, with the Channel ferries and the forty-and-eights replacing the liners and chic trains of real travel, with dugouts standing for hotel- rooms and lobbies and Other Ranks serving the travel-book function of "native" porters and servants. Curiously, at the end of the Second World War the war book has something of the same "travel" element attached to it, the same obsession with topography and the mystery of place, with even something like Lawrence's adhesions to the prepositional, like *into*. Recalling his first idea for *The Naked and the Dead*, Mailer says: "I wanted to write a short novel about a long patrol. . . . Probably [the idea] was stimulated by a few war books I had read: John Hersey's *Into the Valley*, Harry Brown's *A Walk in the Sun.*"

The element of the comic novel is visible not merely in the travel books of Byron and Waugh; it is in *Sea and Sardinia* as well, in much of Douglas, and even, if we can conceive the "seedy" as inherently comic, as a pathetic parody of a civilization not worth imitating, in much of Graham Greene. Anomaly is what unites comic novel and travel experience. A baron "traveling in cosmetics" and shaving in beer because the water in the wagons-lits has run out is an anomaly Anthony Powell met in Yugoslavia once. It fitted perfectly into his comic novel *Venusberg* (1933), where the baron is presented as Count Bobel. The comic novel between the wars would be an impoverished thing without its multitude of anomalous strangers—like Mr. Norris—encountered on actual trains and ships.

If as a form of prose fiction a "romance" is more likely than a novel to be set abroad or in an exotic place, then *romance*, whether "quest," picaresque, or pastoral, will suggest itself as a term to designate an indispensable element of the travel book. One could ask: aren't travel books really romances in the old sense, with the difference that the adventures are located within an actual, often famous, topography to satisfy an audience which demands it both ways—which wants to go adventuring vicariously, as it always has, but which at the same time wants to feel itself within a world declared real by such up-to-date studies as political science, sociology, anthropology, economics, and contemporary history? The proximity of the travel book to the thoroughly empirical picaresque romance, contrived from a multitude of adventures in non-causal series, can perhaps be inferred from Freya Stark's disappointment with Gertrude Bell's *Syria*. She felt the book let her down: "[Bell] did not have enough adventures." (On one of her Persian explorations in 1932 Stark took along *Pilgrim's Progress*, and in Brazil an item in Fleming's travel kit was "1 copy of *Tom Jones*.") As in a romance, the modern traveler leaves the familiar and predictable to wander, episodically, into the unfamiliar or unknown, encountering strange adventures, and finally, after travail and ordeals, returns safely. Somehow, we feel a travel book isn't wholly satisfying unless the traveler returns to his starting point: the action, as in a quest romance, must be completed. We are gratified—indeed, comforted—by the "sense of an ending," the completion of the circuit, as we are at the end of *Labels* or *The Road to Oxiana* or *Journey without Maps*, where the "hero" invites us to enjoy his success in returning home.

All this is to suggest that the modern travel book is what Northrop Frye would call a myth that has been "displaced"—that is, lowered, brought down to earth, rendered credible "scientifically"—and that the myth resembles the archetypal monomyth of heroic adventure defined by Joseph Campbell. The myth of the hero, Campbell explains, is tripartite: first, the setting out, the disjunction from the familiar; second, the trials of initiation and adventure; and third, the return and the hero's reintegration into society. Even if there is no return, the monomyth still assumes tripartite form, as in *Pilgrim's Progress*, whose title-page declares that the hero's "progress, from this world, to that which is to come" will be conceived in three stages: "The manner of his setting out; His Dangerous journey; and Safe Arrival at the Desired Country." The first and last stages of the tripartite experience tend to be moments of heightened ritual or magic, even in entirely "secular" travel writings. Eliot understands this, and so does Auden. Witness stanza 4 of Auden's "Dover" (1937):

> *The eyes of departing migrants are fixed on the sea,*
> *Conjuring destinies out of impersonal water:*
> *"I see all important decision made on a lake,*
> *An illness, a beard, Arabia found in a bed,*
> *Nanny defeated. Money."*

Listening to the ship's engine as he sets out from Southampton for Spain, V. S. Pritchett writes in *Marching Spain* (1928), "Every man who heard those sounds must have seemed to himself as great a hero as Ulysses and pitted against as mysterious a destiny, the strange destiny of the outward bound." Starting on his Brazilian adventure, Peter Fleming notices something odd which he can describe only thus: "We were through the looking- glass." And returning is equally full of portent and mystery. We have seen Waugh throwing his champagne glass overboard, a gesture which, be says, "has become oddly important to me," somehow "bound up with the turgid, indefinite feelings of homecoming." Fleming would suggest that the magical feeling upon returning arises from moving from a form of non-existence back to existence, or recovering one's normal self-consciousness before one's accustomed audience. The traveler "who has for weeks or months seen himself only as a puny and irrelevant alien crawling laboriously over a country in which he has no roots and no background, suddenly [on returning] encounters his other self, a relatively solid and considerable figure, with . . . a place in the minds of certain people." Or, as Auden registers the magical act of reintegration in stanza 5 of "Dover,"

> *Red after years of failure or bright with fame,*
> *The eyes of homecomers thank these historical cliffs:*

"The mirror can no longer lie nor the clock reproach;
In the shadow under the yew, at the children's party,
  Everything must be explained."

Indeed, the stages of the classic monomyth of the adventuring hero cannot avoid sketching an allegory of human life itself. As Campbell notes, the "call to adventure" is a figure for the onset of adolescence; adult life is "the travel"; old age, the "return." For the literary imagination, says Auden, "It is impossible to take a train or an airplane without having a fantasy of oneself as a Quest Hero setting off in search of an enchanted princess or the Waters of Life." That's why we enjoy reading travel books, even if we imagine we're enjoying only the curiosities of Liberia, British Guiana, Persia, or Patagonia. Even the souvenirs brought back so religiously by tourists are brought back "religiously." According to the anthropologist Nelson Graburn, tourists bring back souvenirs in unwitting imitation of the Grail Knight returning with his inestimable prize. Even for mass tourists, "the Holy Grail is . . . sought on the journey, and the success of a holiday is proportionate to the degree that the myth is realized."

But travel books are not merely displaced quest romances. They are also displaced pastoral romances. If William Empson is right to define traditional pastoral as a mode of presentation implying "a beautiful relation between rich and poor," then pastoral is a powerful element in most travel books, for, unless he's a *Wandervogel* or similar kind of layabout (few of whom write books), the traveler is almost always richer and freer than those he's among. He is both a plutocrat *pro tem* and the sort of plutocrat the natives don't mind having around. Byron and Waugh and Greene hire drivers and porters and bearers and pay outrageous prices for decrepit horses and cars; Lawrence pays bus and steamer fares; Norman Douglas keeps employed numerous waiters and *sommeliers*. If the cash nexus can be considered "a beautiful relation," the behavior of these characters is like the behavior of the court class in Renaissance pastoral, and there's a closer resemblance between Sidney's *Arcadia* and a modern travel book than is obvious on the surface. Consider the Lawrence of *Twilight in Italy*, attended by his aristocratic consort. Consider the affectionate patronizing of the Persian peasants in Byron's dialogue involving "The Caliph of Rum." And it is with the pastoral strain in travel books that we can associate the implicit elegiac tendency of these works. Pastoral has built into it a natural retrograde emotion. It is instinct with elegy. To the degree that literary travel between the wars constitutes an implicit rejection of industrialism and everything implied by the concept "modern northern Europe," it is a celebration of a Golden Age, and recalling the Ideal Places of Waugh, Auden, and Priestley, we can locate that Golden Age in the middle of the preceding century. One travels to experience the past, and travel is thus an adventure in time as well as distance.

"The King's life is moving peacefully to its close," the BBC announced in January, 1936, invoking for this most solemn, magical moment the root metaphor of human imaginative experience, the figure of time rendered as space. If, as this essential trope persuades us, life is a journey (to the Eliot of the *Quartets*, a never-ending one), then literary accounts of journeys take us very deeply into the center of instinctive imaginative life. Like no other kinds of writing, travel books exercise and exploit the fundamental intellectual and emotional figure of thought, by which the past is conceived as back and the future as forward. They manipulate the whole alliance between temporal and spatial that we use to orient ourselves in time by invoking the dimension of space. That is, travel books make more or less conscious an activity usually unconscious. Travel books are special because the metaphor they imply is so essential. Works we recognize as somehow "classical" derive much of their status and authority from their open exploitation of this metaphor. Housman is an example:

> Into my heart an air that kills
> From you far country blows:
> What are those blue remembered hills,
> What spires, what farms are those?
>
> That is the land of lost content,
> I see it shining plain,
> The happy highways where I went
> And cannot come again.

"When I was a young man," says Borges, "I was always hunting for new metaphors. Then I found out that good metaphors are always the same. I mean you compare time to a road, death to sleeping, life to dreaming, and those are the great metaphors in literature because they correspond to something essential." An Italian friend of Norman Douglas's, indicating that his fifteen-year-old son has died of tuberculosis, says, "He has gone into that other country."

And if living and dying are like traveling, so are reading and writing. As Michel Butor points out, the eyes of the reader "travel" along the lines of print as the reader is "guided" by the writer, as his imagination "escapes" his own I Hate It Here world. Thus in reading, of all books, a travel book, the reader becomes doubly a traveler, moving from beginning to end of the book while touring along with the literary traveler.

"O where are you going?" said reader to rider, writes Auden in the Epilogue to *The Orators* (1931). His near-rhyme implies the parallelism between reading and riding, a parallelism as suggestive as the one Connolly instinctively falls into when designating the three things his Oxford crowd in the early 20's "had a passion for": "literature, travel, and the visual arts." And writing, as Butor perceives, is like traveling. Figures of travel occupy any writer's imagination as he starts out, makes transitions, digresses, returns, goes forward, divagates, pauses, approaches the subject from a slightly different direction, and observes things from various points of view (like Norman Douglas on his eminences). Thus, as Osbert Sitwell says, "To begin a book is . . . to embark on a long and perilous voyage," but to begin a travel book "doubles the sense of starting on a journey."

Thus to speak of "literary traveling" is almost a tautology, so intimately are literature and travel implicated with each other. Any child senses this, and any adult recalling his childhood remembers moments when reading was revealed to be traveling. Peter Quennell's first awareness that he had actually learned to read occurred at the age of four or five when he was looking through bound volumes of *The Boy's Own Paper* at home. "The story I scrutinized was . . . the work of some unknown author who described an African caravan, journeying to the sound of camel-bells from oasis to oasis. Suddenly, the printed words I painfully spelt out melted into a continuous narrative, whence a procession of fascinating images emerged and wound its way across my mental landscape." Gerald Brenan's mental landscape was formed, he reports, not just by the romances of William Morris, with their "descriptions of imaginary travel," but also by Elisée Reclus's *Universal Geography* in nineteen volumes, which he discovered at school. From Reclus he gathered that "foreign countries alone offered something to the imagination," and he filled notebooks with a plan for a tour of the world "which would last, with continuous traveling, some thirty years." As a boy Robin Maugham read all his uncle's short stories set in the Far East "and then determined," he says, "that one day I would visit the strange, exotic places about which be wrote. This I have done." A reading of Maugham also set Alec Waugh on his traveling career. "Were the South Seas really like that?" he wondered in the summer of 1926 after reading *The Moon and Sixpence* and *The Trembling of a Leaf.* "I had to find out for myself. I bought a round the world ticket that included Tahiti," and "I have been on the move ever since."

Names like Brenan, Quennell, and the Maughams suggest the next question: how serious artistically and intellectually can a travel book be? Is there not perhaps something in the genre that attracts second-rate talents? Certainly the travel book will have little generic prestige in today's atmosphere, where if you identify yourself as a "writer," everyone will instantly assume you're a novelist. The genres with current prestige are the novel and the lyric poem, although it doesn't seem to matter that very few memorable examples of either ever appear. The status of those two kinds is largely an unearned and unexamined snob increment from late-romantic theories of imaginative art as religion-cum-metaphysics. Other kinds of works—those relegated to simple- minded categories like "the literature of fact" or "the literature of argument"—are in lower esteem artistically because the term *creative* has been widely misunderstood, enabling its votaries to vest it with magical powers. Before that word had been promoted to the highest esteem, that is, before the romantic movement, a masterpiece was conceivable in a "non-fictional" genre like historiography or memoir or the long essay or biography or the travel book. As recently as 1918 things were different. Fiction had not yet attained its current high status. *Ulysses* was waiting in the wings, not to appear until 1922. *Á la Recherche du Temps Perdu* had not been translated. *The Magic Mountain* hadn't been written, not to mention *Les Faux-Monnayeurs, The Sound and the Fury,* and *The Sun Also Rises.* In the *Century Magazine* for February, 1918, Henry Seidel Canby felt obliged to plead for the dignity and importance of fiction, which, as an editorial in the *New York Times Review of Books* commented, the reading public was accustomed to treat with "a certain condescension." But now a similar condescension is visited on forms thought to be non-fictional. Martin Green is one who doesn't think travel books are serious. They seem to him the natural métier of the dandy. "In *Work Suspended,*" he says, "Waugh portrayed himself as a writer of detective novels; in *Brideshead Revisited,* as a painter of English country houses; these occupations, and writing travel books, were the métiers of the dandies. Notably lacking in anything large-scale, even in the dandy line—not to mention anything really serious, whether political or literary-critical." Yet between the wars writing travel books was not at all considered incompatible with a serious literary career. And who would not find *Sea and Sardinia* a better book than *The Plumed Serpent,* Forster's *Alexandria* a better book than *Maurice,* Ackerley's *Hindoo Holiday* better than the collected novels of Hugh Walpole? We can hardly condescend to the travel book when it is in that genre that Robert Byron wrote a masterpiece that (in England, at least) has outlived all but a half-dozen novels of its decade.

The problem for the critic is to resist the drowsy habit of laying aside his sharpest tools when he's dealing with things that don't seem to be fiction. It takes someone more like a common reader than a critic, someone like H. M. Tomlinson, to remind us of what's going on in these "non-fictional" genres. "We know that in the literature of travel our language is very rich," he writes; "yet as a rule we are satisfied with our certainty that these books exist. . . . We surmise vaguely that a book of travel must be nearly all background. . . . We shrink from the threat of the vigilance it will exact; we shall have to keep all our wits about us." In short, "We have the idle way of allowing books of travel to pass without the test to which poetry must submit." That "test," we can assume, is the test both of a complicated coherence and of a subtle mediation between texture and form, data and significant shape. Like poems—and like any successful kind of literary performance—successful travel books effect a triumphant mediation between two different dimensions: the dimension of individual physical things, on the one hand, and the dimension of universal significance, on the other. The one is Coleridge's "particular"; the other, his "general." The travel book authenticates itself by the sanction of actualities—ships, trains, hotels, bizarre customs, odd people, crazy weather, startling architecture, curious food. At the same time it reaches in the opposite direction, most often to the generic convention that the traveling must be represented as something more than traveling, that it shall assume a meaning either metaphysical, psychological, artistic, religious, or political, but always ethical. A travel book is like a poem in giving universal significance to a local texture. The gross physicality of a travel book's texture should not lead us to patronize it, for the constant recourse to the locatable is its convention. Within that convention, as we have seen, there is ample room for the activities of the "fictionalizing" imagination. And an active, organic, and, if you will, "creative" mediation between fact and fiction is exactly the activity of the mind exhibited in the travel book, which Samuel Hynes has accurately perceived to be "a dual-plane work with a strong realistic surface, which is yet a parable." In the 30's, he understands correctly, two apparently separated modes of perception, reportage and fable, literal record and parable, tend to coalesce, and nowhere more interestingly than in the travel book. What distinguishes the travel books of the 30's from earlier classics like *Eothen* or even *Arabia Deserta* is the way, Hynes says, these writers between the wars "turned their travels into interior journeys and parables of their times, making landscape and incident [and, we must add, in Byron, architecture]—the factual materials of *reportage*—do the work of symbol and myth—the materials of fable." And since the journey is "the most insistent of 'thirties metaphors, . . . one might say that the travel books simply act out, in the real world, the basic trope of the generation." Acting out a trope, like perceiving the metaphor lodging always in the literal, is the essential act of poetry. It is also the essential act of both traveling and writing about it.

LANGUAGE AND EVENT IN NEW WORLD HISTORY

Wayne Franklin

> It is impossible to dream long in a land of such palpable realities.
> *John Stillman Wright, Letters from the West (1819)*

One border between language and event is the point at which a traveler sets down some fact as a cluster of words. Hence the statement of Columbus in 1503: "On the day of Epiphany I reached Veragua, completely broken in spirit."[1] But this is more than a fact, or is a collection of kinds of fact. If it seems to tell a quite simple story, we must note that tale tends not merely to narrate, but also to explain, whatever it embraces. Even the relation of its parts, or the sequence of its details, has more than a narrative purpose.[2] One may say of that statement from Columbus, for instance, that if he really was at Veragua, it was *not* Epiphany—which in a sense the rest of his sentence suggests.[3] There have been great incongruities in this voyage (as in his whole career), and his letter becomes a conscious inventory of them, a tale which attempts to comprehend what has occurred. Statements throughout the text have the tensely balanced structure seen in the "Veragua" sentence: an assertion of the expected order of things, a location in space and time, an assessment of the real order of events and feelings. "Epiphany" in this case is neither just a date nor just a spiritual occasion, neither pure fact nor pure symbol. It describes instead a meeting point of human (and divine) scheme within the temporal world. By implication, this holy day would be the perfect moment for the realization of the voyager's goals; but by implication, too, it here threatens to become simply another unit of secular time.

"Veragua" seems at first like the means by which that threat is expressed, but in fact it has its own spiritual suggestions. Curiously, it is a possible Spanish compound with intriguing connotations (*ver*, to see; *vera*, border, edge; *veras*, reality truth—and *agua*, water). Columbus himself states, however, that the term is a native one, and he provides for it earlier in his letter a gloss which is even more attractive than any which might be invented from the Spanish: the inhabitants of Nicaragua, he writes, "gave me the names of many places on the sea-coast where they said there was gold and goldfields too. The last of these was Veragua, about twenty leagues away" (Cohen, 287). Suddenly the tension of his later statement is enriched: the day of the Lord's manifestation, the arrival at a place of promised earthly reward, the sense of a letdown, of bare survival—a time, an event, a place, an emotional state. We thus have a structure of ironic modification that centers on a verb which is not without coloration in a world where simple arrival is hard to achieve, and which balances across itself and established European occasion and a realized New World feeling—which transmits through the place which it touches, through that exotic and promising word "Veragua," a complete reversal of expectation. To arrive in such a fashion is to be still distant from what was sought. Yet there is a strange completion here nonetheless, for Veragua itself had impelled the voyage which ended so bitterly along its shore—its role in reality (and in the sentence) was to act as both a departure and a conclusion, a shifting point of reference for the traveler. One may say that everything Columbus did from the first moment he heard this place-name until he found the place itself was an education in language, in the relation of words to things in America.[4]

In Columbus, as in other travel writers, that relation is a complex and involved affair. Though we tend to think of such figures as preeminent "men of action" for whom writing was a necessary rather than a chosen task, their view of what they wrote in fact was quite sophisticated. And they often turned to writing with an urgency which suggests that it was a means of self-understanding, an essential way of shaping their lives after the fact. They seem, too, to have been painfully aware of the many problems which language posed for people separated as they were from their own world. There was the almost universal issue of native languages, to begin with, and hence the constant need for translation (and guesswork) as well as for some conceptual grasp of the proliferation of tongues in the New World.[5] The contact with native groups was a form of cultural shock which was expressed most poignantly in the initial failure of even a verbal understanding between red and white. Likewise, the profusion of unknown natural objects in America placed an extra burden on the traveler's mind and language, as did the frequently tangled web of European events in this hemisphere of strange peoples and strange sights. Wherever he turned, the New World traveler seemed to be faced with strains on the one cultural tool by which he might hope to organize his life and explain it to others who had not shared in it.

Such strains first appeared when a European could find neither the proper words nor suitable Old World analogues for American facts. Thus Cortés had to admit in one of his letters to Charles V that the palace of Montezuma was "so marvelous" that it would be "impossible to describe its excellence and grandeur." This disclaimer is, of course, a description of sorts, since we know from it something about the building which Cortés professes himself unable to portray. And it has a certain conventional tone which one might find in comment about any exceptional *Old* World structure. But Cortés will not let his reader rest with a sense of the excellent and grand qualities of the palace. He goes on: "Therefore, I shall not attempt to describe it at all, save to say that in Spain there is nothing to compare it with."[6] There is here a struggle beyond any convention, a sense of the new which the writer will not abridge. Even more touching, for the insight which it offers into the dilemma faced by Cortés, is his attempt to describe the native market in Mexico City. He begins by listing the items sold in it ("lime, hewn and unhewn stone, adobe bricks, tiles, and cut and uncut woods of various kinds," states one catalog; "onions, leeks, garlic, common cress and watercress, borage, sorrel, teasels and artichokes," runs another), and then concludes in a thick-tongued apology—"Finally, besides those things which I have already mentioned, they sell in the market everything else to be found in this land, but they are so many and so varied that because of their great number and because I cannot remember many of them nor do I know what they are called I shall not mention them" (103–4). At the limits of his known world, Cortés appears to have encountered the boundaries of his familiar language, and of the culture implicit in it.

The literary situation of the New World traveler, even in periods much later than that of Cortés, was to be rich in such themes. The struggle to include New World phenomena within the order of European knowledge, and to do so by "naming" them, remained at the heart of the form well into the nineteenth century. But it would be misleading to describe this problem of "inexpressibility" (or others related to it) only as a literary issue. The difficulty with words was, finally, a difficulty with the things to which particular words referred, or for which no appropriate Europeans terms could be found. The challenge which Cortés faced when he tried to write about his experience reflected the ones which arose when he tried to act in the world that he could not easily describe. Indeed, the recognition that his language was inadequate to what he perceived was itself an event, a consequence of his voyage which became a kind of "static" in his medium—and hence a sign of his general position in America. As an actor and author alike, he underwent a formidable cognitive test. If we can view his political career in the New World as an attempt to make the void of American space (and the intertices of Spanish authority there) yield power, we likewise can see his literary efforts as an allied attempt to fill the almost aggressive silence of the West with words, to convert "noise" into meaningful sound.[7]

In some ways, the stylistic problems which Cortés and other American travelers discovered when they tried to write about their experience were the indirect result of their historical uncertainties. But style in the broader sense, as world view, itself had an effect on the making of history. Particularly in colonial settings, where the replication of old forms is a controlling impetus to new action, language develops a priority of its own. As the means by which colonial agents make their reports to the home government (and do so with a clear understanding of what they are expected to say), language comes to exert a subtle influence on how life in the colony is conceptualized, even perceived or carried on. The range of admissible statement predetermines both the manner of reportage and the conduct of those affairs which will be subject to review. That Cortés knew in general what Charles V would like to hear (as well as what his own opponents in the New World were likely to tell the monarch) certainly affected how he addressed the issues raised by his bold departure from expected action. Moreover, such canons of allowable speech also shaped the manner in which he perceived and acted in the world of Mexico. The reportable was the feasible and the conceivable as well. The special languages of colonial order, of Old World government, of Christianity, of, finally, perception itself—all these dialects surrounded Cortés like a series of expanding yet constraining rings, each of them forcing on him a decorum of act and word. His attempt to persuade Charles V that his expedition was legal was aimed at including his accomplishments within such limits. The problem of "naming" native culture thus was extended into the very heart of all he did in America.[8]

As a vehicle of political and intellectual control, European language imposed similar strictures on any traveler in America. But it also possessed, even in these functions, a certain reassuring power. Removed from the tangible environment of their culture, travelers came to rely on this most portable and most personal of cultural orders as a means of symbolic linkage with their homes. More than any other emblem of identity, language seemed capable of domesticating the strangeness of America. It could do so both by the spreading of Old World names over New World places, people, and objects, and by the less literal act of domestication which the telling of an American tale involved. Moreover, it could provide voyagers just departing for America with a set of articulated goals and designs by which the course of Western events actually might be organized beforehand. This ability to "plot" New World experience in advance was, in fact, the single most important attribute of European language. Like the expectations about what a New World report ought to contain (or omit), it entailed a faith in the almost magical power of words which was part of a larger European assumption about the immutable correctness of Old World culture. The imperative in either case was for the traveler to resist that corruption of home order for which the distance was a synonym. But the plot of any given undertaking was concrete in a way that the generalized canons which Cortés recognized were not. It suggested that certain acts were to be performed, certain ends pursued, certain desires fulfilled. By its own articulate understanding of the present venture as a type of the whole colonial effort, it provided for a detailed test of Old World perceptions. The voyager was converted into a conscious hero of European order, and the ideal sketch of his future career became a romantic allegory of victory in the West.

Under the best of conditions, such a sketch should have been fleshed out by the voyage which it described. The final report already was implicit in the initial design, and in so much detail that the traveler's career should have moved from the word through a circle of experience which would lead him once more to a point of verbal composition. The burden of this circular route would be, in the simplest sense, the endurance of European intent through all the trials of realization. The completed report would indicate that Old World words indeed could control American events, that art could organize a multitude of unseen (and perhaps even unforeseen) circumstances. The predicted plot would cease to exist only in a conditional mood; it would become fully indicative, an accomplished fact.

Particularly in the New World, however, the art of prediction proved to be a very uncertain thing. Few European "artifacts" were as subject to loss or perversion here as the word, especially the word which was aimed at a prior formulation of some actual fate. American travel books tell us, most of all, about the enormous Old World energies which went into the attempt at controlling the West by means of the symbol system of language. As structures of language in their own right, they offer a double commentary on this general effort. And in their own imperfection as texts—their frequent lack of literary polish, their incompletion and outright loss, their often eloquent concern with the failures of verbal art—they portray that effort as at best a mixed success. The nervous silence of Cortés over the sheer profusion of Mexican things hints at a wild energy in native culture for which his own origins, and the language in which those origins are embodied, have left him radically unprepared. More poignantly, the desperate condition of Columbus on Jamaica borders on a silence of a quite different sort, a collapse of personality triggered by psychic and spiritual displacements far beyond those of Cortés. The rich ambiguity of his "Epiphany" stems from a sense of disorientation which makes that word and the whole cultural order it implicates— the "plot" of redemptive history which he hoped to extend by his voyages— seem merely verbal. It is as if the word has lost its best connotations and has begun to acquire a set of almost satanic meanings, meanings that suggest the power of American facts to alter the most essential of Old World definitions. The juxtaposition of "Epiphany" and "Veragua" becomes a model of the loss of control to which so many American travelers found themselves subjected. We sense here the discovered plot of colonial life—not the grand plot of idealized experience, the easy passage through a strange place, but rather the steady attrition of all such formulas, the slow accumulation of knowledge won at great expense. What is almost inexpressible for Columbus is not the phenomenal surface of America but the spiritual depth of his own being. The question no longer concerns what the new lands are; it centers instead on who the voyager is, on how his experience has altered his essential nature. His location thus matters only as a sign of his identity. And his language, difficult and even eccentric, mirrors the extremity of his actual fate. It also suggests the degree to which the tensions between word and thing, art and fact, self and experience, were to become the heart of future New World life, and future American writing.

More than anything else, the West became an epistemological problem for Europe. Though the influx of American gold upset the economy of Spain, its biggest beneficiary, and though the imperial struggle to which America gave birth disrupted the already tense political situation in the whole of Europe, it was simply the fact of "another" world which most thoroughly deranged the received order of European life.[9] The issue was not merely an informational one. It involved so many far-reaching consequences that the very structure of Old World knowledge—assumptions about the nature of learning and the role of traditional wisdom in it—was cast into disarray. While colonial expansion was succeeding in the West, Europe in many ways was retreating from the implications of its American involvement. Faced with a flood of puzzling facts and often startling details, the East was almost literally at a loss for words. Having discovered America, it now needed to make a place for the New World within its intellectual and verbal universe.[10] Like the voyagers who had accomplished this feat, Europe itself was in a state of confusion, a kind of panic which was the natural result of perceptual stress.

But the European discovery also had its more positive surfaces. Such a tangible venture into the unknown typified the modern desire to test received ideas by reference to experience. The finding of new lands (once their newness was accepted) was seen as a signal proof that the ancients had been woefully ignorant of their world, and that contemporary achievements did not reflect uniformly the supposed devolution of culture since classical times.[11] The uncertainty caused by a rapid rearrangement of geographical learning thus might be a promise of future advances. And any new voyages partook in varying degrees of this sanguine exultation. Even if it suggested that a systematic understanding of the world would be hard to construct, the expansion of knowledge about the physical universe emerged as a confident sign that innovation was a worthy and fruitful cultural asset. To depart from the shores of Europe was to depart as well from the confines of ancient error and scholastic deduction.

It was from his sense of this benign meaning which European involvement in America might have that Francis Bacon, primary theorist of a new epistemology and staunch opponent of medieval scholasticism, extrapolated Columbus himself into a symbol of bold modernity. His voyager was decidedly not the man of terminal doubt and despair whom we encounter in the Jamaica letter of 1503. He was instead a figure of hopeful departures, a man whose discovery of a "new world" suggested the possibility that "the remoter and more hidden parts of nature" also might be explored with success. The function of Bacon's *Novum Organum*—his title recalled both *mundis novus* and *novus orbis terrarum*—was to provide for the scientific investigator the kind of encouragement which the arguments of Columbus prior to 1492 had provided for a Europe too closely bound to traditional assumptions. Just as Columbus had sought to convince his contemporaries that, in Bacon's view, "new lands and continents might be discovered besides those which were known before," so Bacon himself was trying to "offer hope" that other new facts might be discovered and understood.[12]

Given his high anticipations, it is understandable that Bacon should have distorted the career of Columbus. But Bacon recognized in his own sphere an uncertainty akin to that which Columbus and other voyagers in fact encountered. He noted that "the universe to the eye of the human understanding is framed like a labyrinth," and he went on to elaborate the metaphor which he derived from classical myth into a figure with distinctly modern overtones. It became, in fact, an image of the traveler's difficult path through nature rather than a reference to the contrived mazes of human art. The labyrinth of the world, he wrote, presented "on every side so many ambiguities of way, such deceitful resemblances of objects and signs, natures so irregular in their

lines and so knotted and entangled," that progressing in it was a very difficult task. Moreover, since "the way . . . through the woods of experience and
particulars" had to be located "by the uncertain light of the sense," perception itself might prove to be a labyrinth of false understandings about an ambiguous world. To make matters worse, those who pretended to "offer
themselves for guides" through the woods were in fact so "puzzled" in their
own right that they actually might "increase the number of errors and wanderers." The only solution—modest in nature but radical in implication—was
to be "guided by a clue," a detail culled from the vast world of experience.
One had to insure that "the whole way from the very first perception of the
senses" would be kept clear of waylaying distractions. Hence one had to have
"a sure plan" for finding that path (12–13).

Ideally, the *Novum Organum* was to be such a plan. But Bacon's own way
had been an uncertain one, as he noted: "I have committed myself to the uncertainties and difficulties and solitudes of the ways and, relying on the divine assistance, have upheld my mind both against the shocks and embattled
ranks of opinion and against my own private and inward hesitations and
scruples, and against the fogs and clouds of nature, and the phantoms flitting
about on every side, in the hope of providing at last for the present and future
generations guidance more faithful and secure." The despair which resulted
from such a lonely condition became one of the abiding themes of his book.
But it was balanced by Bacon's insistence that the desired renewal (or "in-
stauration") of learning could be achieved only by accepting the doubt which
an exposure to experience required. By such means, by "dwelling purely and
constantly among the facts of nature," one might hope to lead people "to
things themselves, and the concordances of things"—and hence away from
the traditional errors produced by habits of inattentive speculation (13–14).
One had to enter experience with a full recognition of its deceits, and one's
own shortcomings; the despair had to be faced and accepted. But it was
Bacon's final point that the world could be trusted to yield in return for one's
labors a sense of order beyond doubt, a sense of "concordance."

Columbus and other travelers offered hope precisely on this last point.
Their experience provided Bacon with a body of richly concrete images by
which he could express his otherwise rather vague method. Yet their use was
not merely decorative. Among other things, Bacon was constructing a model
of travel itself as a worldly and intellectual act: the great discoverer was his
hero as much as his metaphor. Indeed, to turn the argument around, we can
say that science was a metaphor for exploration as well as vice versa, that
Bacon's use of Columbus provided travel with a philosophy which it had not
previously had. It was as an example of the subject-object problem which

consumed Bacon's interest that the traveler became a significant figure for him. Separated from that cultural context which, in Bacon's view, so often warped the individual's sense of the natural world, a traveler appeared to enjoy a certain primary contact with the universe. His very separation was a hopeful sign, even if it also represented the possibility for despair that Bacon recognized, the possibility for utter disorientation.

Most germane here is Bacon's view of language, and particularly of the bearing between words and things. In a very real way, words were the villain of his new method, for the library as a symbolic enclosure of authority stood opposite to that "road" which he urged his readers to pursue.[13] By breaking through the enclosures of traditional space, the American traveler also was breaking the bonds of received language. He was penetrating through words to the things which they so often misrepresented, as well as through the texture of fantasy and speculation which had its only real existence in human speech. Though themselves, his reports were composed in a language of events which was hard, concrete, specific—polar to the language used by those "talkers and dreamers who . . . have loaded mankind with promises" (85). The traveler's disclosure might be broken and uneven, fragmentary and problematic; but these traits would be its signal strength, since (like the "short and scattered sentences" of "the first and most ancient seekers after truth" [84]) they would make his form reflect the actual, honest condition of experience. The science of travel pointed one to an uncertain exegetical path through the given world, not toward an edifice of wit akin to that "fabric of human reason which we employ in the inquisition of nature"—"badly put together and built up, and like some magnificent structure without any foundation" (3). The verbal results of travel, like Bacon's own tentative "aphorisms," would be of value insofar as they suggested the mystery and discontinuity of life itself. The source of literary style was to be the style of experience which Bacon advocated; in the literal New World or the "new continent" of knowledge (104), words were to be the signs of things. And words in this sense finally would move beyond doubt: for, Bacon wrote, "a method rightly ordered leads by an unbroken route through the woods of experience to the open ground of axioms" (80).[14]

The actual traveler's route, of course, rarely was "unbroken." Bacon's stress on the exemplary innovations of Columbus points us, in fact, to that moment in 1503 when, faced with the accumulated "uncertainties and difficulties and solitudes" of his own way, the voyager found himself so far beyond the bounds of his known world that knowledge and words alike were threatened with a severe breakdown. His situation then was a paradigm of the losses which European culture as a whole was to incur in its passage across the ocean. Yet some of those losses were to become for later times the hopeful sign of American distance and difference: the "badly put together and built up" structure of Old World order seemed to have suffered a needed renovation during its transport to America. The grand journey which had produced New World culture thus was seen in part as an act of Baconian growth, a set of related departures which, taken together, composed a plot of stunning comic success.

The motives behind the fabrication of this plot were related to those which moved Bacon himself. The panegyrics with which America was loaded down, particularly after the Revolution (that most conspicuous and conscious New World departure,) suggest by the very pitch of their expression that Americans in fact were aware of the doubtful way they had pursued already and still were to follow. To assert not only that the movement west was benign, but also that it was in essence one movement—united in all its reaches, converging in its shape—was to give to the diverse and often fugitive events of early New World history an aesthetic composure inherent in the experience of transplantation. That the United States came to be itself synonymous with the feeling of "hope" was both a mark of exultation and a sign of the need to be exultant in the face of spatial and cultural uncertainties. Like any individual traveler, the expanding nation felt the continual stress of honest western new facts. When the Federalist Fisher Ames responded to Jefferson's purchase of Louisiana by exclaiming, "We rush like a comet to infinite space," he was voicing a sense of dislocation by no means confined to members of the antifrontier faction. Jefferson himself had his own fears about the West.[15]

Rushing into space, for all the anxiety it might cause, was an established American custom. Travel had served from the beginning as an actual and a metaphoric link among countless individuals and groups. And it would continue to perform similar functions for at least the next hundred years. "If God were suddenly to call the world to judgment," wrote the Argentine educator and statesman Domingo Sarmiento in 1847, "He would surprise two-thirds of the population of the United States on the road like ants. . . . In the United States you will see evidence everywhere of the religious cult which has grown up around that nation's noble and worthy instruments of its wealth: its feet."[16] As long as one could assume that all this motion was not in the main a dispersion of energies and individuals—that it aimed at some agreed-upon social goal—one might view it as a sign of America's "arrival." But agreement about the destination was far less than universal. What was clear was that people were on the move (and on the make), that transience had emerged as a central fact of American life.

The sense of community does not necessarily require a high degree of literal stability in a population. But a high level of movement certainly is not the best condition under which to develop sustained and sustaining values. A persistent paradox in America has been the focus of communal energies on a set of actions and attitudes which are extracommunal by nature. Of these focal points perhaps none has been more pervasively evoked than the traveler's pose, the Columbian stance of eager discovery. As Bacon's argument suggests, the traveler is almost by definition an iconoclast; his departure, even if he goes in the service of "home" purposes, hints not merely at the general authority of experience, but also (and more subversively) at the prospective power of individual life beyond the horizon. The American ritual of travel thus was centered from the start on an act which was antiritualistic in essence, which pointed the single traveler or the small group away from the very place where the continual reenactment of significant deeds would help to solidify communal ties.

One solution to this particular paradox was the investment of travelers with a weight of social conscience that in reality they often lacked. The figure of the pioneer, for example, became a conveniently sanitized American traveler, a person whose primary interest supposedly lay in the almost holy replication of social form. Opposite to this forerunner was the white renegade, the denier of home order; and in between the two was an array of figures whose loyalties were mixed or unclear: the solitary man like Daniel Boone, who despite his longing for solitude was an agent of expansion; the fugitive from home, to whom a certain indulgence was extended; the degenerate wanderer, whose path led to a complete inversion of settled values. This cast of national characters was rich in its range, though rather narrow in its meaning. And conspicuously absent from it was that waylaid traveler about whose existence the records of early America offer abundant evidence. So strong was the need to control the possibility for loss in New World experience (except as the deserved condition of certain stereotyped opponents) that Columbus himself became a man of delayed but final victory. Writing in the wake of the Revolution, Joel Barlow went so far as to resuscitate him in *The Vision of Columbus*, and to reveal to him by that poem, "the numerous blessings which have arisen to mankind from the discovery of America." Acknowledging the mistreatment to which Columbus was subjected in his own era, Barlow sought to dismiss that fact by extending the plot of his life— by making the Revolution itself an installment of his glorious Discovery.[17]

Barlow's rather absurd gesture back to 1492 was the act of a single literary artist. Yet it was typical of a dispersed cultural attempt to emphasize the supposed continuities of American experience. The ability of language to map out a literal traveler's future way was converted in such visions into a power of retrospective plotting. The vocabulary of American memory was selected according to the needs of present life, and in this process the active historical quality of much early New World writing was hidden beneath a new aesthetic or even mythological surface. The whole of colonial life acquired an exalted meaning; it became almost a literary "action," a comedy which was to be repeated with greater finish and sophistication (so the assumption ran) throughout the glorious future.

Such attempts at communal memory and definition resulted, ironically, in a militant forgetfulness, a refusal to read in the national past the record of any terminal disorientation. The sufferings of the "pioneers" became, by a kind of sacrificial arrogation, acts of pious devotion to the brighter American future enjoyed by their memorialists.[18] There were, to be sure, significant hesitations—especially as historians and literary figures began to investigate seriously, in the later nineteenth century, what Washington Irving called (regarding his researches on Columbus) the "complete labyrinth" of early New World prose.[19] But in the popular mind the American story was a simple affair, a tale of progressive achievements and solidified order. Even the narratives of wilderness disaster could be seen as integral parts of a victory, touches of pathos finally clarified by the record of subsequent white possession. Almost nowhere in the popular press was the panegyric decorum broken, and it reached, too, into the efforts of people less easily swayed by such fashionable understandings. Even a "new" historian like F. J. Turner, who sought to convert local history from a stronghold of provincial piety into a means of close and critical knowledge, and who lamented in 1893 the ignorance which partly allowed Americans to draw easy lessons from their past, in fact shared the common sense of New World history as a series of linked and enlarging plots. Industrialization was for him the final stage in an action which began in 1492. And if Turner sounded in his Columbian Exposition speech a note of termination which made the era of Columbus seem distant, perhaps unreachable, he averred in an earlier draft of the address that with "a connected and unified account of the progress of civilization across this continent" would come both a "real national self-consciousness" and a sense of "the significance of the discovery made by Columbus."[20] Though he called for detailed research and for a historical vocabulary attentive to the facts of New World experience, he applied to events a certain prior language which was orthodox and hence, in many ways, blinding.

NOTES

1. For the record, his Spanish is: *Dia de la Epifania llegué á Veragua, ya sin aliento.* I quote from R. H. Major, ed. and trans., *Select Letters of Christopher Columbus* (New York: Corinth Books, 1961 [1847]), p. 181; Major renders *ya sin aliento* as "in a state of exhaustion."

2. Arthur C. Danto, *Analytical Philosophy of History* (Cambridge: Cambridge University Press, 1968), is a suggestive study of narrative language—and particularly of the problems entailed in historical narration. I have relied on its formulations throughout the present book.

3. That is to say, Epiphany was a European fact which was irrelevant to Veragua. Columbus, of course, would not have accepted such a premise outrightly; but see his comment later in this letter: "Here in the Indies I am cut off from the prescribed forms of religion, alone in my troubles, sick, in daily expectation of death and surrounded by a million hostile savages full of cruelty, and so far from the Holy Sacraments of the Blessed Church that my soul will be forgotten if it leaves my body" (J. M. Cohen, ed. and trans., *The Four Voyages of Christopher Columbus* [Baltimore: Penguin Books, 1969], pp. 303-4).

4. Columbus heard of Veragua while he was working his way to the East along the Caribbean coast of Central America. Before actually stopping to investigate the reports of gold and goldfields at Veragua, however, he went past it, then turned around and slowly went back to the place, encountering severe bad weather en route. Ironically, the grandson of Columbus (Luis Colón) was granted in 1536, for renouncing his hereditary claims over all of the West Indies, the title of "Duke of Veragua," along with substantial tracts of land in Central America. See Samuel Eliot Morison, *Admiral of the Ocean Sea* (Boston: Little, Brown, 1942), p. 609.

5. Lee Eldridge Huddleston, *Origins of the American Indians: European Concepts, 1492–1729* (Austin: University of Texas Press, 1967), describes the sometimes absurd speculations of Old World thinkers about the number and nature of American languages; Margaret T. Hodgen, *Early Anthropology in the Sixteenth and Seventeenth Centuries* (Philadelphia: University of Pennsylvania Press, 1964) offers rich comments on allied topics—particularly on the canons of cultural observation and description which hampered the accurate perception of non-European life (see esp. chap. 5, "Collections of Customs: Modes of Classification and Description," pp. 162–206).

6. Cortés, *Letters from Mexico*, ed. and trans. A. R. Pagden (New York; Grossman Pub., 1971), p. 109.

7. The political background of the Cortés Expedition was complex. Technically, Cortés was the subordinate of Diego Velázquez (governor of Cuba) who dispatched him in 1518 to locate the Grivalja fleet which had been sent out the previous year, and to round up Christian captives in Yucatan. But Cortés looked upon the Spanish record in the Caribbean as a sad accumulation of selfish acts and upon Velázquez himself as a prime example of what was wrong with colonial government. Hence he exploited his literal distance from Cuba, converting it into a base of power which he shored up by claiming that, according to ancient Spanish custom, his followers had rejected the corrupt authority of Velázquez and had chosen Cortés as their lawful leader. The expedition went so far as to found the "city" of Vera Cruz as a sign that it constituted a true community, and therefore had the right to elect a commander other than the one provided by colonial hierarchy. Complicating matters was the fact that Velázquez, who opposed the actions of Cortés, himself chafed under the authority of Diego Colón, the son of Columbus and hereditary Admiral of the Indies, and petitioned Charles V (as Cortés did) for a grant of direct power. That Cortés did not receive approval from

Charles until 1522 was a crucial fact which influenced all he did and said up to that date. See Elliott's essay in *Letters from Mexico*.

8. Harry Elmer Barnes, *A History of Historical Writing* (2d rev. ed.; New York: Dover Pub., 1962), discusses the changes caused by the "era of discovery" in the practice of European historiography—changes which upset the "special languages" that I mention (see esp. pp. 136–47). His basic point, with which I agree, is that the need to report on countless topics about which little had been written previously caused a sudden, dramatic expansion of historiographical practice. On the other hand, I share with, Hodgen and others a sense of the subtle ways in which old prejudices and biases affected the white apprehension of nonwhite cultures, and hence survived in the very texture of the "new" histories. Roy Harvey Pearce's study of *The Savages of America* (rev. ed.; Baltimore: Johns Hopkins Press, 1965), is a reminder of how closed European minds, and Old World languages, were when it came to confronting native life—of how old biases might actually be extended by those works which on their surface seemed to mark the departure of Europe from its medieval provincialism.

9. J. H. Elliott, *The Old World and the New: 1492–1650* (Cambridge: Cambridge University Press, 1970), is particularly good on the difficult intellectual reaction of Europe to America.

10. Edmundo O'Gorman, *The Invention of America* (Bloomington: Indiana University Press, 1961), demonstrates superbly the process by which this accommodation was achieved.

11. Federico Chabod's essay on "The Concept of the Renaissance," trans. David Moore in *Machiavelli and the Renaissance* (New York: Harper & Row, 1965), discusses briefly but brilliantly the effect of the discovery on modern views of ancient knowledge.

12. Bacon, *The New Organon and Related Writings*, ed. Fulton H. Anderson (Indianapolis: Bobbs-Merrill, 1960), pp. 13, 91. In trying to answer the opinion that the ancients knew far more than the moderns, Bacon writes: "Nor must it go for nothing that by the distant voyages and travels which have become frequent in our times many things in nature have been laid open and discovered which may let in new light upon philosophy. And surely it would be disgraceful if, while the regions of the material globe—that is, of the earth, of the sea, and of the stars—have been in our times laid widely open and revealed, the intellectual globe should remain shut up within the narrow limits of old discoveries" (p. 81).

13. Of the "library" as a symbolic locale, Bacon wrote, "If a man turn to the library, and wonder at the immense variety of books he sees there, let him but examine and diligently inspect their matter and contents, and his wonder will assuredly be turned the other way. For after observing their endless repetitions, and how men are ever saying and doing what has been said and done before, he will pass from admiration of the variety to astonishment at the poverty and scantiness of the subjects which till now have occupied and possessed the minds of men" (pp. 82–83). The real task now was "the opening and laying out of a road for the human understanding direct from the sense" (p. 79).

14. On the issue of a scientific literary style, see also Bacon's comment that "experience has not yet learned her letters" (p. 97), and those many places where he assaults the "foolish and apish images of worlds" so common in older philosophy (p. 113 and *passim*).

15. I quote Ames from Merrill D. Peterson, *Thomas Jefferson and the New Nation* (New York: Oxford University Press, 1970), p. 772; for Jefferson himself, see below, chap.1.

16. *Travels in the United States in 1847*, trans. and ed. Michael Aaron Rockland (Princeton: Princeton University Press, 1970), pp. 133, 149.

17. *The Vision of Columbus, A Poem in Nine Books* (Hartford: Hudson and Goodwin, 1787), "Dedication" (to Louis XVI). Barlow's involvement in the Scioto land frauds in France shortly after the poem appeared suggests how mixed the "blessings" of America might be, how closely linked panegyrics and promotional imposture often were in New World history; see Durand Echeverria, *Mirage in the West: A History of the French Image of American Society to 1815* (Princeton: Princeton University Press, 1968), pp. 116–74, for the various western frauds perpetrated in France during Barlow's Period.

18. The 1930s leftist Josephine Herbst rendered the kind of arrogation I am thinking of here when she had a character deliver an unctuous speech on "Capital" to a Chamber of Commerce meeting in Deadwood, S.D. "I do not intend to speak lightly of the prospector," the speaker remarks. "Rather I would pay him tribute. He is the Columbus in civilization, tracking the wilderness as Columbus did the sea to discover a new world. He finds and tells the public, others come in and possess the land. They who bought the Comstock mines and manipulated their stocks have grown rich and gained seats in the Senate Chamber while the discoverer died poor, alone and friendless. Such lives have not been a failure"—*Pity Is Not Enough* (New York: Harcourt, Brace, 1932), p. 345.

19. Quoted by Justin Winsor, *Christopher Columbus* (Boston: Houghton, Mifflin, 1891), p. 57.

20. "Problems in American History," in Ray Allen Billington, ed., *Frontier and Section* (Englewood Cliffs, N.J.: Prentice-Hall, 1961), p. 29.

SCRATCHES ON THE FACE OF THE COUNTRY; OR, WHAT MR. BARROW SAW IN THE LAND OF THE BUSHMEN

Mary Louise Pratt

> It is not difficult to transpose from physics to politics [the rule that] it is impossible for two bodies to occupy the same space at the same time.
>
> *Johannes Fabian,* Time and the Other

My title originated in the following passage from John Barrow's *Account of Travels into the Interior of Southern Africa in the Years 1797 and 1798*, published in London in 1801. It is an excerpt from a fairly lengthy portrait describing the Bushmen:

> In his disposition he is lively and chearful; in his person active. His talents are far above mediocrity; and, averse to idleness, they are seldom without employment. Confined generally to their hovels by day, for fear of being surprised and taken by the farmers, they sometimes dance on moonlight nights from setting to the rising of the sun. . . . The small circular trodden places around their huts indicated their fondness for this amusement. His cheerfulness is the more extraordinary, as the morsel he procures to support existence is earned with danger and fatigue. He neither cultivates the ground nor breeds cattle; and his country yields few natural productions that serve for food. The bulbs of the iris, and a few gramineous roots of a bitter and pungent taste, are all that the vegetable kingdom affords him. By the search of these the whole surface of the plains near the horde was scratched.[1]

Any reader recognizes here a very familiar, widespread, and stable form of "othering." The people to be othered are homogenized into a collective "they," which is distilled even further into an iconic 'he' (the standardized adult male specimen). This abstracted "he"/ "they" is the subject of verbs in a timeless present tense, which characterizes anything "he" is or does not as a particular historical event but as an instance of a pregiven custom or trait. (In contexts of conquest, descriptions are likely to focus on the other's amenability to domination and potential as a labor pool, as Barrow's does in part.) Through this discourse, encounters with an Other can be textualized or processed as enumerations of such traits. This is what happens in modern anthropology, where a fieldwork encounter results in a descriptive ethnography. It also happens in ethnography's antecedent, the portrait of manners and customs. Barrow's portrait of the Bushmen is an instance of this old and remarkably stable subgenre, which turns up in a wide range of discursive contexts. Barrow's portrait is directly continuous in many respects with those in Christopher Columbus' letters or in John Mandeville's *Travels* (circa 1350), where we find the following account of the inhabitants of the Isle of Natumeran:

> Men and women of that isle have heads like hounds; and they are called Cynocephales. This folk, thereof all they be of such shape, yet they are full reasonable and subtle of wit. . . . And they gang all naked but a little cloth before their privy members. They are large of stature and good warriors, and they bear a great target, with which they cover all their body, and a long spear in their hand.[2]

The only trace of a face-to-face encounter, real or imagined, in this description is the fact that it begins with the body as seen/scene. Such portraits conventionally do so, commonly with the genitals as the crucial site/sight in the "bodyscape"—as they are in Barrow's Bushmen portrait, where he devotes two full pages to the supposed genital peculiarities of Bushmen men and women.[3]

The portrait of manners and customs is a normalizing discourse, whose work is to codify difference, to fix the Other in a timeless present where all "his" actions and reactions are repetitions of "his" normal habits. Thus, it textually produces the Other without an explicit anchoring either in an observing self or in a particular encounter in which contact with the Other takes place. "He" is a *sui generis* configuration, often only a list of features set in a temporal order different from that of the perceiving and speaking subject. Johannes Fabian has recently used the phrase "denial of coevalness" to refer specifically to this temporal distancing.[4]

Manners-and-customs description could serve as a paradigmatic case of the ways in which ideology normalizes, codifies, and reifies. Such reductive normalizing is sometimes seen as the primary or defining characteristic of ideology. In this view, as Catherine Belsey puts it in her lucid study *Critical Practice*, "the task of ideology is to present the position of the subject as fixed and unchangeable, an element in a given system of differences which is human nature and the world of human experience, and to show possible action as an endless repetition of 'normal' familiar action."[5] That, it would seem, is exactly what Mr. Barrow is doing in his description of the Bushmen. Indeed, he is doing so at an especially critical ideological juncture, for nowhere are the notions of normal, familiar action and given systems of difference in greater jeopardy than on the imperial frontier. There Europeans confront not only unfamiliar Others but unfamiliar selves; there they engage in not just the reproduction of the capitalist mode of production but its expansion through displacement of previously established modes. It is no accident that, in the literature of the imperial frontier, manners-and-customs description has always flourished as a normalizing force and now retains a kind of credibility and authority it has lost elsewhere. It is a mainstay of travel and exploration writing; and under the rubric of ethnography, it has been professionalized into an academic discipline which serves, in part, to mediate the shock of contact on the frontier.

If the discourse of manners and customs aspires to a stable fixing of subjects and systems of differences, however, its project is not and never can be complete. This is true if only for the seemingly trivial reason that manners-and-customs descriptions seldom occur on their own as discrete texts. They usually appear embedded in or appended to a superordinate genre, whether a narrative, as in travel books and much ethnography, or an assemblage, as in anthologies and magazines.[6] In the case of travel writing, which is the main focus of this essay, manners-and-customs description is always in play with other sorts of representation that also bespeak difference and position subjects in their own ways. Sometimes these other positionings complement the ideological project of normalizing description, and sometimes they do not.

In what follows, I propose to examine this interplay of discourses in some nineteenth-century travel writing chiefly about Africa. While Barrow's work is not prominent on anybody's mental bookshelves these days, readers will recognize such names as David Livingstone, John Speke, James Grant, Richard Burton, Mungo Park, or Paul Du Chaillu. During the so-called opening up of central and southern Africa to European capitalism in the first half of the nineteenth century, such explorer-writers were the principal producers of Africa for European imaginations—producers, that is, of ideology in connection with the European expansionist project there. What I hope to underscore in these writings is not their tendency towards single, fixed subject positions or single, fixed systems of difference. Rather, I wish to emphasize the multiplicity of ways of codifying the Other, the variety of (seemingly)

fixed positions and the variety of (seemingly) given sets of differences that
they posit. European penetration and appropriation is semanticized in numerous ways that can be quite distinct, even mutually contradictory. In the
course of examining discursive polyphony in these travel writings, I hope to
stress the need to consider ideology not only in terms of reductive simplification but also in terms of the proliferation of meanings.

In the case of Barrow's *Travels* (and in a great many other books of its
kind), manners-and-customs descriptions of indigenous peoples are appended
to or embedded in the day-to-day narrative of the journey. In contrast to what
we might expect, that day-to-day narrative is most often largely devoted not
to Indiana Jones-style confrontations with the natives but to the considerably less exciting presentation of landscape. Barrow's book exemplifies this
practice. Though he was traveling as a colonial official, charged with mediating disputes between Boer colonists and indigenous peoples, and though he
was traveling with a large party of Europeans, Boers, and Hottentots, human
interaction plays little role in his narrative.[7] Instead, page after page catalogs
without a thrill what Barrow likes to call "the face of the country." For example:

> The termination of the Snowy mountains is about twelve miles to the north-
> eastward of Compassberg; and here a port or pass through them opens upon a plain
> extending to the northward, without a swell, farther than the eye could command.
> Eight miles beyond this pass we encamped for the night, when the weather was
> more raw and cold than we had hitherto experienced on the Sneuwberg. The thick
> clouds being at length dissipated by the sun, the Compassberg shewed itself white
> near the summit with snow.
> The division of Sneuwberg comprehends a great extent of country. The moment
> we had ascended from the plains behind Graaf Reynet to those more elevated of
> Sneuwberg, the difference of the face of the country and its natural productions
> were remarkably striking. [*A*, 1:244–451]

And so it goes for the better part of some three hundred pages. The organization of this passage is basically narrative, but it is a strange, attenuated kind
of narrative because it does everything possible to minimize all human presence, including that of the people whose journey is being told. In the main,
what is narrated proves to be a descriptive sequence of sights/sites, with the
travelers present chiefly as a kind of collective moving eye which registers
these sights. Their presence as agents scarcely registers at all. In the opening
sentence, for instance, we must infer that Barrow and his party traveled the
twelve miles, passed through the mountains, and so on. The cold is presented
chiefly as a fact about the weather, not as a discomfort they endured. The

drama here is produced not by the adventures of the travelers but by the changing "face of the country." Signs of human presence, when they occur, are also expressed as marks upon this face; the human agents responsible for those signs are themselves rarely seen.[8] In the following passage, for example, the villages are less important than the rivers and streams, and there is no sign of inhabitants:

> The following day we passed the Great Fish river, though not without some difficulty, the banks being high and steep, the stream strong, the bottom rocky, and the water deep. Some fine trees of the willow of Babylon, or a variety of that species, skirted the river at this place. The opposite side presented a very beautiful country, well wooded and watered, and plentifully covered with grass, among which grew in great abundance, a species of indigo, apparently the same as that described by Mr. Masson as the *candicans*.
>
> The first night that we encamped in the Kaffr country was near a stream called *Kowsha*, which falls into the Great Fish River. On the following day we passed the villages of *Malloo* and *Tooley*, the two chiefs and brothers we had seen in Zuure Veldt, delightfully situated on two eminences rising from the said streamlet. We also passed several villages placed along the banks of the *Guengka* and its branches, and the next day we came to a river of very considerable magnitude called the *Keiskamma*. [A, 1: 190–91]

Here again, the travelers' struggle to cross the river is not narrated but expressed in a much more mediated fashion, as an enumeration of the traits of the river that produced the difficulty. The speaking and experiencing self is as effaced as it is in the ethnographic portraits.

Barrow's book exemplifies a kind of discursive division of labor common to much travel writing of his time: the main narrative deals with landscape, while indigenous peoples are represented separately in descriptive portraits. This division of labor is hinted at in the passage that I quoted at the beginning of this paper. At two points there, the timeless ethnographic present tense is interrupted by a narrative past tense: (1) the trodden places around the Bushmen's huts *indicated* their fondness for dancing, and (2) by the Bushmen's search for roots, the surface of the surrounding plains *was scratched*. These two past tense verbs refer to the specific occasion of Barrow's visit to the Bushmen. What they historicize, however, is his encounter not with *them* but with traces they have left on the lanscape—-their scratches on "the face of the country."

In this kind of writing, the "face of the country" is presented chiefly in sweeping prospects that open before or, more often, beneath the traveler's eye. Such panoramic views are an important commonplace of European aesthetics, of course, and that undoubtedly accounts for much of their appeal here. In the context of exploration writing like Barrow's, however, such views acquire and serve to familiarize meanings they may not have on the domestic front. Barrow's own language suggests, for example, the fantasy of dominance that is commonly built into this stance. The eye "commands" what falls within its gaze; the mountains "show themselves" or "present themselves"; the country "opens up" before the European newcomer, as does the unclothed indigenous bodyscape.[9] At the same time, this eye seems powerless to act or interact with this landscape. Unheroic, unparticularized, without ego, interest, or desire of its own, it seems able to do nothing but gaze from a periphery of its own creation, like the self-effaced, noninterventionist eye that scans the Other's body.

This discursive configuration, which centers landscape, separates people from place, and effaces the speaking self, is characteristic of a great deal of travel writing in the last century, especially the literature of exploration and especially that which aspired to scientific status. By mid-century it predominates among the Victorian explorers who fought so fiercely (with each other) to "win" the source of the Nile for England (and themselves). Despite his vastly greater involvement with African peoples and his more historical view of things, Livingstone readily writes about southern Africa from the same distanced and self-effaced stance that Barrow assumed. Consider, for instance, this excerpt from his *Narrative of an Expedition to the Zambesi* (1857):

> Ten or fifteen miles north of Morambala stands the dome-shaped mountain Makanga, or Chi-kanda; several others, with granitic-looking peaks, stretch away to the north, and form the eastern boundary of the valley; another range, but of metamorphic rocks, commencing opposite Senna, bounds the valley on the west. After steaming through a portion of this marsh, we came to a broad belt of palm and other trees, crossing the fine plain on the right bank. Marks of large game were abundant. Elephants had been feeding on the palm nuts, which have a pleasant fruity taste, and are used as food by man. Two pythons were observed coiled together among the branches of a large tree, and were both shot. The larger of the two, a female, was ten feet long. They are harmless, and said to be good eating.[10]

Again, the Europeans are present mainly as the deleted subjects of passive verbs ("were observed," "were shot"); indigenous inhabitants are there only in the abstract ("man"); even the rest of the animal kingdom is reduced to traces. The presence of the "harmless" female python and her mate and their unexplained destruction suggest at least one of the ideological dimensions underlying this kind of description—a fantasy of returning the country to an Edenic or even pre-Adamic condition. (I will be looking shortly at some other versions of this fantasy in the work of Alexander von Humboldt and Du Chaillu.)

The explicit project of these explorer-writers, whether scientists or not, is to produce what they themselves referred to as "information." Their task, in other words, was to incorporate a particular reality into a series of interlocking information orders—aesthetic, geographic, mineralogical, botanical, agricultural, economic, ecological, ethnographic, and so on. To the extent that it strives to efface itself, the invisible eye/I strives to make those informational orders natural, to find them there uncommanded, rather than assert them as the products/producers of European knowledges or disciplines. In turn, those knowledges are the producers/products of a project they likewise presuppose and seldom bespeak. It is the project whereby, to use Daniel Defert's terms, Europe "takes consciousness of itself . . . as a planetary process rather than [as] a region of the world."[11] This nineteenth-century exploration writing rejoins two planetary processes that had been ideologically sundered: the expansion of the knowledge edifice of natural history and the expansion of the capitalist world system. While the former had set for itself what Humboldt was to call "the great problem of the physical description of the globe,"[12] the latter was undertaking nothing less than the physical appropriation and transformation of that globe in what Barrow calls "the spirit of commerce and adventurous industry" (A, 1: 1).

In these information-producing travel accounts, the goal of expanding the capitalist world system is, as a rule, acknowledged in prefaces, but only there. Livingstone—the missionary—explicitly states in his preface the connection between information, landscape, and commercial expansion. He declares that his account "is written in the earnest hope that it may contribute to the *information* which will cause the great and fertile continent of Africa to be no longer kept wantonly sealed, but made available as a *scene* of European enterprise" (N, p. 2; my emphasis). In the body of the text, European enterprise is seldom mentioned, but the sight/site as textualized consistently presupposes a global transformation that, whether the I/eye likes it or not, is already understood to be underway. In scanning prospects in the spatial sense—as landscape panoramas—this eye *knows itself* to be looking at prospects in the temporal sense—as possibilities for the future, resources to be developed, landscapes to be peopled or repeopled by Europeans. These prospects are one of the main criteria of relevance in the landscape descriptions. They are what make a plain "fine" or make it noteworthy that a peak is "granitic" or a country "well-wooded." Occasionally the force of these criteria is made explicit. At the conclusion of Speke's description of newly discovered Lake Victoria Nyanza (1864), for instance, the "pleasure of the mere view" vanishes in favor of "those more intense and exciting emotions which are called up by the consideration of the commercial and geographical importance of the *prospect* before me."[13] More commonly, European aspirations are introduced in the form of a reverie that overtakes the seer as he ponders the panorama before him. Speke's partner Grant, arriving at Lake Victoria Nyanza, is inspired to make a sketch, "dotting it with imaginary steamers and ships riding at anchor in the bay," apparently dissatisfied with the African boats already plying its waters.[14] As he scans Lake Tanganyika, Burton declares that the view "wants but a little of the neatness and finish of Art—mosques and kiosks, palaces and villas, gardens and orchards—contrasting with the profuse lavishness and magnificence of nature." The view already includes African "villages, cultivated lands, the frequent canoes of fishermen," but they are not enough for Burton.[15] And again, only the traces of people are apparent—not the people themselves. Such reveries abound in nineteenth-century exploration writing. They are determined, in part, by highly generalized literary conventions. It is conventional, for instance, for romantic prospect poems to move from description into reverie. In exploration writing, however, the reverie convention often very specifically projects the civilizing mission onto the scene.

Apart from such relatively explicit allusions, the will to intervene is also present in more ubiquitous and more mystified ways in these writings. It emanates from an unknown site behind the speaking "I"—behind the periphery of what is seen, from a seat of power that should probably be identified with the state. I find it useful here to recall the current conception of the state as a form of public power separate from both ruler and ruled, constituted most basically by the exclusive right to exercise legitimate violence within a certain defined territory.[16] It is not surprising, then, to find the emissaries of the European states on the imperial frontier concerning themselves, above all, with defining territory and scanning perimeters, even though territorial possession was not yet part of the imperial strategy. Nor is it surprising that these subjects positioned themselves in their discourse as neither ruler nor ruled, neither actor nor acted upon, but as invisible, passive, and personally innocent conduits for information. The normalizing, generalizing voice that produces the ethnographic manners-and-customs portraits is distinct from but complementary to the landscape narrator. This voice scans the prospects of the indigenous body and body politic and, in the ethnographic present, abstracts them out of the landscape that is under contention and away from the history that is being made—a history into which they will later be reinserted as an exploited labor pool.

Throughout much nineteenth-century exploration writing on the imperial frontier, this discursive configuration effaces the European presence and textually splits off indigenous inhabitants from habitat. It is a configuration which, in (mis)recognition of what was materially underway or in anticipation of what was to come, verbally depopulates landscapes. Indigenous peoples are relocated in separate manners-and-customs chapters as if in textual homelands or reservations, where they are pulled out of time to be preserved, contained, studied, admired, detested, pitied, mourned. Meanwhile, the now-empty landscape is personified as the metaphorical "face of the country"—a more tractable face that returns the European's gaze, echoes his words, and accepts his caress.[17] Exploration certainly lends itself to heroic narrative paradigms of adventure, personal prowess, obstacles overcome and prizes won, and explorers in the nineteenth century were certainly seen as heroes. Yet most of them did not write themselves as heroes. Indeed, one of the most striking aspects of this informational branch of travel writing is the way it reverses and refuses heroic priorities: it narrates place and describes people. Its European protagonists are everywhere on the margins of their own story, present not as heroes but as effaced information-producers gazing in from a periphery. This discourse was by no means the only one used in travel writing at the time, and I will mention one of the contending discourses below. But until the last decades of the century, when the notorious scramble for Africa changed the whole character of European intervention, it was one of the most powerful discourses.

An important consequence of the European's self-effacement in this literature is that it is possible to narrate the journey and "to other" the Other while maintaining silence about the actual, specific contacts going on between the European travelers and the indigenous peoples they encounter. No conventional textual space calls on the Europeans to portray their interactions, recount their dialogues, report the Other's voices, or display the concrete working out of relations on the spot. Perhaps the most telling conventional silence surrounds the day-to-day interaction within the traveling party—between the European masters and the indigenous laborers who accompanied and far outnumbered them. The two groups coexisted in ongoing struggle, held together in complex relations of mutual dependency, extreme exploitation, and tremendous instability. As we learn from other accounts, conflict between Europeans and indigenous laborers was an endemic fact of life on frontier expeditions. Relations were constantly breaking down and erupting into violence, constantly being renegotiated or enforced by brutality. And regardless of an individual traveler's own attitudes and intentions, the Europeans in this domain of struggle were charged with installing the edifice of domination and legitimizing its hierarchy.

In a discourse that effaces the European and displaces the African, however, all this can be consigned to an invisible, often trivialized domestic sphere behind the back of the land-scanning eye. Significantly enough, when "life in camp" does get textualized, it often appears in the guise of a sketch of a "typical day": "Soon after we halt, the spot for the English is selected, and all regulate their places accordingly and deposit their burdens" (N, p. 193). As with ethnographic portraits, life in camp is represented in a normalized discourse that bleaches out irregularity, uncertainty, instability, violence. In other cases, the accompanying indigenous laborers appear in the narrative as an exotic, comic, or pathetic spectacle for the eyes of the European. The European remains a steadfastly self-effaced seer, whose only intervention seems to be to define the perimeters of what is seen (in this case, the camp). In such instances, the master/slave relation that organizes the traveling group often expresses itself through the mediated form of an emotional projection. The indigenous labor pool is commonly employed (textually speaking) to express or reproduce the desires and fears of their European masters—to carry their emotional baggage, as it were. Burton, in whom these strategies are much in evidence, writes that on reaching Lake Tanganyika, "all the party seemed to join with me in joy," or that after a day without water, "the impatience and selfishness of thirst showed strongly in the Baloch." Grant measures the beauty of Lake Victoria Nyanza by the fact that "even the listless Wanyamuezi came to have a look at its waters. . . . The Seedees were in raptures."[18]

All the works I have mentioned so far have concerned Africa, but this discursive configuration is by no means peculiar to African travel writing. Indeed, one of the most programmatic instances of the strategies I have been examining here appears in the work of a writer who was gazing on the wilds of South America at the same time that Barrow was writing up his African expeditions. Alexander von Humboldt, foiled by Napoleon Bonaparte in his attempts to arrange a trip to Egypt, secured in 1799 from the court of Spain carte blanche to travel in Spanish America. It was an extraordinary coup— except for coastal shipping, the region had been virtually sealed off to legitimate travelers for over two centuries. Humboldt, accompanied by his friend Aimé Bonpland, was gone nearly five years. If the task of Barrow and the others was to invent Africa for the domestic subjects of the British Empire, Humboldt's discursive challenge was to reinvent Spanish America for a

Europe well aware that Spanish control over the region was coming to an end. It was a time for replacing outdated orthodoxies like the old *leyenda negra* ("black legend") of Spanish cruelty with new ones that would provide the ideological framework for the rush of European (notably British) capital that would take over the region once it gained independence from Spain.

Like his counterparts in Africa, Humboldt traveled and wrote in the name of science and, like them, one of his principal discursive strategies was to reduce America to landscape and marginalize its inhabitants. In the preface to his *Personal Narrative of Travels to the Equinoctial Regions of the New Continent* (1816), he extols the American wilderness and discounts both the indigenous cultures and three hundred years of Spanish colonial society:

> In the ancient world, nations, and the distinctions of their civilization form the principal figures on the canvass; in the new, man and his productions almost disappear amidst the stupendous display of wild and gigantic nature. The human race here presents but a few remnants of indigenous hordes, slightly advanced in civilization; or that uniformity of manners and institutions which has been transplanted by European colonists to foreign shores. [*PN*, 1: xliii–xliv]

The *Personal Narrative*, neither very personal nor very narrative, chiefly deploys Humboldt's own brand of landscape appreciation, aimed at harmonizing science and aesthetics. The work is most remembered for its pages and pages of scientistic rhapsody like this:

> After walking two hours, we arrived at the foot of the high chain of the interior mountains, which stretches from the east to the west; from the Brigantine to the Cerro de San Lorenzo. There, new rocks appear, and with them another aspect of vegetation. Every object assumes a more majestic and picturesque character; the soil, watered by springs, is furrowed in every direction; trees of gigantic loftiness, and covered with lianas, rise from the ravins; their bark, black and burnt by the double action of the light and the oxygen of the atmosphere, forms a contrast with the fresh verdure of the pothos and dracontium, the tough and shining leaves of which are sometimes several feet long, The parasite monocotyledones take between the tropics the place of the moss and lichens of our northern zone. As we advanced, the forms and grouping of the rocks reminded us of the scenes of Switzerland and the Tyrol. [*PN*, 3: 9]

Though Humboldt includes some manners-and-customs portraits, current indigenous inhabitants hold little interest for him despite the fact that, as in similar cases in Africa, large numbers of them were engaged in transporting him, his delicate instruments and bulky collections up the Cordillera and down the Amazon. This silence weighs the more heavily if we recall that Humboldt was by profession a mining inspector and that one of his charges on the South American trip was to scout for exploitable precious metals. It can hardly have escaped him that these "few remnants of indigenous hordes" were the labor pool on whose backs would rest the advancement of capitalism in the region. Indeed, Humboldt might well be trying to escape this fact when he writes people out of the place completely.

But Humboldt, like Barrow, is interested in the traces the natives have left on the "face of the country." Indigenous America attracts Humboldt in the guise of archaeological ruins, and he devotes many pages to the description of sites, artifacts, and mythologies almost completely unknown or forgotten in Europe. Without detracting front Humboldt's considerable achievement, we cannot overlook the ideological import of this effort. It valorizes America by European standards—America too had its great cities—but, by the same token, it reduces current American societies to vestiges of a glorious past. In this framework, disruption and transformation of indigenous ways of life do not destroy anything of current value but simply dispose of scraps or leftovers in preparation for a new transformation.[19]

What that transformation is supposed to be is hardly in doubt, though, as with the African explorers, Humboldt seldom mentions it explicitly within his travel narrative. In his book, too, it turns up in the form of fantasy. Humboldt ends his introduction to the *Personal Narrative* by sketching out the landscape of his dreams, and it too depicts America as the future "scene of European enterprise":

> If then some pages of my book are snatched from oblivion, the inhabitant of the banks of the Oroonoko will behold with extasy, that populous cities enriched by commerce, and fertile fields cultivated by the hands of freemen, adorn those very spots, where, at the time of my travels, I found only impenetrable forests, and inundated lands. [*PN*, 1: l–li]

I have argued that this scientistic, information-oriented branch of travel writing played an extremely important role in producing the domestic subjects of nineteenth-century European capitalist expansion. We would be justified in calling it the hegemonic form of othering at the time, at least on the imperial frontier. But its hegemony was much contested—perhaps more contested than most—because this informational kind of writing suffered from one serious defect: it was terribly boring. Despite many writers' very real talent for description, despite their passionate engagement with nature, despite their often sincere fascination and admiration for indigenous peoples, the commentators on these works never stopped bemoaning how dull they made it all. Humboldt himself was one such commentator. In the introduction to his *Personal Narrative*, he diagnoses the problem as follows:

In proportion as voyages have been made by persons more enlightened, and whose views have been directed towards researches into descriptive natural history, geography, or political economy, itineraries [that is, travel narratives] have partly lost that unity of composition, and that simplicity which characterized those of former ages. It is now become scarcely possible to connect so many different materials with the narration of other events; and that part which we may call dramatic gives way to dissertations merely descriptive. The great number of readers, who prefer an agreeable amusement to solid instruction, have not gained by the exchange. [*PN*, 1: xii–xiii]

This discursive dilemma was much discussed in the literature of the time. While bourgeois readers welcomed the authority of science and the totalizing project of natural history, there was no denying that these had drastically upset the balance of teaching and delighting that had long been considered the great virtue of travel books. Despite his recognition of the loss involved, Humboldt clearly cast his lot with science. His preferred solution to the dilemma was to abandon travel narrative altogether in favor of nonnarrative (or nondramatic) forms such as his famous *Political Essay on the Kingdom of New Spain* (1811) or descriptive sketches like his popular *Views of Nature* which sought to harmonize science and aesthetics. Humboldt undertook his *Personal Narrative* only reluctantly seven years after his trip and abandoned it nine years later, after the third volume.

But contrary to what Humboldt suggests in his preface, "dramatic" travel narrative full of "agreeable amusement" was far from being a relic of "former ages." Indeed, it had entered a full-fledged renaissance in the 1780s; by the time Humboldt was writing, dramatic travel narrative constituted one of the strongest voices contrasting with the scientific, informational tradition Humboldt was trying to codify. Humboldt certainly knew this, and his attempt to consign this writing to "former ages" points up the programmatic thrust of the comments in his preface.

The contrastive voice is that of a kind of travel writing most aptly described as sentimental, which emerges in the 1780s. Early authors of such narratives on Africa include James Bruce, François Le Vaillant, Richard Lander, and Mungo Park. One well-known example, set in South America, was John Stedman's *Narrative of a Five Year's Expedition against the Revolted Negroes of Surinam* (1796), which recounted a famous love story between its hero and a mulatta slave named Joanna. The tale, which Humboldt surely knew, gave rise to a German play, *Die Sklavin in Surinam*, which ran in Frankfurt in 1804; it revived in London in a popular story, "Joanna; or, The Female Slave," and again in 1840 in Eugène Sue's *Aventures D'Hercule Hardi*.

In this sentimental literature, dramatization predominates and heroic paradigms are retained. Its discursive agenda is sharply distinct from that of the informational tradition. The traveler is the protagonist of the journey and the primary focus of the account. It narrates the journey as an epic-style series of trials and challenges, of various kinds of encounters—often erotic ones—where indigenous inhabitants occupy the stage alongside the European. If the other discourse is called informational, this one should be called experiential. It consulates its authority by anchoring itself not in informational orders but in situated human subjects, notably (but not always) the European protagonist.

These features are well illustrated by one of the most characteristic commonplaces of this branch of writing, the courtly encounter. In this conventional scene, the European male portrays himself arriving in a village and presenting himself to the local patriarch and his court. One of the classics of the sentimental genre, Park's *Travels in the Interior Districts of Africa* (1799)—a personal favorite of Humboldt's and one of the most popular travel books of its time—includes several such scenes:

> We reached at length the king's tent, where we found a great number of people, men and women, assembled. Ali was sitting upon a black leather cushion, clipping a few hairs from his upper lip; a female attendant holding up a looking glass before him. He appeared to be an old man, of the Arab cast, with a long white heard; and he had a sullen and indignant aspect. He surveyed me with attention and inquired of the Moors if I could speak Arabic; being answered in the negative he appeared much surprised, and continued silent. The surrounding attendants and especially the ladies were abundantly more inquisitive; they asked a thousand questions, inspected every part of my apparel, searched my pockets and obliged me to unbutton my waistcoat, and display the whiteness of my skin; they even counted my toes and fingers, as if they doubted whether I was in truth a human being.[20]

In its eroticism, its dramatization of contact, the realization of both Europeans and Africans as characters, the situating of the European at the center of a stage—someone else's stage—this passage contrasts strongly with the writing of Barrow and the others. These sentimental texts are characteristically dialogic in the Bakhtinian sense: they represent the Other's voices in dialogue with the voices of the self and often tender the Other some credibility and equality. The European's relations with the Other are governed by a desire for reciprocity and exchange. Estrangement and repulsion are presented as entirely mutual and equally irrational on both sides. Parody and self-parody abound. Park, displaying his tummy and toes, looks as ridiculous as the narcissistic Ali. This discourse does not explicitly seek a unified, authoritative speaking subject. The subject here is split simply by virtue of realizing itself as both protagonist and narrator, and it tends to split itself even further in these accounts. As this passage demonstrates, the self sees, it sees itself seeing, it sees itself being seen. And always it parodies both itself and the Other.

Ethnographic manners-and-customs description occurs in this kind of travel writing too, but it tends to be much more entwined with narrative episodes. Landscape is textualized mainly as a source of comfort or discomfort, danger or safety for the protagonist or as a trigger for an outpouring of emotion. In this famous and highly conventional scene from Park's *Travels*, Park has just been plundered and left for dead by a band of thieves:

> After they were gone I sat for some time looking around me with amazement and terror. Whichever way I turned, nothing appeared but danger and difficulty. I saw myself in the midst of a vast wilderness, in the depth of the rainy season, naked and alone; surrounded by savage animals, and men still more savage. I was five hundred miles from the nearest European settlement. All these circumstances crowded at once on my recollection, and I confess that my spirits began to fail me. [*T*, p. 225]

The "influence of religion" saves Park from despair; the flora and fauna around him become not pieces of information to be gathered but triggers for meditation on human psychology and Providence's benevolent presence:

> At this moment, painful as my reflections were, the extraordinary beauty of a small moss, in fructification, irresistibly caught my eye. I mention this to show from what trifling circumstances the mind will sometimes derive consolation; for though the whole plant was not larger than the top of one of my fingers, I could not contemplate the delicate conformation of its roots, leaves, and capsula, without admiration. *Can that Being (thought I) who planted, watered, and brought to perfection, in this obscure part of the world, a thing which appears of so small importance, look with unconcern upon the situation and sufferings of creatures formed after his own image?—surely not!* [*T*, p. 225]

If the land-scanning, self-effacing producer of information is associated with the state, then this sentimental, experiential voice must be associated with that critical sector of the bourgeois world, the private sphere, home of the solitary, introspecting Individual. Though positioned at the center rather than on a periphery, and though composed of a whole body rather than just an eye, this European too is passive and incapable of intervention. The voice, too, is innocent, though its innocence lies not in its self-effacement but in its isolation and vulnerability. In short, European expansionism is as mystified in this literature as in the informational kind. Park's explicitly commercial assignment—"rendering the geography of Africa more familiar to my countrymen and . . . opening to their ambition and industry new sources of wealth and new channels of commerce"—is readily lost from sight in the drama of personal survival and the satisfying symmetry of reciprocal exchange (*T*, p. 2).

I have focused on Park's book here because it was a popular classic and a touchstone for many writers such as Humboldt, who cited it often. In his introduction to the *Personal Narrative*, Humboldt names Park's *Travels* as an example of the simple (that is, naive) dramatic travel writing that has (supposedly) been overtaken by science. The other example Humboldt gives is that of the Spanish chroniclers of the sixteenth century. Although Humboldt is right to identify his influential contemporary with a different discursive configuration, the attempt to link Park with a lost past must be seen as an attempt to marginalize a discourse that was to remain, throughout the next century, a main challenger to the hegemony of information.

Much more could be said about this subject-centered, experiential discourse and its challenge to scientific, informational travel writing. Comments like Humboldt's—and there are many of them—demonstrate how readily the two discourses were distinguished in the early nineteenth century. In the 1860s, their contrast is nicely reasserted in the frontispieces of two books that were published within months of each other—the first edition of Livingstone's *Narrative of an Expedition to the Zambesi* (1861) and a new edition of Park's *Travels* (1860). Livingstone's frontispiece depicts "a bird's-eye view of the cataracts of the Zambesi"; his title page shows a drawing of a lone, unidentified African. Park's frontispiece depicts himself with five companions arriving at the "majestic Niger"; the title page again shows Park, in the scene quoted earlier, forlorn and destitute while a group of native bandits flees in the background.

Ultimately, the sentimental, experiential discourse, like the private sphere to which it attached, mounted little more than an internal critique of the hegemony of information. But it could be a powerful critique. In 1861, for example, the Franco-American explorer Du Chaillu published his *Explorations and Adventures in Equatorial Africa*, a relentless travesty of the scientific, informational tradition. In the following excerpt, for instance, Du Chaillu marshals the same strategies found in Park's writing to construct an explicit parody of the kind of landscape description I discussed at the beginning of this essay. The passage starts out as a conventional promontory scene and moves into a particularly American fantasy of the civilized future (Du Chaillu is in the Congo):

From this elevation—about 5000 feet above the ocean level—I enjoyed an unob-
structed view as far as the eye could reach. The hills we had surmounted the day
before lay quietly at our feet, seeming mere molehills. On all sides stretched the
immense virgin forests, with here and there the sheen of a water-course. And far
away in the east loomed the blue tops of the farthest range of the Sierra del Crystal,
the goal of my desires. The murmur of the rapids below filled my ears, and, as I
strained my eyes toward those distant mountains which I hoped to reach, I began to
think how this wilderness would look if only the light of Christian civilization
could once be fairly introduced among the black children of Africa. I dreamed of
forests giving way to plantations of coffee, cotton, and spices; of peaceful negroes
going to their contented daily tasks; of farming and manufactures; of churches and
schools

It is obvious why this vision makes contemporary readers uncomfortable;
but it was intended, in its unabashed explicitness about colonialism and its
suggestion of slavery, to make Du Chaillu's contemporaries uncomfortable
too. For the guilty fantasy is punished by a new arrival on the scene—both a
symbol of the Other and the dreamer's own double. The passage continues:

and, luckily raising my eyes heavenward at this stage of my thoughts, [I] saw
pendent from the branch of a tree beneath which I was sitting an immense serpent,
evidently preparing to gobble up this dreaming intruder on his domains.

My dreams of future civilization vanished in a moment. Luckily my gun lay at
hand.[21]

Probably this serpent (not snake) has come directly from the Garden of Eden
to remind everyone that, among other things, the cozy pastoral/plantation
fantasy is forbidden fruit which will lead eventually to expulsion from the
garden. On waking from his reverie, Du Chaillu turns to the real instrument
of the civilizing mission, his gun. He shoots this guilty self (referring to the
serpent as "my black friend"), but that does not save it from the grip of the
colonized themselves. Du Chaillu's bearers immediately roast the snake and
eat it ("dividing the body into proper pieces") in a kind of macabre last sup-
per, a symbolic cannibalism in which the great white father himself is unable
to partake. (Du Chaillu pointedly does not eat snake, or gorilla.) He mocks
himself for being a "poor, starved, but *civilized* mortal," concluding, "so
much for civilization, which is a very good thing in its way, but has no business in an African forest when food is scarce."[22] So the subject splits and authority shifts in this writing—Du Chaillu is now parodier, now parodied,
now dreamer, now demystifier of his own dream, now provider of civilization, now deprived by civilization, now hunter, now hunted.

In contrast and in chorus with the monochromatic and self-effacing stance of information, then, books like Du Chaillu's asserted multivalence, confusion, self-doubt, and self-parody. Indeed, as might be expected, the multivalent sentimental discourse can be found erupting into predominantly informational texts, especially at points of intense ideological contradiction. This brings me back, finally, to Mr. Barrow's visit with the Bushmen. For though that encounter results in a conventional ethnographic portrait like the others in his book, the violence and wild contradictoriness of the encounter itself register in the text as a breakdown of the information-producing subject.

By the time Barrow appears, the Bushmen have become difficult to find and impossible to visit. After decades of being hunted down for sport by Boers bent on genocide, the survivors have become wary and skilled at hiding. The only way to see them is to literally invade one of their camps. Barrow reluctantly hires some Boer farmers to do just that, with the condition they not fire unless fired upon. The Boers' nocturnal attack from a hilltop on the Bushmen "horde" encamped below brings Barrow tumbling off his sunlit promontory, down into the center of things, in a veritable descent into hell:

> We instantly set off on full gallop, and in a moment found ourselves in the middle of the kraal. Day was but just beginning to break; and by the faint light I could discover only a few straw-mats, bent each between two sticks, into a semicircular form; but our ears were stunned with a horrid scream like the war-hoop of savages; the shrieking of women and the cries of children proceeded from every side. I rode up with the commandant and another farmer, both of whom fired upon the kraal. I immediately expressed to the former my very great surprise that he, of all others, should have been the first to break a condition which he had solemnly promised to observe, and that I had expected from him a very different kind of conduct. "Good God!" he exclaimed, "have you not seen a shower of arrows falling among us?" I certainly had seen neither arrows nor people, but had heard enough to pierce the hardest heart. [A, p. 272]

It would be difficult to exaggerate how starkly this episode stands out in Barrow's book. It is the only nocturnal scene in the work, the only instance of direct dialogue, the only occasion when Barrow dramatizes himself as a participant (seer and seen), the only outburst of emotion, the only outbreak of violence, one of the few scenes where people and place coincide, the only time sound prevails over sight, and Barrow asserts a limit on his authority to apprehend and represent his surroundings. What provokes the crisis here, it seems, is the fact that Barrow chooses to exercise his right to legitimate violence—not, however, in order to defend himself or his fellow citizens or the state but simply in order to get a look. The ideology that construes seeing as an inherently passive and innocent act cannot be sustained, and Barrow's discursive order breaks down along with his humanitarian moral order. Into that break the sentimental, dramatic counterdiscourse inserts itself, so that Barrow winds up in a confessional mode. "Nothing," he later says, "could be more unwarrantable, because cruel and unjust, than the attack made by our party upon the kraal" (A, p. 291).

But this confessional mode is certainly not a transformative one, for Barrow's loss of innocence produces no new self, no new position of speech. His descent into colonial hell would be repeated by the writers who followed him, at first as an interruption of the calm textual surface produced by the disembodied gaze. Later, as northern Europe created its own black legend in the horrific, genocidal scramble for Africa, that descent would become the canonical story about Africa—the fall from the sun-drenched dreamy prospect into the heart of darkness.

Partly because it has never been fully professionalized or "disciplined," travel writing is one of the most polyphonous of genres. It therefore richly illustrates the fact that, in practice, ideology works through proliferation as well as containment of meaning. The texts I have discussed in this essay were among the most popular travel books of their day; readers of these books received nothing like a fixed set of differences that normalized self and Other in fixed ways. They were presented with multiple sets of differences, multiple fixed subject positions, multiple ways of legitimizing and familiarizing the process of European expansion. The discourses complemented each other even as they challenged and demystified each other. Even if we agree that, as Rosalind Coward and John Ellis put it, "the production of an ideological *vraisemblable* . . . is the result of a practice of fixing or limiting of the endless productivity of the signifying chain," we must recognize that such practices or fixings often work only because they are multiple and endlessly productive.[23] It takes a lot of ideological *vraisemblables* to keep the world comprehensible, especially in a day-to-day way. Proverbs work, after all, only because there is a proverb for everything—there is always going to be more than one way to skin a cat.

I am grateful to Renato Rosaldo, James Clifford, Herbert Lindenberger, Cynthia Ward, and Wlad Godzich for comments and suggestions on this paper.

NOTES

1. John Barrow, *An Account of Travels into the Interior of Southern Africa in the Years 1797 and 1798*, 2 vols. (New York, 1968), 1:283–84 (the full description of the Bushmen runs sixteen pages); all further references to this work, abbreviated *A*, will be included in the text.

2. John Mandeville, *The Book of John Mandeville*, Hakluyt Society Series 2, vol. 101 (London, 1953), p. 138.

3. This genital fixation is still very much with us, especially as regards the Bushmen. See, for example, Laurens Van der Post's popular *Lost World of the Kalahari* (New York, 1958).

4. Johannes Fabian, *Time and the Other: How Anthropology Makes Its Object* (New York, 1983), p. 35.

5. Catherine Belsey, *Critical Practice*, New Accents Series (London, 1980), p. 90.

6. Ethnographies would seem to be a counterexample to this claim, but in fact one can fairly easily show that ethnographic writing is inextricably tied to personal narrative. Indeed, this tie is a symptom of a serious contradiction between ethnographic methods and ethnographic discourse. See my "Fieldwork in Common Places," in *Writing Culture: The Poetics and Politics of Ethnography*, ed. James Clifford and George Marcus (forthcoming, 1986).

7. In 1795, the British took over the Dutch Cape Colony by force, on the pretext that it was in danger of being occupied by the French, who had just overrun Holland. George Macartney was appointed governor of the newly annexed colony; he took Barrow with him as his personal secretary. Appointed Macartney's representative to the interior, Barrow made several lengthy journeys there to settle internal grievances between Boer settlers and Dutch colonial officials, to establish a sense of the British presence to both Boer and indigenous populations, and to begin documenting the geography of the interior, so far almost completely unmapped. He traveled, as was the customs by ox-drawn wagon, and relied for supplies, fresh oxen, and often lodging on the Boer settlers, who were required to provide such services for state representatives in exchange for powder and shot. The cape was returned to the Dutch in 1802 and retaken by the British in 1806. Barrow eventually succeeded Joseph Banks as head of the African Association (the same body that employed Mungo Park) and ended up much involved in polar exploration. See Christopher Lloyd, *Mr. Barrow of the Admiralty: A Life of Sir John Barrow, 1764–1848* (London, 1970).

8. If such human landmarks are too many or too conspicuous, they must themselves be thematized in this discourse—for instance, as ruins or vestiges of some past civilization.

9. For more on this "monarch of all I survey" strategy, see my "Conventions of Representation: Where Discourse and Ideology Meet," in *Contemporary Perceptions of Language: Interdisciplinary Dimensions*, ed. Heidi Byrnes, Georgetown University Roundtable in Languages and Linguistics (Washington, D.C., 1982), pp. 139–55.

10. David and Charles Livingstone, *Narrative of an Expedition to the Zambesi and its Tributaries; and of the Discovery of the Lakes Shirwa and Nyassa, 1858–1864* (New York, 1866), pp. 101–2; all further references to this work, abbreviated *N*, will be included in the text.

11. Daniel Defert, "La collecte du monde: Pour one étude des récits de voyages du seizième au dix-huitième siècle," in *Collections passions*, ed. Jacques Hainard and Roland Kaeht (Neuchatel 1982), p. 26; my translation.

12. Alexander von Humboldt and Aimé Bonpland, *Personal Narrative of Travels to the Equinoctial Regions of the New Continent during the Years 1799–1804*, trans.

Helen Maria Williams, 3d ed., 2 vols. (London, 1822), 1: viii; all further references to this work, abbreviated *PN*, will be included in the text, with volume and page numbers in parentheses.

13. John Hanning Speke, *What Led to the Discovery of the Source of the Nile* (Edinburgh, 1864), p. 307; my emphasis.

14. James Augustus Grant, *A Walk across Africa; or, Domestic Scenes from My Nile Journal* (Edinburgh, 1864), p. 196; all further references to this work, abbreviated *W*, will be included in the text.

15. Richard F. Burton, *The Lake Regions of Central Africa; A Picture of Exploration*, 2 vols. (New York, 1961), 2:43; all further references to this work, abbreviated *LR*, will be included in the text.

16. My wording here is indebted to Quentin Skinner, *Foundations of Modern Political Thought*, 2 vols. (Cambridge, 1978) as well as to Nicos Poulantzas, *State, Power, Socialism* (London, 1978).

17. This face, moreover, has apparently gotten emptier to Western eyes as time goes by Alberto Moravia wrote in 1972 of the "terrifying monotony" of African landscape: "The face of Africa bears a greater resemblance to that of an infant, with few barely indicated features, than to that of a man, upon which life has imprinted innumerable significant lines; in other words, it bears greater resemblance to the face of the earth in prehistoric times . . . than to the face of the earth as it is today" (*Which Tribe Do You Belong To?* trans. Angus Davidson [New York, 1974], p. 8).

18. Burton, *The Lake Regions*, 2:43; Grant, *A Walk across Africa*, p. 196.

19. I am reminded of the rediscovery of Egypt, which took place at the same time, in the wake of the Napoleonic invasion. There, too, the monuments of the distant past were mainly what was depicted and valorized; the glorious history of ancient Egypt was recaptured for Europe, while contemporary Egyptian life was seen as archaic and vestigial.

20. Park, *Travels in the Interior Districts of Africa, Performed under the Direction and Patronage of the African Association, in the Years 1795, 1796, and 1797* (Edinburgh, 1860), p. 109; all further references to this work, abbreviated *T* will be included in the text. Park was a Scottish physician who was sent out by the African Association which had been formed in 1785. By the time Park made his "successful" journey (i.e., he survived it), several parties sent out on the same mission had already disappeared without a trace. Park's own survival was improbable. Accompanied by a single African servant, as he tells it, he made his way through chiefdoms hostile to strangers of any kind, especially Christians. Often plundered, threatened, held captive, relying for survival on the charity of slave populations, he made his way to the Niger River and observed the crucial datum: its direction of flow (away from, not toward, the Nile). Park did not, however, succeed in reaching Timbuktu, as had been hoped. Several years later, Park led a second, much larger mission into the same region and disappeared without a trace. The story of that mission's demise was slowly pieced together by subsequent travelers.

21. Paul B. Du Chaillu, *Explorations and Adventures in Equatorial Africa* (New York, 1861), p. 83.

22. Ibid.

23. Rosalind Coward and John Ellis, *Language and Materialism: Developments in Semiology and the Theory of the Subject* (London, 1977), p. 67.

THE NEW INTERNATIONALISM

The accelerated global circulation of people, goods, and ideas of the (post)-modern era has given rise to new definitions of travel, the traveler, the community, and the nation by breaking down static definitions and demanding more dynamic, hybrid, and problematic ways of considering them. Experiences of diaspora, exile, and displacement expose the double life, the nuanced identity of the individual who straddles two or more home sites and two or more identities. Finding identity to be dynamic and multidimensional, the essays in this section investigate the hybridity of place and the processes of globalization. Like the term "transnationalism," also associated with Homi Bhabha's work, "new internationalism" describes the movements of peoples and ideas across the globe and the discourses that emerge from them, but without insisting so much on an interventionist politics or aesthetics. More than "Travel and Tourism," the essays here stress the dynamics of power, the hybridity of identity, and the multidimensionality of place and travel.

The section begins with "Border Lives: The Art of the Present" from the introduction of Homi Bhabha's *The Location of Culture* in which he uses the term I take for this section. In his essay, Bhabha argues that the trope by which we, at the end of the twentieth century (and now into the twenty-first century), locate culture is the beyond and the in-between. He argues that we need to focus on "moments or processes that are produced in the articulation of cultural differences," rather than originary narratives, and on the in-between spaces to elaborate strategies of selfhood. To do so takes into account hybridity, process, negotiation, political empowerment. He speaks of the new internationalism that is the history of diaspora, migration, displacement, exile, and that becomes the new basis for making international connections and for revisioning the human community. The in-between space is also a space of intervention where new creative inventions emerge. What he is suggesting is that with the conditions of mass movement and cultural hybridity, we need to rethink what constitutes the nation-state and our artistic representations of life and selfhood in that location. He prefers to think about the locations of cultures, of cultures in transit, rather than static, bounded States.

Geographer Doreen Massey's essay, "A Global Sense of Place," from her *Space, Place, and Gender,* addresses modern globalization and the questions it raises about place and time-space compression for theories and practices of place and mobility. Doing so, she goes beyond conventional theories that focus on the influence of capital on the ways we experience space to argue for a social theory of space. Introducing the term "power geometry," she argues that time-space compression involves complex social differentiations and degrees of control and initiation that include access to mobility. By sketching out the social and power relations of a handful of places, she demonstrates that issues of place, mobility, and power are highly complex and contextualized. She then goes forward to re-theorize place, which has often been defined as static and tied to a sense of rootedness, by de-essentializing place. Taking a look at the many identities in her own community, she argues that place has multiple meanings based on the variety of social relations, the links between people, in a given space. She makes the point that just as social interactions are processes, so too are places processes. Thus she redefines place to argue that it is "constructed out of a particular constellation of social relations, meeting and weaving together at a particular locus." Since these social relations can be stretched out over space, the local is globalized, the outside world becomes a part of the local place.

Edward Said's essay "Reflections on Exile," which first appeared in *Granta,* points out that the experience of exile is one of estrangement and sadness, a "condition of terminal loss" from the native place, which he calls the "true home." Attempting at once to comment on modern, political experiences of exile for masses of people and the experiences of literary people like himself, Said attempts to de-romanticize exile. While he acknowledges the modern ethos of estrangement for all, he strives to keep the experience of the true exile separate from the metaphor. He argues that a kind of dialectic exists between nationalism and exile. Nationalism, "an assertion of belonging in and to a place," is born out of a condition of estrangement. And exiles, because they are cut off from their roots, feel "an urgent need to reconstitute their broken lives," in part by constructing ideologies and identities of exile. Unlike Bhabha, who wants to imagine locations of culture and the porousness of nationness, Said notes that "much of the exile's life is taken up with compensating for disorienting loss by creating a new world to rule": that is why so many exiles seem to be novelists and political activists. Finally, Said suggests that exiles experience the environments of their old world and their new one contrapuntally: "For an exile, habits of life, expression or activity in the new environment inevitably occur against the memory of these things in another environment."

In "Deterritorializations: The Rewriting of Home and Exile in Western Feminist Discourse" (*Cultural Critique*), Caren Kaplan asserts that one does not have to emigrate to be an exile. Using a feminist approach to the conjunction between identity and location/relocation, Kaplan argues that people who move between cultures, languages, and configurations of power possess an "oppositional consciousness," or the ability to read and write culture on multiple levels. This consciousness involves both deterritorialization, or the displacement of identity and meaning that is coterminous with exilic dislocation, and reterritorialization, or the re-inhabitation of a world of our making. To make her point, Kaplan looks at the work of Gloria Anzaldúa, Minnie Bruce Pratt, and Michelle Cliff, all of whom experience majority culture and literature from different minority positions. Working against a romanticization of solitude and exile, Kaplan demonstrates how each of these writers manages the tensions of an oppositional consciousness and relations of power in the postmodern world.

Asking the question, "Is the Ethnic 'Authentic' in the Diaspora?" R. Radhakrishnan considers the situation of Asian- Americans and ponders the reciprocal influence of ethnics on the identity of America. From his book, *Diasporic Mediations: Between Home and Location*, the essay is based around conversations with his son, an "Indian child of the diaspora" who was born in the United States and who wonders if he is Indian or American. To answer his son's questions, Radhakrishnan ponders questions of identity, ethnicity, authenticity, and national allegiance for immigrant Indians. He reminds readers that when people move, identities and perspectives change and that all identities, personal and national, are constituted of multiple perspectives. Warning against essentializing identity or history, he points to some responses to the home country that he considers to be wrong and dangerous: forgetting, trivializing, or romanticizing the past. More appropriate is understanding the political crises in India (or the home country) because they concern Indian-Americans and because diasporic Indians have a "duty to represent India to ourselves and to the United States as truthfully as we can." Radhakrishnan also makes the point that as the identity of the immigrant is affected by the adopted country, the identity of the country is marked by its immigrants. Neither just Indian or American, the Indian-American is also identified by the hyphen, the location in-between.

The condition of being "other," difficult as it may be, is nonetheless celebrated in the essays included here as a politics and aesthetics derived from an oppositional consciousness, the margins, and the in-between places of the postmodern world. Above all, the essays in this section destabilize identity and tradition as they explore a destabilized world. Likewise, some other important studies of the "new internationalism" explore the consequences of transnationalism and globalization. Rosi Braidotti celebrates what she refers to as a nomadic consciousness and intellectualism to suggest not only the global circulation of people but the desired instability of boundaries of many kinds. Women's experiences in a globalized, transnational world are explored in the important collection, *Scattered Hegemonies: Postmodernity and Transnational Feminist Practices*, which disrupts essentialist readings of "woman" as it investigates ways people experience their diasporic locations. Speaking more specifically of the kinds of "goods" that move about the globe, Arjun Appadurai defines five dimensions of the global culture and exposes how they both homogenize the world and yet contribute to specific cultural practices. Taking as his example of the processes of global movements, Black music, Paul Gilroy demonstrates the flows of the diaspora and questions the racial essentialism of identity.

FOR FURTHER READING

Appadurai, Arjun. "Disjuncture and Difference in the Global Cultural Economy." *Public Culture* 2.2 (Spring 1990): 1–24.

Braidotti, Rosi. *Nomadic Subjects: Embodiment and Sexual Difference in Contemporary Feminist Theory*. New York: Columbia UP, 1994.

Gilroy, Paul. "It Ain't Where You're From, It's Where You're At: The Dialectics of Diasporic Identification." *Third Text* 13 (1990–91): 3–16.

Scattered Hegemonies: Postmodernity and Transnational Feminist Practices. Ed. Inderpal Grewal and Caren Kaplan. Minneapolis: U of Minnesota P, 1994.

BORDER LIVES

The Art of the Present

Homi Bhabha

> A boundary is not that at which something stops but, as the
> Greeks recognized, the boundary is that from which *something be-*
> *gins its presencing.*
>
> Martin Heidegger, *'Building, dwelling, thinking'*

It is the trope of our times to locate the question of culture in the realm of
the *beyond*. At the century's edge, we are less exercised by annihilation—the
death of the author—or epiphany—the birth of the 'subject'. Our existence
today is marked by a tenebrous sense of survival, living on the borderlines of
the 'present', for which there seems to be no proper name other than the current and controversial shiftiness of the prefix 'post': *postmodernism, postcolonialism, postfeminism*. . . .

The 'beyond' is neither a new horizon, nor a leaving behind of the past. . . .
Beginnings and endings may be the sustaining myths of the middle years;
but in the *fin de siècle*, we find ourselves in the moment of transit where
space and time cross to produce complex figures of difference and identity,
past and present, inside and outside, inclusion and exclusion. For there is a
sense of disorientation, a disturbance of direction, in the 'beyond': an exploratory, restless movement caught so well in the French rendition of the
words *au-delà*—here and there, on all sides, *fort/da*, hither and thither, back
and forth.[1]

The move away from the singularities of 'class' or 'gender' as primary conceptual and organizational categories, has resulted in an awareness of the
subject positions—of race, gender, generation, institutional location, geopolitical locale, sexual orientation—that inhabit any claim to identity in the
modern world. What is theoretically innovative, and politically crucial, is

the need to think beyond narratives of originary and initial subjectivities and to focus on those moments or processes that are produced in the articulation of cultural differences. These 'in-between' spaces provide the terrain for elaborating strategies of selfhood—singular or communal—that initiate new signs of identity, and innovative sites of collaboration, and contestation, in the act of defining the idea of society itself.

It is in the emergence of the interstices—the overlap and displacement of domains of difference—that the intersubjective and collective experiences of *nationness*, community interest, or cultural value are negotiated. How are subjects formed 'in- between', or in excess of, the sum of the 'parts' of difference (usually intoned as race/class/gender, etc.)? How do strategies of representation or empowerment come to be formulated in the competing claims of communities where, despite shared histories of deprivation and discrimination, the exchange of values, meanings and priorities may not always be collaborative and dialogical, but may be profoundly antagonistic, conflictual and even incommensurable?

The force of these questions is borne out by the 'language' of recent social crises sparked off by histories of cultural difference. Conflicts in South Central Los Angeles between Koreans, Mexican-Americans and African-Americans focus on the concept of 'disrespect'—a term forged in the borderlines of ethnic deprivation that is, at once, the sign of racialized violence and the symptom of social victimage. In the aftermath of the *The Satanic Verses* affair in Great Britain, Black and Irish feminists, despite their different constituencies, have made common cause against the 'racialization of religion' as the dominant discourse through which the State represents their conflicts and struggles, however secular or even 'sexual' they may be.

Terms of cultural engagement, whether antagonistic or affiliative, are produced performatively. The representation of difference must not be hastily read as the reflection of *pre-given* ethnic or cultural traits set in the fixed tablet of tradition. The social articulation of difference, from the minority perspective, is a complex, on-going negotiation that seeks to authorize cultural hybridities that emerge in moments of historical transformation. The 'right' to signify from the periphery of authorized power and privilege does not depend on the persistence of tradition; it is resourced by the power of tradition to be reinscribed through the conditions of contingency and contradictoriness that attend upon the lives of those who are 'in the minority'. The recognition that tradition bestows is a partial form of identification. In restaging the past it introduces other, incommensurable cultural temporalities into the invention of tradition. This process estranges any immediate access to an originary identity or a 'received' tradition. The borderline engagements of cultural difference may as often be consensual as conflictual; they may confound our definitions of tradition and modernity; realign the customary boundaries between the private and the public, high and low; and challenge normative expectations of development and progress.

> I wanted to make shapes or set up situations that are kind of open. . . . My work has a lot to do with a kind of fluidity, a movement back and forth, not making a claim to any specific or essential way of being.[2]

Thus writes Renée Green, the African-American artist. She reflects on the need to understand cultural difference as the production of minority identities that 'split'—are estranged unto themselves—in the act of being articulated into a collective body:

> Multiculturalism doesn't reflect the complexity of the situation as I face it daily. . . . It requires a person to step outside of him/herself to actually see what he/she is doing. I don't want to condemn well-meaning people and say (like those T-shirts you can buy on the street) 'It's a black thing, you wouldn't understand.' To me that's essentialising blackness.[3]

Political empowerment, and the enlargement of the multiculturalist cause, come from posing questions of solidarity and community from the interstitial perspective. Social differences are not simply given to experience through an already authenticated cultural tradition; they are the signs of the emergence of community envisaged as a project—at once a vision and a construction—that takes you 'beyond' yourself in order to return, in a spirit of revision and reconstruction, to the political *conditions* of the present:

> Even then, it's still a struggle for power between various groups within ethnic groups about what's being said and who's saying what, who's representing who? What is a community anyway? What is a black community? What is a Latino community? I have trouble with thinking of all these things as monolithic fixed categories.[4]

If Renée Green's questions open up an interrogatory, interstitial space between the act of representation—who? what? where?—and the presence of community itself, then consider her own creative intervention within this in-between moment. Green's 'architectural' site-specific work, *Sites of Genealogy* (Out of Site, The Institute of Contemporary Art, Long Island City, New York), displays and displaces the binary logic through which identities of difference are often constructed—Black/White, Self/Other. Green makes a metaphor of the museum building itself, rather than simply using the gallery space:

> I used architecture literally as a reference, using the attic, the boiler room, and the stairwell to make associations between certain binary divisions such as higher and lower and heaven and hell. The stairwell became a liminal space, a pathway between the upper and lower areas, each of which was annotated with plaques referring to blackness and whiteness.[5]

The stairwell as liminal space, in-between the designations of identity, becomes the process of symbolic interaction, the connective tissue that constructs the difference between upper and lower, black and white. The hither and thither of the stairwell, the temporal movement and passage that it allows, prevents identities at either end of it from settling into primordial polarities. This interstitial passage between fixed identifications opens up the possibility of a cultural hybridity that entertains difference without an assumed or imposed hierarchy:

> I always went back and forth between racial designations and designations from physics or other symbolic designations. All these things blur in some way.... To develop a genealogy of the way colours and noncolours function is interesting to me.[6]

'Beyond' signifies spatial distance, marks progress, promises the future; but our intimations of exceeding the barrier or boundary—the very act of going *beyond*—are unknowable, unrepresentable, without a return to the 'present' which, in the process of repetition, becomes disjunct and displaced. The imaginary of spatial distance—to live somehow beyond the border of our times—throws into relief the temporal, social differences that interrupt our collusive sense of cultural contemporaneity. The present can no longer be simply envisaged as a break or a bonding with the past and the future, no longer a synchronic presence: our proximate self-presence, our public image, comes to be revealed for its discontinuities, its inequalities, its minorities. Unlike the dead hand of history that tells the beads of sequential time like a rosary, seeking to establish serial, causal connections, we are now confronted with what Walter Benjamin describes as the blasting of a monadic moment from the homogenous course of history, 'establishing a conception of the present as the "time of the now"'.[7]

If the jargon of our times—postmodernity, postcoloniality, postfeminism— has any meaning at all, it does not lie in the popular use of the 'post' to indicate sequentiality—*after*-feminism; or polarity—*anti*-modernism. These terms

that insistently gesture to the beyond, only embody its restless and revisionary energy if they transform the present into an expanded and ex-centric site
of experience and empowerment. For instance, if the interest in postmodernism is limited to a celebration of the fragmentation of the 'grand
narratives' of postenlightenment rationalism then, for all its intellectual
excitement, it remains a profoundly parochial enterprise.

The wider significance of the postmodern condition lies in the awareness
that the epistemological 'limits' of those ethnocentric ideas are also the
enunciative boundaries of a range of other dissonant, even dissident histories and voices—women, the colonized, minority groups, the bearers of po-
liced sexualities. For the demography of the new internationalism is the
history of postcolonial migration, the narratives of cultural and political
diaspora, the major social displacements of peasant and aboriginal communities, the poetics of exile, the grim prose of political and economic refugees.
It is in this sense that the boundary becomes the place from which *something begins its presencing* in a movement not dissimilar to the ambulant,
ambivalent articulation of the beyond that I have drawn out: 'Always and
ever differently the bridge escorts the lingering and hastening ways of men
to and fro, so that they may get to other banks. . . . The bridge *gathers* as a
passage that crosses.'[8]

The very concepts of homogenous national cultures, the consensual or
contiguous transmission of historical traditions, or 'organic' ethnic communities—*as the grounds of cultural comparativism*—are in a profound process
of redefinition. The hideous extremity of Serbian nationalism proves that the
very idea of a pure, 'ethnically cleansed' national identity can only be
achieved through the death, literal and figurative, of the complex interweav-
ings of history, and the culturally contingent borderlines of modern nation-
hood. This side of the psychosis of patriotic fervour, I like to think, there is
overwhelming evidence of a more transnational and translational sense of
the hybridity of imagined communities. Contemporary Sri Lankan theatre
represents the deadly conflict between the Tamils and the Sinhalese through
allegorical references to State brutality in South Africa and Latin America;
the Anglo-Celtic canon of Australian literature and cinema is being rewrit-
ten from the perspective of Aboriginal political and cultural imperatives; the
South African novels of Richard Rive, Bessie Head, Nadine Gordimer, John
Coetzee, are documents of a society divided by the effects of apartheid that
enjoin the international intellectual community to meditate on the unequal,
asymmetrical worlds that exist elsewhere; Salman Rushdie writes the fabu-
list historiography of post-Independence India and Pakistan in *Midnight's*

Children and *Shame*, only to remind us in *The Satanic Verses* that the truest eye may now belong to the migrant's double vision; Toni Morrison's *Beloved* revives the past of slavery and its murderous rituals of possession and self-possession, in order to project a contemporary fable of a woman's history that is at the same time the narrative of an affective, historic memory of an emergent public sphere of men and women alike.

What is striking about the 'new' internationalism is that the move from the specific to the general, from the material to the metaphoric, is not a smooth passage of transition and transcendence. The 'middle passage' of contemporary culture, as with slavery itself, is a process of displacement and disjunction that does not totalize experience. Increasingly, 'national' cultures are being produced from the perspective of disenfranchised minorities. The most significant effect of this process is not the proliferation of 'alternative histories of the excluded' producing, as some would have it, a pluralist anarchy. What my examples show is the changed basis for making international connections. The currency of critical comparativism, or aesthetic judgement, is no longer the sovereignty of the national culture conceived as Benedict Anderson proposes as an 'imagined community' rooted in a 'homogeneous empty time' of modernity and progress. The great connective narratives of capitalism and class drive the engines of social reproduction, but do not, in themselves, provide a foundational frame for those modes of cultural identification and political affect that form around issues of sexuality, race, feminism, the lifeworld of refugees or migrants, or the deathly social destiny of AIDS.

The testimony of my examples represents a radical revision in the concept of human community itself. What this geopolitical space may be, as a local or transnational reality, is being both interrogated and reinitiated. Feminism, in the 1990s, finds its solidarity as much in liberatory narratives as in the painful ethical position of a slavewoman, Morrison's Sethe, in *Beloved*, who is pushed to infanticide. The body politic can no longer contemplate the nation's health as simply a civic virtue; it must rethink the question of rights for the entire national, and international, community, from the AIDS perspective. The Western metropole must confront its postcolonial history, told by its influx of postwar migrants and refugees, as an indigenous or native narrative *internal to its national identity*; and the reason for this is made clear in the stammering, drunken-words of Mr 'Whisky' Sisodia from *The Satanic Verses*: 'The trouble with the Engenglish is that their hiss hiss history happened overseas, so they dodo don't know what it means.'[9] Postcoloniality, for its part, is a salutary reminder of the persistent 'neo-colonial' relations within the 'new' world order and the multinational division of labour. Such a perspective enables the authentication of histories of exploitation and the evolution of strategies of resistance. Beyond this, however, postcolonial critique bears witness to those countries and communities—in the North and the South, urban and rural—constituted, if I may coin a phrase, 'otherwise than modernity'. Such cultures of a postcolonial *contra-modernity* may be contingent to modernity, discontinuous or in contention with it, resistant to its oppressive, assimilationist technologies; but they also deploy the cultural hybridity of their borderline conditions to 'translate', and therefore reinscribe, the social imaginary of both metropolis and modernity. Listen to Guillermo Gomez-Peña, the performance artist who lives, amongst other times and places, on the Mexico/U.S. border:

> hello America
> this is the voice of *Gran Vato Charollero*
> *broadcasting from the hot deserts of Nogales, Arizona*
> zona de libre cogercio
> 2000 megaherz en todas direciones
>
> you are celebrating Labor Day in Seattle
> while the Klan demonstrates
> against Mexicans in Georgia
> *ironia, 100% ironia*[10]

Being in the 'beyond', then, is to inhabit an intervening space, as any dictionary will tell you. But to dwell 'in the beyond' is also, as I have shown, to be part of a revisionary time, a return to the present to redescribe our cultural contemporaneity; to reinscribe our human, historic commonality; *to touch the future on its hither side*. In that sense, then, the intervening space 'beyond', becomes a space of intervention in the here and now. To engage with such invention, and intervention, as Green and Gomez-Peña enact in their distinctive work, requires a sense of the new that resonates with the hybrid chicano aesthetic of 'rasquachismo' as Tomas Ybarra-Frausto describes it:

> the utilization of available resources for syncretism, juxtaposition, and integration. *Rasquachismo* is a sensibility attuned to mixtures and confluence . . . a delight in texture and sensuous surfaces . . . self-conscious manipulation of materials or iconography . . . the combination of found material and satiric wit . . . the manipulation of *rasquache* artifacts, code and sensibilities from both sides of the border.[11]

The borderline work of culture demands an encounter with 'newness' that is not part of the continuum of past and present. It creates a sense of the new as an insurgent act of cultural translation. Such art does not merely recall the past as social cause or aesthetic precedent; it renews the past, refiguring it as a contingent 'in-between' space, that innovates and interrupts the performance of the present. The 'past-present' becomes part of the necessity, not the nostalgia, of living.

Pepon Osorio's *objets trouvés* of the Nuyorican (New York/Puerto Rican) community—the statistics of infant mortality, or the silent (and silenced) spread of AIDS in the Hispanic community—are elaborated into baroque allegories of social alienation. But it is not the high drama of birth and death that captures Osorio's spectacular imagination. He is the great celebrant of the migrant act of survival, using his mixed-media works to make a hybrid cultural space that forms contingently, disjunctively, in the inscription of signs of cultural memory and sites of political agency. *La Cama* (*The Bed*) turns the highly decorated four-poster into the primal scene of lost-and-found childhood memories, the memorial to a dead nanny Juana, the *mise-en-scène* of the eroticism of the 'emigrant' everyday. Survival, for Osorio, is working in the interstices of a range of practices: the 'space' of installation, the spectacle of the social statistic, the transitive time of the body in performance.

Finally, it is the photographic art of Alan Sekula that takes the borderline condition of cultural translation to its global limit in *Fish Story*, his photographic project on harbours: 'the harbour is the site in which material goods appear in bulk, in the very flux of exchange.'[12] The harbour and the stock-market become the *paysage moralisé* of a containerized, computerized world of global trade. Yet, the non-synchronous time-space of transnational 'exchange', and exploitation, is embodied in a navigational allegory:

> Things are more confused now. A scratchy recording of the Norwegian national anthem blares out from a loudspeaker at the Sailor's Home on the bluff above the channel. The container ship being greeted flies a Bahamian flag of convenience. It was built by Koreans working long hours in the giant shipyards of Ulsan. The underpaid and the understaffed crew could be Salvadorean or Filipino. Only the Captain hears a familiar melody.[13]

Norway's nationalist nostalgia cannot drown out the babel on the bluff. Transnational capitalism and the impoverishment of the Third World certainly create the chains of circumstance that incarcerate the Salvadorean or the Filipino/a. In their cultural passage, hither and thither, as migrant workers, part of the massive economic and political diaspora of the modern world, they embody the Benjaminian 'present': that moment blasted out of the continuum of history. Such conditions of cultural displacement and social discrimination—where political survivors become the best historical witnesses—are the grounds on which Frantz Fanon, the Martinican psychoanalyst and participant in the Algerian revolution, locates an agency of empowerment:

> As soon as I *desire* I am asking to be considered. I am not merely here-and-now, sealed into thingness. I am for somewhere else and for something else. I demand that notice be taken of my *negating activity* [my emphasis] insofar as I pursue something other than life; insofar as I do battle for the creation of a human world— that is a world of reciprocal recognitions.
>
> I should constantly remind myself that the real *leap* consists in introducing invention into existence.
>
> In the world in which I travel, I am endlessly creating myself. And it is by going beyond the historical, instrumental hypothesis that I will initiate my cycle of freedom.[14]

Once more it is the desire for recognition, 'for somewhere else and for something else' that takes the experience of history *beyond* the instrumental hypothesis. Once again, it is the space of intervention emerging in the cultural interstices that introduces creative invention into existence. And one last time, there is a return to the performance of identity as iteration, the recreation of the self in the world of travel, the resettlement of the borderline community of migration. Fanon's desire for the recognition of cultural presence as 'negating activity' resonates with my breaking of the time-barrier of a culturally collusive 'present'.

NOTES

1. For an interesting discussion of gender boundaries in the *fin de siècle*, see E. Showalter, *Sexual Anarchy: Gender and Culture in the Fin de Siècle* (London: Bloomsbury, 1990), especially 'Borderlines', pp. 1–18.

2. Renée Green interviewed by Elizabeth Brown, from catalogue published by Allen Memorial Art Museum, Oberlin College, Ohio.

3. Interview conducted by Miwon Kwon for the exhibition 'Emerging New York Artists', Sala Mendonza, Caracas, Venezuela (xeroxed manuscript copy).

4. Ibid., p. 6.

5. Renée Green in conversation with Donna Harkavy, Curator of Contemporary Art at the Worcester Museum.

6. Ibid.

7. W. Benjamin, 'Theses on the philosophy of history', in his *Illuminations* (London: Jonathan Cape, 1970), p. 265.

8. M. Heidegger, 'Building, dwelling, thinking', in *Poetry, Language, Thought* (New York: Harper & Row, 1971), pp. 152–3.

9. S. Rushdie, *The Satanic Verses* (London: Viking, 1988), p. 343.

10. G. Gomez-Peña, *American Theatre*, vol. 8, no. 7, October 1991.

11. T. Ybarra-Frausto, 'Chicano movement/chicano art' in I. Karp and S. D. Lavine (eds.) (Washington and London: Smithsonian Institution Press, 1991), pp. 133–4.

12. A. Sekula, *Fish Story*, manuscript, p. 2.

13. Ibid., p. 3.

14. F. Fanon, *Black Skin, White Masks*, Introduction by H. K. Bhabha (London: Pluto, 1986), pp. 218, 229, 231.

A GLOBAL SENSE OF PLACE

Doreen Massey

This is an era—it is often said—when things are speeding up, and spreading out. Capital is going through a new phase of internationalization, especially in its financial parts. More people travel more frequently and for longer distances. Your clothes have probably been made in a range of countries from Latin America to South-East Asia. Dinner consists of food shipped in from all over the world. And if you have a screen in your office, instead of opening a letter which—care of Her Majesty's Post Office—has taken some days to wend its way across the country, you now get interrupted by e-mail.

This view of the current age is one now frequently found in a wide range of books and journals. Much of what is written about space, place and postmodern times emphasizes a new phase in what Marx once called 'the annihilation of space by time'. The process is argued, or—more usually—asserted, to have gained a new momentum, to have reached a new stage. It is a phenomenon which has been called 'time-space compression'. And the general acceptance that something of the sort is going on is marked by the almost obligatory use in the literature of terms and phrases such as speed-up, global village, overcoming spatial barriers, the disruption of horizons, and so forth.

One of the results of this is an increasing uncertainty about what we mean by 'places' and how we relate to them. How, in the face of all this movement and intermixing, can we retain any sense of a local place and its particularity? An (idealized) notion of an era when places were (supposedly) inhabited by coherent and homogeneous communities is set against the current fragmentation and disruption. The counterposition is anyway dubious, of course; 'place' and 'community' have only rarely been coterminous. But the occasional longing for such coherence is none the less a sign of the geographical fragmentation, the spatial disruption, of our times. And occasionally, too, it has been part of what has given rise to defensive and reactionary responses—certain forms of nationalism, sentimentalized recovering of sanitized 'heritages', and outright antagonism to newcomers and 'outsiders'. One of the effects of such responses is that place itself, the seeking after a sense of place, has come to be seen by some as necessarily reactionary.

But is that necessarily so? Can't we rethink our sense of place? Is it not possible for a sense of place to be progressive; not self-enclosing and defensive, but outward-looking? A sense of place which is adequate to this era of time-space compression? To begin with, there are some questions to be asked about time-space compression itself. Who is it that experiences it, and how? Do we all benefit and suffer from it in the same way?

For instance, to what extent does the currently popular characterization of time-space compression represent very much a western, colonizer's, view? The sense of dislocation which some feel at the sight of a once well-known local street now lined with a succession of cultural imports—the pizzeria, the kebab house, the branch of the middle-eastern bank—must have been felt for centuries, though from a very different point of view, by colonized peoples all over the world as they watched the importation, maybe even used, the products of, first, European colonization, maybe British (from new forms of transport to liver salts and custard powder), later U.S., as they learned to eat wheat instead of rice or corn, to drink Coca-Cola, just as today we try out enchiladas.

Moreover, as well as querying the ethnocentricity of the idea of time-space compression and its current acceleration, we also need to ask about its causes: what is it that determines our degrees of mobility, that influences the sense we have of space and place? Time-space compression refers to movement and communication across space, to the geographical stretching-out of social relations, and to our experience of all this. The usual interpretation is that it results overwhelmingly from the actions of capital, and from its currently increasing internationalization. On this interpretation, then, it is time space and money which make the world go round, and us go round (or not) the world. It is capitalism and its developments which are argued to determine our understanding and our experience of space.

But surely this is insufficient. Among the many other things which clearly influence that experience, there are, for instance, 'race' and gender. The degree to which we can move between countries, or walk about the streets at night, or venture out of hotels in foreign cities, is not just influenced by 'capital'. Survey after survey has shown how women's mobility, for instance, is restricted—in a thousand different ways, from physical violence to being ogled at or made to feel quite simply 'out of place'—not by 'capital', but by men. Or, to take a more complicated example, Birkett, reviewing books on women adventurers and travellers in the nineteenth and twentieth centuries, suggests that 'it is far, far more demanding for a woman to wander now than ever before'.[1] The reasons she gives for this argument are a complex mix of colonialism, ex-colonialism, racism, changing gender relations and relative wealth. A simple resort to explanation in terms of 'money' or 'capital' alone could not begin to get to grips with the issue. The current speed-up may be strongly determined by economic forces, but it is not the economy alone which determines our experience of space and place. In other words, and put simply, there is a lot more determining how we experience space than what 'capital' gets up to.

What is more, of course, that last example indicated that 'time-space compression' has not been happening for everyone in all spheres of activity. Birkett again, this time writing of the Pacific Ocean:

> Jumbos have enabled Korean computer consultants to fly to Silicon Valley as if popping next door, and Singaporean entrepreneurs to reach Seattle in a day. The borders of the world's greatest ocean have been joined as never before. And Boeing has brought these people together. But what about those they fly over, on their islands five miles below? How has the mighty 747 brought them greater communion with those whose shores are washed by the same water? It hasn't, of course. Air travel might enable businessmen to buzz across the ocean, but the concurrent decline in shipping has only increased the isolation of many island communities. . . . Pitcairn, like many other Pacific islands, has never felt so far from its neighbours.[2]

In other words, and most broadly, time-space compression needs differentiating socially. This is not just a moral or political point about inequality, although that would be sufficient reason to mention it; it is also a conceptual point.

Imagine for a moment that you are on a satellite, further out and beyond all actual satellites; you can see 'planet earth' from a distance and, unusually for someone with only peaceful intentions, you are equipped with the kind of technology which allows you to see the colours of people's eyes and the numbers on their numberplates. You can see all the movement and tune in to all the communication that is going on. Furthest out are the satellites, then aeroplanes, the long haul between London and Tokyo and the hop from San Salvador to Guatemala City. Some of this is people moving, some of it is physical trade, some is media broadcasting. There are faxes, e-mail, film-distribution networks, financial flows and transactions. Look in closer and there are ships and trains, steam trains slogging laboriously up hills somewhere in Asia. Look in closer still and there are lorries and cars and buses, and on down further, somewhere in sub-Saharan Africa, there's a woman—

amongst many women—on foot, who still spends hours a day collecting water.

Now, I want to make one simple point here, and that is about what one might call the *power geometry* of it all; the power geometry of time-space compression. For different social groups, and different individuals, are placed in very distinct ways in relation to these flows and interconnections. This point concerns not merely the issue of who moves and who doesn't, although that is an important element of it; it is also about power in relation *to* the flows and the movement. Different social groups have distinct relationships to this anyway differentiated mobility: some people are more in charge of it than others; some initiate flows and movement, others don't; some are more on the receiving-end of it than others; some are effectively imprisoned by it.

In a sense at the end of all the spectra are those who are both doing the moving and the communicating and who are in some way in a position of control in relation to it—the jet-setters, the ones sending and receiving the faxes and the e-mail, holding the international conference calls, the ones distributing the films, controlling the news, organizing the investments and the international currency transactions. These are the groups who are really in a sense in charge of time-space compression, who can really use it and turn it to advantage, whose power and influence it very definitely increases. On its more prosaic fringes this group probably includes a fair number of western academics and journalists—those, in other words, who write most about it.

But there are also groups who are also doing a lot of physical moving, but who are not 'in charge' of the process in the same way at all. The refugees from El Salvador or Guatemala and the undocumented migrant workers from Michoacán in Mexico, crowding into Tijuana to make a perhaps fatal dash for it across the border into the U.S. to grab a chance of a new life. Here the experience of movement, and indeed of a confusing plurality of cultures, is very different. And there are those from India, Pakistan, Bangladesh, the Caribbean, who come half way round the world only to get held up in an interrogation room at Heathrow.

Or—a different case again—there are those who are simply on the receiving end of time-space compression. The pensioner in a bed-sit in any inner city in this country, eating British working-class-style fish and chips from a Chinese take-away, watching a U.S. film on a Japanese television; and not daring to go out after dark. And anyway the public transport's been cut.

Or—one final example to illustrate a different kind of complexity—there are the people who live in the *favelas* of Rio, who know global football like

the back of their hand, and have produced some of its players; who have contributed massively to global music, who gave us the samba and produced the
lambada that everyone was dancing to last year in the clubs of Paris and
London; and who have never, or hardly ever, been to downtown Rio. At one
level they have been tremendous contributors to what we call time-space
compression; and at another level they are imprisoned in it.

This is, in other words, a highly complex social differentiation. There are
differences in the degree of movement and communication, but also in the degree of control and of initiation. The ways in which people are placed within
'time-space compression' are highly complicated and extremely varied.

But this in turn immediately raises questions of politics. If time-space
compression can be imagined in that more socially formed, socially evalua-
tive and differentiated way, then there may be here the possibility of developing a politics of mobility and access. For it does seem that mobility, and
control over mobility, both reflects and reinforces power. It is not simply a
question of unequal distribution, that some people move more than others,
and that some have more control than others. It is that the mobility and control of some groups can actively weaken other people. Differential mobility
can weaken the leverage of the already weak. The time-space compression of
some groups can undermine the power of others.

This is well established and often noted in the relationship between capital and labour. Capital's ability to roam the world further strengthens it in relation to relatively immobile workers, enables it to play off the plant at Genk
against the plant at Dagenham. It also strengthens its hand against struggling
local economies the world over as they compete for the favour of some investment. The 747s that fly computer scientists across the Pacific are part of
the reason for the greater isolation today of the island of Pitcairn. But also,
every time someone uses a car, and thereby increases their personal mobility,
they reduce both the social rationale and the financial viability of the public
transport system—and thereby also potentially reduce the mobility of those
who rely on that system. Every time you drive to that out-of-town shopping
centre you contribute to the rising prices, even hasten the demise, of the corner shop. And the 'time-space compression' which is involved in producing
and reproducing the daily lives of the comfortably-off in First World societies—not just their own travel but the resources they draw on, from all over
the world, to feed their lives—may entail environmental consequences, or hit
constraints, which will limit the lives of others before their own. We need to
ask, in other words, whether our relative mobility and power over mobility
and communication entrenches the spatial imprisonment of other groups.

But this way of thinking about time-space compression also returns us to the question of place and a sense of place. How, in the context of all these socially varied time-space changes do we think about 'places'? In an era when, it is argued, 'local communities' seem to be increasingly broken up, when you can go abroad and find the same shops, the same music as at home, or eat your favourite foreign-holiday food at a restaurant down the road—and when everyone has a different experience of all this—how then do we think about 'locality'?

Many of those who write about time-space compression emphasize the insecurity and unsettling impact of its effects, the feelings of vulnerability which it can produce. Some therefore go on from this to argue that, in the middle of all this flux, people desperately need a bit of peace and quiet—and that a strong sense of place, of locality, can form one kind of refuge from the hubbub. So the search after the 'real' meanings of places, the unearthing of heritages and so forth, is interpreted as being, in part, a response to desire for fixity and for security of identity in the middle of all the movement and change. A 'sense of place', of rootedness, can provide—in this form and on this interpretation—stability and a source of unproblematical identity. In that guise, however, place and the spatially local are then rejected by many progressive people as almost necessarily reactionary. They are interpreted as an evasion; as a retreat from the (actually unavoidable) dynamic and change of 'real life', which is what we must seize if we are to change things for the better. On this reading, place and locality are foci for a form of romanticized escapism from the real business of the world. While 'time' is equated with movement and progress, 'space'/'place' is equated with stasis and reaction.

There are some serious inadequacies in this argument. There is the question of why it is assumed that time-space compression will produce insecurity. There is the need to face up to—rather than simply deny—people's need for attachment of some sort, whether through place or anything else. None the less, it is certainly the case that there is indeed at the moment a recrudescence of some very problematical senses of place, from reactionary nationalisms, to competitive localisms, to introverted obsessions with 'heritage'. We need, therefore, to think through what might be an adequately progressive sense of place, one which would fit in with the current global-local times and the feelings and relations they give rise to, *and* which would be useful in what are, after all, political struggles often inevitably based on place. The question is how to hold on to that notion of geographical difference, of uniqueness, even of rootedness if people want that, without it being reactionary.

There are a number of distinct ways in which the 'reactionary' notion of place described above is problematical. One is the idea that places have single, essential, identities. Another is the idea that identity of place—the sense of place—is constructed out of an introverted, inward-looking history based on delving into the past for internalized origins, translating the name from the Domesday Book. Thus Wright recounts the construction and appropriation of Stoke Newington and its past by the arriving middle class (the Domesday Book registers the place as 'Newtowne'): 'There is land for two ploughs and a half. . . . There are four villanes and thirty seven cottagers with ten acres'. And he contrasts this version with that of other groups—the white working class and the large number of important minority communities.[3] A particular problem with this conception of place is that it seems to require the drawing of boundaries. Geographers have long been exercised by the problem of defining regions, and this question of 'definition' has almost always been reduced to the issue of drawing lines around a place. I remember some of my most painful times as a geographer have been spent unwillingly struggling to think how one could draw a boundary around somewhere like the 'east midlands'. But that kind of boundary around an area precisely distinguishes between an inside and an outside. It can so easily be yet another way of constructing a counterposition between 'us' and 'them'.

And yet if one considers almost any real place, and certainly one not defined primarily by administrative or political boundaries, these supposed characteristics have little real purchase.

Take, for instance, a walk down Kilburn High Road, my local shopping centre. It is a pretty ordinary place, north-west of the centre of London. Under the railway bridge the newspaper stand sells papers from every county of what my neighbours, many of whom come from there, still often call the Irish Free State. The postboxes down the High Road, and many an empty space on the wall, are adorned with the letters IRA. Other available spaces are plastered this week with posters for a special meeting in remembrance: Ten Years after the Hunger Strike. At the local theatre Eamon Morrissey has a one-man show; the National Club has the Wolfe Tones on, and at the Black Lion there's Finnegan's Wake. In two shops I notice this week's lottery ticket winners: in one the name is Teresa Gleeson, in the other, Chouman Hassan.

Thread your way through the often almost stationary traffic diagonally across the road from the newsstand and there's a shop which as long as I can remember has displayed saris in the window. Four life-sized models of Indian women, and reams of cloth. On the door a notice announces a forthcoming concert at Wembley Arena: Anand Miland presents Rekha, live, with Aamir Khan, Salman Khan, Jahi Chawla and Raveena Tandon. On another ad, for the end of the month, is written, 'All Hindus are cordially invited'. In another newsagents I chat with the man who keeps it, a Muslim unutterably depressed by events in the Gulf, silently chafing at having to sell the *Sun*. Overhead there is always at least one aeroplane—we seem to be on a flight-path to Heathrow and by the time they're over Kilburn you can see them clearly enough to tell the airline and wonder as you struggle with your shopping where they're coming from. Below, the reason the traffic is snarled up (another odd effect of time-space compression!) is in part because this is one of the main entrances to and escape routes from London, the road to Staples Corner and the beginning of the M1 to 'the North'.

This is just the beginnings of a sketch from immediate impressions but a proper analysis could be done of the links between Kilburn and the world. And so it could for almost any place.

Kilburn is a place for which I have a great affection; I have lived there many years. It certainly has 'a character of its own'. But it is possible to feel all this without subscribing to any of the static and defensive—and in that sense reactionary—notions of 'place' which were referred to above. First, while Kilburn may have a character of its own, it is absolutely not a seamless, coherent identity, a single sense of place which everyone shares. It could hardly be less so. People's routes through the place, their favourite haunts within it, the connections they make (physically, or by phone or post, or in memory and imagination) between here and the rest of the world vary enormously. If it is now recognized that people have multiple identities then the same point can be made in relation to places. Moreover, such multiple identities can either be a source of richness or a source of conflict, or both.

One of the problems here has been a persistent identification of place with 'community'. Yet this is a misidentification. On the one hand, communities can exist without being in the same place—from networks of friends with like interests, to major religious, ethnic or political communities. On the other hand, the instances of places housing single 'communities' in the sense of coherent social groups are probably—and, I would argue, have for long been—quite rare. Moreover, even where they do exist this in no way implies a single sense of place. For people occupy different positions within any community. We could counterpose to the chaotic mix of Kilburn the relatively stable and homogeneous community (at least in popular imagery) of a small mining village. Homogeneous? 'Communities' too have internal structures. To take the most obvious example, I'm sure a woman's sense of place in a mining village—the spaces through which she normally moves, the meeting places, the connections outside—are different from a man's. Their 'senses of the place' will be different.

Moreover, not only does 'Kilburn', then, have many identities (or its full identity is a complex mix of all these) it is also, looked at in this way, absolutely *not* introverted. It is (or ought to be) impossible even to begin thinking about Kilburn High Road without bringing into play half the world and a considerable amount of British imperialist history (and this certainly goes for mining villages too). Imagining it this way provokes in you (or at least in me) a really global sense of place.

And finally, in contrasting this way of looking at places with the defensive reactionary view, I certainly could not begin to, nor would I want to, define 'Kilburn' by drawing its enclosing boundaries.

So, at this point in the argument, get back in your mind's eye on a satellite; go right out again and look back at the globe. This time, however, imagine not just all the physical movement, nor even all the often invisible communications, but also and especially all the social relations, all the links between people. Fill it in with all those different experiences of time-space compression. For what is happening is that the geography of social relations is changing. In many cases such relations are increasingly stretched out over space. Economic, political and cultural social relations, each full of power and with internal structures of domination and subordination, stretched out over the planet at every different level, from the household to the local area to the international.

It is from that perspective that it is possible to envisage an alternative interpretation of place. In this interpretation, what gives a place its specificity is not some long internalized history but the fact that it is constructed out of a particular constellation of social relations, meeting and weaving together at a particular locus. If one moves in from the satellite towards the globe, holding all those networks of social relations and movements and communications in one's head, then each 'place' can be seen as a particular, unique, point of their intersection. It is, indeed, a *meeting* place. Instead then, of thinking of places as areas with boundaries around, they can be imagined as articulated moments in networks of social relations and understandings, but where a large proportion of those relations, experiences and understandings are constructed on a far larger scale than what we happen to define for that moment as the place itself, whether that be a street, or a region or even a continent. And this in turn allows a sense of place which is extroverted, which includes a consciousness of its links with the wider world, which integrates in a positive way the global and the local.

This is not a question of making the ritualistic connections to 'the wider system'—the people in the local meeting who bring up international capitalism every time you try to have a discussion about rubbish-collection—the point is that there are real relations with real content—economic, political, cultural—between any local place and the wider world in which it is set. In economic geography the argument has long been accepted that it is not possible to understand the 'inner city', for instance its loss of jobs, the decline of manufacturing employment there, by looking only at the inner city. Any adequate explanation has to set the inner city in its wider geographical context. Perhaps it is appropriate to think how that kind of understanding could be extended to the notion of a sense of place.

These arguments, then, highlight a number of ways in which a progressive concept of place might be developed. First of all, it is absolutely not static. If places can be conceptualized in terms of the social interactions which they tie together, then it is also the case that these interactions themselves are not motionless things, frozen in time. They are processes. One of the great one-liners in Marxist exchanges has for long been, 'Ah, but capital is not a thing, it's a process.' Perhaps this should be said also about places; that places are processes, too.

Second, places do not have to have boundaries in the sense of divisions which frame simple enclosures. 'Boundaries' may of course be necessary, for the purposes of certain types of studies for instance, but they are not necessary for the conceptualization of a place itself. Definition in this sense does not have to be through simple counterposition to the outside; it can come, in part, precisely through the particularity of linkage *to* that 'outside' which is therefore itself part of what constitutes the place. This helps get away from the common association between penetrability and vulnerability. For it is this kind of association which makes invasion by newcomers so threatening.

Third, clearly places do not have single, unique 'identities'; they are full of internal conflicts. Just think, for instance, about London's Docklands, a place which is at the moment quite clearly *defined* by conflict: a conflict over what its past has been (the nature of its 'heritage'), conflict over what should be its present development, conflict over what could be its future.

Fourth, and finally, none of this denies place nor the importance of the uniqueness of place. The specificity of place is continually reproduced, but it is not a specificity which results from some long, internalized history. There are a number of sources of this specificity—the uniqueness of place.[4] There is the fact that the wider social relations in which places are set are themselves geographically differentiated. Globalization (in the economy, or in culture, or in anything else) does not entail simply homogenization. On the contrary, the globalization of social relations is yet another source of (the reproduction of) geographical uneven development, and thus of the uniqueness of place. There is the specificity of place which derives from the fact that each place is the focus of a distinct *mixture* of wider and more local social relations. There is the fact that this very mixture together in one place may produce effects which would not have happened otherwise. And finally, all these relations interact with and take a further element of specificity from the accumulated history of a place, with that history itself imagined as the product of layer upon layer of different sets of linkages, both local and to the wider world.

In her portrait of Corsica, *Granite Island*, Dorothy Carrington travels the island seeking out the roots of its character.[5] All the different layers of peoples and cultures are explored; the long and tumultuous relationship with France, with Genoa and Aragon in the thirteenth, fourteenth and fifteenth centuries, back through the much earlier incorporation into the Byzantine Empire, and before that domination by the Vandals, before that being part of the Roman Empire, before that the colonization and settlements of the Carthaginians and the Greeks . . . until we find . . . that even the megalith builders had come to Corsica from somewhere else.

It is a sense of place, an understanding of 'its character', which can only be constructed by linking that place to places beyond. A progressive sense of place would recognize that, without being threatened by it. What we need, it seems to me, is a global sense of the local, a global sense of place.

Mexico City
published in 1991

NOTES

1. D. Birkett, *New Statesman & Society*, 13 June 1990, pp. 41–2.
2. D. Birkett, *New Statesman & Society*, 15 March 1991, p. 38.
3. P. Wright, *On Living in an Old Country* (London, Verso, 1985), pp. 227, 231.
4. D. Massey, *Spatial Divisions of Labour: Social Structures and the Geography of Production* (Basingstoke, Macmillan, 1984).
5. D. Carrington, *Granite Island: A Portrait of Corsica* (Harmondsworth, Penguin, 1984).

REFLECTIONS ON EXILE

Edward W. Said

Exile is strangely compelling to think about but terrible to experience. It is the unhealable rift forced between a human being and a native place, between the self and its true home: its essential sadness can never be surmounted. And while it is true that literature and history contain heroic, romantic, glorious, even triumphant episodes in an exile's life, these are no more than efforts meant to overcome the crippling sorrow of estrangement. The achievements of exile are permanently undermined by the loss of something left behind for ever.

But if true exile is a condition of terminal loss, why has it been transformed so easily into a potent, even enriching, motif of modern culture? We have become accustomed to thinking of the modern period itself as spiritually orphaned and alienated, the age of anxiety and estrangement. Nietzsche taught us to feel uncomfortable with tradition, and Freud to regard domestic intimacy as the polite face painted on patricidal and incestuous rage. Modern Western culture is in large part the work of exiles, émigrés, refugees. In the United States, academic, intellectual and aesthetic thought is what it is today because of refugees from fascism, communism and other regimes given to the oppression and expulsion of dissidents. The critic George Steiner has even proposed the perceptive thesis that a whole genre of twentieth-century Western literature is 'extraterritorial', a literature by and about exiles, symbolizing the age of the refugee. Thus Steiner suggests

> It seems proper that those who create art in a civilization of quasi-barbarism, which has made so many homeless, should themselves be poets unhoused and wanderers across language. Eccentric, aloof, nostalgic, deliberately untimely. . . .

In other ages, exiles had similar cross-cultural and transnational visions, suffered the same frustrations and miseries, performed the same elucidating and critical tasks—brilliantly affirmed, for instance, in E. H. Carr's classic study of the nineteenth-century Russian intellectuals clustered around Herzen, *The Romantic Exiles*. But the difference between earlier exiles and those of our own time is, it bears stressing, scale: our age—with its modern warfare, imperialism and the quasi-theological ambitions of totalitarian rulers—is indeed the age of the refugee, the displaced person, mass immigration.

Against this large, impersonal setting, exile cannot be made to serve notions of humanism. On the twentieth-century scale, exile is neither aesthetically nor humanistically comprehensible: at most the literature about exile objectifies an anguish and a predicament most people rarely experience at first hand; but to think of the exile informing this literature as beneficially humanistic is to banalize its mutilations, the losses it inflicts on those who suffer them, the muteness with which it responds to any attempt to understand it as 'good for us'. Is it not true that the views of exile in literature and, moreover, in religion obscure what is truly horrendous: that exile is irremediably secular and unbearably historical; that it is produced by human beings for other human beings; and that, like death but without death's ultimate mercy, it has torn millions of people from the nourishment of tradition, family and geography?

To see a poet in exile—as opposed to reading the poetry of exile—is to see exile's antinomies embodied and endured with a unique intensity. Several years ago I spent some time with Faiz Ahmad Faiz, the greatest of contemporary Urdu poets. He was exiled from his native Pakistan by Zia's military regime, and found a welcome of sorts in strife-torn Beirut. Naturally his closest friends were Palestinian, but I sensed that, although there was an affinity of spirit between them, nothing quite matched—language, poetic convention, or life-history. Only once, when Eqbal Ahmad, a Pakistani friend and a fellow-exile, came to Beirut, did Faiz seem to overcome his sense of constant estrangement. The three of us sat in a dingy Beirut restaurant late one night, while Faiz recited poems. After a time, he and Eqbal stopped translating his verses for my benefit, but as the night wore on it did not matter. What I watched required no translation: it was an enactment of a homecoming expressed through defiance and loss, as if to say, 'Zia, we are here'. Of course Zia was the one who was really at home and who would not hear their exultant voices.

Rashid Hussein was a Palestinian. He translated Bialik, one of the great modern Hebrew poets, into Arabic, and Hussein's eloquence established him in the post-1948 period as an orator and nationalist without peer. He first worked as a Hebrew language journalist in Tel Aviv, and succeeded in establishing a dialogue between Jewish and Arab writers, even as he espoused the cause of Nasserism and Arab nationalism. In time, he could no longer endure the pressure, and he left for New York. He married a Jewish woman, and began working in the PLO office the United Nations, but regularly outraged his superiors with unconventional ideas and utopian rhetoric. In 1972 he left for the Arab world, but a few months later he was back in the United States: he had felt out of place in Syria and Lebanon, unhappy in Cairo. New York sheltered him anew, but so did endless bouts of drinking and idleness. His life was in ruins, but he remained the most hospitable of men. He died after a night of heavy drinking when, smoking in bed, his cigarette started a fire that spread to a small library of audio cassettes, consisting mostly of poets reading their verse. The fumes from the tapes asphyxiated him. His body was repatriated for burial in Musmus, the small village in Israel where his family still resided.

These and so many other exiled poets and writers lend dignity to a condition legislated to deny dignity—to deny an identity to people. From them, it is apparent that, to concentrate on exile as a contemporary political punishment, you must therefore map territories of experience beyond those mapped by the literature of exile itself. You must first set aside Joyce and Nabokov and think instead of the uncountable masses for whom UN agencies have been created. You must think of the refugee-peasants with no prospect of ever returning home, armed only with a ration card and an agency number. Paris may be a capital famous for cosmopolitan exiles, but it is also a city where unknown men and women have spent years of miserable loneliness: Vietnamese, Algerians, Cambodians, Lebanese, Senegalese, Peruvians. You must think also of Cairo, Beirut, Madagascar, Bangkok, Mexico City. As you move further from the Atlantic world, the awful forlorn waste increases: the hopelessly large numbers, the compounded misery of 'undocumented' people suddenly lost, without a reliable history. To reflect on exiled Muslims from India, or Haitians in America, or Bikinians in Oceania, or Palestinians throughout the Arab world means that you must leave the modest refuge provided by subjectivity and resort instead to the abstractions of mass politics. Negotiations, wars of national liberation, people bundled out of their homes and prodded, bussed or walked to enclaves in other regions: what do these experiences add up to? Are they not manifestly and almost by design irrecoverable?

We come to nationalism and its essential association with exile. Nationalism is an assertion of belonging in and to a place, a people, a heritage. It affirms the home created by a community of language, culture and customs;

and, by so doing, it fends off exile, fights to prevent its ravages. Indeed, the interplay between nationalism and exile is like Hegel's dialectic of servant and master, opposites informing and constituting each other. All nationalisms in their early stages develop from a condition of estrangement. The struggles to win American independence, to unify Germany or Italy, to liberate Algeria were those of national groups separated—exiled—from what was construed to be their rightful way of life. Triumphant, achieved nationalism then justifies, retrospectively as well as prospectively, a history selectively strung together in a narrative form: thus all nationalisms have their founding fathers, their basic, quasi-religious texts, their rhetoric of belonging, their historical and geographical landmarks, their official enemies and heroes. This collective ethos forms what Pierre Bourdieu, the French sociologist, calls the *habitus*, the coherent amalgam of practices linking habit with inhabitance. In time, successful nationalisms consign truth exclusively to themselves and relegate falsehood and inferiority to outsiders (as in the rhetoric of capitalist versus communist, or the European versus the Asiatic).

And just beyond the frontier between 'us' and the 'outsiders' is the perilous territory of not-belonging: this is to where in a primitive time peoples were banished, and where in the modern era immense aggregates of humanity loiter as refugees and displaced persons.

Nationalisms are about groups, but in a very acute sense exile is a solitude experienced outside the group: the deprivations felt at not being with others in the communal habitation. How, then, does one surmount the loneliness of exile without falling into the encompassing and thumping language of national pride, collective sentiments, group passions? What is there worth saving and holding on to between the extremes of exile on the one hand, and the often bloody-minded affirmations of nationalism on the other? Do nationalism and exile have any intrinsic attributes? Are they simply two conflicting varieties of paranoia?

These are questions that cannot ever be fully answered because each assumes that exile and nationalism can be discussed neutrally, without reference to each other. They cannot be. Because both terms include everything from the most collective of collective sentiments to the most private of private emotions, there is hardly language adequate for both. But there is certainly nothing about nationalism's public and all-inclusive ambitions that touches the core of the exile's predicament.

Because exile, unlike nationalism, is fundamentally a discontinuous state of being. Exiles are cut off from their roots, their land, their past. They generally do not have armies or states, although they are often in search of them. Exiles feel, therefore, an urgent need to reconstitute their broken lives, usu-

ally by choosing to see themselves as part of a triumphant ideology or a re-
stored people. The crucial thing is that a state of exile free from this triumphant ideology—designed to reassemble an exile's broken history into a
new whole—is virtually unbearable, and virtually impossible in today's
world. Look at the fate of the Jews, the Palestinians and the Armenians.

Noubar is a solitary Armenian, and a friend. His parents had to leave
Eastern Turkey in 1915, after their families were massacred: his maternal
grandfather was beheaded. Noubar's mother and father went to Aleppo, then
to Cairo. In the middle-sixties, life in Egypt became difficult for non-
Egyptians, and his parents, along with four children, were taken to Beirut by
an international relief organization. In Beirut, they lived briefly in a pension
and then were bundled into two rooms of a little house outside the city. In
Lebanon, they had no money and they waited: eight months later, a relief
agency got them a flight to Glasgow. And then to Gander. And then to New
York. They rode by Greyhound bus from New York to Seattle: Seattle was
the city designated by the agency for their American residence. When I
asked, 'Seattle?', Noubar smiled resignedly, as if to say better Seattle than
Armenia—which he never knew, or Turkey where so many were slaughtered,
or Lebanon where he and his family would certainly have risked their lives.
Exile is sometimes better than staying behind or not getting out: but only
sometimes.

Because *nothing* is secure. Exile is a jealous state. What you achieve is precisely what you have no wish to share, and it is in the drawing of lines
around you and your compatriots that the least attractive aspects of being in
exile emerge: an exaggerated sense of group solidarity, and a passionate hostility to outsiders, even those who may in fact be in the same predicament as
you. What could be more intransigent than the conflict between Zionist Jews
and Arab Palestinians? Palestinians feel that they have been turned into exiles by the proverbial people of exile, the Jews. But the Palestinians also
know that their own sense of national identity has been nourished in the
exile milieu, where everyone not a blood-brother or sister is an enemy, where
every sympathizer is an agent of some unfriendly power, and where the slight-
est deviation from the accepted group line is an act of the rankest treachery
and disloyalty.

Perhaps this is the most extraordinary of exile's fates: to have been exiled
by exiles: to relive the actual process of up-rooting at the hands of exiles. All
Palestinians during the summer of 1982 asked themselves what inarticulate
urge drove Israel, having displaced Palestinians in 1948, to expel them con-

tinuously from their refugee homes and camps in Lebanon. It is as if the re-constructed Jewish collective experience, as represented by Israel and modern Zionism, could not tolerate another story of dispossession and loss to exist alongside it—an intolerance constantly reinforced by the Israeli hostility to the nationalism of the Palestinians, who for forty-six years have been painfully reassembling a national identity in exile.

This need to reassemble an identity out of the refractions and discontinuities of exile is found in the earlier poems of Mahmud Darwish, whose considerable work amounts to an epic effort to transform the lyrics of loss into the indefinitely postponed drama of return. Thus he depicts his sense of homelessness in the form of a list of unfinished and incomplete things:

> But I am the exile.
> Seal me with your eyes.
> Take me wherever you are—
> Take me whatever you are.
> Restore to me the colour of face
> And the warmth of body
> The light of heart and eye,
> The salt of bread and rhythm,
> The taste of earth . . . the Motherland,
> Shield me with your eyes.
> Take me as a relic from the mansion of sorrow.
> Take me as a verse from my tragedy;
> Take me as a toy, a brick from the house
> So that our children will remember to return.

The pathos of exile is in the loss of contact with the solidity and the satisfaction of earth: homecoming is out of the question.

Joseph Conrad's tale 'Amy Foster' is perhaps the most uncompromising representation of exile ever written. Conrad thought of himself as an exile from Poland, and nearly all his work (as well as his life) carries the unmistakable mark of the sensitive émigré's obsession with his own fate and with his hopeless attempts to make satisfying contact with new surroundings. 'Amy Foster' is in a sense confined to the problems of exile, perhaps so confined that it is not one of Conrad's best-known stories. This, for example, is the description of the agony of its central character, Yanko Goorall, an Eastern European peasant who, en route to America, is shipwrecked off the British coast:

It is indeed hard upon a man to find himself a lost stranger helpless, incomprehensible, and of a mysterious origin, in some obscure corner of the earth. Yet amongst all the adventurers shipwrecked in all the wild parts of the world, there is not one, it seems to me, that ever had to suffer a fate so simply tragic as the man I am speaking of, the most innocent of adventurers cast out by the sea. . . .

Yanko has left home because the pressures were too great for him to go on living there. America lures him with its promise, though England is where he ends up. He endures in England, where he cannot speak the language and is feared and misunderstood. Only Amy Foster, a plodding, unattractive peasant girl, tries to communicate with him. They marry, have a child, but when Yanko falls ill, Amy, afraid and alienated, refuses to nurse him; snatching their child, she leaves. The desertion hastens Yanko's miserable death, which like the deaths of several Conradian heroes is depicted as the result of a combination of crushing isolation and the world's indifference. Yanko's fate is described as 'the supreme disaster of loneliness and despair'.

Yanko's predicament is affecting: a foreigner perpetually haunted and alone in an uncomprehending society. But Conrad's own exile causes him to exaggerate the differences between Yanko and Amy. Yanko is dashing, light and bright-eyed, whereas Amy is heavy, dull, bovine; when he dies, it is as if her earlier kindness to him was a snare to lure and then trap him fatally. Yanko's death is romantic: the world is coarse, unappreciative; no one understands him, not even Amy, the one person close to him. Conrad took this neurotic exile's fear and created an aesthetic principle out of it. No one can understand or communicate in Conrad's world, but paradoxically this radical limitation on the possibilities of language doesn't inhibit elaborate efforts to communicate. All of Conrad's stories are about lonely people who talk a great deal (for indeed who of the great modernists was more voluble and 'adjectival' than Conrad himself?) and whose attempts to *impress* others compound, rather than reduce, the original sense of isolation. Each Conradian exile fears, and is condemned endlessly to imagine, the spectacle of a solitary death illuminated, so to speak, by unresponsive, uncommunicating eyes.

Exiles look at non-exiles with resentment. *They* belong in their surroundings, you feel, whereas an exile is always out of place. What is it like to be born in a place, to stay and live there, to know that you are of it, more or less forever?

Although it is true that anyone prevented from returning home is an exile, some distinctions can be made between exiles, refugees, expatriates and émigrés. Exile originated in the age-old practice of banishment. Once banished, the exile lives an anomalous and miserable life, with the stigma of being an outsider. Refugees, on the other hand, are a creation of the twentieth-century state. The word 'refugee' has become a political one, suggesting large herds of innocent and bewildered people requiring urgent international assistance, whereas 'exile' carries with it, I think, a touch of solitude and spirituality.

Expatriates voluntarily live in an alien country, usually for personal or social reasons. Hemingway and Fitzgerald were not forced to live in France. Expatriates may share in the solitude and estrangement of exile, but they do not suffer under its rigid proscriptions. Émigrés enjoy an ambiguous status. Technically, an émigré is anyone who emigrates to a new country. Choice in the matter is certainly a possibility. Colonial officials, missionaries, technical experts, mercenaries and military advisers on loan may in a sense live in exile, but they have not been banished. White settlers in Africa, parts of Asia and Australia may once have been exiles, but as pioneers and nation-builders the label 'exile' dropped away from them.

Much of the exile's life is taken up with compensating for disorienting loss by creating a new world to rule. It is not surprising that so many exiles seem to be novelists, chess players, political activists, and intellectuals. Each of these occupations requires a minimal investment in objects and places a great premium on mobility and skill. The exile's new world, logically enough, is unnatural and its unreality resembles fiction. Georg Lukács, in *Theory of the Novel*, argued with compelling force that the novel, a literary form created out of the unreality of ambition and fantasy, is *the* form of 'transcendental homelessness'. Classical epics, Lukács wrote, emanate from settled cultures in which values are clear, identities stable, life unchanging. The European novel is grounded in precisely the opposite experience, that of a changing society in which an itinerant and disinherited middle-class hero or heroine seeks to construct a new world that somewhat resembles an old one left behind for ever. In the epic there is no *other* world, only the finality of *this* one. Odysseus returns to Ithaca after years of wandering; Achilles will die because he cannot escape his fate. The novel, however, exists because other worlds *may* exist, alternatives for bourgeois speculators, wanderers, exiles.

No matter how well they may do, exiles are always eccentrics who *feel* their difference (even as they frequently exploit it) as a kind of orphanhood. Anyone who is really homeless regards the habit of seeing estrangement in everything modern as an affectation, a display of modish attitudes. Clutching difference like a weapon to be used with stiffened will, the exile jealously insists on his or her right to refuse to belong.

This usually translates into an intransigence that is not easily ignored. Willfulness, exaggeration, overstatement: these are characteristic styles of being an exile, methods for compelling the world to accept your vision— which you make more unacceptable because you are in fact unwilling to have it accepted. It is yours, after all. Composure and serenity are the last things associated with the work of exiles. Artists in exile are decidedly un- pleasant, and their stubbornness insinuates itself into even their exalted works. Dante's vision in *The Divine Comedy* is tremendously powerful in its universality and detail, but even the beatific peace achieved in the *Paradiso* bears traces of the vindictiveness and severity of judgement embodied in the *Inferno*. Who but an exile like Dante, banished from Florence, would use eternity as a place for settling old scores?

James Joyce *chose* to be in exile: to give force to his artistic vocation. In an uncannily effective way—as Richard Ellmann has shown in his biography— Joyce picked a quarrel with Ireland and kept it alive so as to sustain the strictest opposition to what was familiar. Ellmann says that 'whenever his relations with his native land were in danger of improving, [Joyce] was to find a new incident to solidify his intransigence and to reaffirm the rightness of his voluntary absence'. Joyce's fiction concerns what in a letter he once de- scribed as the state of being 'alone and friendless'. And although it is rare to pick banishment as a way of life, Joyce perfectly understood its trials.

But Joyce's success as an exile stresses the question lodged at its very heart: is exile so extreme and private that any instrumental use of it is ulti- mately a trivialization? How is it that the literature of exile has taken its place as a *topos* of human experience alongside the literature of adventure, education or discovery? Is this the *same* exile that quite literally kills Yanko Goorall and has bred the expensive, often dehumanizing relationship be- tween twentieth-century exile and nationalism? Or is it some more benign variety?

Much of the contemporary interest in exile can be traced to the somewhat pallid notion that non-exiles can share in the benefits of exile as a redemp- tive motif. There is, admittedly, a certain plausibility and truth to this idea. Like medieval itinerant scholars or learned Greek slaves in the Roman Empire, exiles—the exceptional ones among them—do leaven their environ- ments. And naturally 'we' concentrate on that enlightening aspect of 'their' presence among us, not on their misery or their demands. But looked at from the bleak political perspective of modern mass dislocations, individual exiles force us to recognize the tragic fate of homelessness in a necessarily heartless world.

A generation ago, Simone Weil posed the dilemma of exile as concisely as it has ever been expressed. 'To be rooted,' she said, 'is perhaps the most important and least recognized need of the human soul.' Yet Weil also saw that most remedies for uprootedness in this era of world wars, deportations and mass exterminations are almost as dangerous as what they purportedly remedy. Of these, the state—or, more accurately, statism—is one of the most insidious, since worship of the state tends to supplant all other human bonds.

Weil exposes us anew to that whole complex of pressures and constraints that lie at the centre of the exile's predicament, which, as I have suggested, is as close as we come in the modern era to tragedy. There is the sheer fact of isolation and displacement, which produces the kind of narcissistic masochism that resists all efforts at amelioration, acculturation and community. At this extreme the exile can make a fetish of exile, a practice that distances him or her front all connections and commitments. To live as if everything around you were temporary and perhaps trivial is to fall prey to petulant cynicism as well as to querulous lovelessness. More common is the pressure on the exile to join—parties, national movements, the state. The exile is offered a new set of affiliations and develops new loyalties. But there is also a loss— of critical perspective, of intellectual reserve, of moral courage.

It must also be recognized that the defensive nationalism of exiles often fosters self-awareness as much as it does the less attractive forms of self-assertion. Such reconstitutive projects as assembling a nation out of exile (and this is true in this century for Jews and Palestinians) involve constructing a national history, reviving an ancient language, founding national institutions like libraries and universities. And these, while they sometimes promote strident ethnocentrism, also give rise to investigations of self that inevitably go far beyond such simple and positive facts as 'ethnicity'. For example, there is the self-consciousness of an individual trying to understand why the histories of the Palestinians and the Jews have certain patterns to them, why in spite of oppression and the threat of extinction a particular ethos remains alive in exile.

Necessarily, then, I speak of exile not as a privilege, but as an *alternative* to the mass institutions that dominate modern life. Exile is not, after all, a matter of choice: you are born into it, or it happens to you. But, provided that the exile refuses to sit on the sidelines nursing a wound, there are things to be learned: he or she must cultivate a scrupulous (not indulgent or sulky) subjectivity.

Perhaps the most rigorous example of such subjectivity is to be found in the writing of Theodor Adorno, the German-Jewish philosopher and critic. Adorno's masterwork, *Minima Moralia*, is an autobiography written while in exile; it is subtitled *Reflexionen aus dem beschädigten Leben* (*Reflections from a Mutilated Life*). Ruthlessly opposed to what he called the 'administered' world, Adorno saw all life as pressed into ready-made forms, prefabricated 'homes'. He argued that everything that one says or thinks, as well as every object one possesses, is ultimately a mere commodity. Language is jargon, objects are for sale. To refuse this state of affairs is the exile's intellectual mission.

Adorno's reflections are informed by the belief that the only home truly available now, though fragile and vulnerable, is in writing. Elsewhere, 'the house is past. The bombings of European cities, as well as the labour and concentration camps, merely precede as executors, with what the immanent development of technology had long decided was to be the fate of houses. These are now good only to be thrown away like old food cans.' In short, Adorno says with a grave irony, 'it is part of morality not to be at home in one's home.'

To follow Adorno is to stand away from 'home' in order to look at it with the exile's detachment. For there is considerable merit in the practice of noting the discrepancies between various concepts and ideas and what they actually produce. We take home and language for granted; they become nature, and their underlying assumptions recede into dogma and orthodoxy.

The exile knows that in a secular and contingent world, homes are always provisional. Borders and barriers, which enclose us within the safety of familiar territory, can also become prisons, and are often defended beyond reason or necessity. Exiles cross borders, break barriers of thought and experience.

Hugo of St Victor, a twelfth-century monk from Saxony, wrote these hauntingly beautiful lines:

> It is, therefore, a source of great virtue for the practised mind to learn, bit by bit, first to change about invisible and transitory things, so that afterwards it may be able to leave them behind altogether. The man who finds his homeland sweet is still a tender beginner; he to whom every soil is as his native one is already strong; but he is perfect to whom the entire world is as a foreign land. The tender soul has fixed his love on one spot in the world; the strong man has extended his love to all places; the perfect man has extinguished his.

Erich Auerbach, the great twentieth-century literary scholar who spent the war years as an exile in Turkey, has cited this passage as a model for anyone wishing to transcend national or provincial limits. Only by embracing this attitude can a historian begin to grasp human experience and its written records in their diversity and particularity; otherwise he or she will remain committed more to the exclusions and reactions of prejudice than to the freedom that accompanies knowledge. But note that Hugo twice makes it clear that the 'strong' or 'perfect' man achieves independence and detachment by *working through* attachments, not by rejecting them. Exile is predicated on the existence of, love for, and bond with, one's native place; what is true of all exile is not that home and love of home are lost, but that loss is inherent in the very existence of both.

Regard experiences as if they were about to disappear. What is it that anchors them in reality? What would you save of them? What would you give up? Only someone who has achieved independence and detachment, someone whose homeland is 'sweet' but whose circumstances makes it impossible to recapture that sweetness, can answer those questions. (Such a person would also find it impossible to derive satisfaction from substitutes furnished by illusion or dogma.)

This may seem like a prescription for all unrelieved grimness of outlook and, with it, a permanently sullen disapproval of all enthusiasm or buoyancy of spirit. Not necessarily. While it perhaps seems peculiar to speak of the pleasures of exile, there are some positive things to be said for a few of its conditions. Seeing 'the entire world as a foreign land' makes possible originality of vision. Most people are principally aware of one culture, one setting, one home; exiles are aware of at least two, and this plurality of vision gives rise to an awareness of simultaneous dimensions, an awareness that—to borrow a phrase from music—is *contrapuntal*.

For an exile, habits of life, expression or activity in the new environment inevitably occur against the memory of these things in another environment. Thus both the new and the old environments are vivid, actual, occurring together contrapuntally. There is a unique pleasure in this sort of apprehension, especially if the exile is conscious of other contrapuntal juxtapositions that diminish orthodox judgement and elevate appreciative sympathy. There is also a particular sense of achievement in acting as if one were at home wherever one happens to be.

This remains risky, however: the habit of dissimulation is both wearying and nerve-racking. Exile is never the state of being satisfied, placid, or secure. Exile, in the words of Wallace Stevens, is 'a mind of winter' in which the pathos of summer and autumn as much as the potential of spring are nearby but unobtainable. Perhaps this is another way of saying that a life of exile moves according to a different calendar, and is less seasonal and settled than life at home. Exile is life led outside habitual order. It is nomadic, decentred, contrapuntal; but no sooner does one get accustomed to it than its unsettling force erupts anew.

DETERRITORIALIZATIONS

The Rewriting of Home and Exile in Western Feminist
Discourse

Caren Kaplan

Women have a history of reading and writing in the interstices of masculine
culture, moving between use of the dominant language or form of expression
and specific versions of experience based on their marginality. Similarly, men
and women who move between the cultures, languages, and the various configurations of power and meaning in complex colonial situations possess
what Chela Sandoval calls "oppositional consciousness," the ability to read
and write culture on multiple levels.[1] Such a view of cultural marginality ne-
cessitates the recognition of specific skills. As bell hooks writes:

> Living as we did—on the edge—we developed a particular way of seeing reality.
> We looked both from the outside in and from the inside out. We focused our atten-
> tion on the center as well as the margin. We understood both. . . .[2]

This location is fraught with tensions; it has the potential to lock the subject
away in isolation and despair as well as the potential for critical innovation
and particular strengths.

According to Immanuel Wallerstein, the political economy of margin and
center relies on the relationship between the two terms.[3] Ulf Hannerz has
expanded this model to describe a "world system of cultures" where marginal societies (here one can insert the terms "third world" or "underdeveloped") are not the passive recipients of ready-made images and consumer
goods. Rather, these are complex, sophisticated cultures which filter and mediate first world imports, recreating local meanings, producing hybrid cultural artifacts and subjects.[4]

A world which brings people, information, objects, and images across
enormous distances at rapid speeds destabilizes the conventions of identity

traditionally found in the culture of the first world during the first half of this century. "Deterritorialization" is one term for the displacement of identities, persons, and meanings that is endemic to the postmodern world system. Gilles Deleuze and Felix Guattari use the term "deterritorialization" to locate this moment of alienation and exile in language and literature. In one sense it describes the effects of radical distanciation between signifier and signified. Meaning and utterances become estranged. This defamiliarization enables imagination, even as it produces alienation, "to express another potential community, to force the means for another consciousness and another sensibility."[5] The paradoxical nature of this utopian moment in displacement can be realized in language or in the literature that Deleuze and Guattari designate as "minor." This is not a literature of "masters" or "masterpieces." Deleuze and Guattari assert: "We might as well say that minor no longer designates specific literatures but the revolutionary conditions for every literature within the heart of what is called great (or established) literature."[6] This writing dismantles notions of value, genre, canon, etc. It travels, moves between centers and margins.[7] Within the constructs of Deleuze and Guattari's theory, this process can be seen as both deterritorialization and reterritorialization—not imperialism but nomadism.[8]

The value of this conception lies in the paradoxical movement between minor and major—a refusal to admit either position as final or static. The issue is positionality. In modern autobiographical discourses, for example, the self that is constructed is often construed to be evolving in a linear fashion from a stable place of origin towards a substantial present. In postmodern autobiographical writing such a singular, linear construction of the self is often untenable or, at the very least, in tension with competing issues.

Much of contemporary feminist theory proposes a strategy of reading and an analysis of positionality similar to Deleuze and Guattari's conception of "becoming minor." In working with issues of race, class, and sexualities, as well as gender, feminist discourses have come to stress difference and oscillation of margin and center in the construction of personal and political identities. In fact, the difficulty of defining and totalizing the full range of feminist concerns marks the enriched diversity of this field at this particular historical juncture.

For the first world feminist critic, therefore, the challenge at this particular time is to develop a discourse that responds to the power relations of the world system, that is, to examine her location in the dynamic of centers and margins. Any other strategy merely consolidates the illusion of marginality while glossing over or refusing to acknowledge centralities. Thus, the first world feminist critic may be marginal *vis à vis* the literary establishment or the academy that employs her, yet she may also be more closely linked to these institutions than a non-western or third world feminist critic. Interpretations based on dualities and dialectical oppositions may not provide adequate models for explaining our differences and our respective positions in full complexity.

How do we begin to make methods of describing, explaining, and understanding this world of differences in order to make the connections necessary to change prevailing power relations? Deleuze and Guattari begin their investigation by focusing on the potential in language itself—"How many people live today in a language that is not their own?" they ask.[9] Displaced, marginal people—immigrants, subjects of external and internal colonialism, subjects of racial, gendered, or sexual oppression—recognize this issue in the full spectrum of affirmative and negative aspects. Gloria Anzaldúa, an American writer who describes herself as a Chicana, a feminist, and a lesbian, describes the damage of this system as well as the possibility of developing a strategic response:

> Because white eyes do not want to know us, they do not bother to learn our language, the language which reflects us, our culture, our spirit. The schools we attended or didn't attend did not give us the skills for writing nor the confidence that we were correct in using our class and ethnic languages. I, for one, became adept at, and majored in English to spite, to show up, the arrogant racist teachers who thought all Chicano children were dumb and dirty. . . . And though I now write my poems in Spanish as well as English I feel the rip-off of my native tongue. . . .[10]

Anzaldúa's project has several dimensions: the recognition of a minor literature written from a viewpoint based on the experience of marginality, the full identification with that minor position, and the acknowledgment that her capacity to use the dominant or major language has strategic value. Ripped-off, defensive of her right to her native tongue, certainly embittered, Anzaldúa writes through Sandoval's oppositional consciousness. Here she uses English for a purpose—stretching the language somewhat out of its major shape. In this instance, a major language has a minor use; it deconstructs its own preconditions in its very employment. Deleuze and Guattari explore this process when they write:

> This is the problem of immigrants, and especially of their children, the problem of minorities, the problem of a minor literature, but also a problem for all of us: how to tear a minor literature away from its own language, allowing it to challenge the language and making it follow a sober revolutionary path? How to become a nomad and an immigrant and a gypsy in relation to one's own language?[11]

When first world critics advocate a process of "becoming minor" it is necessary to ask: where are we located in this movement of language and literature? What are we losing with such a move? What do we stand to gain? Do
we have freedom of movement and where does this freedom come from? For
example, I would have to pay attention to whether or not it is possible for me
to *choose* deterritorialization or whether deterritorialization has chosen me.
For if I choose deterritorialization, I go into literary/linguistic exile with all
my cultural baggage intact. If deterritorialization has chosen me—that is, if I
have been cast out of home or language without forethought or permission,
then my point of view will be more complicated. Both positions are constructed by the world system but they are not equal. Of course, Deleuze, and
Guattari are suggesting that we are all deterritorialized on some level in the
process of language itself and that this is a point of contact between "us all."
Yet we have different privileges and different compensations for our positions in the field of power relations. My caution is against a form of theoretical tourism on the part of the first world critic, where the margin becomes a
linguistic or critical vacation, a new poetics of the exotic. One can also read
Deleuze and Guattari's resistance to this romantic trope in their refusal to
recognize a point of origin. Theirs is a poetics of travel where there is no return ticket and we all meet, therefore, en train. Reterritorialization without
imperialism? Can language provide a model of this process? Who dares let go
of their respective representations and systems of meaning, their identity
politics and theoretical homes, when it is, as Kafka rightly noted, "a matter
of life and death here?"[12]

What is lost in Deleuze and Guattari's formulation is the acknowledgment that oppositional consciousness (with its benefits and costs) stems
from the daily, lived experience of oppression. Language can constantly remind us of the differences encoded in social relations. It may well be the site
of the problem "for us all," but I am confused by the universalizing of the
term "us." Who is the "us" that is circulating in the essay "What Is a Minor
Literature?"

I have found several more cogent discussions of deterritorialization and
oppositional consciousness in the recent writings of some contemporary
feminists. I will focus on two writers, in particular, to illustrate this method
of feminist discourse, but there are many others who could easily be invoked
for this discussion.[13] One writer I would like to discuss, Minnie Bruce Pratt,
is a white American born in the South. Her essay "Identity: Skin Blood
Heart" explores the difficulty and the costs of maintaining a notion of identity based on racist and heterosexual privilege. In the autobiographical
process of memory and review in this essay Pratt questions the conditions of

her "home" in the past and looks for a different representation of identity
and location. In *Claiming an Identity They Taught Me to Despise* Michelle
Cliff, born in Jamaica and writing in New York, constructs an autobiographical poetics that moves relentlessly towards a minor position. What is most
interesting about both these memoirs is their inability to remain in any one
position—past, utopian, present, minor, major—they explore the social relations that create all of these locations.

Location is a crucial metaphor in Pratt's considerations of identity. The
first words we read are: "I live in a part of Washington D.C. that white sub-
urbanites called 'the jungle' . . ."[14] Where Pratt as a white, lesbian feminist
lives is always central to her description and explanation of a change in consciousness and way of being. She begins at the end of her story, in Washington D.C., her present location. But she soon moves us to Alabama where she
grew up during the era of civil rights struggles. She simultaneously evokes
the world of her childhood while dismantling the conditions of her early life.
A desire to be and feel "at home" is examined in light of who and what made
the conditions of security and contentment possible. In particular, Pratt focuses on the radical separation between people of different skin colors in her
community. This separation was justified to her when she was a girl by a
rigid system of racist explanation and rationalization. Pratt relates how she
felt safe in this world, accepting its terms, never pushed to question the
structure of its legitimation.

Protection and security come to be contextualized when Pratt finds herself feeling increasingly threatened by sexism and homophobia. Habituated
to white southern gentility, Pratt has a rude awakening when she transgresses the boundaries of her culture. She finds that she no longer merits protection or consideration:

> Raised to believe that I could be where I wanted and have what I wanted, as a
> grown woman I thought I could simply claim what I wanted. . . . I had no under-
> standing of the limits that I lived within, nor of how much my memory and my ex-
> perience of a safe space was to be based on places secured by omission, exclusion, or
> violence, and on my submitting to the limits of that place.[15]

The incident which prompts this reflection involves the loss of Pratt's
children in a custody battle. Her parents withdraw their emotional support
from her at the same time. In this process of estrangement and loss, Pratt
feels expelled from the warm circle of the home she had known. "I felt," she
writes, "like my life was cracking around me."[16] Reflecting on the costs of
the security she has taken for granted, she chooses to go another route—

rather than return to the terms she had taken for granted, Pratt chooses to learn about the social relations that create the terms.

Pratt's autobiographical essay elaborates a dynamic feminist theory of location and positionality. Moving away from "home" to deconstruct the terms of social privilege and power, such a feminist practice favors the process of the move over the ultimate goal. The uncertainty of this situation is preferable, Pratt argues, to the sensation of being homesick while at "home."

For the first world feminist critic the process of becoming minor has two primary aspects. First, I must acknowledge that there are things that I do not know. Second, I must find out how to learn about what I have been taught to avoid, fear, or ignore. A critique of where I come from, my home location, takes me away from the familiar. Yet, there is no pure space of total deterritortalization. I must look carefully at what I carry with me that could help me with the process. This is crucial if I am to avoid appropriating the minor through romanticization, envy, or guilt. Becoming minor is not a process of emulation. As Pratt writes: "I am compelled *by my own life* to strive for a different place than the one we have lived in."[17]

This is work that feminists have to do for themselves—sometimes in concert with others, sometimes alone. What we gain from this process is an understanding of what connects us as well as how we are different from each other—here re-written as a refusal of the terms of radical separation. Exploring all the differences, keeping identities distinct, is the only way we can keep power differentials from masquerading as universals. We will have different histories, but we will often have similar struggles. To recognize with whom we need to work instead of against is a continual process.

The first stage in this process is refusing the privilege of universalizing theories. Some of us may experience ourselves as minor in a world that privileges the masculine gender. But our own centrality in terms of race, class, ethnicity, religious identity, age, nationality, sexual preference, and levels of disabilities is often ignored in our own work. All women are not equal, and we do not all have the same experiences (even of gender oppression). When we insist upon gender alone as a universal system of explanation we sever ourselves from other women. How can we speak to each other if we deny our particularities? Recognizing the minor cannot erase the aspects of the major, but as a mode of understanding it enables us to see the fissures in our identities, to unravel the seams of our totalities. First world feminist criticism is struggling to avoid repeating the same imperializing moves that we claim to protest. We must leave home, as it were, since our homes are often sites of

racism, sexism, and other damaging social practices. Where we come to locate ourselves in terms of our specific histories and differences must be a
place with room for what can be salvaged front the past and what can be
made new. What we gain is a reterritorialization; we reinhabit a world of our
making (here "our" is expanded to a coalition of identities—neither universal nor particular). In this spirit Pratt writes: "One gain for me as I change: I
learn a way of looking at the world that is more accurate, complex, multi-
layered, multi-dimensioned, more truthful: to see the world of overlapping
circles. . . . "[18]

In *Claiming an Identity They Taught Me to Despise* Michelle Cliff describes the process of finding a social space to inhabit that will not deny any
of the complicated parts of her identity and history.[19] Radically deterritorialized from a Carribean culture and a race by a family conspiracy of silence and
denial, she explores the parameters of identity and the limits of privilege.
Separated from her home and family by geography, education, and experience, Cliff articulates the boundaries between homelessness and origin, between exile and belonging. She must, as she puts it, "untangle the filaments
of my history."[20]

The first move Cliff makes in her autobiographical memoir is a return to
the territory of her childhood. This trip into memory uncovers a primal in-
junction. "Isolate yourself," she was told:

> If they find out about you it's all over. Forget about your great-grandfather with
> the darkest skin. . . . Go to college. Go to England to study. Learn about the Italian
> Renaissance and forget that they kept slaves. Ignore the tears of the Indians. Black
> Americans don't understand us either. . . . Blend in. . . .[21]

In order to understand her refusal to blend in, Cliff begins to explore what is
at stake in her mother's efforts to obscure her racial identity. She has to learn
the history of white, black, and mulatto people in Jamaica, the island where
she was born. It is a history of divisions, violence, and suppression. A creole
culture with no single origin, Jamaica exists in many levels and time periods.
Cliff moves through several of these identities. She rewrites her history to
"claim" an identity through her powers of storytelling and imagination.

Turning her memories of childhood over and over, Cliff begins with the
terrain of the island. Looking for a firm foundation for her identity she finds
instead that the geography of that time is "obsolete." There is no possibility
of return to that innocent land. Instead, she moves through each place she
has lived, asking, "What is here for me: where do these things lead?"[22] At
first Cliff discovers the pain that her family had struggled to spare her.
Behind each nostalgic memory lies a history of oppression:

> Behind the warmth and light are dark and damp/ . . . behind the rain and river
> water, periods of drought/underneath the earth are the dead/ . . . underneath the
> distance is the separation/ . . . behind the fertility are the verdicts of insanity/ . . .
> underlying my grandmother's authority with land and scripture is obedience to a
> drunken husband . . .[23]

Her new view of her past and her life has to contain all of these images and
kinds of knowledge. They become materials for Cliff to discover and use, stories to listen to again, photographs to review, a landscape to rewrite. Mining
her memories of both Jamaica and New York she is no longer able to remain
separated from the full range of experiences and identities available to her in
the past and present.

In the section of the text entitled "Against Granite" Cliff refines the possibilities of reterritorialization. Imagining an archive where historians are
restoring "details of an unwritten past" she writes:

> Out back is evidence of settlement: a tin roof crests a hill amid mountains—or-
> ange and tangerine trees form a natural border. A river where women bathe can be
> seen from the historian's enclave. The land has been cultivated; the crops are ready
> for harvest. In the foreground a young black woman sits on grass which flourishes.
> Here women pick freely from the trees.[24]

The inhabitants of this imaginary settlement are women, the "historians"
who keep an eye on the border guards who threaten to invade their camp.
Cliff names the threat to this vision of postcolonial feminist space:
"slicers/suturers/invaders/abusers/sterilizers/infibulators/castrators/dividers/
enclosers . . ."[25] Reflecting her new passion for historical specificity, Cliff's
naming project becomes more explicit: "Upjohn, Nestle, Riker's, Welfare,
Rockland State, Jesus, the Law of the Land—and yes, and also—Gandhi and
Kenyatta." Cliff constitutes a kind of collective history based on gender as
well as on race and class. It is a history of women who are threatened variously and complexly by forces ranging from an American drug company to
the masculinist proponents of certain nationalist liberation struggles. This
kind of epistemological shift helps to enact a politics of identity that is flexible enough to encompass the ironies and contradictions of the modern world
system.

The notion of settlement delineated in this section of the text is a fictional terrain, a reterritorialization that has passed through several versions
of deterritorialization to posit a powerful theory of location based on contingency, history, and change. One of the final images written in the text is a
garden that resonates with many cultural associations, Western and non-
Western. In Cliff's text the garden is a piece of land where she can work and

live. The parameters are fluid, there are no "slicers" or "dividers" here. "To garden is a solitary act," she writes.[26] Yet, this activity does not replicate the enclosed space of the modern ego, exiled from the world. The garden is, Cliff writes:

> Not a walled place—in fact, open on all sides.
> Not secret—but private.
> A private open space.[27]

This is a new terrain, a new location, in feminist poetics. Not a room of one's own, not a fully public or collective self, not a domestic realm—it is a space in the imagination which allows for the inside, the outside, and the liminal elements of inbetween. Not a romanticized pastoral nor a modernist urban utopia—Cliff's garden is the space where writing occurs without loss or separation. It is "next to," or juxtaposed, to the other plots of postmodern fictions and realities. Feminist writing in this expanded sense of "minor" acts against the romanticization of solitude and the suppression of differences. It points towards a rewriting of the connections between different parts of the self in order to make a world of possibilities out of the experience of displacement.

NOTES

1. Chela Sandoval, (n.d.), "Women Respond to Racism: A Report on the National Women's Studies Association Conference, Storrs, Connecticut," Occasional Papers Series: *The Struggle Within* (Oakland, Ca.: Center for Third World Organizing).

2. Bell Hooks, *Feminist Theory: From Margin to Center* (Boston: South End Press, 1984).

3. Immanuel Wallerstein, *The Modern World System* (New York: Academic Press, 1974).

4. Ulf Hannerz, "The World System of Culture: The International Flow of Meaning and Its Local Management," mss., 1985. For a related discussion see James Clifford, "Histories of the Tribal and the Modern," *Art in America* (April 1985): 164–77, 215.

5. Gilles Deleuze and Felix Guattari, "What Is a Minor Literature?" in *Kafka: Towards a Minor Literature*, trans. Dana Polan (Minneapolis: Univ. of Minnesota Press, 1986), 17.

6. Ibid., 18.

7. For an elaboration of the notion of the circulation of ideas and theories see Edward Said, "Traveling Theory" in *The World, the Text, the Critic* (Cambridge: Harvard Univ. Press, 1983), 226–47.

8. In his essay on Deleuze and Guattari's *Mille Plateaux* Stephen Muecke describes/cites their formulation of ex-centric nomad societies as models of "becoming and heterogeneity" as opposed to "the stable, the eternal, the identical and the con-

stant." "It is a paradoxical 'model' of becoming." Cf. Stephen Muecke, "The Discourse of Nomadology: Phylums in Flux," *Art and Text* 14 (1984): 27.

9. Deleuze and Guattari, 19.

10. Gloria Anzaldúa, "Speaking in Tongues: A Letter to Third World Women Writers," in *This Bridge Called My Back: Writings by Radical Women of Color*, Cherríe Moraga and Gloria Anzaldúa, eds. (Watertown, Ma.: Persephone Press, 1981), 165–66.

11. Deleuze and Guattari, 19.

12. Ibid., 17.

13. See the work of: Cherríe Moraga, Audre Lorde, Elly Bulkin, Barbara Smith, Lillian Smith, Mitsuye Yamada, Chela Sandoval, Bernice Reagon, Adrienne Rich, Gloria Hull, Jewelle L. Gomez, Becky Birtha, Cheryl Clark, June Jordan, Katie King, Barbara Harlow, Nellie Wong, Bell Hooks, Osa Hidalgo, Lata Mani, Ruth Frankenberg, Lisa Bloom, Debbie Gordon, Biddy Martin, Chandra Talpade Mohanty, Alicia Partnoy, and many others.

14. Minnie Bruce Pratt, "Identity: Skin Blood Heart," in *Yours in Struggle: Three Feminist Perspectives on Anti-Semitism and Racism*, Elly Bulkin, Minnie Bruce Pratt, and Barbara Smith, eds. (Brooklyn, N.Y.: Long Haul Press, 1984), 2.

15. Ibid., 25–26.

16. Ibid., 39.

17. Ibid., 48–49.

18. Ibid., 17.

19. Michelle Cliff, *Claiming an Identity They Taught Me to Despise* (Watertwon, Ma.: Persephone Press, 1980).

20. Ibid., 7.

21. Ibid.

22. Ibid., 20.

23. Ibid., 21.

24. Ibid., 29–30.

25. Ibid., 30.

26. Ibid., 55.

27. Ibid., 52.

IS THE ETHNIC "AUTHENTIC" IN THE DIASPORA?

R. Radhakrishnan

My eleven-year-old son asks me, "Am I Indian or American?" The question excites me, and I think of the not-too-distant future when we will discuss the works of Salman Rushdie, Toni Morrison, Amitav Ghosh, Jamaica Kincaid, Bessie Head, Amy Tan, Maxine Hong Kingston, and many others who have agonized over the question of identity through their multivalent narratives. I tell him he is *both* and offer him brief and down-to-earth definitions of ethnicity and how it relates to nationality and citizenship. He follows me closely and says, "Yeah, Dad [or he might have said "*Appa*"], I am both," and a slight inflection in his voice underscores the word "both," as his two hands make a symmetrical gesture on either side of his body. I am persuaded, for I have seen him express deep indignation and frustration when friends, peers, teachers, and coaches mispronounce his name in cavalier fashion. He pursues the matter with a passion bordering on the pedagogical, until his name comes out correctly on alien lips. I have also heard him narrate to his "mainstream" friends stories from the *Ramayana* and the *Mahabharatha* with an infectious enthusiasm for local detail, and negotiate nuances of place and time with great sensitivity. My son comes back to me and asks, "But you and Amma [or did he say "Mom"?] are not U.S. citizens?" I tell him that we are Indian citizens who live here as resident aliens. "Oh, yes, I remember we have different passports," he says and walks away.

At a recent Deepavali (a significant Hindu religious festival) get together of the local India Association (well before the horrendous destruction of the Babri Masjid by Hindu zealots) I listen to an elderly Indian man explain to a group of young first-generation Indian-American children the festival's significance. He goes on and on about the contemporary significance of Lord Krishna, who has promised to return to the world in human form during times of crisis to punish the wicked and protect the good. During this lecture, I hear not a word to distinguish Hindu identity from Indian identity, not a word about present-day communal violence in India in the name of Hindu fundamentalism, and not even an oblique mention of the ongoing crisis in Ayodhya. In a sense, these egregious oversights and omissions do not matter, for the first-generation American kids, the intended recipients of this ethnic lesson, hardly pay attention: they sleep, run around, or chatter among themselves, their mouths full of popcorn. I do not know whether I am more angry with the elderly gentleman for his disingenuous ethnic narrative, or with the younger generation, who in their putative assimilation do not seem to care about ethnic origins.

I begin with these two episodes because they exemplify a number of issues and tensions that inform ethnicity. I imagine that the main problem that intrigued my son was this: How could some*one* be both *one* and something *other*? How could the unity of identity have more than one face or name? If my son is both Indian and American, which *one* is he *really*? Which is the real self and which the other? How do these two selves coexist and how do they weld into one identity? How is ethnic identity related to national identity? Is this relationship hierarchically structured, such that the "national" is supposed to subsume and transcend ethnic identity, or does this relationship produce a hyphenated identity, such as African-American, Asian-American, and so forth, where the hyphen marks a dialogic and nonhierarchic conjuncture? What if identity is exclusively ethnic and not national at all? Could such an identity survive (during these days of bloody "ethnic cleansing") and be legitimate, or would society construe this as a nonviable "difference," that is, experientially authentic but not deserving of hegemony?

The Indian gentleman's address to his audience of first-generation Indian-Americans raises several insidious and potentially harmful conflicts. First it uses religious (Hindu) identity to empower Indian ethnicity in the United States, which then masquerades as Indian nationalism. What does the appeal to "roots and origins" mean in this context, and what is it intended to achieve? Is ethnicity a mere flavor, an ancient smell to be relived as nostalgia? Is it a kind of superficial blanket to be worn over the substantive U.S. identity? Or is Indianness being advocated as a basic immutable form of being that triumphs over changes, travels, and dislocations?

The narrative of ethnicity in the United States might run like this. During the initial phase, immigrants suppress ethnicity in the name of pragmatism and opportunism. To be successful in the New World, they must actively assimilate and, therefore, hide their distinct ethnicity. This phase, similar to the Booker T. Washington era in African-American history, gives way to a Du

Boisian period that refuses to subsume political, civil, and moral revolutions under mere strategies of economic betterment. In the call for total revolution that follows, immigrants reassert ethnicity in all its autonomy. The third phase seeks the hyphenated integration of ethnic identity with national identity under conditions that do not privilege the "national" at the expense of the "ethnic." We must keep in mind that in the United States the renaming of ethnic identity in national terms produces a preposterous effect. Take the case of the Indian immigrant. Her naturalization into American citizenship simultaneously minoritizes her identity. She is now reborn as an ethnic minority American citizen.

Is this empowerment or marginalization? This new American citizen must think of her Indian self as an ethnic self that defers to her nationalized American status. The culturally and politically hegemonic Indian identity is now a mere qualifier: "ethnic." Does this transformation suggest that identities and ethnicities are not a matter of fixed and stable selves but rather the results and products of fortuitous travels and recontextualizations? Could this mean that how identity relates to place is itself the expression of a shifting equilibrium? If ethnic identity is a strategic response to a shifting sense of time and place, how is it possible to have a theory of ethnic identity posited on the principle of a natural and native self? Is ethnicity nothing but, to use the familiar formula, what ethnicity does? Is ethnic selfhood an end in itself, or is it a necessary but determinate phase to be left behind when the time is right to inaugurate the "postethnic"? With some of these general concerns in mind, I would now like to address the Indian diaspora in the United States.

This chapter began with a scenario both filial and pedagogic. The child asks a question or expresses some doubt or anxiety and the parent resolves the problem. The parent brings together two kinds of authority: the authority of a parent to transmit and sustain a certain pattern generationally and the authority of a teacher based on knowledge and information. Thus, in my response to my son, "You are both," I was articulating myself as teacher as well as parent. But how do I (as a parent) know that I know? Do I have an answer by virtue of my parenthood, or does the answer have a pedagogic authority that has nothing to do with being a parent? In other words, how is my act of speaking for my daughter or son different from a teacher speaking for a student? Is knowledge *natural* or is it a questioning of origins? In either case, is there room for the student's own self-expression? How are we to decide whether or not the "conscious" knowledge of the teacher and the "natural" knowledge of the parent are relevant in the historical instance of the child/student?

Let's look at yet another episode as a counterpoint to my teacherly episode with my son. During the last few years, I have talked and listened to a number of young, gifted Indian children of the diaspora who, like my son, were born here and are thus "natural" American citizens. I was startled when they told me that they had grown up with a strong sense of being exclusively Indian; and the reason was that they had experienced little during their growing years that held out promise of first-class American citizenship. Most of them felt they could not escape being *marked* as different by virtue of their skin color, their family background, and other ethnic and unassimilated traits. Many of them recited the reality of a double life, ethnic private life and the "American" public life, with very little mediation between the two. For example, they talked about being targets of racial slurs and racialized sexist slurs, and they remembered not receiving the total understanding of their parents who did not quite "get it." Sure, the parents understood the situation in an academic and abstract way and would respond with the fierce rhetoric of civil rights and antiracism, but the fact was that the parents had not gone through similar experiences during their childhoods. Although the home country is indeed replete with its own divisions, phobias, and complexes, the racial line of color is not one of them. Thus, if the formulaic justification of parental wisdom is that the parent "has been there before," the formula does not apply here. Is the prescriptive wisdom of "you are both" relevant?

Within the diaspora, how should the two generations address each other? I would suggest for starters that we candidly admit that learning and knowledge, particularly in the diaspora, can only be a two-way street. The problem here is more acute than the unavoidable "generation gap" between students/ young adults and teachers/parents. The tensions between the old and new homes create the problem of divided allegiances that the two generations experience differently. The very organicity of the family and the community, displaced by travel and relocation, must be renegotiated and redefined. The two generations have different starting points and different givens. This phenomenon of historical rupture within the "same" community demands careful and rigorous analysis. The older generation cannot afford to invoke India in an authoritarian mode to resolve problems in the diaspora, and the younger generation would be ill advised to indulge in a spree of forgetfulness about "where they have come from." It is vital that the two generations empathize and desire to understand and appreciate patterns of experience not their own.

What does "being Indian" mean in the United States? How can one be and live Indian without losing clout and leverage as Americans? How can one transform the so-called mainstream American identity into the image of the many ethnicities that constitute it? We should not pretend we are living in some idealized "little India" and not in the United States. As Maxine Hong Kingston demonstrates painfully in *The Woman Warrior*, both the home country and the country of residence could become mere "ghostly" locations, and the result can only be a double depoliticization. For example, the anguish in her book is *relational*; it is not exclusively about China or the United States. The home country is not "real" in its own terms and yet it is real enough to impede Americanization, and the "present home" is materially real and yet not real enough to feel authentic. Whereas at home one could be just Indian or Chinese, here one is constrained to become Chinese-, Indian-, or Asian-American. This leads us to the question: Is the "Indian" in Indian and the "Indian" in Indian-American the same and therefore interchangeable? Which of the two is authentic, and which merely strategic or reactive? To what extent does the "old country" function as a framework and regulate our transplanted identities within the diaspora? Should the old country be revered as a pregiven absolute, or is it all right to invent the old country itself in response to our contemporary location? Furthermore, whose interpretation of India is correct: the older generation's or that of the younger; the insider's version or the diasporan?

These questions emphasize the reality that when people move, identities, perspectives, and definitions change. If the category "Indian" *seemed secure*, positive, and affirmative within India, the same term takes on a reactive, strategic character when it is pried loose from its nativity. The issue then is not just "being Indian" in some natural and self-evident way ("being Indian" naturally is itself a highly questionable premise given the debacle of nationalism, but that is not my present concern), but "cultivating Indianness" self-consciously for certain reasons; for example, the reason could be that one does not want to lose one's past or does not want to be homogenized namelessly, or one could desire to combat mainstream racism with a politicized deployment of one's own "difference." To put it simply, one's very being becomes polemical. Is there a true and authentic identity, more lasting than mere polemics and deeper than strategies?

Before I get into an analysis of this problem, I wish to sketch briefly a few responses to the home country that I consider wrong and quite dangerous. First, from the point of view of the assimilated generation, it is all too easy to want to forget the past and forfeit community in the name of the "free individual," a path open to first-generation citizens. As Malcolm X, Du Bois, and others have argued, it is in the nature of a racist, capitalist society to isolate and privatize the individual and to foster the myth of the equal and free individual unencumbered by either a sense of community or a critical sense of the past. As the Clarence Thomas nomination has amply demonstrated, the theme of "individual success" is a poisoned candy manufactured by capitalist greed in active complicity with a racist disregard for history. We cannot afford to forget that we live in a society that is profoundly antihistorical, and that leaders represent us who believe that we have buried the memories of Vietnam in the sands of the Gulf War, which itself is remembered primarily as a high-tech game intended for visual pleasure. We must not underestimate the capacity of capitalism, superbly assisted by technology, to produce a phenomenology of the present so alluring in its immediacy as to seduce the consumer to forget the past and bracket the future.

The second path is the way of the film *Mississippi Masala*, reveling uncritically in the commodification of hybridity. The two young lovers walk away into the rain in a Hollywood resolution of the agonies of history. Having found each other as "hybrids" in the here and now of the United States, the two young adults just walk out of their "prehistories" into the innocence of physical, heterosexual love. The past *sucks*, parents *suck*, Mississippi *sucks*, as do India and Uganda, and the only thing that matters is the bonding between two bodies that step off the pages of history, secure in their "sanctioned ignorance," to use Gayatri Chakravorty Spivak's ringing phrase. What is disturbing about the "masala" resolution is that it seems to take on the question of history, but it actually trivializes histories (there is more than one implicated here) and celebrates a causeless rebellion in the epiphany of the present. Just think of the racism awaiting the two lovers. In invoking the term "masala" superficially, the movie begs us to consume it as exotica and make light of the historical ingredients that go into making "masala." My point here is that individualized escapes (and correspondingly, the notion of the "history of the present" as a total break from the messy past) may serve an emotional need, but they do not provide an understanding of the histories of India, Uganda, or the racialized South.

What about the options open to the generation emotionally committed to India? First, it is important to make a distinction *between information about and knowledge of India* and an *emotional investment in India*. What can be shared cognitively between the two generations is the former. It would be foolish of me to expect that India will move my son the same way it moves me. It would be equally outrageous of me to claim that somehow my India is more real than his; my India is as much an invention or production as his. There is more than enough room for multiple versions of the same reality. But here again, our inventions and interpretations are themselves products of history and not subjective substitutes for history. The discovery of an "authentic" cannot rule over the reality of multiple perspectives, and, moreover, we cannot legislate or hand down authenticity from a position of untested moral or political high ground.

Second, my generation has to actively learn to find "Indianness" within and in conjunction with the minority-ethnic continuum in the United States. To go back to my conversations with the younger generation, it is important to understand that many of them confess to finding their "ethnic Indian" identity (as distinct from the "Indian" identity experienced at home) not in isolation but in a coalition with other minorities. It is heartening to see that a number of students identify themselves under the third world umbrella and have gone so far as to relate the "third world out there" and "the third world within." (I am aware that the term "third world" is deeply problematic and often promotes an insensitive dedifferentiation of the many histories that comprise the third world, but this term when used by the groups that constitute it has the potential to resist the dominant groups' divide-and-rule strategies.)

My generation is prone, as it ages, to take recourse to some mythic India as a way of dealing with the contemporary crises of fragmentation and racialization in the United States. Instead, we could learn from first-generation Indians who have developed solidarity and community by joining together in political struggle. The crucial issue for the older generation here is to think through the politics of why we are here and to deliberate carefully about which America they want to identify with: the white, male, corporate America or the America of the Rainbow Coalition. In cases where economic betterment is the primary motivation for immigration into the United States, and especially when these cases are successful, it is easy to deny the reality of our racially and *color*fully marked American citizenship. Even as I write, communities are targeting schoolteachers with "foreign" accents for dismissal.

Third, it is disingenuous of my generation to behave as though one India exists "out there" and our *interpretation of India* is it. This is a generation both of and distant from India, therefore the politics of proximity has to negotiate dialectically and critically with the politics of distance. We may not like this, but it is our responsibility to take our daughters and sons seriously when they ask us, Why then did you leave India? I believe with Amitav Ghosh (I refer here to his novel *The Shadow Lines*) that places are both real and imagined, that we can know places that are distant as much as we can misunderstand and misrepresent places we inhabit. As Arjun Appadurai, among others, has argued, neither distance nor proximity guarantees truth or alienation. One could live within India and not care to discover India or live "abroad" and acquire a nuanced historical, appreciation of the home country, and vice versa. During times when the demographic flows of peoples across territorial boundaries have become more the norm than the exception, it is counterproductive to maintain that one can only understand a place when one is in it. It is quite customary for citizens who have emigrated to experience distance as a form of critical enlightenment or a healthy "estrangement" from their birthland, and to experience another culture or location as a reprieve from the orthodoxies of their own "given" cultures. It is also quite normal for the same people, who now have lived a number of years in their adopted country, to return through critical negotiation to aspects of their culture that they had not really studied before and to develop criticisms of their chosen world. Each place or culture gains when we open it to new standards.

In saying this I am not conceding to individuals the right to rewrite collective histories that determine individual histories in the first place, nor am I invoking diasporan cultural politics as a facile answer to the structural problem of asymmetry and inequality between "developed" and "underdeveloped" nations. My point is that the diaspora has created rich possibilities of understanding different histories. And these histories have taught us that identities, selves, traditions, and natures do change with travel (and there is nothing decadent or deplorable about mutability) and that we can achieve such changes in identity intentionally. In other words, we need to make substantive distinctions between "change as default or as the path of least resistance" and "change as conscious and directed self-fashioning."

Among these mutable, changing traditions and natures, who are we to ourselves? Is the identity question so hopelessly politicized that it cannot step beyond the history of strategies and counterstrategies? Do I know in some abstract, ontological, transhistorical way what "being Indian" is all about and on that basis devise strategies to hold on to that ideal identity, or do I—when faced by the circumstances of history—strategically practice Indian identity to maintain uniqueness and resist anonymity through homogenization? For that matter, why can't I be "Indian" without having to be "authentically Indian"? What is the difference and how does it matter? In the diasporan context in the United States, ethnicity is often forced to take on the discourse of authenticity just to protect and maintain its space and history. Would "black" have to be authentic if it were not pressured into a reactive mode by the dominance of "white"? It becomes difficult to determine if the drive toward authenticity comes from within the group as a spontaneous self-affirming act, or if authenticity is nothing but a paranoid reaction to the "naturalness" of dominant groups. Why should "black" be authentic when "white" is hardly even seen as a color, let alone pressured to demonstrate its authenticity?

Let us ask the following question: If a minority group were left in peace with itself and not dominated or forced into a relationship with the dominant world or national order, would the group still find the term "authentic" meaningful or necessary? The group would continue being what it is without having to authenticate itself. My point is simply this: When we say "authenticate," we also have to ask, "Authenticate to whom and for what purpose?" Who and by what authority is checking our credentials? Is "authenticity" a home we build for ourselves or a ghetto we inhabit to satisfy the dominant world?

I do understand and appreciate the need for authenticity, especially in first world advanced capitalism, where the marketplace and commodities are the norm. But the rhetoric of authenticity tends to degenerate into essentialism. I would much rather situate the problem of authenticity alongside the phenomenon of relationality and the politics of representation. How does authenticity speak for itself: as one voice or as many related voices, as monolithic identity or as identity hyphenated by difference? When someone speaks as an Asian-American, who exactly is speaking? If we dwell in the hyphen, who represents the hyphen: the Asian or the American, or can the hyphen speak for itself without creating an imbalance between the Asian and the American components? What is the appropriate narrative to represent relationality?

Back to my son's question again: True, both components have status, but which has the power and the potential to read and interpret the other on its terms? If the Asian is to be Americanized, will the American submit to Asianization? Will there be a reciprocity of influence whereby American identity itself will be seen as a form of openness to the many ingredients that constitute it, or will "Americanness" function merely as a category of marketplace pluralism?

Very often it is when we feel deeply dissatisfied with marketplace pluralism and its unwillingness to confront and correct the injustices of dominant racism that we turn our diasporan gaze back to the home country. Often, the gaze is uncritical and nostalgic. Often, we cultivate the home country with a vengeance. Several dangers exist here. We can cultivate India in total diasporan ignorance of the realities of the home country. By this token, anything and everything is India according to our parched imagination: half-truths, stereotypes, so-called traditions, rituals, and so forth. Or we can cultivate an idealized India that has nothing to do with contemporary history. Then again, we can visualize the India we remember as an antidote to the maladies both here and there and pretend that India hasn't changed since we left its shores. These options are harmful projections of individual psychological needs that have little to do with history. As diasporan citizens doing double duty (with accountability both here and there) we need to understand as rigorously as we can the political crises in India, both because they concern us and also because we have a duty to represent India to ourselves and to the United States as truthfully as we can.

Our ability to speak for India is a direct function of our knowledge about India. The crisis of secular nationalism in India, the ascendancy of Hindu fundamentalism and violence, the systematic persecution of Muslims, the incapacity of the Indian national government to speak on behalf of the entire nation, the opportunistic playing up of the opposition between secularism and religious identity both by the government and the opposition, the lack of success of a number of progressive local grassroots movements to influence electoral politics—these and many other such issues we need to study with great care and attention. Similarly, we need to make distinctions between left-wing movements in India that are engaged in critiquing secularism responsibly with the intention of opening up a range of indigenous alternatives, and right-wing groups whose only intention is to kindle a politics of hatred. Diasporan Indians should not use distance as an excuse for ignoring happenings in India. It is heartening to know that an alliance for a secular and democratic South Asia has recently been established in Cambridge, Massachusetts.

The diasporan hunger for knowledge about and intimacy with the home country should not turn into a transhistorical and mystic quest for origins. It is precisely this obsession with the sacredness of one's origins that leads peoples to disrespect the history of other people and to exalt one's own. Feeling deracinated in the diaspora can be painful, but the politics of origins cannot be the remedy.

Time now for one final episode. Watching Peter Brooks's production of the Hindu epic *Mahabharatha* with a mixed audience, I was quite surprised by the different reactions. We were viewing this film after we had all seen the homegrown TV serials *The Ramayana* and the *Mahabharatha*. By and large, initially my son's generation was disturbed by the international cast that seemed to falsify the Hindu/the Indian (again, a dangerous conflation) epic. How could an Ethiopian play the role of Bheeshma and a white European (I think Dutch) represent Lord Krishna? And all this so soon after they had been subjected to the "authentic version" from India? But soon they began enjoying the film for what it was. Still, it deeply upset a number of adults of my generation. To many of them, this was not the real thing, this could not have been the real Krishna. My own response was divided. I appreciated and enjoyed humanizing and demystifying Krishna, endorsed *in principle* globalizing a specific cultural product, and approved the production for not attempting to be an extravaganza. On the other hand, I was critical of some of its modernist irony and cerebral posturing, its shallow United Nations-style internationalism, its casting of an African male in a manner that endorsed certain black male stereotypes, and finally a certain Western, Eurocentric arrogance that commodifies the work of a different culture and decontextualizes it in the name of a highly skewed and uneven globalism.

Which is the true version? What did my friend mean when he said that this was not the real thing? Does he have some sacred and unmediated access to the real thing? Is his image any less an ideological fabrication (or the result of Hindu-Brahmanical canonization) than that of Peter Brooks? Did his chagrin have to do with the fact that a great epic had been produced critically, or with the fact that the producer was an outsider? What if an Indian feminist group had produced a revisionist version? Isn't the insider's truth as much an invention and an interpretation as that of the outsider? How do we distinguish an insider's critique from that of the outsider? If a Hindu director had undertaken globalizing the Hindu epic, would the project have been different or more acceptable or more responsive to the work's origins? But on the other hand, would a Western audience tolerate the Indianization of Homer, Virgil, or Shakespeare? Questions, more questions. I would rather proliferate questions than seek ready-made and ideologically overdetermined answers. And in a way, the diaspora is an excellent opportunity to think through some of these vexed questions: solidarity and criticism, belonging and distance, insider spaces and outsider spaces, identity as invention and identity as natural, location-subject positionality and the politics of representation, rootedness and rootlessness.

When my son wonders who he *is*, he is also asking a question about the future. For my part, I hope that his future and that of his generation will have many roots and many pasts. I hope, especially, that it will be a future where his identity will be a matter of rich and complex negotiation and not the result of some blind and official decree.

THE POLITICS OF RELOCATION

Expanding the idea of the "politics of location" articulated by the poet Adrienne Rich, this section investigates a more kinetic "politics of *reloca-tion.*" Just as Rich recognized that location is individual and particular and involves issues of politics (power), aesthetics, and identity, so too the essays in this section recognize the particulars of mobility. They demonstrate that how one experiences relocation, immigration, migration, or mobility is in large part shaped by the community to which one belongs and the circumstances that compel movement. Beginning with an overview of the effects of reloca-tion and immigration, by Thayer Scudder and Gustavo Pérez-Firmat, the essays in this section interrogate the paradigms of travel and home, power and identity, factoring in locations of gender, race, and historical moment. They demonstrate the dynamics of power in forced relocations and migrations, and the negotiations of the disempowered to retain or construct homesites.

The section begins with Thayer Scudder's analysis of the negative effects of forced relocation for modern Navajo Indians, taken from his *The Impacts of Forced Relocation on Navajos.* Commissioned by the Navajo Nation in 1974 to investigate the projected consequences of compulsory relocation from the Joint Use Area occupied by both Hopi and Navajo Indians, Scudder finds that the forced relocation of low-income rural populations with strong ties to the land, as in the case of the Navajo, is a "traumatic experience." Relocation, he argues, undermines "people's faith in themselves," creates dependency on relocation agencies, disrupts families, and undermines the influence and authority of local leaders. These factors work together to cause multidimensional stress—physiological, psychological, and sociocultural stress—that has deleterious effects on both the individual and the group; in this case, the Navajo Nation. Scudder's piece, while specifically about the Navajo, suggests ways of discussing other peoples forcefully moved from their homes at the same time that it counters the positive transformation of self that Leed and those who discuss leisure travel intimate.

The next essay, "The Desi Chain" by Gustavo Pérez-Firmat, delineates three stages of adaptation by an immigrant group to its new homeland, here Cuban-Americans. From the introduction to his *Life on the Hyphen: The Cuban-American Way*, the essay considers the forces of tradition and translation, of continuity and displacement, in shaping Cuban-American culture. In assessing what exiles go through in the new country, he discusses the one-and-a-half generation, those born in Cuba but who grew to be adults in America and who experience "life on the hyphen." Marginal to both the native and adopted cultures, this generation of emigrants is nonetheless able to circulate within and through both the old and the new cultures and, thus, is actually marginal to neither culture. Rather than adopting a model of opposition to discuss the relations between minority and majority cultures, as do Said and Kaplan, Pérez-Firmat suggests that for Cuban-Americans a model of collaboration and equilibrium between the claims of both cultures is more accurate. He then goes on to delineate three stages of adaptation by an immigrant group to its new homeland. The first is "substitutive" and is marked by nostalgia and the effort to create substitutes or copies of the home culture. The second stage is "destitution" when the sense of displacement crushes the fantasy of rootedness that the first stage tried to build. The third stage is "institution," or the establishment of a new relation between person and place that emphasizes the here and now. While these are largely chronologic stages, they can coexist within a single person, and individuals and communities can swing between one attitude and another.

The last essays consider migration and migration narratives within and to the United States by Chicano/as, Native Americans and African Americans, further demonstrating that relocation is both political and particular, that there is no essential "travel experience." In "The Homeland, Aztlán," from her book *Borderlands/La Frontera: The New Mestiza*, Gloria Anzaldúa traces the history of movement and migration of Chicano/as and the permeability of borders in the American Southwest. Her point is that despite changes in the political control of the Southwest, people have historically moved across geographic borders and have crossed hereditary borders to create a hybrid, the *mestizo/a*. She also investigates border culture, where boundaries are set up to distinguish one group of people from another, the safe from the unsafe. She says that the borderland that emerges "is a vague and undetermined place created by the emotional residue of an unnatural boundary. It is in a constant state of transition. The prohibited and the forbidden are its inhabitants." A writer who combines poetry with prose, personal introspection with history, English with Spanish, Anzaldúa problematizes such terms as origin, home, legal/illegal migration, boundary, and refuge when she points out that the

Mexican migrants the U.S. labels "illegal" are in reality returning to their ancient homeland, a place not of refuge but of danger to them.

In "Native American Novels: Homing In" (collected in Brian Swann and Arnold Krupat's *Recovering the Word: Essays in Native American Literature*), William Bevis calls into question assumptions made by white writers about place, time, self-identity, and travel, that one "finds" oneself by leaving home. While most white novels, Bevis notes, are "eccentric, centrifugal, diverging, expanding," most Native American novels are "incentric, centripetal, converging, contracting." In Native American novels, the hero comes home to a place and a time that bespeak tradition, authority, and society. It is here that the hero finds identity (a self that is transpersonal) and knowledge. Thus knowledge and identity are tied to experiences of place and time, as most theorists have argued, but in a different relation than in non-Native texts and practices. The focus is on a social or tribal interpretation rather than an individualist one. Bevis supports his argument with references to the now classic Native American novels of the twentieth century by D'Arcy McNickle, N. Scott Momaday, Leslie Marmon Silko, and James Welch.

The last two essays concern the experience of African Americans, starting with Carl Pedersen's "Sea Change: The Middle Passage and the Transatlantic Imagination" (from *The Black Columbiad: Defining Moments in African American Literature and Culture*, edited by Werner Sollors and Maria Diedrich). In it Pedersen investigates the meaning of the Middle Passage between Africa and the Americas by looking at a number of literary texts, from Olaudah Equiano's *Interesting Narrative* to Martin Delany's tale of a failed slave revolt at sea to Charles Johnson's 1990 novel *Middle Passage* and George Lamming's *Natives of My Person*. By drawing on literary works and by including Caribbean authors in his sketch of the Middle Passage, Pedersen demonstrates how the historical events of the Atlantic slave trade and voyages between Africa and the Americas are transformed in literature and imagination. He sees the Middle Passage as transformative, a space where past and present, Europe and Africa, memory and imagination meet to construct new discourses and hybrid identities. He argues that the Middle Passage is a space of memory and mediated reconstruction, not an end but the beginning of a new cultural configuration formulated by resistance. Like Bhabha's liminal spaces, the Middle Passage is an in-between site where new identities and discourses are forged.

Farah Jasmine Griffin's essay, the introduction to her book *"Who Set You Flowin'?": The African-American Migration Narrative*, outlines the pivotal moments of the African-American migration narrative and the direction the rest of her book will take. Griffin argues that the migration narrative is one of the dominant forms of African-American cultural production as artists and thinkers continue to come to terms with the massive dislocation of Black people, particularly during the Great Migration from the rural South to Northern cities. She delineates four pivotal moments in the narratives she examines (musical, visual, literary) and in all phases she notes the negotiations the migrants make with power structures. The first stage is the event that propels the action northward, the catalyst for leaving the South or provincial Midwest, often depicted as brute power in the form of a lynching, beating, rape. The second stage is the initial confrontation with the urban landscape where the migrant is faced with new relations to time, space, technology, and race relations and where power "is more subtle and sophisticated." The third moment of the narrative is the portrayal of ways migrants negotiate the urban landscape and the construction of "safe havens" from the negative effects of the cityscape. The fourth moment considers the effects of migration and the future possibilities or limitations for the migrant. Implicit in all of the moments of the narrative, which are not necessarily linear or treated in the same way from narrative to narrative, are the figures of the "ancestors" and the "stranger." These figures represent the tensions between attachment to and detachment from the past (often represented as the South) and the larger community in negotiations with new places and identities.

The essays in this section, thus, demonstrate how migration impinges on individual and collective identity when people are uprooted from locations that have individual, cultural, ethnic, and sacred meaning for them, the deracination that occurs when place identity, a component of personal identity, is disrupted. They also interrogate the meaning and design of travel and travel narratives, suggesting as does William Bevis that coming home is also a seminal travel and ontological experience, and as Pedersen does that imagination can reconstruct the gap between memory and history.

Investigations of the politics of relocation, which focuses attention on issues of location and travel for specific populations, abound, even when limited to the American context. An issue that Lisa Lowe and Ronald Takaki raise is the racialization of immigration. They demonstrate that when immigrants from non-European areas, like Asia, converge on the United States, the politics and rhetoric of the country react by attempting to define the nation along racial and ethnic rather than national lines. Studies of women's experiences, such as Annette Kolodny's and bell hooks's, indicate how one's gendered and racial positions within society also affect mobility, adding to Rich's and Anzaldúa's analyses of sexual orientation, or lesbianism, as a location from which the world is experienced and the self defined. Kolodny argues that women who moved to the American western frontiers used a different symbology to represent their experiences than did their male counterparts, while hooks transforms the margins of society—the "other" side of the tracks—into sites of resistance for Black women against the hegemonic order.

FOR FURTHER READING

hooks, bell. "Choosing the Margin as a Space of Radical Openness." *Yearning: Race, Gender, and Cultural Politics.* Boston: South End P, 1990. 145–53.

Kolodny, Annette. *The Land Before Her: Fantasy and Experience of the American Frontiers, 1630–1860.* Chapel Hill: U of North Carolina P, 1984.

Lowe, Lisa. *Immigrant Acts: On Asian American Cultural Politics.* Durham: Duke UP, 1996.

Rich, Adrienne. "Notes toward a Politics of Location." *Blood, Bread, and Poetry: Selected Prose 1979–1985.* New York: W. W. Norton, 1986. 210–31.

Takaki, Ronald. *Strangers from a Different Shore: A History of Asian Americans.* New York: Penguin, 1989.

Women, America, and Movement: Narratives of Relocation. Ed. Susan L. Roberson. Columbia: U of Missouri P, 1998.

THE RELOCATION OF LOW-INCOME RURAL COMMUNITIES WITH STRONG TIES TO THE LAND

Thayer Scudder

NEGATIVE EFFECTS OF RELOCATION

The results of over twenty-five studies around the world indicate without exception that the compulsory relocation of low-income rural populations with strong ties to their land and homes is a traumatic experience. For the majority of those who have been moved, the profound shock of compulsory relocation is much like the bereavement caused by the death of a parent, spouse, or child. This multidimensional stress has been shown to have a number of negative effects.

Relocation undermines a people's faith in themselves—they learn, to their humiliation, that they are unable to protect their most fundamental interests. In the Navajo case, these interests include the preservation of their land (both for themselves and, of great importance, for their children), their homes, their system of livestock management with its associated lifestyle, and their links with the environment they were born to.

Partly because they have lost, at least temporarily, their self-respect and initiative, and because they did not request removal in the first place, many relocatees tend to become dependent on the agency or agencies responsible for their removal. This dependency syndrome has plagued innumerable resettlement programs, and it can be expected to plague Navajo relocation under P.L. 93–531, since funds currently are not budgeted, let alone allocated, for economic development and social services.

The trauma of relocation disrupts the family unit and the lives of each of its members. It undermines the influence and authority of the household head since he or she is shown to be incapable of preserving the family's lifestyle. Individual family members may suffer from severe depression.

217

Violence, alcohol abuse, and mental and physical illness are all too often intimately associated with forced removal.

Relocation also undermines the influence and authority of local leaders. Throughout the world, politicians and officials find themselves in a "Catch-22" situation when their constituents are threatened with compulsory relocation. Since the majority of potential relocatees resist relocation in one way or another, their leaders are discredited if they cooperate with the relocation authorities. On the other hand, these leaders are also discredited if relocation occurs despite their resistance. In the Navajo case, both chapter and tribal officials are placed in an almost impossible position. If they withdraw land from the reservation for resettlement purposes, their actions will be seen as aiding and abetting relocation or as lowering the chances for passing amendments to P.L. 93-531, such as those that provide for purchase of additional land outside the reservation. On the other hand, if they resist relocation, their sincerity and effectiveness will still be questioned should relocation eventually occur. Under these circumstances, the present stance of the tribal authorities is understandable: it seems better to resist or attempt to modify relocation since in the long run such efforts may pay off, whereas agreeing to relocation now will discredit both the elected tribal council delegates from the former JUA and the tribal government itself.

Relocation creates serious conflicts between the relocatees, the hosts, and outsiders. These conflicts are characteristic of all rural projects involving compulsory relocation, and they can be expected to be especially serious among the Navajos. This is due to their restricted land base (with population densities more than double those in the areas surrounding the reservation, according to Gilbreath's 1973 analysis of the Navajo economy), their ranching style of life, and the current overgrazing of much of the reservation. When Navajo chapters hesitate and sometimes refuse to approve homesite leases for even small numbers of relocatees, they are not behaving in a uniquely unfeeling fashion. Indeed, such behavior is a common feature of all relocation projects in which relocatees wish to move or must move onto lands that are already occupied. Their arrival obviously reduces the per capita availability of land. It also increases the pressure on existing services—including water supplies, clinics, and schools—so that the hosts are often worse off after relocation.

The negative costs of relocation, like ripples, spread far beyond their points of origin. They demoralize families, break up kin groups, and divide whole communities and regions. In the Navajo case, these effects are already manifest and can be expected to influence the lives of the Navajo people for years to come.

RESISTANCE TO RELOCATION

The negative effects outlined above have been documented repeatedly in connection with programs of compulsory relocation. Possibly because they anticipate major disadvantages, the majority of relocatees the world over do not wish to move; indeed, they resist removal, sometimes violently. Unfortunately, it is impossible to forecast whether or not violence will occur in a specific case. In coping with the stress of relocation, potential relocatees often behave as if nothing were going to happen; rather, they continue to carry on their lives as in the past. We found some Navajos in the former JUA behaving in this fashion. For example, one household head told us, "Until the time comes—, we will not discuss relocation." With no plans for relocation, he and the adult members of his family were part of that minority of household heads who had not yet applied for relocation benefits. An elderly man born before the turn of the century, he had no intention of moving. When such a family is forcibly evicted, it is impossible to predict what will happen, but the situation is potentially explosive.

In a similar situation in Africa studied by Colson and Scudder, a series of incidents under a "benevolent" relocation agency touched off violence that left eight potential relocatees dead and at least thirty-two injured. More recently, potential relocatees among the Kalingas in the Philippines have attacked government forces and scientists, killing at least twelve. Navajo threats of violence have already been heard. The octogenarian previously quoted threatened possible violence should relocation be forced. In addition, 16.1 percent (ten people) of the Navajos from the Hopi side of the partition line who sought mental health treatment from the Indian Health Service during a recent six-month period stated that the execution of relocation would be met with resistance (Martin Topper, personal communication). Such threats do not mean that physical violence against others will in fact occur, but the possibility cannot be discounted. Because compulsory relocation is a basic threat to the well-being of those involved, a "flashpoint" situation can occur with or without outside agitation.

MULTIDIMENSIONAL STRESS

Those who plan and execute programs of compulsory relocation are usually relatively educated, wealthy, and mobile individuals, often without strong ties to a particular geographical area or community. In the United States, they also tend to be the descendants of Anglo-Saxon or East European immigrants. They tend either to be unaware of, or at least to underestimate,

the negative effects of compulsory relocation on less mobile, poorly educated, low-income populations, especially when such populations have a
strong attachment to their homes, land, and livelihood, as is the case with
the Navajo. The highly mobile planners are also apt to forget that their own
movements tend to cause stress for their families, especially when children
must leave school and associates and when nonworking spouses must leave
friends and familiar surroundings for a new locale. Yet in such cases the
move is freely discussed among family members and is usually of a voluntary
nature.

While in the long run a majority of those who are subject to compulsory
relocation may become better off (though not necessarily because of relocation), in the short run the effects of relocation are invariably adverse.
Furthermore, the relocatees' position in life can be expected to improve only
if they have access to training programs and employment opportunities.
These developmental components are not provided for under P.L. 93–531, despite the fact that the former Joint Use Area has one of the highest unem-
ployment rates in the United States (76 percent of those sixteen and older
have no wage or salary employment, according to Wood, Vannette, and An-
drews 1979: 104).

Compulsory relocation invariably involves multidimensional stress. This
stress begins as soon as the first rumors of possible relocation arise. It increases during the months immediately preceding removal and remains at a
high level during much of the transition period. Throughout this time, relocatees often behave like those who are mourning the death of a loved one.
They turn in upon themselves, relying on family members and close friends.
They cling to the familiar and try to recreate their old routines and lifestyles
in their new home. Relocatees behave as if their world is a closed system;
they try to move the shortest distance possible and then only into familiar
surroundings. This phenomenon has been commonly observed in urban re-
development projects throughout the United States: whenever possible, relocatees move into adjacent neighborhoods.

Clinging to the familiar in the form of known persons, routines, and surroundings would appear to be a means of coping with the multidimensional
stress of relocation. In a world turned upside down, the familiar provides assur-
ance until the transition period comes to an end. After that, the individual—if
he or she is still alive—is able to turn outward again. For the purposes of our
analysis, multidimensional stress can be broken down into three components:
physiological stress, psychological stress, and sociocultural (including economic) stress. These three components are synergistically interrelated.

Physiological stress results in increased morbidity rates, for both mental and physical illness. It may also result in increased mortality rates.

Psychological stress has two aspects, one directed toward the past and the other directed toward the future. The first has been labeled by Fried (1963) as the "grieving for a lost home" syndrome. It is especially serious among the elderly and among younger women, although its effect on children has never been adequately researched. The second aspect is a strong anxiety about the future, including a feeling of uncertainty that can be most debilitating. In situations of uncertainty, people feel that they are out of context. Because they do not know "the rules of the game," they cannot calculate the odds associated with different coping strategies—so risk-taking becomes impossible. They cease to explore, become disoriented, and draw in upon themselves. With the loss of their independence, initiative, and self-respect, such relocatees tend to develop a dependency relationship with the agency or agencies that moved them, a relationship that is hard to break and that delays the end of the transition period.

Sociocultural stress is not as well understood as the other two components. It is caused by the disruption, disorganization, and simplification of the behavioral patterns, institutions, and organizational processes of a community and of the society of which it is a part. A major aspect of this sort of stress is the undermining of local leadership. Another aspect is the temporary or permanent disruption of established behavioral patterns, including forms of livelihood that give meaning to life. These are stopped with relocation because they are tied to particular pieces of land. For instance, there are special sites where wild plants are gathered for eating and ritual purposes; other sites are reserved for carrying out certain rituals. In the Navajo case, the cessation of sheep herding is especially serious, particularly for the elderly; it signals the disappearance of the whole way of life associated with the ownership of grazing permits and the care of livestock.

The types of multidimensional stress outlined above are associated with the transition period that invariably accompanies compulsory relocation. For the majority of relocatees, this period extends at least two years from the date of relocation. It seldom lasts more than a single generation, since children born in the relocation setting tend to adapt to that setting. The Navajos, however, may follow a path similar to that of the Palestinian Arabs. In both cases, there is a very strong identification with their land and an overriding desire by adults to pass that land on to their children. For these people, inability to accept expulsion from their homes may go on for several generations.

THE DESI CHAIN

Gustavo Pérez-Firmat

> Ricky to Lucy: "Lucy, honey, if I wanted things Cuban I'd stayed in
> Havana. That's the reason I married you, 'cause you're so different
> from everyone I'd known before."

A couple of years ago the cover story of an issue of *People* magazine was devoted to Gloria Estefan, who is well known as the most important moving
part in the Miami Sound Machine. At the time, Estefan was staging what the
magazine termed an "amazing recovery" from a serious traffic accident that
had left her partially paralyzed. Gloria herself was upbeat about her
prospects, and the point of the story was to reassure all of the rhythm nation
that little Gloria would conga again.[1]

I begin with this anecdote for two reasons: the first is that Estefan's
celebrity gives a fair indication of the prominent role that Cuban Americans
are playing in the increasing—and inexorable—latinization of the United
States; by now, few Americans will deny that, sooner or later, for better or for
worse, the rhythm is going to get them. My other reason for bringing up the
People story has to do with the photograph on the cover, which shows Gloria
holding two dalmatians whose names happen to be Lucy and Ricky. Like one
of the Miami Sound Machine's recent albums, the photograph cuts both
ways: it suggests not only the prominence but also the pedigree of Cuban-
American pop culture. After all, if Gloria Estefan is the most prominent
Cuban-American performer in this country today—a "one woman Latin
boom," as the *New York Times* put it[2]—Ricky Ricardo is certainly her strong
precursor. Surprising as it may seem, Desi Arnaz's TV character has been the
single most visible Hispanic presence in the United States over the last forty
years. Indeed, several generations of Americans have acquired many of their
notions of how Cubans behave, talk, lose their temper, and treat or mistreat

their wives by watching Ricky love Lucy. Just last semester, I had a Cuban-American student who claimed he had learned to be a Cuban male by watching *I Love Lucy* reruns from his home in Hialeah.

But the connection between Estefan and Ricky goes further than this. The Miami Sound Machine's first cross-over hit was "Conga"—the 1986 song that contained the memorable refrain:

Come on shake your body, baby, do the conga,
I know you can't control yourself any longer.

Well, the person who led the first conga ever danced on American soil was none other than Desi Arnaz, who performed this singular feat in a Miami Beach nightclub in 1937.[3] Alluding to this historic (and quite possibly hysteric) event, Walter Winchell later said, in a wonderful phrase, that a conga line should be called instead a Desi Chain. It is well to remember, then, that a few years ago when Gloria Estefan entered the *Guinness Book of World Records* for having led the longest conga line ever, she was only following in Desi's footsteps, only adding another kinky link to the Desi Chain.

I can summarize the significance of this photograph by saying that it illustrates in a particularly clear manner the two forces that shape Cuban-American culture, which I will call *traditional* and *translational*. As a work of tradition, the photograph points to the genealogy of Cuban-American culture; it reminds us that Gloria Estefan is only the latest in a long line of Cuban-American artists who have come, seen, and conga'd in the United States. As a work of translation, it reminds us of the sorts of adjustments that have to occur for us to be able to rhyme "conga" and "longer." In this the photograph is typical, for ethnic cultures are constantly trying to negotiate between the contradictory imperatives of tradition and translation.

"Tradition," a term that derives from the same root as the Spanish *traer*, to bring, designates convergence and continuity, a gathering together of elements according to underlying affinities or shared concerns. By contrast, "translation" is not a homing device but a distancing mechanism. In its topographical meaning, translation is displacement, in Spanish, *traslación*. This notion has been codified in the truism that to translate is to traduce (*traduttore, traditore*); implicit in the concept is the suggestion that to move is to transmute, that any linguistic or cultural displacement necessarily entails some mutilation of the original. In fact, in classical rhetoric *traductio*—which is of course Spanish for translation—was the term used to refer to the repetition of a word with a changed meaning. Translation/*traslación*, traduction/*traducción*—the mis-leading translation of these cognates is a powerful reminder of the intricacies of the concept.

The subject of this [essay] is how tradition and translation have shaped Cuban-American culture, which is built on the tradition of translation, in both the topographical and linguistic senses of the word. My name for this tradition will be the Desi Chain, since Desi Arnaz is its initial link. To be sure, the Cuban presence on the North American continent is at least as old as the Florida city of St. Augustine, which was founded in 1565.[4] But it is one thing to be Cuban in America, and quite another to be Cuban American. My subject is the latter, a contemporary development. The scope of this [essay] is limited, therefore, to the last half-century, for it is during this period that Cuban-American culture has evolved into a recognizable and coherent cluster of attitudes and achievements.

Another thing that Desi Arnaz and Gloria Estefan have in common is that both left Cuba before they reached adulthood. Born in Cuba but made in the U.S.A., they belong to an intermediate immigrant generation whose members spent their childhood or adolescence abroad but grew into adults in America. Because this group falls somewhere between the first and second immigrant generations, the Cuban sociologist Rubén Rumbaut has labeled it the "1.5" or "one-and-a-half" generation.

> Children who were born abroad but are being educated and come of age in the United States form what may be called the "1.5" generation. These refugee youth must cope with two crisis-producing and identity-defining transitions: (1) adolescence and the task of managing the transition from childhood to adulthood, and (2) acculturation and the task of managing the transition from one sociocultural environment to another. The "first" generation of their parents, who are fully part of the "old" world, face only the latter; the "second" generation of children now being born and reared in the United States, who as such become fully part of the "new" world, will need to confront only the former. But members of the "1.5" generation form a distinctive cohort in that in many ways they are marginal to both the old and the new worlds, and are fully part of neither of them.[5]

One of the theses of this [essay] is that Cuban-American culture has been to a considerable extent an achievement of the 1.5 generation. Many of the links in the Desi Chain are made up of one-and-a-halfers, for their intercultural placement makes them more likely to undertake the negotiations and compromises that produce ethnic culture. Life on the hyphen can be anyone's prerogative, but it is the one-and-a-halfer's destiny. I diverge from Rumbaut, though, in stressing the beneficial consequences of this intermediate location. Although it is true enough that the 1.5 generation is "marginal" to both its native and its adopted cultures, the inverse may be equally accurate: only the 1.5 generation is marginal to *neither* culture. The 1.5 individual is unique in that, unlike younger and older compatriots, he or she may actually find it possible to circulate within and through both the old and the new cultures. While one-and-a-halfers may never feel entirely at ease in either one, they are capable of availing themselves of the resources—linguistic, artistic, commercial—that both cultures have to offer. In some ways they are *both* first and second generation. Unlike their older and younger cohorts, they may actually be able to choose cultural habitats. The one-and-a-halfer's incompleteness—more than one, less than two—is something that I will have occasion to discuss later on; but for now I want to highlight the opportunities for distinctive achievement created by this fractional existence.

One-and-a-halfers are translation artists. Tradition bound but translation bent, they are sufficiently immersed in each culture to give both ends of the hyphen their due. As a one-and-a-halfer myself, I realize that this view is self-serving; but it does not seem unusual that hyphenated cultures should emerge from a sensibility that is not universally shared within an immigrant group. Only those immigrants who arrived here between infancy and adulthood share both the atavism of their parents and the Americanness of their children. I see it in my own family. My parents, who are now in their early seventies, have no choice but to be Cuban. No matter how many years they have resided away from the island—and if they live long enough soon there will come a time when they will have lived longer in Miami than they did in Havana—they are as Cuban today as they were when they got off the ferry in October 1960. My children, who were born in this country of Cuban parents and in whom I have tried to inculcate some sort of *cubanía*, are American through and through. They can be "saved" from their Americanness no more than my parents can be "saved" from their Cubanness. Although technically they belong to the so-called ABC generation (American-Born Cubans), they are Cubans in name only, in last name. A better acronym would be the reverse: CBA (Cuban-Bred Americans). Like other second-generation immigrants, they maintain a connection to their parents' homeland, but it is a bond forged by my experiences rather than their own. For my children Cuba is an enduring, perhaps an endearing, fiction. Cuba is for them as ethereal as the smoke and as persistent as the smell of their grandfather's cigars (which are not even Cuban but Dominican).

In order to describe the blending of cultures that has taken place in many parts of the world, and particularly in the Americas, anthropologists have employed the terms "acculturation" and "transculturation." Acculturation stresses the acquisition of culture; transculturation calls attention to the passage from one culture to another.[6] Drawing on these two notions, I will use the term "biculturation" to designate the type of blending that is specific, or at least characteristic, of the one-and-a-half generation. In my usage, biculturation designates not only contact of cultures; in addition, it describes a situation where the two cultures achieve a balance that makes it difficult to determine which is the dominant and which is the subordinate culture. Unlike acculturation or transculturation, biculturation implies an equilibrium, however tense or precarious, between the contributing cultures. Cuban-American culture is a balancing act. One-and-a-halfers are no more American than they are Cuban—and vice versa. Their hyphen is a seesaw: it tilts first one way, then the other. The game ends at some point (the one-and-a-half generation passeth away), and the board then comes to rest on one side. But in the meantime it stays in the air, uneasily balancing one weight against the other.

I realize that mine is not a fashionable view of relations between "majority" and "minority" cultures. Contemporary models of culture contact tend to be oppositional: one culture, say white American, vanquishes another, say Native American. But the oppositional model, accurate as it may be in other situations, does not do justice to the balance of power in Cuban America. I like to think of Cuban-American culture as "appositional" rather than "oppositional," for the relation between the two terms is defined more by contiguity than by conflict. I am not referring here to the political relations between Cuba and the United States, to which this statement, obviously and sadly, does not apply. And neither do I want to discount the persistent anti-Americanism that has loomed so large in the island's history. My context of reference is the experience of Cubans in this country, lives lived in collusion rather than collision. Over the last several decades, in the United States, Cuba and America have been on a collusion course. The best products of this collaboration display an intricate equilibrium between the claims of each culture. Equilibrium does not necessarily mean stasis, however, and I am not talking about dull, motionless coexistence. Fractions are fractious, and one-and-a-halfers are notorious for being restless and uppity.

I am also not talking about anything that a given individual or community actually elects. Before becoming a prerogative, biculturation is a fate—the fate typical of individuals who reach this country too young to be Cuban and too old to be American. But this fate, once it is accepted and assumed, becomes a prerogative. It's an election after the fact. You choose what you cannot avoid. You elect what you cannot elude. You rearrange fate into feat. A Cuban proverb says: "Si del cielo te caen limones, aprende a hacer limonada." If God gives you lemons, learn to make lemonade. In many ways the interstitial placement of the one-and-a-half generation is a lemon, since you do not feel entirely at home in either setting. Spiritually and psychologically you are neither *aquí* nor *allá*, you are neither Cuban nor Anglo. You're "cuban-glo," a word that has the advantage of imprecision, since one can't tell where the "Cuban" ends and the "Anglo" begins. Having two cultures, you belong wholly to neither one. You are both, you are neither: *cuba-no/america-no*. What is more, you can actually choose the language you want to work, live, love, and pun in. For myself, there have been many times I wish I didn't have this option, for choosing can be painful and complicated—those lemons were really limes, weren't they? Nonetheless, the equipment that comes with the option creates the conditions for distinctive cultural achievement. One-and-a-halfers gain in translation. One-and-a-halfers feed on what they lack. Their position as equilibrists gives them the freedom to mix and match pieces from each culture: they are "equi-libre."

An immigrant group, especially if the expatriation has been involuntary, passes through three stages in its adaptation to a new homeland. Initially the immigrant tries to deny the fact of displacement. I will call this first stage "substitutive," for it consists of an effort to create substitutes or copies of the home culture. This is translation in the topographical sense only, an undertaking that engenders all of those faint doubles of foreign places that speckle the American urban landscape—the little Italies and little Haitis and little Havanas with which we are all familiar. But the adjective "little" here is equivocal, for it says not only that these enclaves are smaller than their models but that they are diminished in ways more important than square miles or population. What's "little" about little Havana is not only its size (Miami is actually the second most populous Cuban city), but its diminished status as a deficient or incomplete copy of the original. No matter how great the effort, substitution is always partial. In Miami one can find stores and restaurants that claim lifespans much in excess of the duration of the Castro regime. These claims rest on a particular kind of historical elision that overlooks personal, historical, and geographical discontinuities. The Miami version of a restaurant called El Carmelo does not have a whole lot in common with its Havana homonym; it's not the same *place*, and it's not even the same *food*, for the Miami menu by now includes such offerings as the Nicaraguan dessert *tres leches*.

Yet the substitutive impulse of newly arrived exiles makes them ignore the evidence of the senses, including their taste buds. Because the reality of exile may be too costly to accept, the exile aspires to reproduce, rather than recast, native traditions. No immigrant ever arrives with only the clothes on his or her back. Even those Cubans who arrived penniless brought with them all kinds of baggage. Willie Chirino, a popular Cuban-American singer and composer, says in a song that he left Cuba with the following: Beny Moré, the Trío Matamoros, Miguelito Cuní, a *colibrí*, a palm tree, a *bohío*, and a book by José Martí. He even "relocalized" in Miami his native province of Pinar del Río. Chirino did not bring much luggage, but he certainly arrived with a lot of baggage, for his list is a gallery of Cuban icons. Most revealing about the list is that several of the people it mentions, like Beny Moré and the surviving members of the Matamoros Trio, never did leave Cuba. Typically his bill of cultural goods denies political and geographical ruptures. The speaker of Chirino's song inhabits, or would like to inhabit, a Cuba of the mind, a fantasy island untouched by time or history.

The compensatory theme of the substitutive stage is "we are (still) there." This is why, even after more than thirty years of exile, it sometimes seems that Little Havana exists in a time warp. This phenomenon is related to what Lisandro Pérez has termed "institutional completeness."[7] An "ethnic en-clave" like Miami provides for all of its members' needs. As Pérez points out, your life begins in the hands of a Cuban obstetrician and it ends in the hands of a Cuban undertaker. In between, you have little need of contact with the outside, non-Cuban world. The completeness of the enclave has enabled the reproduction in Miami of what many still call, whimsically, *la Cuba de ayer* (yesterday's Cuba). I find this effort to recreate yesterday's Cuba in today's America both heroic and pathetic. Heroic because it tries to rise above his-tory and geography. Pathetic because it is doomed to fail. No matter how in-tense and persistent, substitution cannot go on forever. At some point—after months or years or maybe decades—the immigrant begins to find it impossi-ble to sustain, even precariously, the fiction of rootedness. Unsettling events reimpose a sense of reality. Someone dies and has to be buried outside the Cuban family plot; your children bring home friends (or worse: spouses!) who cannot trill their *rs*; the old radio stations switch to music that follows a dif-ferent beat. The enclave is no longer *en clave*.

When events like these become habitual, the substitutive fantasy col-lapses. No amount of duplicate landmarks can cover up the fact that you are no longer there, and what's more, that you may never return. This is the clever point of Arturo Cuenca's *This Isn't Havana*, where the colloquial English-language phrase is placed over a photograph of the Little Havana restaurant La Equina de Tejas, which was modeled after the one in Cuba. Barely visible, the overlaid text is a ghostly presence, a geographical reality-principle that says, "You're not there." The name of the restaurant, "The Corner of Tiles," refers to a street corner in Havana, not Miami; and the fact that "Tejas" is also Spanish for Texas adds to the equivocal geography of this uncommon place. Tile Corner or Texas Corner—either way, it isn't Havana. If René Magritte's *Ceci n'est pas une pipe* underscores that the copy is not the thing, Cuenca's *This Isn't Havana*—whose title perhaps alludes to Magritte's painting—makes the related point that the exile needs to live and reside in the same place. You can't have your *coquito* in Cuba and eat in Miami too.

The Cuban-American poet Ricardo Pau-Llosa once wrote, "The exile knows his place, and that place is the imagination."[8] I would add that the exile is someone who thinks imagination is a place. The problem is, imagination is *not* a place. You can't live there, you can't buy a house there, you can't raise your children there. Grounded in compensatory substitutions, the recreation of Havana in Miami is an act of imagination. Sooner or later reality crashes though, and the exile loses the place that never was. His or her reaction to the collapse of substitution is vertigo, disorientation. If La Equina de Tejas is not Havana, what is it? If you aren't there, where are you? I do not mean that exiled individuals literally do not know where they are, but that emotionally they have gotten used to believing otherwise. The painful knowledge that they live in exile has been attenuated by the comforting feeling that they never left. You walk into a restaurant on Eighth Street and not only does it have the same name as one in Cuba, but it probably has a map of Havana on the wall and a Cuban flag over the counter. You *know* you're in Miami, but still you *feel* at home.

But as exile lengthens, these feelings begin to fray. Gradually the awareness of displacement crushes the fantasy of rootedness. This ushers in the second stage, for which I will use the term "destitution." In its common usage a destitute person is someone bereft of wealth or possessions; but since destitution derives from *stare*, to stand, it literally means not having a place to stand on. This is what second-stage exiles feel: that the ground has been taken out from under them, that they no longer know their place, that they have in fact lost their place. Rather than nostalgic, they now feel estranged and disconnected. The provisional comforts of substitution have vanished. Now every time you drive by La Equina de Tejas, in your mind's eye you see a sign that says instead, "This Isn't Havana." If the theme of the first moment was "we are there," the theme of the second moment is "we are nowhere."

Mercifully, time passes and "nowhere" begins to feel like home. While the ground under your feet may be unfamiliar, it's still ground, a place to stand on. As the years go by the foreign country loses its foreignness and "nowhere" breaks down into a "now" and a "here," into a concrete time and place. If this isn't Havana, it must be someplace else. Destitution gives way to institution, to the establishment of a new relation between person and place. To institute is to stand one's ground, to dig in and endure. Thus, the theme of the third stage is not "we are there" or "we are nowhere," but rather, "here we are." I take this phrase from Emerson, for this is an Emersonian moment, a moment to lay foundations. For many years there has been a popular Cuban-American band in Miami called Clouds; in 1984 the band changed its name to Clouds of Miami. The addition of the locative phrase signals the transition from destitution to institution. Whereas the band's original name signified uprootedness, the feeling of being up in the air, the revised name brings Clouds down to earth by anchoring them in a specific locale. The cover of Clouds' first album after the name change showed cumuli drifting against the Miami skyline. Although the sensation of rootlessness does not dissipate altogether, it acquires a name and an address.

Since these three moments or stages chart an individual's or a community's slow acceptance of life in a new country, they tend to succeed each other. In Miami the three moments have roughly corresponded to the three decades since the Cuban Revolution. The sixties was a time of nostalgia and substitution; by the seventies, when it had become evident that Castro was there to stay, the prevailing attitude was destitution; and in the eighties, with the maturation of a younger generation of Cuban Americans, destitution gave way to institution. But this chronological progression belies the crucial fact that these attitudes commingle and alternate. For one thing, not everybody reaches exile at the same time or at the same age; for another, individuals as well as communities swing back and forth from one moment to another. It may be, in fact, that all three attitudes are already present from the moment one steps on foreign soil. Even then, feelings of nostalgia and disorientation are probably tempered by a sense of emplacement. Nonetheless, there has been a discernible evolution in the attitudes of Cubans in the United States. Once an exile, always an exile; but it doesn't follow that once an exile, always *only* an exile. What changes is the relative prominence of these attitudes. To this day Cuban Miami is by turns nostalgic, estranged and foundational; but it used to be far more nostalgic than it is now.

NOTES

1. Steve Dougherty, "One Step at a Time," *People*, June 25, 1990.

2. Enrique Fernandéz, "Spitfires, Latin Lovers, Mambo Kings," *New York Times*, April 19, 1992.

3. Desi Arnaz, *A Book* (New York: William Morrow, 1976), 61–62. This claim is not uncontested. In *Rhumba Is My Life* (New York: Didier, 1948), Xavier Cugat also takes credit for having introduced the conga to America (198). So does Arthur Murray, who claims to have brought it over from France (Sylvia G. L. Dannett and Frank R. Rachel,

Down Memory Lane: Arthur Murray's Picture Story of Social Dancing [New York: Greenberg, 1954], 140)! These assertions need to be taken cautiously, especially given that Arthur Murray also liked to claim that he "created most of the steps used in the rumba" (163). In *The Latin Tinge* (New York: Oxford University Press, 1979), John Storm Roberts points out that by the week of New Year's 1937–1938, which is when Arnaz claimed to have introduced the conga, Eliseo Grenet's "La Conga" had been published in English under the title "Havana Is Calling Me" (82). The publication of a song is something different from the introduction and popularization of a dance, however. The dance instructor Rudolfo D'Avalos has also been credited with introducing the conga (Angela M. Rosanova, *Ballroom Dancing Made Easy* [New York: Vantage, 1954], 84).

4. For a historical overview of the Cuban presence in the United States, see Carlos Ripoll, *Cubans in the United States* (New York: Eliseo Torres, 1987).

5. Rubén G. Rumbaut, "The Agony of Exile: A Study of the Migration and Adaptation of Indochinese Refugee Adults and Children," in *Refugee Children: Theory, Research, and Services*, ed. Frederick L. Ahearn, Jr., and Jean L. Athey (Baltimore: Johns Hopkins University Press, 1991), 61. On the importance of adolescence as a dividing line among immigrants, see also Michael Piore, *Birds of Passage* (Cambridge: Cambridge University Press, 1979), 65–69.

6. See Ralph Beals, "Acculturation," in *Anthropology Today*, ed. A. L. Kroeber (Chicago: University of Chicago Press, 1953), 621–41; Gonzalo Aguirre Beltrán, *El proceso de aculturación* (Mexico City: Universidad Nacional Autónoma de México, 1957); and Fernando Ortiz, "Del fenómeno social de la transculturación y de su importancia en Cuba," *Revista Bimestre Cubana* 46 (1940): 272–78.

7. Lisandro Pérez, "Cuban Miami," in *Miami Now! Immigration, Ethnicity, and Social Change*, ed. Guillermo J. Grenier and Alex Stepick III (Gainesville: University Press of Florida, 1992), 83–108.

8. Ricardo Pau-Llosa, "Identity and Variations: Cuban Visual Thinking in Exile since 1959," in *Outside Cuba / Fuera de Cuba*, ed. Ileana Fuentes-Pérez, Graciella Cruz Taura, Ricardo Pau-Llosa (New Brunswick: Office of Hispanic Arts, Mason Gross School of the Arts, Rutgers University, 1988), 41.

THE HOMELAND, AZTLÁN

Gloria Anzaldúa

El otro México

El otro México que acá hemos construido
el espacio es lo que ha sido
territorio nacional.
Esté el esfuerzo de todos nuestros hermanos
y latinoamericanos que han sabido
progressar.

Los Tigres del Norte[1]

"The *Aztecas del norte* . . . compose the largest single tribe or nation of Anishinabeg (Indians) found in the United States today. . . .
Some call themselves Chicanos and see themselves as people
whose true homeland is Aztlán [the U.S. Southwest]."[2]

Wind tugging at my sleeve
feet sinking into the sand
I stand at the edge where earth touches ocean
where the two overlap
a gentle coming together
at other times and places a violent clash.

Across the border in Mexico
stark silhouette of houses gutted by waves,
cliffs crumbling into the sea,
silver waves marbled with spume
gashing a hole under the border fence.

Miro el mar atacar
la cerca en Border Field Park
con sus buchones de agua,

an Easter Sunday resurrection
of the brown blood in my veins.

Oigo el llorido del mar, el respiro del aire,
    my heart surges to the beat of the sea.
        In the gray haze of the sun
            the gulls' shrill cry of hunger,
                the tangy smell of the sea seeping into me.

                I walk   through the hole in the fence
                        to the other side.
        Under my fingers I feel the gritty wire
                rusted by 139 years
                    of the salty breath of the sea.

Beneath the iron sky
Mexican children kick their soccer ball across,
run after it, entering the U.S.

            I press my hand to the steel curtain—
        chainlink fence crowned with rolled barbed wire—
    rippling from the sea where Tijuana touches San Diego
        unrolling over mountains
                and plains
                    and deserts,
this "Tortilla Curtain" turning into *el río Grande*
        flowing down to the flatlands
            of the Magic Valley of South Texas
            its mouth emptying into the Gulf.

1,950 mile-long open wound
                dividing a *pueblo*, a culture,
                running down the length of my body,
                    staking fence rods in my flesh,
                    splits me   splits me
                        me raja   me raja

            This is my home
            this thin edge of
                barbwire.

            But the skin of the earth is seamless.
            The sea cannot be fenced,

el mar does not stop at borders.
To show the white man what she thought of his
arrogance,
Yemaya blew that wire fence down.

This land was Mexican once,
was Indian always
and is.
And　will be again.

Yo soy un puente tendido
del mundo gabacho al del mojado,
lo pasado me estirá pa' 'trás
y lo presente pa' 'delante.
Que la Virgen de Guadalupe me cuide
Ay ay ay, soy mexicana de este lado.

The U.S.-Mexican border *es una herida abierta* where the Third World grates against the first and bleeds. And before a scab forms it hemorrhages again, the lifeblood of two worlds merging to form a third country—a border culture. Borders are set up to define the places that are safe and unsafe, to distinguish *us* from *them*. A border is a dividing line, a narrow strip along a steep edge. A borderland is a vague and undetermined place created by the emotional residue of an unnatural boundary. It is in a constant state of transition. The prohibited and forbidden are its inhabitants. *Los atravesados* live here: the squint-eyed, the perverse, the queer, the troublesome, the mongrel, the mulato, the half-breed, the half dead; in short, those who cross over, pass over, or go through the confines of the "normal." Gringos in the U.S. Southwest consider the inhabitants of the borderlands transgressors, aliens— whether they possess documents or not, whether they're Chicanos, Indians or Blacks. Do not enter, trespassers will be raped, maimed, strangled, gassed, shot. The only "legitimate" inhabitants are those in power, the whites and those who align themselves with whites. Tension grips the inhabitants of the borderlands like a virus. Ambivalence and unrest reside there and death is no stranger.

In the fields, *la migra*. My aunt saying, "*No corran*, don't run. They'll think you're *del otro lao*." In the confusion, Pedro ran, terrified of being caught. He couldn't speak English, couldn't tell them he was fifth generation American. *Sin papeles*—he did not carry his birth certificate to work in the fields. *La migra* took him away while we watched. *Se lo llevaron*. He tried to smile when he looked back at us, to raise his fist. But I saw the shame pushing his head down, I saw the terrible weight of shame hunch his shoulders. They deported him to Guadalajara by plane. The furthest he'd ever been to Mexico was Reynosa, a small border town opposite Hidalgo, Texas, not far from McAllen. Pedro walked all the way to the Valley. *Se lo llevaron sin un centavo al pobre. Se vino andando desde Guadalajara.*

During the original peopling of the Americas, the first inhabitants migrated across the Bering Straits and walked south across the continent. The oldest evidence of humankind in the U.S.—the Chicanos' ancient Indian ancestors—was found in Texas and has been dated to 35,000 B.C.[3] In the Southwest United States archeologists have found 20,000-year-old campsites of the Indians who migrated through, or permanently occupied, the Southwest, Aztlán—land of the herons, land of whiteness, the Edenic place of origin of the Azteca.

In 1000 B.C., descendants of the original Cochise people migrated into what is now Mexico and Central America and became the direct ancestors of many of the Mexican people. (The Cochise culture of the Southwest is the parent culture of the Aztecs. The Uto-Aztecan languages stemmed from the language of the Cochise people.)[4] The Aztecs (the Nahuatl word for people of Aztlán) left the Southwest in 1168 A.D.

Now let us go.
>   *Tihueque, tihueque,*
Vámonos, vámonos.
>   *Un pájaro cantó.*
Con sus ocho tribus salieron
>   *de la "cueva del origen."*
los aztecas siguieron al dios
>   *Huitzilopochtli.*

Huitzilopochtli, the God of War, guided them to the place (that later became Mexico City) where an eagle with a writhing serpent in its beak perched on a cactus. The eagle symbolizes the spirit (as the sun, the father); the serpent symbolizes the soul (as the earth, the mother). Together, they symbolize the struggle between the spiritual/celestial/male and the underworld/earth/ feminine. The symbolic sacrifice of the serpent to the "higher" masculine powers indicates that the patriarchal order had already vanquished the feminine and matriarchal order in pre-Columbian America.

At the beginning of the 16th century, the Spaniards and Hernán Cortés invaded Mexico and, with the help of tribes that the Aztecs had subjugated, conquered it. Before the Conquest, there were twenty-five million Indian people in Mexico and the Yucatan. Immediately after the Conquest, the Indian population had been reduced to under seven million. By 1650, only one-and-a-half-million pure-blooded Indians remained. The *mestizos* who were genetically equipped to survive small pox, measles, and typhus (Old World diseases to which the natives had no immunity), founded a new hybrid race and inherited Central and South America.⁵ *En 1521 nació una nueva raza, el mestizo, el mexicano* (people of mixed Indian and Spanish blood), a race that had never existed before. Chicanos, Mexican-Americans, are the offspring of those first matings.

Our Spanish, Indian, and *mestizo* ancestors explored and settled parts of the U.S. Southwest as early as the sixteenth century. For every gold-hungry *conquistador* and soul-hungry missionary who came north from Mexico, ten to twenty Indians and *mestizos* went along as porters or in other capacities.⁶ For the Indians, this constituted a return to the place of origin, Aztlán, thus making Chicanos originally and secondarily indigenous to the Southwest. Indians and *mestizos* from central Mexico intermarried with North American Indians. The continual intermarriage between Mexican and American Indians and Spaniards formed an even greater *mestizaje.*

El destierro/THE LOST LAND

Entonces corré la sangre
no sabe el indio que hacer,
le van a quitar su tierra,
la tiene que defender,
el indio se cae muerto,
y el afuerino de pie.
Levántate, Manquilef.

Arauco tiene una pena
más negra que su chamal,
ya no son los españoles
los que les hacen llorar,
hoy son los propios chilenos
los que les quitan su pan.
Levántate, Pailahuan.

—Violeta Parra, *"Arauco tiene una pena"*⁷

In the 1800s, Anglos migrated illegally into Texas, which was then part of Mexico, in greater and greater numbers and gradually drove the *tejanos* (native Texans of Mexican descent) from their lands, committing all manner of atrocities against them. Their illegal invasion forced Mexico to fight a war to keep its Texas territory. The Battle of the Alamo, in which the Mexican forces vanquished the whites, became, for the whites, the symbol for the cowardly and villainous character of the Mexicans. It became (and still is) a symbol that legitimized the white imperialist takeover. With the capture of Santa Anna later in 1836, Texas became a republic. *Tejanos* lost their land and, overnight, became the foreigners.

> *Ya la mitad del terreno*
> *les vendió el traidor Santa Anna,*
> *con lo que se ha hecho muy rica*
> *la nación americana.*
>
> *¡Qué acaso no se conforman*
> *con el oro de lay minas!*
> *Ustedes muy elegantes*
> *y aquí nosotros en ruinas.*
>   —from the Mexican corrido,*"Del peligro de la Intervención"*[8]

In 1846, the U.S. incited Mexico to war. U.S. troops invaded and occupied Mexico, forcing her to give up almost half of her nation, what is now Texas, New Mexico, Arizona, Colorado and California.

With the victory of the U.S. forces over the Mexican in the U.S.-Mexican War, *los norteamericanos* pushed the Texas border down 100 miles, from *el río Nueces* to *el río Grande*. South Texas ceased to be part of the Mexican state of Tamaulipas. Separated from Mexico, the Native Mexican-Texan no longer looked toward Mexico as home; the Southwest became our homeland once more. The border fence that divides the Mexican people was born on February 2, 1848 with the signing of the Treaty of Guadalupe-Hidalgo. It left 100,000 Mexican citizens on this side, annexed by conquest along with the land. The land established by the treaty as belonging to Mexicans was soon swindled away from its owners. The treaty was never honored and restitution, to this day, has never been made.

> The justice and benevolence of God
> will forbid that . . . Texas should again
> become a howling wilderness
> trod only by savages, or . . . benighted
> by the ignorance and superstition,
> the anarchy and rapine of Mexican misrule.
> The Anglo-American race are destined
> to be forever the proprietors of

this land of promise and fulfillment.
Their laws will govern it,
their learning will enlighten it,
their enterprise will improve it.
Their flocks range its boundless pastures,
for them its fertile lands will yield . . .
luxuriant harvests . . .
The wilderness of Texas has been redeemed
by Anglo-American blood & enterprise.
                                        —William H. Wharton[9]

The Gringo, locked into the fiction of white superiority, seized complete
political power, stripping Indians and Mexicans of their land while their feet
were still rooted in it. *Con el destierro y el exilo fuimos desuñados, destron-
cados, destripados*—we were jerked out by the roots, truncated, disembow-
eled, dispossessed, and separated from our identity and our history. Many,
under the threat of Anglo terrorism, abandoned homes and ranches and went
to Mexico. Some stayed and protested. But as the courts, law enforcement officials, and government officials not only ignored their pleas but penalized
them for their efforts, *tejanos* had no other recourse but armed retaliation.

After Mexican-American resisters robbed a train in Brownsville, Texas on
October 18, 1915, Anglo vigilante groups began lynching Chicanos. Texas
Rangers would take them into the brush and shoot them. One hundred Chicanos were killed in a matter of months, whole families lynched. Seven thousand fled to Mexico, leaving their small ranches and farms. The Anglos,
afraid that the *mexicanos*[10] would seek independence from the U.S., brought
in 20,000 army troops to put an end to the social protest movement in South
Texas. Race hatred had finally fomented into an all out war.[11]

My grandmother lost all her cattle,
they stole her land.

"Drought hit South Texas," my mother tells me. "*La tierra se puso bien
seca y los animales comenzaron a morrirse de se'. Mi papá se murió de un
heart attack *dejando a mamá* pregnant *y con ocho huercos,* with eight kids
and one on the way. *Yo fuí la mayor, tenía diez años.* The next year the
drought continued *y el ganado* got hoof and mouth. *Se calleron* in droves *en
las pastas y el* brushland, *pansas blancas* ballooning to the skies. *El siguiente
año* still no rain. *Mi pobre madre viuda perdió* two-thirds of her *ganado.* A
smart *gabacho* lawyer took the land away *mamá* hadn't paid taxes. No *hab-*

laba inglés, she didn't know how to ask for time to raise the money." My father's mother, Mama Locha, also lost her *terreno*. For a while we got $12.50 a year for the "mineral rights" of six acres of cemetery, all that was left of the ancestral lands. Mama Locha had asked that we bury her there beside her husband. *El cemeterio estaba cercado.* But there was a fence around the cemetery, chained and padlocked by the ranch owners of the surrounding land. We couldn't even get in to visit the graves, much less bury her there. Today, it is still padlocked. The sign reads: "Keep out. Trespassers will be shot."

In the 1930s, after Anglo agribusiness corporations cheated the small Chicano landowners of their land, the corporations hired gangs of *mexicanos* to pull out the brush, chaparral and cactus and to irrigate the desert. The land they toiled over had once belonged to many of them, or had been used communally by them. Later the Anglos brought in huge machines and root plows and had the Mexicans scrape the land clean of natural vegetation. In my childhood I saw the end of dryland farming. I witnessed the land cleared; saw the huge pipes connected to underwater sources sticking up in the air. As children, we'd go fishing in some of those canals when they were full and hunt for snakes in them when they were dry. In the 1950s I saw the land, cut up into thousands of neat rectangles and squares, constantly being irrigated. In the 340-day growth season, the seeds of any kind of fruit or vegetable had only to be stuck in the ground in order to grow. More big land corporations came in and bought up the remaining land.

To make a living my father became a sharecropper. Rio Farms Incorporated loaned him seed money and living expenses. At harvest time, my father repaid the loan and forked over 40% of the earnings. Sometimes we earned less than we owed, but always the corporations fared well. Some had major holdings in vegetable trucking, livestock auctions and cotton gins. Altogether we lived on three successive Rio farms; the second was adjacent to the King Ranch and included a dairy farm; the third was a chicken farm. I remember the white feathers of three thousand Leghorn chickens blanketing the land for acres around. My sister, mother and I cleaned, weighed and packaged eggs. (For years afterwards I couldn't stomach the sight of an egg.) I remember my mother attending some of the meetings sponsored by well-meaning whites from Rio Farms. They talked about good nutrition, health, and held huge barbeques. The only thing salvaged for my family from those years are modern techniques of food canning and a food-stained book they printed made up of recipes from Rio Farms' Mexican women. How proud my mother was to have her recipe for *enchiladas coloradas* in a book.

El cruzar del mojado/ILLEGAL CROSSING

> *"Ahora si ya tengo una tumba para llorar,"* dice Conchita, upon
> being reunited with her unknown mother just before the mother
> dies
> —from Ismael Rodriguez' film, *Nosotros los pobres*[12]

La crisis. Los gringos had not stopped at the border. By the end of the nineteenth century, powerful landowners in Mexico, in partnership with U.S.
colonizing companies, had dispossessed millions of Indians of their lands.
Currently, Mexico and her eighty million citizens are almost completely dependent on the U.S. market. The Mexican government and wealthy growers
are in partnership with such American conglomerates as American Motors,
IT&T and Du Pont which own factories called *maquiladoras.* One-fourth of
all Mexicans work at *maquiladoras;* most are young women. Next to oil,
maquiladoras are Mexico's second greatest source of U.S. dollars. Working
eight to twelve hours a day to wire in backup lights of U.S. autos or solder
minuscule wires in TV sets is not the Mexican way. While the women are in
the *maquiladoras,* the children are left on their own. Many roam the street,
become part of *cholo* gangs. The infusion of the values of the white culture,
coupled with the exploitation by that culture, is changing the Mexican way
of life.

The devaluation of the *peso* and Mexico's dependency on the U.S. have
brought on what the Mexicans call *la crisis. No hay trabajo.* Half of the
Mexican people are unemployed. In the U.S. a man or woman can make eight
times what they can in Mexico. By March, 1987, 1,088 pesos were worth one
U.S. dollar. I remember when I was growing up in Texas how we'd cross the
border at Reynosa or Progreso to buy sugar or medicines when the dollar was
worth eight *pesos* and fifty *centavos.*

La travesía. For many *mexicanos del otro lado,* the choice is to stay in
Mexico and starve or move north and live. *Dicen que cada mexicano siem-*
pre sueña de la conquista en los brazos de cuatro gringas rubias, la con-
quista del país poderoso del norte, los Estados Unidos. En cada Chicano y
mexicano vive el mito del tesoro territorial perdido. North Americans call
this return to the homeland the silent invasion.

> "A la cueva volverán"
> —El Puma *en la cancion "Amalia"*

South of the border, called North America's rubbish dump by Chicanos,
mexicanos congregate in the plazas to talk about the best way to cross.

Smugglers, *coyotes, pasadores, enganchadores* approach these people or are sought out by them. *"¡Qué dicen muchachos a echársela de mojado?"*

> "Now among the alien gods with
> weapons of magic am I."
> —Navajo protection song, sung when going into battle.[13]

We have a tradition of migration, a tradition of long walks. Today we are witnessing *la migración de los pueblos mexicanos*, the return odyssey to the historical/mythological Aztlán. This time, the traffic is from south to north.

El retorno to the promised land first began with the Indians from the interior of Mexico and the *mestizos* that came with the *conquistadores* in the 1500s. Immigration continued in the next three centuries, and, in this century, it continued with the *braceros* who helped to build our railroads and who picked our fruit. Today thousands of Mexicans are crossing the border legally and illegally; ten million people without documents have returned to the Southwest.

Faceless, nameless, invisible, taunted with "Hey cucaracho" (cockroach). Trembling with fear, yet filled with courage, a courage born of desperation. Barefoot and uneducated, Mexicans with hands like boot soles gather at night by the river where two worlds merge creating what Reagan calls a frontline, a war zone. The convergence has created a shock culture, a border culture, a third country, a closed country.

Without benefit of bridges, the *"mojados"* (wetbacks) float on inflatable rafts across *el río Grande*, or wade or swim across naked, clutching their clothes over their heads. Holding onto the grass, they pull themselves along the banks with a prayer to *Virgen de Guadalupe* on their lips: *Ay virgencita morena, mi madrecita, dame tu bendición.*

The Border Patrol hides behind the local McDonalds on the outskirts of Brownsville, Texas or some other border town. They set traps around the river beds beneath the bridge.[14] Hunters in army-green uniforms stalk and track these economic refugees by the powerful nightvision of electronic sensing devices planted in the ground or mounted on Border Patrol vans. Cornered by flashlights, frisked while their arms stretch over their heads, *los mojados* are handcuffed, locked in jeeps, and then kicked back across the border.

One out of every three is caught. Some return to enact their rite of passage as many as three times a day. Some of those who make it across undetected fall prey to Mexican robbers such as those in Smugglers' Canyon on the American side of the border near Tijuana. As refugees in a homeland that does not want them, many find a welcome hand holding out only suffering, pain, and ignoble death.

Those who make it past the checking points of the Border Patrol find themselves in the midst of 150 years of racism in Chicano *barrios* in the Southwest and in big northern cities. Living in a no-man's-borderland, caught between being treated as criminals and being able to eat, between resistance and deportation, the illegal refugees are some of the poorest and the most exploited of any people in the U.S. It is illegal for Mexicans to work without green cards. But big farming combines, farm bosses and smugglers who bring them in make money off the "wetbacks'" labor—they don't have to pay federal minimum wages, or ensure adequate housing or sanitary conditions.

The Mexican woman is especially at risk. Often the *coyote* (smuggler) doesn't feed her for days or let her go to the bathroom. Often he rapes her or sells her into prostitution. She cannot call on county or state health or economic resources because she doesn't know English and she fears deportation. American employers are quick to take advantage of her helplessness. She can't go home. She's sold her house, her furniture, borrowed from friends in order to pay the *coyote* who charges her four or five thousand dollars to smuggle her to Chicago. She may work as a live-in maid for white, Chicano or Latino households for as little as $15 a week. Or work in the garment industry, do hotel work. Isolated and worried about her family back home, afraid of getting caught and deported, living with as many as fifteen people in one room, the *mexicana* suffers serious health problems. *Se enferma de los nervios, de alta presión.*[15]

La mojada, la mujer indocumentada, is doubly threatened in this country. Not only does she have to contend with sexual violence, but like all women, she is prey to a sense of physical helplessness. As a refugee, she leaves the familiar and safe homeground to venture into unknown and possibly dangerous terrain.

> This is her home
> this thin edge of
> barbwire.

NOTES

1. Los Tigres del Norte is a *conjunto band.*
2. Jack D. Forbes, *Aztecas del Norte: The Chicanos of Atzlán.* (Greenwich, CT:

Fawcett Publications, Premier Books, 1973), 13, 183; Eric R. Wolf, *Sons of Shaking Earth* (Chicago, IL: University of Chicago Press, Phoenix Books, 1959), 32.

3. John R. Chávez, *The Lost Land: The Chicano Images of the Southwest* (Albuquerque, NM: University of New Mexico Press, 1984), 9.

4. Chávez, 9. Besides the Aztecs, the Ute, Gabrillino of California, Pima of Arizona, some Pueblo of New Mexico, Comanche of Texas, Opata of Sonora, Tarahumara of Sinaloa and Durango, and the Huichol of Jalisco speak Uto-Aztecan languages and are descended from the Cochise people.

5. Reay Tannahill, *Sex in History* (Briarcliff Manor, NY: Stein and Day/Publishers/Scarborough House, 1980), 308.

6. Chávez, 21.

7. Isabel Parra, *El Libro Major de Violeta Parra* (Madrid, España: Ediciones Michay, S.A., 1985), 156-7.

8. From the Mexican *corrido*, "Del peligro de la Intervencion." Vicente T. Mendoza, *El Corrido Mexicano* (Mexico. D.F.: Fondo De Cultura Economica, 1954), 42.

9. Arnoldo De León, *They Called Them Greasers: Anglo Attitude Toward Mexicans in Texas, 1821-1900* (Austin, TX: University of Texas Press, 1983), 2-3.

10. The Plan of San Diego, Texas, drawn up on January 6, 1915, called for the independence and segregation of the states bordering Mexico: Texas, New Mexico, Arizona, Colorado, and California. Indians would get their land back. Blacks would get six states from the south and form their own independent republic. Chávez, 79.

11. Jesús Mena, "Violence in the Rio Grande Valley," *Nuestro* (Jan/Feb 1983), 41-42.

12. *Nosotros los pobres* was the first Mexican film that was truly Mexican and not an imitation European film. It stressed the devotion and love that children should have for their mother and how its lack would lead to the dissipation of their character. This film spawned a generation of mother-devotion/ungrateful-sons films.

13. From the Navajo "Protection Song" (to be sung upon going into battle). George W. Gronyn, ed., *American Indian Poetry: The Standard Anthology of Songs and Chants* (New York, NY: Liveright, 1934), 97.

14. Grace Halsell, *Los ilegales*, trans. Mayo Antonio Sánchez (Editorial Diana Mexica, 1979).

15. Margarita B. Melville, "Mexican Women Adapt to Migration," *International Migration Review*, 1978.

NATIVE AMERICAN NOVELS

Homing In

William Bevis

> But you know Crows measure wealth a little differently than non-Indians. . . . Wealth is measured by one's relatedness, one's family, and one's clan. To be alone, that would be abject poverty to a Crow.
>
> Janine Windy Boy-Pease, from the film *Contrary Warriors: A Story of the Crow Tribe*, Rattlesnake Productions, © 1985

How Native American is the Native American novel? And in what ways? Novels are certainly not traditional Native American arts, and we have only begun to ask how novels can be significantly Native American in anything but subject matter and politics. Should we say that Native Americans write not "Native American novels" but "novels about Native Americans"? The questions recall debates over "Black literature" in the 1960s: How deeply has a minority point of view entered these arts?

In the handling of plot and nature the novels of McNickle, Momaday, Silko, and Welch are Native American. This sounds simple, and in some ways it is; however, both "plot" and "nature" lead to culturally conditioned concepts and to pervasive differences in white and Native American points of view. As we shall see in their "homing" plots and their surprisingly "humanized" nature, these works are drenched in a tribalism most whites neither understand nor expect in the works of contemporary Indians, much less when they are professors (all four novelists have taught at universities). I will present the arguments on plot and on nature referring mainly to the novels of McNickle and Welch. They wrote about northern plains tribes only two mountain ranges apart; I will draw most evidence and comparisons from tribes between the Salish in western Montana and the Crows in eastern Montana, thereby hoping to minimize problems introduced by tribal variety.

This essay is neither proscriptive nor exhaustive. Native American novels *need* not have the characteristics I am proposing; many other possible characterizations—such as Momaday's calling Silko's *Ceremony* a "telling" rather than a novel, or Lincoln's comparison of Welch's surrealism to trickster tales—may well be apposite, yet are not discussed here. What we seek is the special appropriateness of "homing" plots and a humanized nature to Native Americans past and present, an appropriateness that is manifest in their novels.

HOMING

American whites keep leaving home: *Moby Dick, Portrait of a Lady, Huckleberry Finn, Sister Carrie, The Great Gatsby*—a considerable number of American "classics" tell of leaving home to find one's fate farther and farther away. To be sure, Ahab or Gatsby might have been better off staying put, and their narrators might finally be retreating homeward, but the story we tell our children is of lighting out for the territories. A wealth of white tradition lies behind these plots, beginning with four centuries of colonial expansion. The Bildungsroman, or story of a young man's personal growth, became in America, especially, the story of a young man or woman leaving home for better opportunities in a newer land. In *Letters from an American Farmer*, St. Jean de Crevecoeur defined Americans as a people who leave the old to take the new: "*He* is an American, who, leaving behind all his ancient prejudices and manners, takes new ones from the mode of life he has embraced, the new government he obeys, and the new rank he holds" (in Bradley et al. 1974:184). The home we leave, to Crevecoeur, is not only place; it is a past, a set of values and parents, an "ancien regime."

Such "leaving" plots—not really picaresque because they are directed toward a new mode of life—embody quite clearly the basic premise of success in our mobile society. The individual advances, sometimes at all cost, with little or no regard for family, society, past, or place. The individual is the ultimate reality, hence individual consciousness is the medium, repository, and arbiter of knowledge; "freedom," our primary value, is a matter of distance between oneself and the smoke from another's chimney. Isolation is the poison in this mobile plot, and romantic love seems to be its primary antidote. Movement, isolation, personal and forbidden knowledge, fresh beginnings; the basic ingredients of the American Adam have dominated our art, even if many of our artists are dissenters from mainstream myths of success. The free individual may be a tragic failure, but his is the story we tell and always in our ears is Huck's strange derision "I been there before."

In marked contrast, most Native American novels are not "eccentric," centrifugal, diverging, expanding, but "incentric," centripetal, converging, contracting. The hero comes home. "Contracting" has negative overtones to us, "expanding" a positive ring. These are the cultural choices we are considering. In Native American novels, coming home, staying put, contracting, even what we call "regressing" to a place, a past where one has been before, is not only the primary story, it is a primary mode of knowledge and a primary good.

Let us begin with the simplest consideration, the plots of the six most prominent Native American novels, and then see how these plots thicken. In D'Arcy McNickle's *The Surrounded*, Archilde comes home from Portland— where he "can always get a job now any time" playing the fiddle in a "show house" (1936:2)—to the Salish and Kootenai ("Flathead") reservation in Western Montana. He has made it in the white world, and has come "to see my mother . . . in a few days I'm going again" (p. 7). From the very beginning, however, family ties, cultural ties, ties to place, and growing ties to a decidedly "reservation" (versus assimilated) girl are spun like webs to bind him down. He does not leave, and finally is jailed by the white man's law. It seems to be a "tar baby" plot; Archilde takes one lick and then another at his own backward people, and suddenly he is stuck. At first, being assimilated into a white world, he had expected to remain mobile, thinking of "wherever he might be in times to come. Yes, wherever he might be!" (p. 5). McNickle's repetition underscores the plot: whites leave, Indians come home.

Although the white point of view would find in such a homing-as-failure plot either personal disaster or moral martyrdom (e.g., Silas Lapham, Isabel Archer), McNickle's point of view toward his home village of St. Ignatius is more complex: that of a Salish Indian turned anthropologist, B.I.A. administrator and a founder of the National Congress of American Indians and the Newberry Library in Chicago. His novel does not present Archilde as simply sucked into a depressing situation, although he certainly is; the novel applauds his return to Indian roots. At first Archilde is "on the outside of their problems. He had grown away from them, and even when he succeeded in approaching them in sympathy, he remained an outsider—only a little better than a professor come to study their curious ways of life" (1936:193). He has, in short, the charm of an anthropologist. When he stays, however, to gratify his mother's wish for a traditional feast and to help his Spanish father harvest the wheat, "It was a way of fulfilling the trust placed in him. He was just learning what that meant, that trust" (p. 177). And as he watches his mother dress her grandson for the feast, he begins to appreciate the old ways, and to enter a different time:

> Watching his mother's experienced hands, he could guess how she had lived, what she had thought about in her childhood. A great deal had happened since those hands were young, but in making them work in this way, in the way she had been taught, it was a little bit as if the intervening happenings had never been. He watched the hands move and thought these things. For a moment, almost, he was not an outsider, so close did he feel to those ministering hands. (pp. 215–16)

We can hardly wish such beauty to be "outmoded," and although Archilde cannot save his mother or with any convenience apply her old "mode of life" to himself, the point of view of the novel offers profound respect for the past, family, and tradition; more troublingly, it asks us to admire Archilde's chosen involvement on the reservation even as it leads to personal doom. At first this plot may seem "Romantic" and "Primitivist," but as we shall see, it is not.

The plot of *The Surrounded* is typical. In McNickle's other novel of contemporary Indians, *Wind from an Enemy Sky* (1978; first published after his death), a young boy on the same reservation is abducted by whites to a Mission school (not uncommon—it happened to McNickle). Four years later he returns, an outsider, to his very traditional grandfather and tribe. The plot hangs on the tribe's attempt to recover from white authorities a lost Feather Boy medicine bundle. In the course of the book, the young boy and the reader gain increasing respect for this futile and regressive effort to "bring back our medicine, our power" (p. 18), a perfect example of an activity whites cannot easily appreciate. Grounds for our respect for such regression would usually be existential or heroic, but again, something different is going on. As in *The Surrounded*, action focuses in concentric circles from the outside world to the few miles between McDonald peak and the Flathead river; just as Archilde had recovered his traditional mother, so young Antoine is initiated by his conservative grandfather into the tribe. The traditional Indians, however, once more win the past only to lose the war.

Three of the other novels also tell of a wanderer in the white world coming home. In Momaday's *House Made of Dawn* (1966), an Indian serviceman comes back to the reservation, drinks and kills, drifts in Los Angeles, and finally returns to the pueblo to give his grandfather a traditional burial and participate in the annual healing race, which his grandfather had once run. In Welch's *Winter in the Blood* (1974), a thirty-ish Indian who has quit his job in an Oregon hospital returns to the ranch in northern Montana, to a desperate

round of drunken bar hopping that leads, finally to discovering his grandfather, pulling out of his lethargy, and throwing the traditional tobacco pouch
in his grandmother's grave. In Leslie Silkos's *Ceremony* (1977), an Indian serviceman returns from Japan to the Southwest Laguna tribe, and slowly
breaks from a pattern of drinking and madness to participating in a healing
ceremony guided by an old medicine man, a ceremony that begins with a
quest for cattle and ends with an amended story and rain for the desert land.
In the last of the six novels, Welch's *The Death of Jim Loney* (1979), an Indian
in northern Montana refuses to leave—despite pressure and opportunity—his
hopeless town and native land. He shrinks back into the darkest corner of all,
as his circle spirals inward to one place, one past, and suicide. In all these
books, Indian "homing" is presented as the opposite of competitive individualism, which is white success:

> But Rocky was funny about those things. He was an A-student and all-state in
> football and track. He had to win; he said he was always going to win. So he lis-
> tened to his teachers, and he listened to the coach. They were proud of him. They
> told him, "Nothing can stop you now except one thing: don't let the people at
> home hold you back." (Silko 1977:52)

First let us agree on the obvious: In the six novels, an Indian who has been
away or could go away comes home and finally finds his identity by staying.
In every case except Loney's, a traditional tribal elder who is treated by the
novel with great respect precipitates the resolution of the plot. In every case
except Loney's that elder is a relative—usually parent or grandparent—with
whom the protagonist forms a new personal bond. In every case including
Loney's, the ending sought by the protagonist is significantly related to tribal
past and place. With or without redemption, these "homing" plots all present tribal past as a gravity field stronger than individual will.

What is interesting is not this simple "structuralist" pattern, but its implications and the attitudes toward it within the novels. Tribalism is
respected, even though it is inseparable from a kind of failure. Under examination, that "homing" to tribe is complex: Tribalism is not just an individual's past, his "milieu" or "background." Tribe is not just lineage or kinship;
home is not just a place. "Grounded Indian literature is tribal; its fulcrum is
a sense of relatedness. To Indians tribe means family, not just bloodlines but
extended family, clan, community, ceremonial exchanges with nature, and
an animate regard for all creation as sensible and powerful" (Lincoln 1983:8).
These books suggest that "identity," for a Native American, is not a matter
of finding "one's self," but of finding a "self" that is transpersonal and includes a society, a past, and a place. To be separated from that transpersonal

time and space is to lose identity. These novels are important, not only because they depict Indian individuals coming home while white individuals leave but also because they suggest—variously and subtly and by degrees—a tribal rather than an individual definition of "being."

The tribal "being" has three components: society, past, and place. The "society" of the tribe is not just company; it is law. Catherine, Archilde's aging mother in *The Surrounded*, makes clear that what they have lost are the customs, rituals, and practices of law which bind people together into more than a population. In the central feast scene, the Indians lament the banning of dances, ceremonies, and practices by secular and religious authorities, just as conquered white Americans might lament the loss of courts, due process, and private ownership of land. The tone of the discussion is that, under white rule, "mere anarchy is loosed upon the world." *Wind from an Enemy Sky* is filled with discussions of white attempts to break Indian law:

> What kind of law is that? Did we have such a law? When a man hurt somebody in camp, we went to that man and asked him what he was going to do about it. If he did nothing, after we gave him a chance, we threw him away. He never came back. But only a mean man would refuse to do something for the family he hurt. That was a good law, and we still have it. We never threw it away. Who is this white man who comes here and tells us what the law is? Did he make the world? Does the sun come up just to look at him? (McNickle 1978:89)

Just as in American law, these tribal guarantees of rights within the nation are not necessarily extended to foreigners (other tribes). So in *Wind*, the young Indian's murder of the white man tending the white dam is met by the Chief with a shrug, the casual counterpart of colonial invasion: "The man up there was not one of us. He has people to mourn for him. Let his own people be troubled" (p. 65).

In each of these novels, the protagonist seeks a meaningful relation to a meaningful structure: He becomes a healthy man through accepted social ritual (Silko, Momaday) and a self-respecting man through deeds traditional to his people and needed by them (McNickle, and Welch's pouch on the grave in *Winter in the Blood*). Self-realization is not accomplished by the individual or by romantic bonding only; that would be incomprehensible. In *Wind*, Henry Jim tries assimilation, which means individualization, by farming his own land, living in his own frame house (with rooftop widow's walk overlooking the valley—the government had decided to showcase Henry Jim), and by white standards he succeeds as an individual. But:

> The government man said it would be a good thing. He wanted the Indians to see what it is like to have a nice house like that. In those days I had the foolish

thought that a man stands by himself, that his kinsmen are no part of him. I did not go first to my uncles and my brothers and talk it over with them. . . . I didn't notice it at first, but one day I could see that I was alone. . . . Brothers, I was lonesome, sitting in my big house. I wanted to put my tepee up in the yard, so people would come to see me, but my son and his wife said it would be foolish, that people would only laugh. . . . Two days ago I told my son to put up this tepee; it is the old one from my father's time. "Put up the tepee," I said, "the stiff-collars can stay away. I want to die in my own house."

Every voice in the circle murmured. Antoine looked up, stealthily scanning each face, and he could feel what was there among them. It shamed them that they had stayed away and had been hard against this old man. It shamed them, and they were in grief. (McNickle 1978:117–18)

So the first assumption of tribalism is that the individual is completed only in relation to others, that man is a political animal (lives through a relationship to a village-state), and the group which must complete his "being" is organized in some meaningful way. That meaning, not just land, is what has been lost: "now in old age she looked upon a chaotic world—so many things dead, so many words for which she knew no meaning; . . . How was it that when one day was like another there should be, at the end of many days, a world of confusion and dread and emptiness?" (McNickle 1936:22).

The second component of tribalism is its respect for the past. The tribe, which makes meaning possible, endures through time and appeals to the past for authority. Tribal reality is profoundly conservative; "progress" and "a fresh start" are not *native* to America: "Modeste was silent for a long time. Then he announced that he too . . . had turned back to that world which was there before the new things came" (McNickle 1936:210). Most of the Western tribes shared a belief in a "distant past": "Back in time immemorial things were different, the animals could talk to human beings and many magical things still happened" (Silko 1977:99). Old Betonie in *Ceremony*, the grandfather in *House Made of Dawn*, Catherine in *The Surrounded*, Bull in *Wind from an Enemy Sky*, and Grandfather Yellow Calf, who talks to the deer in Welch's more skeptical *Winter in the Blood*—all are in touch with a tradition tracing from the distant past, and all extend this connection to the young protagonists. Only Loney fails to find a connected ancestor, and only Loney fails.

In these novels, whites, mobile in time as well as space, have left their own past behind. The liberal Indian agent in *Wind*, Rafferty, reflects on Henry Jim's request:

And he asks me to help bring back this old bundle, whatever it is—this old symbol. It's been gone twenty-five or thirty years, but he thinks the people should have it.

Nobody in Marietta, Ohio, would make such a request—in Marietta, if it's like towns I know, they're trying to get away from the past. (McNickle 1978:36)

Most instructive is McNickle's recital of a Christian welcome to Mission school:

> You students, now, you listen to me. I want you to appreciate what we're doing for you. We're taking you out of that filth and ignorance, lice in your heads, all that, the way you lived before you came here. . . . Forget where you came from, what you were before; let all that go out of your minds and listen only to what your teachers tell you. (p. 106)

Quite apart from the tyranny of such hair-scouring and brainwashing is the stupidity of the white demands from an Indian point of view. Indians were understandably startled at white heterogeneity, at the political and religious differences among whites, at their rapid and ill-considered change of all within their grasp. In opposing the past, whites were opposing a fundamental reality and were likely to fail: "They're just like young bears, poking their noses into everything. Leave them alone and they'll go away. . . . Wait until a hard winter comes . . . they would go away and the world would be as it had been from the beginning, when Feather Boy visited the people and showed them how to live" (McNickle 1978:131, 135).

Native Americans had excellent grounds for valuing the past, grounds that do not seem as impractical, quaint, or primitive as faith in Feather Boy. The source of respect for the past in Indian life and novels is respect for authority. Since Socrates and the growth of the ideals of free inquiry and the practices of ingenious manipulation, we have hardly known such stability. At least in the last four hundred years, few Europeans have absorbed the respect for parents, elders, customs, and government, the belief in the *benevolence of power* that Plains Indians knew. The aging Crow Chief Plenty-coups spoke to Frank Linderman in 1930:

> "This talking between our mothers, firing us with determination to distinguish ourselves, made us wish we were men. It was always going on—this talking among our elders, both men and women—and we were ever listening. On the march, in the village, everywhere, there was praise in our ears for skill and daring. Our mothers talked before us of the deeds of other women's sons, and warriors told stories of the bravery and fortitude of other warriors until a listening boy would gladly die to have his name spoken by the chiefs in council, or even by the women in their lodges.
>
> "More and more we gathered by ourselves to talk and play. . . . We had our leaders just as our fathers had, and they became our chiefs in the same manner that men become chiefs, by distinguishing themselves."

The pleasure which thoughts of boyhood had brought to his face vanished now. His mind wandered from his story. "My people were wise," he said thoughtfully. "They never neglected the young or failed to keep before them deeds done by illustrious men of the tribe. Our teachers were willing and thorough. They were our grandfathers, fathers, or uncles. All were quick to praise excellence without speaking a word that might break the spirit of a body who might be less capable than others. Those who failed at any lesson got only more lessons, more care, until he was as far as he could go." (Linderman 1974 [1932]: 8-9)

That is far from the America which Crevecoeur viewed, and such respect for the old ways necessarily mocks change.

A culture believing that power corrupts, naturally encourages dissent. A culture believing that power is benign, naturally respects its elders. We should not see the regressive plots of these novels as returns only to a "distant past" of Edenic unity, magic, and medicine bundles. Right down to the raising of young and the conduct of tribal councils, Native Americans successfully practiced a system that engendered respect for the immediate as well as distant past. That is, the past, too, was part of tribal authority and culture and therefore part of identity. Each plot of all six novels hinges on the insufferability of individuality in time as well as space: Severed from the past, the present is meaningless, outcast, homeless. The connotations of "regression" are cultural; not all people equate their "civilization" with "discontents," and therefore a return to a previous status quo is not necessarily a romantic "escape" from an unbearable present of cultural or individual maturity and anxiety. Indeed, Native Americans said and still say that Marietta's attempt "to get away from the past" is the escapist fantasy that will not succeed.

I suggested earlier that, to white Americans, the individual is often the ultimate reality, that therefore individual consciousness is the medium, repository, and arbiter of knowledge, and that our "freedom" can be hard to distinguish from isolation. In contrast, I suggested that Native Americans valued a "transpersonal self," and that this "transpersonal self" composed of society, past, and place conferred identity and defined "being." Why not, the skeptic might ask, use a vocabulary of "individual" and "context," and simply explore the differing degrees of emphasis on each by the cultures in question? That might be possible, but such discourse presumes both the separability and independent value of each category, as if the individual is a meaningful category with or without context. That an individual exists is not contested, and Native American life and novels present all the variety of personality expected in our species; but the individual alone has no meaning. In all six novels, the free individual without context is utterly lost, so it would be misleading to apply to him so hallowed an English term as "individual." No "free individual" who achieves white success in these six books is really admired—not Rocky, Henry Jim (the closest case would be Kate in *Loney*)—and certainly the free "mode of life" they have "chosen" is not preferred to tribal context. So, to call Welch's narrator in Minough's bar, or Tayo back from the war, or Abel in Los Angeles, or Loney at the football game an "individual," implying all the weight of dignity, promise, and law which is carried by that term in white culture, is misleading. In every one of these books the protagonist seeks an identity that he can find *only* in his society, past, and place; unlike whites, he feels no meaningful being, alone. Individuality is not even the scene of success or failure; it is nothing.

In a similar way, "knowledge" is formed and validated tribally in Native American life and in these books, although of course the individual cortex does the thinking. Consider the vision quest, the most radically isolated "knowing" an Indian was encouraged to seek. Alone for days, fasting and punishing the body, the young man sought the hallucinatory dream or vision which would help him realize his identity by revealing his spirit helpers and special animal henchmen, and which also would supply information to the tribe. Quite apart from the obvious tribal acculturation involved in even the acquisition of such knowledge (a context often overlooked in American knowledge gained by individual "free inquiry"), its *interpretation*, that is, the conversion of traditionally sought phenomena to knowledge, was usually tribal. Plenty-coups, for instance, had his private dream but depended on the tribal council to determine what it meant: "By articulating his visionary experience so that it can be socially embodied, the dreamer frees himself from a burden of power while enhancing his tribal culture" (Kroeber 1983:330). Tayo's mythic romance and the narrator's visit to Grandfather in *Winter* place their acquisitions of crucial knowledge in a social and family context. Old Two Sleeps in *Wind* dissolves into the natural world (loses individuality) to gain his knowledge, and what is gained is so tribal that the entire encampment spends the winter months watching his furrowed brow, waiting for his vision to come forth.

Not only is knowledge usually sought, interpreted, and applied in a social context in these books, but useful knowledge is also knowledge from and of the past. From Henry Jim's point of view:

> It was not just an old story intended for the passing of an afternoon. As he had announced, he had come to ask for something—and a white man, a government man, might not understand the importance of the thing he asked unless the story was carried back to the beginnings. Today talks in yesterday's voice, the old people said. The white man must hear yesterday's voice. (McNickle 1978:28)

These plots are regressive because Native American knowledge is regressive; the traditional elders of *Ceremony, House, Surrounded, Wind,* and *Winter* (tragically, such lineage fails to develop for Loney) teach the protagonists the only knowledge which proves useful in each book. "I been there before" is a primary virtue. It does not seem too strong to say that in these books both meaningful "being" and meaningful "knowledge" are supra-individual, aspects of tribe.

The third component of tribalism inherent in these novels is place. In all six novels the protagonist ends *where* as well as *when* he began. Even in Welch's works, the most contemporarily realistic of the novels, the reservation is not just a place where people are stuck; it is *the* home. Curiously, all six novels are from inland West reservations and all six come from tribes not drastically displaced from their original territories or ecosystems. Place is not only an aspect of these works; place may have made them possible.

In each book the specific details of that one place are necessary to the protagonist's growth and pride. In *Ceremony,* "All things seemed to converge" on the Enchanted Mesa: "The valley was enclosing this totality, like the mind holding all thoughts together in a single moment" (Silko 1977:248–49). In *House,* that one particular road must be run; in McNickle the Mission Mountains must be the last stand; in Welch, the gate where Mose was killed, the ditch where his father froze, and Loney's Little Rockies, on the reservation, must be the scenes of growth.

Conversely, white disregard and disrespect for place is crucial to these books:

> ... the cities, the tall buildings, the noise and the lights, the power of their weapons and machines. They were never the same after that: they had seen what the white people had made from the stolen land. (Silko 1977:177)

> These mountains, trees, streams, the earth and the grass, from which his people learned the language of respect—all of it would pass into the hands of strangers, who would dig it up, chop it down, burn it up. (McNickle 1978:130–31)

Fey and McNickle, in their scholarly work, identified the concept of individual, transferable title to the land as the "prime source of misunderstanding" between whites and Indians (1959:26). McNickle thought that Indians understood land payment as a gift and perhaps as a rental fee for land use, but that probably, even late in the nineteenth century out West, Indians could not conceive of private land ownership. The Cherokees, by 1881, had learned and dissented: "the land itself is not a chattel" (p. 27). Fey and McNickle eloquently state the difference between the white transmutation of land to money (does that medicine work?) and the Native American view: "Even today, when Indian tribes may go into court and sue the United States for inadequate compensation or no compensation for lands taken from them, they still are dealing in alien concepts. One cannot grow a tree on a pile of money, or cause water to gush from it; one can only spend it, and then one is homeless" (p. 28).

Thus, all six novels depict Indians coming home and staying home, but "home" is not the "house" of white heaven, as dreamed by Catherine in *The Surrounded*: "everything they wanted, big houses all painted, fine garments ... rings ... gold," all out of sight of neighbors. Home to the Indian is a society: "Then I went to the Indian place and I could hear them singing. Their campfires burned and I could smell meat roasting (McNickle 1936:209). In all of these novels the protagonists succeed largely to the degree in which they reintegrate into the tribe, and fail largely to the degree in which they remain alone. Although such aspirations toward tribal reintegration may be treated by a novelist sentimentally, or romantically, or as fantasy, these aspirations are not *inherently* sentimental or romantic. Rather, they constitute a profound and articulate continuing critique of modern European culture, combined with a persistent refusal to let go of tribal identity; a refusal to regard the past as inferior; a refusal—no matter how futile—of even the wish to assimilate.

Whites may wonder why Indians are still living, as it were, in the past of having a past. It is a reasonable question, and it influences our reading of these novels. Only a little over one hundred years ago, in 1884, Montana Territory was fenced, the railroad came, the cattle market boomed, and the last buffalo was shot. Elders who remembered that winter of '84 ("Starvation Winter") lived into the 1930s; some of their children are now sixty to eighty years old. Indian students right now have relatives who heard from the lips of the living what it was like to ride a horse, belly deep in grass, across unfenced plains dark with buffalo. Several of my Crow students speak English as a second language; many members of all tribes have relatives who tell the old stories.

Even to occasional university professors such as the four authors under consideration, tribalism is not necessarily so distant as many whites think; these authors are not resurrecting archaic rituals for symbolic purposes, but telling of entire communities and drifting individuals still feeling the pull of tribal identity, tribal despair, tribal pride. There were surges of white interest in Indians in the 1880s, at the time of Helen Hunt Jackson and the final massacres; in the thirties, as the last fieldwork recalling pre-White culture faded; in the sixties, as Indians and whites grew politically active. But in between,

Native Americans were forgotten, and each surge of interest or neglect has resurrected the same issues: allotment, assimilation, termination of reservations, despair. The "Indian Question" is not an old question, beyond living memory, nor is it answered. The major threats of a hundred years ago still threaten, and many Native American tribes are still a people unwilling to buy wholesale the white ways or to abandon their own: "In many areas whites are regarded as a temporary aspect of tribal life and there is unshakable belief that the tribe will survive the domination of the white man and once again rule the continent" (Deloria 1970: 13).

REFERENCES

Broyard, Anatole. "Books of the Times," *New York Times*, Nov. 28, 1979.

Chapman, Abraham, ed. 1975. *Literature of the American Indians*. New York: New American Library.

Crevecoeur, St. Jean de. 1782. *Letters from an American Farmer*. Quoted in Sculley Bradley, Richard Croom Beatty, E. Hudson Long, and George Perkins. 1974. *The American Tradition in Literature*, vol. 1, 4th ed. New York: Grosset and Dunlop.

Deloria, Vine, Jr. 1970. *We Talk, You Listen*. New York: Macmillan.

Dialogues with Northwest Writers. 1982. *Northwest Review* 20 (2–3).

Erdrich, Louise. 1984. *Love Medicine*. New York: Holt, Rinehart and Winston.

Fey, Harold E., and D'Arcy McNickle. 1959. *Indians and Other Americans*. New York: Harper.

Garcia, Andrew. 1967. *Tough Trip Through Paradise*. Sausalito: Comstock.

Guthrie, A. B., Jr. 1947. *The Big Sky*. Boston: Houghton Mifflin.

Kroeber, Karl. 1983. "Poem, Dream, and the Consuming of Culture." In *Smoothing the Ground*, ed. Brian Swann. Berkeley, Los Angeles, London: University of California Press.

Krupat, Arnold. 1983. "The Indian Autobiography: Origins, Type and Function." In *Smoothing the Ground*, ed. Brian Swann. Berkeley, Los Angeles, London: University of California Press, 1983.

Lincoln, Kenneth. 1983. *Native American Renaissance*. Berkeley, Los Angeles, London: University of California Press.

Linderman, Frank. 1962 [1930]. *Plenty-Coups*. Lincoln: University of Nebraska Press. (Originally published as *American, the Life Story of a Great Indian, Plenty-Coups, Chief of the Crows*.)

———. 1974 [1932]. *Pretty-Shield*. Lincoln: University of Nebraska Press. (Originally published as *Red Mother*.)

McNickle, D'Arcy. 1936. *The Surrounded*. New York: Dodd, Mead.

———. 1978. *Wind from an Enemy Sky*. San Francisco: Harper & Row.

Momaday, N. Scott. 1966. *House Made of Dawn*. New York: Harper & Row.

Silko, Leslie. 1977. *Ceremony*. New York: Viking.

Standing Bear, Luther. 1978 [1933]. *Land of the Spotted Eagle*. Lincoln: University of Nebraska Press.

Strelke, Barbara. 1975. "N. Scott Momaday: Racial Memory and Individual Imagination." In *Literature of the American Indians*, ed. Abraham Chapman. New York: New American Library.

Swann, Brian, ed. 1983. *Smoothing the Ground*. Berkeley, Los Angeles, London: University of California Press.

Vittorini, Elio. 1949. *In Sicily*, trans. Wilfred David. New York: New Directions.

Welch, James. 1979. *The Death of Jim Loney*. New York: Harper & Row.

————. 1974. *Winter in the Blood*. New York: Harper & Row.

————. n.d. *Fools Crow*. Harmondsworth: Penguin (forthcoming).

SEA CHANGE

The Middle Passage and the Transatlantic Imagination

Carl Pedersen

In his 1862 essay "Walking" Henry David Thoreau, taking a page from Greek mythology, views the gap between Europe and America as a sea of oblivion that demarcates the restricted space of the Old World from the boundless space of the New: "The Atlantic is a Lethean stream, in our passage over which we have had an opportunity to forget the Old World and its institutions."[1] Yet ironically, in constructing this ideology of unremembering, Thoreau is nonetheless compelled to draw on a particularly European frame of reference, familiar to most educated European Americans of his day. Furthermore, he demonstrates, in Wayne Franklin's phrase, the ability of European language to plot New World experience in advance. The course of Thoreau's walking headed away from Europe: "Eastward I go only by force; but westward I go free."[2] Thoreau's formulation of the trajectory of American cultural development is linear and unproblematic: the movement westward is unmitigated by burdensome memories that would slow the settler on the journey to spiritual regeneration. In this paradigm the sea has washed away the past.

According to legend, retold in Paule Marshall's *Praisesong for the Widow* and Julie Dash's film *Daughters of the Dust*, Ibo warriors, transported to the shores of the Carolinas by the slave ships, took one look at this new world and turned their gaze eastward. They decided to return home: "Chains didn't stop those Ibo. They just kept on walking, like the water was solid ground."[3] For African Americans the Atlantic was a different kind of space. Instead of a breach separating past from present, it constituted a transformative Middle Passage where an African past and the American future, one in danger of fading from memory, the other imposing its hegemonic will, were constantly in

258

conflict over contested spheres of power. If, following the Thoreauvian paradigm, slave owners and slave traders had willingly severed their bonds with
the past, they seemed determined to expunge forcibly the African past
among their captives, sensing, perhaps unconsciously, that memory could be
a means of resistance and liberation. Breaking free of these ideological fet-
ters, the slave imagination was articulating an alternative discourse rooted in
memory and yearning for a return.

Thoreau notwithstanding, the African Middle Passage haunted the white
imagination. "Poised against the *Mayflower* is the slave ship," as William
Carlos Williams would have it,[4] and this juxtaposition is evident in Herman
Melville's "Benito Cereno," and even invades the aesthetic consciousness of
non-American representations of the slave ships, such as Prosper Merimée's
"Tamango," and J. W. F. Turner's painting *Slavers Throwing Overboard the
Dead and Dying*. Writing at about the same time as Thoreau, Martin Delany
hinted at the existence of an Atlantic world that provided a way out of physical and cultural bondage in the Americas: "Africa is our fatherland and we
its legitimate descendents . . . I have outgrown, long since, the boundaries of
North America, and with them have also outgrown the boundaries of their
claims."[5] A little more than a century after Delany the Barbadian poet
Edward Kamau Brathwaite would declare that only by returning to Africa
could he discover his native Caribbean.[6] Brathwaite's journey to Ghana confirmed his belief that Caribbean culture had a strong African undercurrent
which had been suppressed by the European colonizing powers. Thus the
Middle Passage emerges as more of a bridge than a breach, a space-in-
between where memory entails reconstructing the horrors of the voyage
westward and retracing the journey of Africans to the Americas.

Since Fernand Braudel's pathbreaking study *The Mediterranean and the
Mediterranean World* (1949), in which history is integrated by the sea, it has
become a commonplace in historical and geographical studies to investigate
the slave trade in terms of interconnected Atlantic zones. More recently John
Thornton and D. W. Meinig have mapped out an Atlantic space of political,
economic, and cultural interdependence that bears little resemblance to
Thoreau's Lethean stream.[7] In part inspired by these reconceptualizations of
the Atlantic World, I am concerned with charting a complementary literary
geography of an African American transatlantic imagination. Following
Delany's notion of expanding boundaries, I intend to examine selected works
from African American and Afro-Caribbean literatures that engage in an exploration of an Atlantic world which can ultimately widen the symbolic dimensions of the Middle Passage. For, to dwell for one final moment on
Thoreau's imagery, if the Atlantic is seen as a Lethean stream for European

voyagers to the Americas, it has subsequently in slave historiography, at least up to Stanley Elkins in the 1950s, also been thought of as a Lethean stream for enslaved African Americans. If there was an African past, it had been left behind, and slaves were held in bondage by European representations. Because Africa, as Hegel would have it, stood outside of history, enslaved Africans in the Americas could enter history only by blindly replicating European culture. In this view Africans were culturally malleable, veritable putty in the hands of their owners. If, by contrast, they were deemed incapable of attaining this culture, they would be forever consigned to the dark realm of savagery.

The contribution of Afro-Caribbean critical writing has been largely ignored in the recent literature of slavery and the literary imagination. With C. L. R. James as an intellectual trailblazer, writers such as Edward Kamau Brathwaite, George Lamming, Wilson Harris, Edouard Glissant, Derek Walcott, and others have produced a sizable body of critical work that either implicitly or explicitly addresses the idea of a Middle Passage. Taken together, this work furthermore offers an eloquent refutation of the notorious claim by V. S. Naipaul that "nothing was created in the West Indies."[8] One early assessment of the meaning of the Middle Passage in the transatlantic imagination is the Guyanese novelist Wilson Harris's little-known essay from 1970 "History, Fable, and Myth in the Caribbean and Guianas." Pointing to what he calls a "cleavage . . . between historical convention . . . and the arts of the imagination," Harris focuses on a particular cultural practice which explains the larger significance of the Middle Passage experience: the limbo. This dance, according to Harris, was born on the slave ships because of the lack of space. From an environment of coercion, which would seemingly allow no cultural room to move, a new configuration emerges in the form of the slave contorted into a human spider, provoking a "dislocation of a chain of miles" which opens up space not for a replication of the African past, but rather for "the renascence of a new corpus of sensibility that could translate and accommodate African and other legacies within a new architecture of cultures." Connecting limbo with the Jamaican spider figure Anancy and Haitian vodun, Harris emphasizes the dynamism of reconfiguration and transformation, not the stasis of essentialism or emasculation. Paradoxically, the cramped figure of the slave dancing the limbo heralds a "re-assembly" that promotes "a new growth." The new kind of space that was constituted during the Middle Passage is constantly rearticulated and points "to the necessity for a new kind of drama, novel, and poem."[9] Harris's concept of reassembly is echoed in Derek Walcott's 1992 Nobel lecture, in which he counters Naipaul's negative view with an alternative vision: "Break a vase, and the love that reassembles the fragments is stronger than that love which took its symmetry for granted when it was whole. The glue that fits the pieces is the sealing of its original shape. It is such a love that reassembles our African and Asiatic fragments, the cracked heirlooms whose restoration shows its white scars."[10] The geography of Walcott's polyglot Antilles contains an African memory of the Middle Passage and of slavery that defies attempts to deny its existence. This memory provides a rich source for the imagination, for, as Walcott has declared elsewhere, "every event becomes an exertion of memory and is thus subject to invention."[11]

An early narrative anticipating Harris's new kind of writing, and one that can be claimed as part of the African, Caribbean, American, and British literary traditions, thereby touching all four Atlantic zones as defined by Thornton and Meinig, is *The Interesting Narrative of the Life of Olaudah Equiano*, first published in 1789. Incorporating many key elements of Atlantic history and culture, Equiano's narrative is one of the first examples of Harris's limbo gateway joining the African past with the African American present. Equiano's journey takes him from the interior of Africa to the coast, across the Atlantic to Barbados, then to a Virginia plantation, and finally to England. The many Middle Passages that propel his story are part of a narrative strategy that hovers between the demands of his audience and his sponsors and his own writerly ambitions which subvert these demands. In this sense the text itself replicates and reacts to constrictions of space, both physical and mental, imposed by economic imperatives and dominant discourse. The authority which Equiano acquires in the course of his many voyages functions as a narrative representation of his growing confidence as a writer.

By contrasting Africa with Europe, Equiano forces his readers to encounter culture from a multiple perspective. From the time of his childhood in an Ibo village to the moment when he distills his experiences in his *Narrative*, Equiano's life is one of Middle Passages. Each stage of his account underscores the tension between firsthand memory and mediated reconstruction. Thus, for example, his recollection of his Ibo childhood is informed by his reading of the works of the Quaker antislavery writer Anthony Benezet. In the opening passages dealing with Africa, images of social harmony and cooperative labor clash with the slave division of labor and the insatiable avarice which characterize English society.

During the journey to the Americas Equiano finds himself caught between the horror of the Middle Passage and a sense of wonder at European technology that made it seem as if he were "in another world." So intense is this conflict between unreality and abject terror that Equiano longs for death. Nonetheless, embarking on a later voyage across the Atlantic eastward from

Virginia to England, Equiano recounts how fear and trepidation gave way to empowerment and resistance: "When I got on board this large ship, I was indeed amazed to see the quantity of men and guns. However my surprise began to diminish, as my knowledge increased; and I ceased to feel those apprehensions and alarms which took such strong possession of me when I came first among the Europeans, and for some time after. I began now to pass to an opposite extreme; and was so far from being afraid of any thing new which I saw, that after I had been some time in this ship, I even began to long for an engagement."[12] Equiano, of course, was not alone in undergoing such a transformation. An earlier allusion to Greek mythology, employed by slaveholders and prevalent at the time that Equiano was writing his autobiography, referred to the potential for rebellion in the Atlantic world as a many-headed Hydra that linked black and white laborers, both slave and free.[13] The Atlantic system was creating connections that its designers had not foreseen.

During the nineteenth century the widespread fear of slave rebellion in the Americas was an unconscious acknowledgment from the slaveholders that the Middle Passage was not an end but rather the beginning of a new cultural configuration formulated by resistance. Resistance took many forms: dance, folktales, or religion, as Harris stresses, the development of nation-language, defined by Brathwaite as "the *submerged* area of that dialect which is much more closely allied to the African aspect of existence in the Caribbean,"[14] and slave revolts on land and at sea. Equiano's empowerment is echoed in two narratives of the transatlantic imagination in the nineteenth century, Frederick Douglass's short novel *The Heroic Slave*, (1853) and Martin Robison Delany's novel *Blake; or, The Huts of America* (1859–1862).

Douglass's only work of fiction recounts a Middle Passage not from Africa to the Americas but from the United States to the Caribbean in his reconstruction of the revolt on the brig the *Creole* in 1841. The leader of the revolt, Madison Washington, recognizes, as did Equiano, that the ship at sea represents not only oppression but the possibility of emancipation, for "you cannot write the bloody laws of slavery on those restless billows. The ocean, if not the land, is free."[15] Even the failed revolt on board the *Vulture* in Delany's novel has the rebellious blacks and an Atlantic storm joined in opposition to the crew of the slave ship: "The black and frowning skies and raging hurricane above; the black and frowning slaves with raging passions below, rendered it dreadful without, fearful within, and terrible all around."[16] In these narratives the sea functions as a trope marking the unruly space between the past memory of Africa and the present reality of slavery in terms of active resistance.

In *Being and Race*, a book of literary criticism, Charles Johnson observes that much contemporary African American writing is "a meditation on remembrance." Citing David Bradley's *Chaneysville Incident* as a prime example of this obsession with memory, Johnson notes how in Bradley's novel "the racial past begins to appear . . . as partly a product of imagination, a plastic and malleable thing freighted with ambiguity."[17] In line with Harris and Walcott, facts for Johnson can yield meaning only by a conscious effort of the imagination. His 1990 novel, *Middle Passage*, displays the effort of a transatlantic imagination transforming the Middle Passage experience into a microcosm of Atlantic history and an allegory of growing self-awareness. Structured as a series of entries into a ship's log over a period of a little more than two months in 1830, *Middle Passage* recounts the exploits of Rutherford Calhoun, a free black and petty thief from Illinois. In New Orleans he stows away on the *Republic* only to discover that it is a slave ship under the command of Ebenezer Falcon, whom Calhoun equates with the young nation: "He, like the fledgling republic itself, felt expansive, eager to push back frontiers, even to slide betimes into bullying others and taking, if need be, what was not offered."[18] For Calhoun as well the sea represents a reaffirmation of the frontier spirit of the settlers, an escape from the oppressiveness of eastern culture. In the course of the *Republic*'s voyage to Africa and back to New Orleans, Calhoun realizes that he is caught in the economic and cultural web of the slave trade. Commercial interests make the crew of the *Republic* no freer than their African captives, the Allmuseri and their god. Drawing a parallel between the physical contortions and mental transformations of the Africans, Calhoun observes that they are "no longer Africans, yet not Americans either."[19] Representing an alternative history ultimately undermining Calhoun's confidence in frontier ideology, the rebellion of the Allmuseri and the sinking of the *Republic* during a storm transform him into a "cultural mongrel." The Middle Passage is not confined to the hold of the slave ship; it invades the consciousness of all who enter the Atlantic zone.

The prerogatives of empire supposedly enabled dominant cultures to block out alternative histories and narratives. A central point of the Middle Passage, however, is that it effectively transformed the cultures of Europeans and Africans alike, binding them in an uneven yet symbiotic relationship. In his novel *Natives of My Person* (1971) George Lamming describes a voyage that would attempt to deny that relationship. In his allegorical exploration of the meaning of the slave trade, Lamming attempts to penetrate the seventeenth-century mind in order to arrive at an understanding of the root causes of the European urge for colonization and slavery. As early as 1960 he had offered one possible explanation: "The slave whose skin suggests the savaged deformity of his nature becomes identical with the Carib Indian who feeds on human flesh. Carib Indian and African slave, both seen as the wild fruits of Nature, share equally that spirit of revolt which Prospero by sword or Language is determined to conquer."[20]

What the commandant of the *Reconnaissance* proposes on this new voyage is nothing less than to undo the past by undertaking a mission that will "reverse all previous philosophies."[21] Like Ebenezer Falcon, the commandant has been on numerous voyages to capture slaves on the African coast and to exterminate the indigenous peoples of the Caribbean. He now plans to undertake an unauthorized voyage to establish an ideal community on the imaginary island of San Cristobal, one of the places he had ravished. Memory, however, thwarts the realization of the commandant's vision of a future with no past. Using journal entries and flashbacks Lamming records how the officers of the ship, like the commandant, have committed atrocities against their captives which affect their present actions.

In Lamming's view all human relationships are haunted by the memory of the slave trade. He continually draws parallels between the officers' ruthless treatment of slaves and of women. Colonization possesses a logic that extends from white over black, to the masculine over the feminine, and finally to the mind over the self. Even without the physical presence of slaves, the mission of the *Reconnaissance* is doomed.

Paule Marshall once observed that her first three novels "constitute a trilogy, describing, in reverse, the slave trade's triangular route back to the motherland, the source."[22] The difference between Marshall's effort of the transatlantic imagination and the futility of the mission of the *Reconnaissance* is obvious. The former eagerly encourages memory, the latter militantly seeks to deny it. Yet the longing for a physical or imaginative return can ultimately succumb to the same essentialist propensities as the officers of the *Reconnaissance*. Wright and, more recently, Eddy Harris returned from their reverse Middle Passages to Africa with any racial fantasies about the continent largely dispelled. As Harris concluded at the end of his journey of self-discovery: "Africa is the birth of mankind. Africa is the land of my ancestors. But Africa is not home. I hardly know this place at all."[23] Yet Afrocentrists such as Molefi Kete Asante tend to downplay if not entirely ignore African complicity in the slave trade, are keen to register "pure," unmitigated African retentions in the Americas, and seek to introduce a coherent African worldview into the school curriculum. The virtue of Wilson Harris's model of a transatlantic imagination is that it celebrates hybridity. Instead of refuting the history of the slave trade, he seeks to incorporate this experience in charting the development of a new African diasporic culture. In this conception the Middle Passage extends from the sands of the Sahara to the rivers of the Americas, from the Sudan to the Cunje and the Mississippi. Memory opens Harris's limbo gateway to the exploration of the space-in-between and its many tributaries.

The implications of the limbo gateway are wide-ranging. It eliminates the fixed boundaries between the literary and the extraliterary as it engages historical events in narrative terms. A parallel can be drawn between Harris's fusion of history and literature into a notion of cultural syncretism and Bakhtin's dialogism. Seen in linguistic terms, efforts to possess meaning as a fixed entity in the discourse of a single voice divorced from social interaction are doomed to failure. Similarly, in terms of the development of the Atlantic world, efforts to suppress the voices of the hold result in incomplete, monologic history. Between the fixed points of Europe, Africa, and the Americas, dialogic discourse in its many forms subverts colonial domination by becoming part of its consciousness.

Toni Morrison has mapped out a critical geography expressing the dialogic relationship between the Africanist presence in the United States and the white imagination in her book of literary criticism, *Playing in the Dark*. In her own work, and in the work of many African Americans and African Caribbeans, it is the effort of memory that confirms the resilience of an Africanist presence, not essentialized but the creation of a Middle Passage experience. In an interview with Paul Gilroy, Morrison provides an acute description of the Lethean currents of Americanist thought: "We live in a land where the past is always erased and America is the innocent future in which immigrants can come and start over, where the slate is clean. The past is absent or it's romanticized. This culture doesn't encourage dwelling on, let alone coming to terms with, the truth about the past. That memory is much more in danger now than it was thirty years ago."[24] In contrast, the transatlantic imagination sees the Middle Passage as a transformative process that bridges the geographical space from East to West and from West to East, fills the space between memory and history, reconstructs the space left by historiographical omission, and negotiates the space between colonizer and colonized. By reassembling the fragments of history and restoring the writing on the slate, memory comes to terms with a troubled past.

NOTES

1. Henry David Thoreau, "Walking," in *The Portable Thoreau*, ed. Carl Bode (New York: Viking, 1947), p. 604.

2. Wayne Franklin, *Discovers, Explorers, Settlers* (Chicago: University of Chicago Press, 1979), p. 5. Thoreau, "Walking," p. 603.

3. Julie Dash, *"Daughters of the Dust": The Making of an African American Woman's Film* (New York: New Press, 1992), p. 142. Paule Marshall, *Praisesong for the Widow* (New York: Plume, 1983), pp. 38–39. Another version of this story, repeated in folktales and rearticulated in Toni Morrison's *Song of Solomon*, has the Africans flying back to their homeland.

4. William Carlos Williams, *In the American Grain* (New York: New Directions, 1956), p. 208.

5. Martin Delany, *Official Report of the Niger Valley Exploring Party* (1859), quoted in Paul Gilroy, *The Black Atlantic: Modernity and Double Consciousness* (London: Verso, 1993), p. 26.

6. Edward Kamau Brathwaite, "Timehri," *Savacou*, 2 (September 1970): 38.

7. Fernand Braudel, *The Mediterranean and the Mediterranean World* (London: Collins, 1972–73). John Thornton, *Africa and Africans in the Making of the Atlantic World, 1400–1680* (New York: Cambridge University Press, 1992). D. W. Meinig, *The Shaping of America*, vol. 1 (New Haven: Yale University Press, 1986).

8. V. S. Naipaul, *The Middle Passage* (New York: Macmillan, 1963), p. 28.

9. Wilson Harris, "History, Fable, and Myth in the Caribbean and Guianas" (Georgetown, Guyana: The National History and Arts Council, Ministry of Information and Culture, 1970), pp. 8, 9, 10, 11.

10. Derek Walcott, *The Antilles: Fragments of Epic Memory* (New York: Farrar, Straus, and Giroux, 1993), unpaginated.

11. Derek Walcott "The Muse of History," in *Is Massa Day Dead? Black Moods in the Caribbean.* ed. Orde Coombs (Garden City, N.Y.: Anchor, 1974), p. 2.

12. Olaudah Equiano, *The Interesting Narrative of the Life of Olaudah Equiano*, in *The Classic Slave Narratives*, ed. Henry Louis Gates, Jr. (New York: New American Library, 1987), pp. 36, 45.

13. Peter Linebaugh and Marcus Rediker, "The Many-Headed Hydra: Sailors, Slaves, and the Atlantic Working Class in the Eighteenth Century," *Journal of Historical Sociology*, 3, no. 3 (September 1990): 225–52.

14. Edward Kamau Brathwaite, *History of the Voice* (London: New Beacon, 1984), p. 13.

15. Frederick Douglass, "The Heroic Slave," in *The Negro Carvan*, ed. Sterling A. Brown, Arthur P. Davis, and Ulysses Lee (New York: Dryden Press, 1943), p. 26.

16. Martin Delany, *Blake, or The Huts of America* (Boston: Beacon Press, 1970), p. 234.

17. Charles Johnson, *Being and Race* (Bloomington: Indiana University Press, 1988), pp. 74, 79.

18. Charles Johnson, *Middle Passage* (New York: Atheneum, 1990), p. 50.

19. Ibid., p. 125.

20. George Lamming, *The Pleasures of Exile* (London: Allison & Busby, 1984), p. 13.

21. George Lamming, *Natives of My Person* (London: Allison & Busby, 1986), p. 250.

22. Paule Marshall, "Shaping the World of My Art," quoted in Gay Wilentz, *Black Women Writers in Africa and the Diaspora* (Bloomington: Indiana University Press, 1992), p. 100.

23. Eddy L. Harris, *Native Stranger: A Black American's Journey into the Heart of Africa* (New York: Simon & Schuster, 1992), p. 312.

24. "Living Memory: Meeting Toni Morrison," quoted in Gilroy, *Black Atlantic*, p. 222.

WHO SET YOU FLOWIN'?

The African-American Migration Narrative

Farah Jasmine Griffin

> This new phase of Negro American life . . . will doubtless prove to
> be the most significant event in our local history since the Civil
> War.
>
> Carter G. Woodson (1918)

> Move. Walk. Run.
>
> Toni Morrison (1987)

> Take me to another place, take me to another time.
>
> Arrested Development (1992)

> The fundamental theme of New World African modernity is nei-
> ther integration nor separation but rather migration and emigra-
> tion.
>
> Cornel West (1993)

From the publication of Paul Laurence Dunbar's *Sport of the Gods* in 1902 to
Toni Morrison's *Jazz* in 1992, the migration narrative emerges as one of the
twentieth century's dominant forms of African-American cultural production.[1] Through migration narratives—musical, visual, and literary—African-
American artists and intellectuals attempt to come to terms with the
massive dislocation of black peoples following migration. Given the impact
of migration and urbanization on African-Americans in particular and
American society in general, it is not surprising that this century has witnessed the emergence of this new form.

Most often, migration narratives portray the movement of a major character or the text itself from a provincial (not necessarily rural) Southern or
Midwestern site (home of the ancestor) to a more cosmopolitan, metropoli-
tan area. Within the migration narrative the protagonist or a central figure

who most influences the protagonist is a migrant. The representation of the migration experience depends on the genre and form of the narrative as well as the historical and political moment of production. Also, each artist's conception of power is directly related to the construction of his or her text.

The narrative is marked by four pivotal moments: (1) an event that propels the action northward, (2) a detailed representation of the initial confrontation with the urban landscape, (3) an illustration of the migrant's attempt to negotiate that landscape and his or her resistance to the negative effects of urbanization, and (4) a vision of the possibilities or limitations of the Northern, Western, or Midwestern city and the South. These moments may occur in any given order within the context of the narrative; in other words, it is not necessary that there be a straightforward linear progression from the South to a vision of the consequences of migration, although this is most often the case.

The migration narrative shares with the slave narrative notions of ascent from the South into a "freer" North. Like the slave narrative and the fiction it inspired, the migration narrative has its own set of narrative conventions. If the slave narrative revolves around the auction block, the whipping, the separation of families, and miscegenation, the migration narrative provides us with lynching scenes, meetings with ancestors, and urban spaces like kitchenettes, dance halls, and street corners. The migration narrative is marked by an exploration of urbanism, an explication of sophisticated modern power, and, in some instances, a return South. Finally, the migration narrative takes shape in a variety of art forms: autobiography, fiction, music, poetry, photography, and painting.

Although literary critics have noted migration as an important theme in African-American fiction, until recently they have been less attentive to the relationship between migration and African-American literary production. The study of twentieth-century black migration has been the province of social scientists, historians, and scholars of African-American music and folklore. Prompted by Robert Stepto's From Behind the Veil: A Study of Afro-American Narrative (1979), in the past decade, literary and cultural critics Susan Willis, Hazel Carby, Lawrence Rodgers, and Charles Scruggs have started the important project of situating twentieth-century migration as a major factor in African-American cultural productions.[2]

Hazel Carby's work is particularly noteworthy. Carby documents the emergence and development of a black women's blues culture that created "a music that spoke the desires which were released in the dramatic shift in social relations that occurred in a historical moment of crisis and dislocations."[3] For Carby, the 1920s marked a time when established black North-

ern intellectuals were confronted with large numbers of migrants who challenged earlier notions of sexuality, leadership, and any sense of a monolithic
black culture.

Charles Scruggs stresses migration as an important starting point in the
study of black literature of the city. Lawrence Rodgers is the first to identify
migration with the emergence of a new genre of African-American literature:
the Great Migration novel.

This [essay] departs from the foregoing studies in its interdisciplinary
focus and in its discussion of a variety of literary, musical, and visual works
that were created during the height of the Great Migration and the years that
followed it. I have chosen to call these texts migration narratives. The paradigm "migration narrative" provides a conceptual umbrella under which to
gather these African-American creative artifacts. In addition to identifying
the migration narrative as a dominant form of African-American cultural
production in the twentieth century, I have tried to create a way of talking
about African-American art that provides comprehensive space for the diversity of gender, class, and sexuality. Through critical readings of migration
narratives, I reveal paradigms like "ancestors" and "strangers" that cross
class, gender, and genre. This interpretation finds no one static migration
narrative; instead these narratives are as diverse as the people and the times
that create them.

Most migration narratives offer a catalyst for leaving the South. Although
there are different reasons for migrating, in all cases the South is portrayed as
an immediate, identifiable, and oppressive power. Southern power is exercised by people known to its victims—bosses, landlords, sheriffs, and, in the
case of black women, even family members. To the extent that power is exercised psychically, it relies on the potential victim's fear of the violence that
awaits him or her. In fictional texts especially, Southern power is inflicted on
black bodies in the form of lynching, beating, and rape. It is dramatized in the
spectacle and torture of elaborate lynching and burning rituals.[4] The degree
to which Southern power is stressed differs from genre to genre, but there is
a consensus that this power is unsophisticated in nature.[5]

Although the narratives tend to represent the South as a site of terror and
exploitation, some of them also identify it as a site of the ancestor. The role
of the ancestor in the Southern sections of the migration narrative is of great
significance to the development of the text. If the ancestor's role is mitigated,
then it is likely that throughout the course of the narrative, the South will be
portrayed as a site of racial horror and shame. In this instance, the ancestor
will be of little use on the Northern landscape. If, on the other hand, the

early Southern sections stress the significance of an ancestor, or the blood of any recently deceased black person, then the South becomes a place where black blood earns a black birthright to the land, a locus of history, culture, and possible redemption. If the South is thus established as a place of birthright, then the ancestor will be a significant influence in the migrant's life in the North.

After leaving the South, the next pivotal moment in the migration narrative is the initial confrontation with the urban landscape. This confrontation often shapes the fate of the South (embodied in the migrants themselves, the ancestor, and any retention of the South) in the city. The confrontation with the urban landscape—usually experienced as a change in time, space, and technology as well as a different concept of race relations—results in a profound change in the way that the mechanisms of power work in the city. Here, it seems, power is more subtle and sophisticated. The more sophisticated use of power is not beyond resorting to acts of physical violence on black bodies. The prevalence of police brutality in urban areas is one example of this. In this instance it is often necessary for migrants to evoke the presence of an ancestor or certain aspects of their Southern folk culture in order to combat the harsh confrontation with the urban landscape.

I have borrowed the concept "ancestor" from Toni Morrison, who argues: "[Ancestors] are sort of timeless people whose relationships to the characters are benevolent, instructive, and protective, and they provide a certain kind of wisdom."[6] I want to extend Morrison's definition of the ancestor to include an understanding of the full ramifications of the term. The ancestor is present in ritual, religion, music, food, and performance. His or her legacy is evident in discursive formations like the oral tradition. The ancestor might be a literal ancestor; he or she also has earthly representatives, whom we might call elders. The ancestor's presence in Southern cultural forms such as song, food, and language sometimes provides the new migrant a cushion with which to soften the impact of urbanization. In *Moorings and Metaphors: Figures of Culture and Gender in Black Women's Literature*, Karla Holloway argues that the ancestor figure "serves as a recursive touchstone" and that "the ancestral presence constitutes a posture of remembrance" (p. 115).

Toni Morrison's Pilate Dead and Julie Dash's Nana Peazant are the quintessential representatives of the ancestor. Pilate is the central female figure of Morrison's *Song of Solomon*. As the daughter of Macon Dead I she is a direct descendant of the flying African. She embodies the history of the Dead clan in her earring and her song. Self-born, possessing no sign of her connection, she is nonetheless the most connected character in the text. She sits on the boundaries, dwells in the borderlands. In her mind she houses not only the songs and stories of the past, but also the remedies, the recipes for nurturance and survival. Pilate is both root and leaf, the transitional space between the ground where the ancestors reside and the sky to which they direct all who revere them. She is both tall and short; both eloquent and illiterate. She speaks freely to the dead, the living, and the unborn.

Similarly, the character Nana Peazant in Julie Dash's film *Daughters of the Dust* possesses the qualities of the ancestor. As family griot, Nana holds her family's history in a box filled with "scraps of memory," her Yoruba-based religious rituals, and her stories. This elder advises her migrating grandchildren: "I'm the one that can give you strength. . . . Take me wherever you go. I'm your strength."

Ancestors are a specific presence in the text. They are found in both its content and its form. Toni Morrison best articulates the role of the migration narrative as repository of the ancestor when she says that her storytelling, like that of the characters in *Song of Solomon*, is an attempt to preserve and pass on the stories and the songs of the African-American past.[7] As far as she is concerned, urbanization and "the press toward upward social mobility would mean to get as far away from that kind of knowledge as possible." According to Morrison, such a fiction "recognizes what the conflicts are, what the problems are. But it need not solve those problems because it is not a case study."[8] In an interview, Morrison even suggested that fiction as ancestor serves as a space for enlightenment, sustenance, and renewal: "There is a confrontation between old values of the tribes and newer urban values. It's confusing. There has to be a mode to do what the music did for blacks, what we used to be able to do with each other in private and in that civilization that existed underneath the white civilization."[9]

While Morrison's fiction seeks to be the repository of the ancestor and eschews becoming a "case study," other migration narratives strive toward a more objective stance. These are dominated by the "stranger." On the pages of the written migration narrative and in the lyrics of many of the musical ones, the migrant often meets a literal stranger who offers (mis)guidance, advice, and a new worldview. The stranger exists in a dialectical relationship with the ancestor. While the ancestor originates in the South and lives in the North, for the most part the stranger is a Northern phenomenon.

My concept of the stranger is greatly influenced, but not circumscribed by, the stranger "who stays" in the work of the German-Jewish sociologist Georg Simmel. Simmel's stranger is a figure whose membership within a group involves being at once outside and within its boundaries.

Simmel characterizes the stranger who stays as "a potential wanderer . . .

[who,] although he has gone no further, has not quite got over the freedom of coming and going. He is fixed within a certain spatial circle—or within a group whose boundaries are analogous to spatial boundaries."[10] Simmel's stranger does not initially belong to the group; instead, he brings qualities into it that are not, and cannot be, indigenous. The stranger is a cosmopolitan figure.

Simmel created his concept of the stranger as a means of understanding the process of migration and urbanization in a European context. In American sociology, "the stranger" evolves into "the marginal man" and is best described in the work of Robert Park.[11] For Park, human migrations produced new personalities, one of which he characterized as the newly emancipated individual, or the marginal man. For this character type, "energies that were formerly controlled by custom and tradition are released. . . . [Such persons] become . . . not merely emancipated, but enlightened."[12] Park continues, "The emancipated individual invariably becomes in a certain sense and to a certain degree a cosmopolitan. He learns to look upon the world in which he was born and bred with something of the detachment of a stranger. He acquires, in short, an intellectual bias." This figure has severed all ties with the ancestor, yet, under Park's definition, this will not inhibit but will further his access to freedom.

In relation to the dominant white society, all migrants are strangers—foreigners driven by persecution to wander in search of a new home. However, within the context of the African-American community, the stranger is that figure who possesses no connections to the community. Migrants who seek to be strangers can never occupy that space fully, but those who come closest "change their discomforts into a base of resistance."[13]

Like Simmel's "stranger," the omniscient narrators of these texts play the role of journalists, streetwise reporters who detach themselves and present the readers with a case for consideration and action. Gwendolyn Brooks has in fact likened herself to a reporter in her attempts to record the daily lives of ordinary black urbanites. Ann Petry used her skills as a newspaper reporter documenting black Harlem of the forties to write her classic novel *The Street*, and with *Native Son* Richard Wright provides us with the novel-as-stranger par excellence. In "Blueprint for Negro Writing," Wright argues that writers are "agents of social change who possess unified personalities, organized emotions [and an] obdurate will to change the world."[14] Wright credited the social sciences for providing him with objective, critical frameworks in which to place his stories.[15]

Richard Wright is an exemplar of the migrant as stranger. In his essay "How Bigger Thomas Was Born," Wright explains how he himself avoided becoming Bigger. Wright's description resembles that of Julia Kristeva's stranger, who, according to Kristeva, "had he stayed home, might have become an outlaw." Wright the protagonist shares with Bigger a sense of disconnection from the stifling folk tradition of the race. The protagonists Bigger and Wright mark the negative and positive consequences of stranger status, respectively. Bigger is devoid of any human connection and does not fill that void with a critical consciousness until he has already become an outlaw. Wright becomes the stranger who possesses the critical consciousness and who occupies the position of cosmopolite.

In terms of form, the texts seem to oscillate between the two encounters with the stranger and the ancestor. In fact, the most sophisticated texts, like Morrison's *Song of Solomon* and Jean Toomer's *Cane*, strive to be sites of the ancestor. Wright's *Native Son* and Petry's *The Street* strive to occupy the space of the stranger, the observer, the social scientist shedding light on a familiar but strange situation. Stevie Wonder's "Living for the City" embodies the conflict between the stranger and the ancestor in both its content and its musical form. The figurations of ancestors and strangers provide useful conceptual tools for understanding the migration narratives; they are both masculine and feminine, male and female, concrete and abstract. In their extremes, ancestors and strangers are polar opposites; in more sophisticated texts they overlap. Sometimes the stranger and the ancestor seem to exist in the same figure. In fact, the most effective ancestors possess qualities of the stranger and the most effective strangers can pass as ancestors. For instance, Pilate glides through the pages of *Song of Solomon* walking a line between the familiar, ancestral mode and that of the "stranger."

The third moment of the migration narrative is the portrayal of the way migrants negotiate the urban landscape. Once situated on the urban landscape, domestic, street, and psychic space are all sites of contestation for migrants and the powers that seek to control them. Again, the ancestor is of great significance in this struggle. These spaces are often sites where the ancestor is invoked; at other times they are sites from which he or she is banished. Often, rejection of the ancestor leads to further alienation, exile, the status of stranger, or sometimes death. The ancestor in turn is a site of negotiation for the construction of a new self. The creation of a new self may be one of the most crucial aspects of resistance to the complexities of the North. However, for many, the sites of the ancestor are stifling and provincial and as such they inhibit the progress and the development of the protagonist.

These spaces are either the locus for producing and maintaining the negative effects of urbanization—fragmentation, dislocation, and material and spiritual impoverishment—or "safe havens" from these negative effects. In the latter instance, they help the migrant to construct an alternate urban subjectivity. (Subject is here used to connote an object of social and historical forces as well as a historical agent.)

I borrow the term "safe spaces" from Patricia Hill Collins, who defines them as places where black women "speak freely" and where domination does not exist as a "hegemonic ideology." She identifies as safe spaces extended families, churches, and African-American community organizations, as well as cultural traditions like the black women's blues and literary traditions. According to Collins these spaces form a site of "resisting objectification as Other." Collins claims such sites "house a culture of resistance."[16]

My use of "safe space" seeks to complicate Collins's definition. First, hegemonic ideology can exist even in spaces of resistance. Second, these sites are more often the locus of sustenance and preservation than of resistance. While sustenance and preservation are necessary components of resistance, I do not believe they are in and of themselves resistant acts. Moreover, safe spaces can be very conservative spaces as well. For my purposes safe spaces provide a way of understanding the possibilities of such sites in the migration narrative. However, the narratives often point out the irony of the term "safe." For instance, in some cases the black church is not necessarily a safe space for black women in light of its gender hierarchy, its stand against birth control and abortion, and its homophobia. In other cases the church is the only site that recognizes and affirms black humanity.

In the migration narrative, safe spaces are available to both male and female characters.[17] At their most progressive, they are spaces of retreat, healing, and resistance; at their most reactionary, they are potentially provincial spaces which do not encourage resistance but instead help to create complacent subjects whose only aim is to exist within the confines of power that oppress them. In many instances these spaces contain both possibilities. In some cases safe spaces are sites where the South is invoked—not just in its horror, terror, and exploitation, but as a place that housed the values and memories that sustained black people. The South emerges as the home of the ancestor, the place where community and history are valued over Northern individualism.

Safe spaces are both material and discursive. Narrative safe spaces are often resistant to traditional narrative form. They appear in song, food, elements of oral culture, the silences around ritual, and in dream sequences. Literal safe spaces in the city are places where rituals can be enacted to invoke the presence of the ancestor in the North: Pilate's kitchen in *Song of*

Solomon, Mary's boarding house in *Invisible Man,* the Savoy Ballroom in Harlem, the Jungle Room on Sixty-eighth Street in Manhattan, where new migrants shouted "Let's go home" to band leader James P. Johnson in a call for Southern Music.[18] These are all safe spaces where the ancestor is invoked. In this sense, the South is no longer simply a "historical locus" but also a figurative one.

On the other hand, for writers like Richard Wright and James Baldwin, sites like the library provide "safe" space as well as exposure to a world from which their protagonists are excluded.[19] This newfound knowledge can both empower and anger them. In any case, they are aware of the racism of the dominant society as well as the provincial nature of their own communities.

Because safe spaces are created by as well as resistant to sophisticated urban power, they have a tenuous and contradictory existence. A woman's safe space—the home, for instance—might be inhibiting for a man. Similarly, a woman might find the culture of the street, which nurtures an urban black manhood, somewhat dangerous and detrimental to her well-being. Both men and women might find that these spaces are under the control of people and forces that oppress them.

The fourth moment of the migration narrative provides a consideration of the sophistication of modern urban power, an evaluation of the consequences of migration and urbanization, and a vision of future possibilities. For many artists, the North ensures the death and demise of the migrant; for others migration is one step on the road to a cosmopolitan status. Still others, like the rap band Arrested Development, require a return to the South as a means of acquiring racial, historical, and cultural redemption.

The moments described here are constantly revised and challenged. At any given time different interpretations exist side by side. Nevertheless, one interpretation usually emerges as dominant.[20] The major shift in the representation of the migration is prompted by a shift in the understanding of power and the different forms it takes in the North and the South.

During the years following the Harlem Renaissance throughout the Depression to World War II, Richard Wright's version of the migration narrative was the dominant portrayal. For Wright, the South is never a site of possibility for the migrant. Unless he acquires a critical consciousness of the stranger, unless he distances himself from folk culture, he is assured a certain literal or metaphorical "death on the city pavements." Although Zora Neale Hurston provides an alternative to Wright in that her fiction is situated in a racially monolithic South, Wright's is nonetheless the dominant vision. I measure Wright's hegemony not only by the critical attention received by his work, or by the accolades of Book-of-the-Month Club selection and best-seller lists, but also by the degree to which he influenced other African-American writers: Although authors like Chester Himes, William Demby, and Ann Petry differ from Wright in significant ways, they nonetheless have been influenced by him.

The period following the war serves as a kind of transition from Wright's dominance to the emergence of Ralph Ellison. This era is marked by the publication of Ralph Ellison's *Invisible Man* and James Baldwin's *Go Tell It on the Mountain*. Despite both writers' very public disavowals of Wright's influence on their work—indeed neither presents a picture as bleak as that of Wright—they nonetheless share his vision in many ways. Baldwin shares Wright's sense of the stifling nature of black life, yet both he and Ellison appreciate the complexities of African-American life much more than Wright. In so doing, they also suggest the possibilities of the South by privileging the importance of certain elements of black Southern culture to the survival of urban blacks.

Following the Civil Rights and Black Power movements, Toni Morrison's version of the migration narrative emerges as the dominant one. In her work the South becomes not only a site of racial redemption and identity but also the place where Africa is most present. It is not surprising that this emerges as the dominant portrayal of African-American migration following the Civil Rights Movement. If, in fact, the South is a premodern power, it is more susceptible to the forms of social protest that take place there during the Civil Rights Movement. Therefore, it is more likely to be affected by social change. Because of this it can be reconsidered as a burial ground, as a place of cultural origins, home of the ancestors, as a place to be redeemed. The North, however, as a more complex and omniscient power, is not susceptible to the same strategies of the Civil Rights Movement; thus the failure of Martin Luther King in Chicago. Artists who recognize this begin to represent the South in ways only alluded to by their predecessors and to reimagine the possibilities the South holds for African-American people.

Morrison is not the first to have the South reemerge as a site of African-American history and culture; Ralph Ellison, Albert Murray, and Alice Walker precede her. However, Morrison is the first whose texts not only tell the story of the ancestor in the South, but also embody the ancestor.[21] In this way, her significance is not only in the story she tells, but also in the way in which she tells it. I measure Morrison's dominance by the number of scholarly books and articles devoted to her work, the almost automatic appearance of her work on best-seller lists, and her winning of the Pulitzer Prize and the Nobel Prize for Literature.

Although one interpretation of migration may reign at any given moment, it is always challenged by other visions. At times those challenges come from other forms; for instance, film or music may challenge the dominance of a literary artist's interpretation. Oftentimes the challenge comes from within genres; thus one novelist challenges another. Challenges may even come within the work of one artist. . . . Toni Morrison revises and rewrites many of the tropes that she helps to establish.

NOTES

1. While the experience of migration is different and varied, the many portrayals of this moment have enough in common to constitute them as a new form of cultural production.

2. Susan Willis, *Specifying Black Women Writing the American Experience* (Madison: University of Wisconsin Press, 1987). Willis argues that "no other body of writing . . . so intimately partakes of the transformation from rural to urban society or so cogently articulates the change in its content as well as its form" (p. 4); Hazel Carby, *Reconstructing Womanhood: The Emergence of the Black Woman Novelist* (New York: Oxford University Press, 1987); "'It jus Be's Dat Way Sometime': The Sexual Politics of Women's Blues," in *Unequal Sisters: A Multicultural Reader in U.S. Women's History* ed. Ellen Carol DuBois and Vicki L. Ruiz (New York: Routledge, 1990), pp. 238–49 (first published in *Radical America* 20 [1986]: 9–24); "Policing the Black Woman's Body in an Urban Context," *Critical Inquiry* 18 (Summer 1992): 738–55; Lawrence R. Rodgers, "Dorothy West's *The Living Is Easy* and the Ideal of Southern Folk Community," *African American Review* 26 (Spring 1992): 167–68; "Paul Laurence Dunbar's *The Sport of the Gods*: The Doubly Conscious World of Plantation Fiction, Migration, and Ascent," *American Literary Realism* 24 (Spring 1992): 42–57 (Rodgers is also the author of a very important dissertation from which these two articles are drawn: "The Afro-American Great Migration Novel," Ph.D. dissertation, University of Wisconsin-Madison, 1989); Charles Scruggs, *Sweet Home: Invisible Cities in the Afro-American Novel* (Baltimore: Johns Hopkins University Press, 1993).

3. Carby, "Policing the Black Woman's Body," p. 754.

4. Trudier Harris has detailed the portrayal of lynchings in African-American fiction in *Exorcising Blackness: Historical and Literary Lynching and Burning Rituals* (Bloomington: Indiana University Press, 1984).

5. Michel Foucault, *Discipline and Punish: The Birth of the Prison* (New York: Pantheon Books 1977), pp. 8–16. While Foucault notes that "by the end of the 18th century and the beginning of the 19th century the gloomy festival of punishment was dying out, though here and there it flickered momentarily into life," in the American South these "festivals" occurred well into the twentieth century. Foucault continues, "Most changes [in punishment are] achieved by 1840 but the hold on the body did not entirely disappear in the mid-19th century." Beneath the qualifying phrases of these two statements lies the continuous history of the torture and punishment of black people in the New World. Foucault is talking about violence imposed by the state, the acts committed against black people in the American South were usually acts of vigilantism, although they were sanctioned by the state.

6. Toni Morrison, "Rootedness: The Ancestor in Afro-American Fiction," in *Black Women Writers at Work: A Critical Evaluation*, ed. Mari Evans (Garden City, N.Y.: Anchor Press, 1984), p. 343.

7. See Theodore O. Mason "The Novelist as Conservator: Stories and Comprehension in Toni Morrison's *Song of Solomon*," *Contemporary Literature* 29 (1988): 565–81. Mason notes: "Morrison is an example of the novelist as conservator. She is a writer particularly interested in depicting, and thereby preserving and perpetuating, the cultural practices of black communities" (p. 565).

8. Morrison, "Rootedness," p. 345.

9. Thomas Leclair, "'The Language Must Not Sweat': A Conversation with Toni Morrison," in *Toni Morrison: Critical Perspectives Past and Present*, ed. Henry Louis Gates Jr., and K. A. Appiah (New York: Amistad Press, 1993).

10. Georg Simmel, "The Stranger," in *On Individuality and Social Forms*, ed. Donald Levine (Chicago: University of Chicago Press, 1971), p. 143; "The Metropolis and the Mental Life," in Richard Bennett, ed., *Classic Essays on the Culture of Cities* (New York: Appleton-Century-Crofts, 1969).

11. Jerry G. Watts has noted very important differences between Simmel's Stranger and Park's Marginal Man. "Park's marginal man was a racial or cultural hybrid. He lived an 'outsider' inside two worlds. He is a person who 'aspires to be but is denied full membership in the new group.'" Simmel's stranger by contrast has no assimilation desires. He remains a potential wanderer who stays. Whereas Park's marginal man was a tormented man suffering from 'spiritual instability, intensified self-consciousness, restlessness and malaise,' the stranger endured no such anxieties. Instead, he was described as a judge and trusted confidant." Jerry Watts, *Victim's Revolt*, unpublished manuscript, pp. 4–5. See also E. Franklin Frazier, *The Negro Family in Chicago* (Chicago: University Chicago Press, 1932).

12. Robert Park, "The Marginal Man," in *Race and Culture* (London: Free Press of Glencoe, 1950), p. 351.

13. Julia Kristeva, *Strangers to Ourselves* (New York: Columbia University Press, 1991). See also Abdul R. JanMohamed, "Negating the Negation as a Form of Affirmation in Minority Discourse: The Construction of Richard Wright as Subject," *Cultural Critique* 7 (Fall 1987): 245–66.

14. Richard Wright, "Blueprint for Negro Writing," *New Challenge*, Fall 1937, pp. 53–65.

15. Carla Cappetti explores Wright's relationship to sociology in detail in *Writing Chicago: Modernism, Ethnography, and the Novel* (New York: Columbia University Press, 1993).

16. Patricia Hill Collins, *Black, Feminist Thought* (Boston: Unwin Hyman, 1990), p. 97.

17. bell hooks identifies a similar concept in her essay "Homeplace: A Site Resistance," in *Yearning: Race, Gender and Cultural Politics* (Boston: South End Press, 1990), pp. 41–51. According to hooks these spaces are the domain of black women. They differ from the Marxist conception of the worker's home as a site where the oppressed are sustained in order to maintain their place in the social order. In contrast, hooks's homeplaces lay the foundation for radical resistance.

18. Leroi Jones, *Blues People: The Negro Experience in White America and the Music That Developed From It* (New York: William Morrow, 1968), p. 107.

19. Because of racial segregation in the South, even the library is not always a safe space for Richard Wright. See *Black Boy* (New York: Harper and Row, 1945).

20. Interpretations that are dominant in mainstream culture are not always dominant in African-American culture. Where possible, I have selected texts that fall into both categories. This is easier to do with musical works than with books. Until re-

cently there were no mechanisms that charted the popularity of books by black authors with black audiences. In light of this, I measure a book's dominance in African-American culture by its influence on other African-American writers, and by reviews in African-American publications.

21. Alice Walker, *The Third Life of Grange Copeland* (New York: Harcourt Brace Jovanovich, 1970); Albert Murray, *South to a Very Old Place* (New York: McGraw-Hill, 1971).

22. The migration of African-Americans from the South to the North during the early years of the century is representative of the larger movements of former enslaved and colonized peoples into Western metropolises following World War II. This movement is perhaps one of the most significant moments in the modern history of the West. The historical significance of these migrations is not limited to the people who participated in them. The mass movement of peoples of color to major urban centers of the West changed the forces of these cities and profoundly influenced Western culture as well. Certainly there are texts from throughout the black diaspora that may also be considered a variation on the migration narrative.

23. Chester Himes, *If He Hollers Let Him Go* (Garden City, N.Y.: Doubleday, Doran, 1946); Charles Burnett *Killer of Sheep* (Independent, 1977); *To Sleep With Anger* (Samuel Goldwyn, 1990); Carrie Mae Weems, *Family Pictures and Stories, 1978–84*. Exhibition Catalogue (Washington, D. C.: National Museum of Women in the Arts, 1993).

ESSAYISTS

GLORIA ANZALDÚA is the author of *Borderlands/La Frontera: The New Mestiza* (1987), in which the essay collected here appears. She is also editor with Cherríe Moraga of *This Bridge Called My Back: Writings by Radical Women of Color* (1981) and of *Making Face/Making Soul/Hacieno Caras: Creative and Critical Perspectives by Women of Color* (1990). Anzaldúa has taught courses on feminism, Chicano studies, and creative writing at a number of universities, including the University of Texas, Vermont College of Norwich University, and San Francisco State University. She has recently published *Interviews/Entrevistas* (2000).

JEAN BAUDRILLARD is one of France's leading intellectuals and critics of modern society, especially as related to the media and consumer culture. Among his many studies are *Simulacra and Simulations* (1994), *Cool Memories* (1987), and *Seduction* (1979). *America* (1988), from which his selection is taken, is an impressionistic account of his tourist gaze and analysis of postmodern culture. He also published a response to the Gulf War, *The Gulf War Did Not Take Place* (1991).

WILLIAM BEVIS is professor of American literature, emeritus, at the University of Montana. Interested in Montana and Western writers, Bevis has published *Ten Tough Trips: Montana Writers and the West* (1990) and served on the editorial board of *Last Best Place*, an anthology of Montana writing (1988). In addition, he has published *Mind of Winter: Wallace Stevens, Meditation and Literature* (1989), *Borneo Log* (1995), and a novel, *Shorty Harris, or, the Price of Gold* (1999). The essay included in this collection, appeared in *Recovering the Word: Essays on Native American Literature*, edited Brian Swann and Arnold Krupat (1987).

HOMI BHABHA is the Chester D. Tripp Professor in the Humanities at the University of Chicago, where he is a professor of English, art history, and south Asian languages and civilizations and serves on the Committee on the History of Culture. One of the first scholars to articulate postcolonial theory, Bhabha has written widely on the status of the colonized subject. He is the editor of *Nation and Narration* (1990), the author of *The Location of Culture* (1994), and the co-author of *Colonizer and the Colonized* (2001).

MICHEL BUTOR, French novelist and essayist, is a leading figure of the *nouveau roman*. He has taught at universities in Egypt, Manchester, Salonika, and Geneva, where in 1975 he was appointed "professor extraordinaire." Among his literary awards are the Fénélon Prize, Renaudot Prize, and Grand Prize for Literary Criticism. Consistent with his efforts to question perception, his essay from *Mosaic* redefines what we mean by travel and the place of reading and writing in relation to movement and place. Among his many other works are *Mobile: A Study for a Representation of the United States* (1963) and his best-known novel, *La Modification* (1957).

MICHEL DE CERTEAU was a French polymath Jesuit priest and held the chair of Historical Anthropology of Beliefs at the École des hautes études en sciences sociales. His book *The Practice of Everyday Life* (1974, trans. 1984), from which the essay "Spatial Stories" is taken, is an important contribution to the understanding of media audiences and cultural studies. Other books by de Certeau include *Cultural in the Plural* (1974), *The Writing of History* (1975), and *Heterologies: Discourses on the Other* (1986). Michel de Certeau died in 1986.

HÉLÈNE CIXOUS is a feminist theorist, novelist, playwright, and educational innovator. A professor of English literature at Paris VIII, she founded the university's Centre d'Études Féminines, and directs doctoral programs in English literature and in the Centre. Known for developing the concept of l'écriture féminine, she is also a prolific writer whose works include *"Coming to Writing" and Other Essays, Inside,* and *Three Steps on the Ladder of Writing* (1993), from which the piece included here is taken.

ERIK COHEN is the George S. Wise Professor, Emeritus, of Sociology at Hebrew University of Jerusalem. He has conducted sociological and anthropological research in Israel, Peru, the Pacific Islands, and Thailand. Recent publications include *Thai Tourism: Hill Tribes, Islands and Open-ended Prostitution* (1996), *The Commercialized Crafts of Thailand* (2000), and *The Chinese Vegetarian Festival in Phuket* (forthcoming 2001). He was also an associate editor of *Encyclopedia to Tourism* (2000).

WAYNE FRANKLIN is Davis Distinguished Professor and chair of English at Northeastern University. He is also editor of the University of Iowa's American Land and Life Series and one of the editors of the *Norton Anthology of American Literature*. A specialist in American culture, he is the author of *Discoverers, Explorers, Settlers: Diligent Writers of Early America* (1979), from which the selection is taken, and of *A Rural Carpenter's World* (1990), and is editor of *Mapping American Culture* (1995).

PAUL FUSSELL is University of Pennsylvania's Donald T. Regan Professor of English Emeritus. He has received the National Book Award, National Book Critics Circle Award, and the Emerson Award. His book *Abroad: British Literary Traveling between the Wars* (1980), from which this selection comes, set the standard for travel study. Among his other books are *The Great War and Modern Memory* (1977), *Boy Scout Handbook and Other Observations* (1982), and *Thank God for the Atom Bomb and Other Essays* (1988). He is also the editor of the *Norton Book of Travel* (1987). More recently, he has published his autobiography, *Doing Battle* (1996).

FARAH JASMINE GRIFFIN is associate professor of English at the University of Pennsylvania. She is the author of *Who Set You Flowin'?: The African American Migration Narrative* (1995), from which her selection is taken. She is also the co-editor of *Stranger in the Village: Two Centuries of African American Travel Writing* (1998) and editor of *Beloved Sisters and Loving Friends: The Rebecca Primus-Addie Brown Correspondence* (1999).

CAREN KAPLAN is associate professor of women's studies at the University of California, Berkeley. Interested in transnational feminist cultural studies, she has published *Scattered Hegemonies: Postmodernity and Transnational Feminist Practices*, edited with Inderpal Grewal (1994), *Questions of Travel: Postmodern Discourses of Displacement* (1996), and *Between Woman and Nation: Nationalisms, Transnational Feminisms and the State*, edited with Norma Alarcón and Minoo Moallem (1999). The essay selected here appeared in *Cultural Critique* (1987).

ERIC LEED is retired professor of history at Florida International University. A specialist in modern European history, Leed compiled the history of the dynamics of travel, *The Mind of the Traveller: From Gilgamesh to Global Tourism* (1991), from which his selection comes. He is also the author of *Shores of Discovery: How Expeditionaries Have Constructed the World* (1995) and *No Man's Land: Combat and Identity in World War I* (1979).

DEAN MACCANNELL is chair and professor of environmental design at the University of California, Davis. *The Tourist: A New Theory of the Leisure Class* (1976; 1999) is a classic examination of tourism through the perspective of sociological theory and semiotics. Recently republished, with a new afterword by MacCannell, *The Tourist* continues to influence theories of society and travel. MacCannell has also written *Empty Meeting Grounds* (1992) and *Time of the Sign: A Semiotic Interpretation of Modern Culture*, with Juliet Flower MacCannell (1982).

DOREEN MASSEY is professor of geography at Open University, London. Interested in the theorization of space and place, Massey has published extensively. Among her publications are *Spatial Division of Labor: Social Structures and the Geography of Production* (1984); *Space, Place and Gender* (1994), from which her piece is taken; *Human Geography Today*, of which she is co-editor (1999); and *Cities for the Many not the Few*, co-authored with A. Amin and N. Thrift (2000). She is also the co-founder and co-editor of *Soundings: A Journal of Politics and Culture*.

CARL PEDERSEN is associate professor of English and director of the Center for American Studies at the University of Southern Denmark. He is co-editor of *American Studies in Scandanavia*. His most recent publication (with Maria Diedrich and Henry Louis Gates, Jr., editors) is *Black Imagination and the Middle Passage* (1999).

GUSTAVO PÉREZ-FIRMAT, a professor at Duke University from 1979 to 1999, is now David Feinson Professor of Humanities at Columbia University, where he teaches in the department of Spanish and Portuguese. The piece selected for this collection comes from the introduction of his book *Life on the Hyphen: The Cuban-American Way* (1994), which won the Eugene M. Kayden University Press National Book Award. His other books include *Cuban Condition: Translation and Identity in Modern Cuban Literature* (1989), his autobiography *Next Year in Cuba: A Cubano's Coming of Age in America* (1995), and *My Own Private Cuba* (1999).

MARY LOUISE PRATT holds the Oliver H. Palmer Chair in Humanities as a professor in the Spanish and Portuguese and comparative literature departments at Stanford University. She is co-author of *Linguistics for Students of Literature* (1980) and *Women, Culture and Politics in Latin America* (1990). She is also the author of *Imperial Eyes: Travel Writing and Transculturalism* (1992) and *Mujer y ciudadanía: historia de discursos, 1820–1997* (forthcoming). She teaches courses in Latin American literature, colonialism, postcolonialism, cultural studies, and travel literature.

R. RADHAKRISHNAN is professor of English at the University of Massachusetts, Amherst, where he teaches courses on critical theory, postcoloniality, poststructuralism, and cultural studies. The essay included here comes from his book *Diasporic Mediations: Between Home and Location* (1996). He is also the author of *Theory in an Uneven World* (2001) and has a number of essays that have appeared in such journals as *Social Text, Cultural Critique,* and *MELUS*. He is currently working on a book-length project on the ethics and aesthetics of hybridity.

EDWARD W. SAID is professor of English and Comparative Literature at Columbia University, teaching across the fields of history, music, and literature. He was president of the Modern Language Association in 1999, has been a consultant to the United Nations, and served from 1977 to 1991 on the Palestine National Council. Among his books are *Orientalism* (1978), *World, the Text, and the Critic* (1983), *Culture and Imperialism* (1993), *Out of Place: A Memoir* (1999), and *Reflections on Exile* (2000). The essay included here was originally published in *Granta* (1984).

THAYER SCUDDER is professor of anthropology, emeritus, at California Institute of Technology. A scholar in the field of involuntary community relocation, he has worked with various United Nations associations as well as the World Bank. Among his awards are the Solon T. Kimball Award for Public and Applied Anthropology (1984), the Edward J. Lehman Award (1991), and the Bronislaw Malinowski Award (1999). His books include *The Gwembe Tonga* (1962), *Secondary Education and the Formation of an Elite* (1979), *No Place to Go: Effects of Forced Relocation on Navajos* (1982), from which the selection for this collection is taken, *For Prayer and Profit: The Changing Role of Beer in Gwembe District* (1988), and *African Experience with River Basin Development* (1993).

ACKNOWLEDGMENTS

From *Borderlands/La Frontera: The New Mestiza*, © 1987 by Gloria Anzaldúa. Reprinted by permission of Aunt Lute Books.

From *America* by Jean Baudrillard (1988). Reprinted by permission of Verso Publishing.

From "Native American Novels: Homing In" by William Bevis. Reprinted by permission of William Bevis.

The Location of Culture by Homi Bhabha, 1994, Routledge. Reprinted with the permission of Taylor & Francis Books.

"Travel and Writing" by Michel Butor, *Mosaic* 8.1 (1974), pp. 1–16. Reprinted by permission of *Mosaic*.

From *Three Steps on the Ladder of Writing* by Hèléne Cixous. © 1993 Columbia University Press. Reprinted by permission of the publisher.

Erik Cohen, "Phenomenology of Tourist Experiences," *Sociology*, 13.2 (1979), pp. 179–201. World Copyright: The British Sociological Association, 1979. Reprinted with the permission of Cambridge University Press.

From *The Practice of Everyday Life* by Michel de Certeau, translated by Steven Rendall, "Spatial Stories." Copyright © 1984 The Regents of the University of California. Reprinted by permission of the University of California Press.
Permission is also granted by Steven F. Rendall, translator.

From *Discoverers, Explorers, Settlers: Diligent Writers of Early America* by Wayne Franklin. Copyright © 1979 by The University of Chicago Press. Reprinted by permission of The University of Chicago Press.

From *Abroad: British Literary Traveling Between the Wars* by Paul Fussell, copyright © 1980 by Oxford University Press, Inc. Used by permission of Oxford University Press, Inc.

From *Who Set You Flowin?: The African-American Migration Narrative* by Farah Jasmine Griffin, copyright ©1996 by Farah Jasmine Griffin. Used by permission of Oxford University Press, Inc.

Caren Kaplan, "Deterritorializations: The Rewriting of Home and Exile in Western Feminist Discourse" in *Cultural Critique* 6 (Spring 1987) pp. 187–198. Reprinted by permission of the University of Minnesota Press.

From *The Mind of the Traveller: From Gilgamesh to Global Tourism* by Eric Leed. Copyright © 1991 by Basic Books, Inc. Reprinted by permission of Basic Books, a member of Perseus Books, L.L.C.

From *The Tourist: A New Theory of the Leisure Class* by Dean MacCannell. Copyright © 1976 Schocken Books. Reprinted by Permission of the University of California Press.

"A Global Sense of Place" from *Space, Place and Gender* (1994) by permission of Doreen Massey.

Reprinted by permission of the publisher from "Sea Change: The Middle Passage and the Transatlantic Imagination" by Carl Pedersen in *The Black Columbiad: Defining Moments in African American Literature and Culture*, edited by Werner Sollors and Maria Diedrich, Cambridge, Mass.: Harvard University Press, Copyright © 1995 by the President and Fellows of Harvard College.

From *Life on the Hyphen: The Cuban-American Way* by Gustavo Pérez-Firmat. Copyright © 1994. By permission of the University of Texas Press.

Mary Louise Pratt, "Scratches on the Face of the Country; or, What Mr. Barrow Saw in the Land of the Bushmen" in *Critical Inquiry* 12.1 (Autumn

1985), pp. 119–143. © 1985 by The University of Chicago. Reprinted by permission of the University of Chicago Press.

"Is the Ethnic 'Authentic' in the Diaspora?" by R. Radhakrishnan from *The State of Asian America* edited by Karin Aguilar-San Juan (1994), pp. 219–233. Reprinted by permission of South End Press.

"Reflections on Exile." Copyright © 1984 Edward Said, first published in *Granta*, reprinted with permission of The Wylie Agency, Inc.

"The Relocation of Low-Income Rural Communities with Strong Ties to the Land" from *No Place to Go: Effects of Compulsory Relocation on Navajos* (1982) by permission of Thayer Scudder.

INDEX

LaVergne, TN USA
07 January 2010
169234LV00004B/116/A